Edinburgh Law and Society Series

The Emancipation of Prisoners

A Socio-Historical Analysis of the Dutch Prison Experience

HERMAN FRANKE

EDINBURGH UNIVERSITY PRESS

Edinburgh University Press Ltd
22 George Square, Edinburgh

Typeset in Linotron Plantin
by Koinonia Limited, Bury, and
printed and bound in Great Britain
by The University Press, Cambridge

A CIP record for this book is
available from the British Library

ISBN 0 7486 0614 9

Contents

List of Tables

Abbreviations

AC	*Alkmaars(ch)e Courant* (the Alkmaar Daily)
AD	*Algemeen Dagblad* (General Daily)
AH	*Algemeen Handelsblad* (General Commercial Paper, a Dutch newspaper)
AMC	*Amsterdams(ch)e Courant* (Amsterdam Daily)
art.	article
BWO	Bond voor Wetsovertreders (Union for Lawbreakers)
CBS	Centraal Bureau voor de Statistiek (Central Bureau of Statistics)
CDA	Christen-Democratisch Appel (Christian Democratic Appeal)
CHU	Christelijk-Historische Unie (Christian–Historical Union)
D'66	Democraten '66 (Democrats '66)
HdSG	*Handelingen der Staten-Generaal* (Official Parliamentary Reports)
KB	Koninklijk Besluit (Royal Decree)
KVP	Katholieke Volkspartij (Roman Catholic People's Party)
MvBR	*Maandblad voor Berechting en Reclassering* (Monthly for the trial and the after-care of prisoners)
MVBZ	Ministerie van Binnenlandse Zaken (Department of Home Affairs)
MvhG	*Maandblad voor het Gevangeniswezen* (Monthly for the Prison System)
MVJ	Ministerie van Justitie (Ministry of Justice)
NJB	*Nederlandsch Juristenblad* (Dutch Lawyers' Journal)
NJV	Nederlandse Juristen Vereniging (Dutch Society of Lawyers)
NRC	*Nieuwe Rotterdams(ch)e Courant* (New Rotterdam Daily)
OHC	*Oprechte Haarlemsche Courant* (The Fair Haarlem Daily)
PvdA	Partij van de Arbeid (Labour Party)
Sb	Staatsblad (statute-book)
SDAP	Sociaal Democratische Arbeiders Partij (Socialist Democratic Labour Party)
TvCr	*Tijdschrift voor Criminologie* (Journal of Criminology)

TVS	*Tijdschrift voor Strafrecht* (Journal of Criminal Law)
VK	*de Volkskrant* (People's Daily)
VN	*Vrij Nederland* (Free Netherlands, a weekly)
VVD	Volkspartij voor Vrijheid en Democratie (People's Party for Freedom and Democracy)
WvhR	*Weekblad van het Recht* (Weekly of the Law)
WVS	Wetboek van Strafrecht (Penal Code)

Glossary

BEJEGENING   attendance, social intercourse
BERAADSLAGINGEN   deliberations, debates
BIJLAGEN   Appendices
BULLEPEES   a whip made of a hard muscle of a bull
COLLEGE VAN REGENTEN   Board of Trustees of a prison
CORRECTIONELE GEVANGENIS (SEN)   house(s) of correction
EERSTE KAMER   the Dutch Upper House, senate
GEVANGENIS (SEN)   prison (s)
HANDELINGEN   transactions, proceedings
HUIS(HUIZEN) VAN ARREST   House(s) of detention for arrested persons
HUIS (HUIZEN) VAN BEWARING   remand prison(s)
HUIS (HUIZEN) VAN CORRECTIE   house(s) of correction
HUIZEN (HUIS) VOOR MILITAIRE EN BURGERLIJKE VERZEKERING   Houses
   (house) where military men and civilians were taken into custody
KONINKLIJK BESLUIT   Royal Decree
LIEFDE EN HOOP   Charity and Hope (a periodical)
MAANDBLAD VOOR BERECHTING EN RECLASSERING   Monthly for Adjudi-
   cation (Trial) and Rehabilitation (After-care and probation)
MEMORIE VAN ANTWOORD   Memorandum in Reply
MEMORIE VAN TTOELICHTING   Explanatory Memorandum
NEDERLANDS JURISTENBLAD   Dutch Lawyers' Journal
NEDERLANDSCHE JAARBOEKEN VOOR REGTSGELEERDHEID EN WETGEVING
   Dutch Yearlies for Jurisprudence and Legislation
NIEUWE RICHTING   New Direction (in penal law)
ONTOEREKENBAAR   not imputable, unaccountable, of unsound mind
RASPHUIS   a prison for male criminals in which prisoners were
   originally (and sometimes even at the beginning of the 19th century)
   forced to rasp wood
RIJKSOPVOEDINGSGESTICHT   youth custody centre (community home)
   run by the state; broadly the same as Borstal institution
RIJKSWERKINRICHTING   work institution of the state; labour colony for
   beggars and vagrants

SPINHUIS   a prison for female criminals in which they were originally (and sometimes even down to the 19th century) forced to spin

STRAF   punishment

STRAFGEVANGENIS   prison for punishment, penitentiary

TBR/TBS-MEASURE   sentence to compulsory treatment and placement in a secure clinic for an indeterminate period

TUCHTHUIS   a former prison for severe criminals

TWEEDE KAMER   the Dutch Lower House or House of Commons

VERBETERHUIS (HUIZEN)   house(s) of correction

VRAGEN DES TIJDS   Present-day Problems (a periodical)

WEEKBLAD VAN HET REGT(RECHT)   Weekly of the Law

WERKHUIS (HUIZEN)   workhouse(s)

Preface

In 1994, the American Senate's acceptance of President Clinton's anti-crime bill was celebrated as a victory. At last the war on crime had started! The president stated that the bill would guarantee more safety on the streets in the near future. From a socio-historical – and certainly from a Dutch – perspective, the optimism in the USA was rather amazing. Two main elements in the anti-crime bill concerned an extension of the death penalty and the building of more prisons. In The Netherland, capital punishment had been abolished as early as 1870, and the detention rate was about ten times lower than in the USA even befofe Clinton announced a huge expansion of prison capacity. The crime rates are correspondingly lower in The Netherlands; for example, the homicide rate in the USA was also about ten times higher than ours and it far exceeds the homicide rate in all other European countries, where far fewer people are imprisoned than in the USA. Throughout Western Europe capital punishment has been abolished or is at any rate no longer practised.

In my opinion, this all shows that Europe has little to learn from the USA in solving problems of crime and punishment. On the other hand, politicians and public-opinion leaders in the USA could profit from the centuries of penal experience in Europe. This experience indicates that the relationship between crime and punishment is much less direct and simple than the majority in the USA seems to be convinced of, even in circles of lawyers and penal experts. It is simply not the case that more prisons lead to less crime, and it is also not true that capital punishment prevents people from committing serious crimes. The level of crime has to do with changing characteristics of society as a whole (e.g. to what extent the state succeeds in establishing a monopoly in the use of violence), and penal changes should be seen as socio-cultural developments rather than as well-thought-out strategies to fight crime more efficiently.

In this book, I have analysed in detail two centuries of Dutch prison experience and thinking about crime. Although during the last two decades the detention rate in The Netherlands has risen very steeply and its penal climate has become harsher, it still has one of the lowest detention rates in the western world. Moreover, prisoners in The Netherlands have more rights and are treated more humanely than in most other European countries, let alone the USA, Latin America, Africa and Asia. The Dutch authorities have very recently given up temporarily (and only in some specific circumstances) their principle of one prisoner to a cell. They preferred alternative sanctions, fewer prison sentences and even the release of arrested criminals to overcrowding their prisons and having prisoners share their cells with other inmates. Prison riots are very rare in The Netherlands and have never been as serious or violent as, for example, in France, Belgium, Britain or the USA. One can understand this rather unique position of the Dutch prison system better – in my opinion, best – by knowing how it developed historically. I hope this book will contribute to a broadening of our insight into problems of crime and punishment in modern society so that we can reduce these problems by causing less human pain. Crime is a bad thing, and we should not make it even worse by being too tough on it.

I started to write the extended Dutch version of this book more than ten years ago when I met Carla Schoo. I am still in love with her, and I want to thank her for her unceasing moral support. Her daughter – my 'daughter as a gift' – Anne Dekker also helped me, simply by growing up in my presence as a lovely person. From all the colleagues and friends who gave advice, stimulated me, listened to me, and commented on (or reviewed) earlier Dutch versions (or parts) of this book, I want to mention especially Henk Bonger, Carolien Bouw, Frank Bovenkerk, Kees Bruin, David Downes, Sjoerd Faber, Cyrille Fijnaut, Willem Frijhoff, Joop Goudsblom, Nico Jörg, Paul Kapteyn, Constantijn Kelk, Martin Moerings, Krijn Niekerk, Sibo van Ruller, Pieter Spierenburg and Hans Tulkens. Very special thanks go to Elisabeth Lissenberg for her detailed and accurate comment on an earlier English version. Koos van Weringh has stimulated me much in writing this book and did much to propagate my ideas about imprisonment, placing me under a lifelong obligation. I am grateful to Peter Young for his detailed comment and his efforts to get this book published in English. I am also grateful to Tony Peters, who advised me to shorten and translate into English the Dutch version of this book, and introduced and praised me to the academic editors of the Law and Society Series at Edinburgh University Press. Last but not least, I want to thank Kate Simms for translating this book into English. She did a wonderful job, not only in being so accurate and concerned, but also in not becoming angry when I kept whining about details for hours.

The editors of the *British Journal of Criminology* have kindly allowed material first published in this journal to be reproduced in some sections of Chapter 11 in a slighly revised form. I am grateful to the Faculty of Law of the University of Amsterdam and the prison-department

(Delinquentenzorg en Jeugdinrichtingen) of the Dutch Ministry of Justice for having financed the English translation of this book.

H.F.

Introduction

And, though at present my friends may find it a hard thing to believe, it is true none the less, that for them living in freedom and idleness and comfort it is more easy to learn the lessons of humility than it is for me, who begin the day by going down on my knees and washing the floor of my cell. For prison life with its endless privations and restrictions makes one rebellious. The most terrible thing about it is not that it breaks one's heart – hearts are meant to be broken – but that it turns one's heart to stone. One sometimes feels that it is only with a front of brass and a lip of scorn that one can get through the day at all.[1]

The prison sentence has grown in significance since the end of the eighteenth century. Debtors, suspects, beggars, vagrants, lunatics, prostitutes and other marginal figures in prison found themselves more and more often in the company of criminals who had been sentenced by a judge to imprisonment. Michael Ignatieff calculated that the number of convicted offenders in London's *Old Bailey* increased from 1.2 to 28.3 per cent between 1760 and 1794. The rapid increase in numbers of convicted offenders in France moved Michel Foucault to speak of the 'birth' of the prison. The significance of the prison sentence grew in Dutch and German provinces as well, but it had already been imposed there far more often in the seventeenth and eighteenth centuries than in other West European countries.[2]

The relative importance of prison sentences in the Dutch republic was perhaps linked to the fact that the first workhouses on the European continent were established in Amsterdam (1596) and other Dutch cities, something which, in the view of the historian Pieter Spierenburg, was the result of a more secularised attitude to the poor and an increasing pacification of society. These developments were interconnected, directly and indirectly, with processes of urbanisation and state formation.[3]

The formation of national states certainly also contributed, albeit at a later stage, to the decreasing use of banishment. Until the late eighteenth century, this had been a very important form of punishment, notwith-standing the fact that gangs of banished people made life outside city gates unsafe. As national authority tightened its grip on the exercise of criminal justice, banishment came to be seen as a senseless exchange of criminals between cities and provinces. Henricus Calkoen, called the 'Dutch Beccaria' (see start of Chapter 2), was of the opinion in 1780 that this punishment led to nothing more 'than an exchange of rogues, one for the other, whereby no one gains, but, on the contrary, everyone loses.'[4] He thought that confinement, instead of banishment, would save the execu-tioner a lot of work. In the eighteenth century, these understandable objections were not yet reflected in sentences passed by magistrates,[5] but after the French occupation (1810-13), this punishment was virtually unused, even though it remained in the Penal Code until 1886. At that time, it was also becoming more difficult to banish convicts to other states or continents.[6]

This gradual phasing out of banishment clearly illustrates the growing interdependence between cities, provinces and states over the span of a few centuries. It became increasingly difficult to see this shuffling back and forth of criminals as a solution. Thus, the prison sentence grew in significance, a development given impetus by growing resistance to public corporal and capital punishment. This resistance was also connected, though somewhat less directly, to the formation of national states and increasing interdependence between their members. However, feelings of aversion rather than rational or practical objections formed the core of this resistance.

This connection between historical changes in the structure of human societies and the emotional life of individuals is a central theme of the work of Norbert Elias. In his main work *Ueber den Prozess der Zivilisation* (The Civilizing Process), he shows how, in the upper levels of society, codes of behaviour for eating, sleeping, drinking, making love, relieving oneself and so on changed in a quite specific was from the late Middle Ages onwards. The civilizing process has taken place largely in an un-planned and haphazard way and has certainly not been a consequence of 'purposive education'; it did not happen, however, completely without order. Elias shows how a growing number of human activities were thrust behind the scenes of social life and came to be laden with feelings of shame. The regulation of the whole instinctual and affective life by steady self-control became 'more and more stable, more even and more all-embracing'. Elias analyses this civilizing process in the context of the rise of the national states. In the course of this process, people came to be increasingly interdependent, which led to a growing reticence in daily social intercourse and made stricter and stricter demands on their self-control. Members of the upper classes tried continually to distinguish and distance themselves from the middle classes (as did the middle from the lower classes) by an exemplary self-control, conduct and etiquette, and particularly from those bent on climbing the social ladder by closely copying these upper-class rules of conduct. Increasing interdependency and the urge to distinguish oneself socially provided, as it were, the impetus for the civilizing process.

The new rules for conduct were experienced at first as social constraints imposed from the outside . Later, such constraint became something which people imposed upon themselves, from within. The changed structures for social intercourse went hand in hand with changes in emotion management and self-image - in short, in the structure of personality.[7]

Some of the feelings which Elias analyzes are concerned with aggression and the use of physical violence. He demonstrates convincingly that, as the use of violence came to be monopolized by government officials within the national states, daily life became less and less violent.[8] Pacified social spaces were created which were normally free from acts of violence. Government also restricted itself, in times of peace, to milder forms of violence. In The Netherlands in the nineteenth century, the police regularly took severe and violent action against insurrections and riots. Popular uprisings in Groningen (1847) and Amsterdam (1886), for instance, ended with dozens dead and many wounded. Government use of force in the twentieth century and particularly after the Second World War became increasingly problematic and met with growing social resistance.[9] Prison warders at the beginning of the nineteenth century were still in possession of firearms (which were later replaced by swords), and presently warders carry only truncheons, the use of which is strictly regulated.[10] These developments were mirrored by a growing aversion towards the visible use of physical violence. Civilized opponents called its use barbarian and primitive. Spierenburg and I have tried to show how the growing resistance to physical violence in the second half of the eighteenth century found expression in protests against public corporal and capital punishment.[11] Mutilating penalties such as drawing and quartering, breaking on the wheel and amputation did not warrant inclusion in the first Dutch *crimineel wetboek* (penal code) of 1809. Week-long exhibitions of corpses of criminals hung in so-called 'gallows fields' had already been forbidden under the Batavian Republic (1795–1806), some years earlier. The abolition of corporal (1854) and capital punishment (1870) followed a period of fiery debates in press and parliament in the nineteenth century. The last execution of criminals in The Netherlands took place in 1860.

It was not only because other forms of punishment had become problematic and had encountered resistance that the prison sentence came to occupy an increasingly important position in the penal system.[12] Pedagogical possibilities seemingly inherent in the system also appealed to penal reformers. New goals such as the building of character, disciplining and moral improvement, themselves aspects of the civilizing process, could only be realized in prisons and not on the scaffold. Thus, the prison sentence established itself as the most important penal measure apart from the fine.[13]

This book is concerned with changes in the prison system from the late eighteenth century onwards, as developments described above began to accelerate. The central themes are the treatment of prisoners, their legal position and the degree to which they had any power and rights. My descriptions of changing prison practices, new aims, policy changes, political and scientific discussions and shifting public opinion will focus on the influence of these developments upon what I have called the 'process of emancipation' of prisoners.

While there are many justifications for the continued position of the prison sentence[14] in modern society, my descriptions and interpretations are concerned primarily with changes within the prison system. Emile Durkeim's notion that people cannot live together without creating moral boundaries which repeatedly have to be reinforced by imposing sanctions and penalties circumscribes my study. 'A theory of punishment which gives no place to historical change and says nothing about penal forms leaves too many questions unanswered', Garland rightly states in *Punishment and Modern Society*:[15] What I have tried to elucidate is not the 'why' of punishment in general but that of *changes* in punishment and punishment practices, focusing on imprisonment. I have made use of many sources: reports of parliamentary proceedings, judicial reports, ministerial circulars and letters, newspapers, brochures, books, scientific journals and popular magazines, prison statistics, public archives, radio and television programmes and films. In the course of two centuries, terms used to describe h*uizen van bewaring'*(remand prisons) and *strafgevangenissen* (prisons for convicts) have varied greatly, both in the vernacular and in official reports. Sometimes I have used these terms, but, to prevent confusion, I have used the word 'prison' consistently as a collective noun for all buildings in which suspects or convicts were locked up.

The Emancipation of Prisoners

Prisoners are allowed fewer rights and much less freedom than other groups in society. That is why they are prisoners. Still, the development of their position over more than two centuries can be productively described in terms of a process of emancipation. From contemptible, almost bestial creatures who died of hunger and misery in poorly-heated, unhygienic hovels and underground holes, Dutch prisoners have become reasonably well-housed detainees who now publish their own newspaper, defend their interests through a union and can lodge a legally regulated appeal (via a complaints procedure) to an independent authority. Relatives of prisoners and ex-convicts have even joined forces in forming a lobby group. Commissions of detainees exist, as do minimum standards for the treatment of prisoners. Articles written by prisoners make their way on to the pages of daily newspapers.

Two centuries ago, almost no one was concerned with the fate of prisoners, except perhaps the guards who were earning too little from them. Today an army of social workers, lawyers, warders, pastoral helpers, probation workers, criminologists, psychiatrists and psychologists stand at the ready to protest should their rights and position be threatened.

There are scholars who feel, however, that appearances are deceptive. They see many changes in the prison system as refined forms of oppression. They feel that only the economic conditions and political interests of the upper classes have been behind most changes. Others see many changes as the intentional consequence of ethical considerations or purely judicial arguments. What is remarkable in the work of these scholars is that they ignore an unintentional but very important consequence of all the legally established changes in the prison system since the end of the eighteenth century, regardless of moral or other social motives. This is that these changes gave rise to extensive parliamentary debate, scientific discussion and public attention. Experts and laymen were forced to concern themselves with the problems surrounding criminals and their punishment. Through this process, prisoners - often without actively striving for it - repeatedly received that which other oppressed groups could only achieve with demonstrations and violence: public attention culminating in a fundamental and lasting improvement in their position and greater understanding of their needs. Fewer and fewer rights which free citizens possess were denied to them.

Power and Emancipation

The words 'power' and 'emancipation' will often be used in my description of this history of the prison system, but I wish to avoid defining these concepts precisely. Like Wittgenstein, I think that general concepts derive their meaning and content from the use which is made of them. They focus the attention on certain phenomena just as a spotlight lights up its surroundings: clearly and sharply in the middle, vaguely and filled with shadows on the edges.[16] The meaning of 'power' and 'emancipation', as these concepts are used in this book, is rather flexible and diffuse. To extend the analogy, the spotlight is not focused on a set place but is hand-operated and moveable. Still, something further can be said about these concepts. Power has a relational meaning in this book; it will be understood, in the words of Elias, as 'a structural characteristic of a relationship, all-pervading and, as a structural characteristic, is neither good nor bad'.[17]

Power is not a thing that is possessed or not, and it has no desires and longings of its own, as Michel Foucault seems to postulate. Power is concerned with the opportunity to control the position or behaviour of others. Such opportunities are never totally absent, and no one has a monopoly on them; but huge differences in power exist. 'In so far as we are more dependent on others than they are on us, more directed by others than they are by us, they have power over us, whether we have become dependent on them by their use of naked force or by our need to be loved, our need for money, healing, status, a career or simply for excitement,' says Elias.

The central theme of this book is the changing balance of power between prisoners and their punishers. I describe how prisoners slowly earned small degrees of power, consequently diminishing that of their punishers. The balance of power between prisoners and punishers seems to have shifted in favour of the prisoners over a period of two centuries, even though there is no question of equality. On this point, my interpretation is diametrically opposed to that of Foucault. Indeed, he contends in *Discipline and Punish* that changes within the prison system have led to a more refined and sophisticated exercise of power over prisoners.[18] This conflict of interpretations is connected with Foucault's sociological, or, in my opinion, non-sociological assumptions. Foucault's use of power as something all-pervasive that attempts to increase its own strength makes him unable to see shifts in the balance of power between individuals affecting potential power, opportunities for power, sources of power, and, especially, the growing power of the 'powerless'. That increasing sensitivity to the sufferings of others could constitute a source of power for those who suffer is an insight that, of necessity, escapes Foucault's attention. In this book, *the power of pain* is, indeed, a central theme.

The meaning of 'emancipation', as this emerges from my descriptions, is intimately connected with everyday uses of this word, but it also possesses all their inherent sensitizing force. In some passages, I use 'emancipation' to mean freeing oneself from oppressed power; in others, legal equality and recognition of equal rights; and, in yet others, the recognition of specific needs. But I always deal with changes which widen prisoners' opportunities of controlling and influencing the behaviour of their punishers. I did not wish to use the concept to stress that prisoners *ought* to be emancipated, though I do believe that their position is still open to improvement. Neither do I mean that an end to their emancipation will present itself in the future, in the sense of their complete liberation. Prisoners will always be prisoners, and their situation differs fundamentally from that of free citizens. The concept of emancipation is used descriptively to focus attention, not normatively. Emancipation represents a development through which increasing numbers of people are forced to take into account the needs and desires of the group which is emancipating itself. In this context, the emancipation of prisoners resembles the emancipation of other groups, but it has, as I shall demonstrate, very specific dynamics which correspond to the aims and nature of imprisonment. Their emancipation process moreover must develop within narrow boundaries: prisoners, by definition, can never do completely what free citizens can. But, within those boundaries, they have managed to create a position from which they exert more influence upon their own treatment than most progressive prison reformers would have deemed possible in the last century.

It is important to realize that the emancipation process of prisoners took place largely without the active and purposive contribution of prisoners and punishers. Often, completely unconnected aims motivated penitentiary changes, and prisoners had to acquiesce for quite some time. Nevertheless, I attempt to show that those changes reveal a certain structure and direction. Only late in the twentieth century, as will become apparent, did the emancipation of prisoners become infused with an active, goal-oriented character in the sense of an emancipation movement. But this movement has to be placed in the context of the largely unplanned process of their emancipation.

Humanization and Civilization

During their emancipation process, prisoners have suffered much, and prison life still gives rise to serious mental disturbances, self-mutilation and suicide. Such suffering is extensively described in this book. These descriptions make it difficult to perceive changes within the prison system as a humanizing and civilizing process. Physical suffering inflicted on criminals on the scaffold was probably much easier to bear than the lasting solitude in cells which appeared later. Nevertheless, prison reformers, politicians, lawyers and historians have repeatedly persisted in trying to understand changes in the punishment of criminals from the late Middle Ages until the present time in such a light.[19] It is still said that the level of civilization of a people can be judged from the treatment which it affords its criminals.[20]

The terms 'humanization' and 'civilization' express, more often than not, a moral judgement about the treatment of criminals in earlier times and in other countries, and obscure detached understanding. If one takes into account the context in which they are used, one can still derive a reasonable feeling for what was meant, ignoring the moral judgements. The humane, 'civilized' punishment of criminals is taken to mean that little or no use is made of physical violence; psychological torture is restricted to a minimum; reason predominates over emotion.

This use of the term seems to be similar to the meaning given to it by

Elias. It is important, however, to realize that differences exist between
the rather precise meaning of Elias's 'civilizing process' and the vague
meaning ascribed to the everyday use of the term 'civilization'. As it is
used in everyday political discourse, 'civilization' has a normative aspect.
To claim, for example, that the prison system is more civilized, more
humane, is to claim that it is better than those that existed before or exists
elsewhere today. This hodiecentred, evolutionary and also ethnocentred
use of the concept is avoided, but not always successfully, by Elias in his
description and analysis of the civilizing process.[21] In connecting the
civilizing process to developments within the prison system in this book,
I hope that I, too, will have avoided these connotations. This has not been
easy when describing the opinions, feelings and behaviour of punishers
and prisoners conspicuously in conflict with what nowadays is deemed
morally acceptable and sensible. However, I have tried to draw attention
to these conflicting ideas and to clarify them.[22]

Between Involvement and Detachment

Those who have punished others or have been punished may find that I
have not always struck the correct balance between involvement and
detachment. This has been unavoidable. Crime and punishment are
concerned with feelings, normative judgements and sentiments. Changes
in penitentiary developments are, I am convinced, not really understandable without discussing the emotions involved. In my history of the Dutch
prison system, both judgements and expressions of feeling appear, but I
have tried as much as possible to interpret these sociologically with regard
to political, scientific and other social developments. Using long-term
sociological analysis, I wanted, for instance, to come to some understanding of the fact that politicians and experts in the nineteenth century
showed themselves unfeeling and blind to the psychological misery
accompanying long-term solitude. Politicians, scholars and prison governors wrote and did things in the past that we would now consider
reprehensible and morally objectionable. They possessed images of themselves and of others which surprise us. A number of the crimes for which
people were given year-long sentences are hardly liable to prosecution
today. I can only make these changes understandable by alternating
between a position of great objectivity and one of great involvement. I
have repeatedly attempted to find a workable middle position between the
two extremes. I have, of course, not really been able to escape from the
prison of the time in which I live. Neither were the punishers who have
their say in this book able to escape from theirs. All of this means that the
prisoners were caught in these views as much as between four walls for
two centuries.

NOTES

1. Wilde, 1987 (1949), p. 163.
2. Ignatieff, 1978, p. 81; Foucault, 1979, pp. 231–2 (for the exercise of French criminal law in the eighteenth and nineteenth centuries, see also Petit (ed.), parts ii and iii, 1984, and Petit, 1990); Spierenburg, 1991, esp. Chapter 7; Faber, 1983.
3. Spierenburg, 1984 (Rotterdam) and 1991.
4. Calkoen, 1780, pp. 182–3.
5. Cf. Faber, 1983, p. 205.
6. France held on to the punishment an unusually long time and only abolished deportation to New Caledonia and later to French Guyana only in 1938. In 1946, the *bagnes* were given up for good: cf. Wright, 1983, p. 188.
7. Elias, 1982 (1939), pp. 229–333: 229–30 (quotations); Goudsblom, 1977, pp. 126–52.
8. Cf. Chesnais, 1981; Franke, 1994.
9. Reenen, 1979.
10. Cf. Eggink, 1958, pp. 129–31.
11. Cf. Spierenburg, 1984 (*The Spectacle of Suffering*) and Franke, 1985. The process of abolition (of public scaffold punishment) in England has been described by Cooper, 1974.
12. Weisser points this out as well, 1984, pp. 162–4. Corporal and capital punishments were less frequently imposed, in his opinion, 'owing to the moral, social and political realities of the time'. Transportation was no longer 'a viable form of punishment'. Thus, only the prison sentence remained as 'an effective system'.
13. Cf. Young (forthcoming).
14. Nagel distinguished in 1977 almost sixty such functions, varying from deterrence and retaliation to 'the honouring of remorse', 'rendering infantile' or 'stigmatizing'.
15. Garland, 1990, p. 35.
16. Wittgenstein, 1977, pp. 23, 66–9; cf. Blok, 1976, p. 24.
17. Elias, 1978 (1970), p. 93.
18. See also Foucault, 1976, 1979; cf. Dekker, 1985, for a Foucaultian view of the history of reformatories (Netherlands Mettray) in the nineteenth century.
19. See for instance Balkema/Corstens, 1986, pp. 303–6; Pompe, 1930, pp. 7–18; Griever, 1979, pp. 33–4; Blok, 1925, pp. 5–6; Veringa, 1964, pp. 4–5.
20. Cf. Rutherford, 1989, p. 17; Wright, 1983, p. vi, recorded the expression as early as 1831 from the lips of a French politician.
21. Cf. *Sociologische Gids*, vol. 29, no. 3/4, 1982; see also Goudsblom, 1987, pp. 167–82.
22. About this problem, see Elias, 1987 (1956), pp. 3–41.

1

Prison Life, 1775–1825: Popular Curiosity and Professional Interest

When help and clemency I implore,
Commiseration with my doleful lot;
You avert your eyes from mine in scorn,
You taunt and scoff, you bitt'rly mock
Accursed be the crime you're seeing,
I must remain a human being,
For God has given me human thought,
Oh, and I, within this dungeon walled,
My pain infinitely recalled,
Am left no shred of hope at all,
God, an end to life is what I've sought.[1]

Two centuries ago, prisoners did not need to count on understanding from influential persons outside the prison. Any interest in the lot of prisoners was very limited, certainly as far as the upper classes were concerned, but there was no lack of popular curiosity. The movement of prisoners took place then out in the open, like many aspects of social life that are now hidden from public view. The prisoners walked, often chained to each other, through cities and villages, exposed to the derision and mockery of the population. Large distances were traversed by a boat towed by horses or on an open cart, always in the presence of an ostentaciously uniformed authority, so that everyone knew these were transports of the fallen. Only wealthy prisoners could save themselves from lumbering along public roads in chains, by hiring a carriage.[2]

These transports resembled the 'parade' of those put away for life which Feuerbach wanted to hold every year.[3] Public humiliation was meant as a deterrant.[4] Transports also played an established role in penal practice in The Netherlands. Some unfortunates died on the roads, others needed months to recover from the gruelling journeys, especially when these took place in the winter. Public transportation of prisoners led to complaints and attempts to abolish this practice long into the nineteenth century. It was apparent that the prisoners themselves were deeply disgraced and felt severely punished by this practice.[5] The fact that their predicament sometimes aroused pity or led to gifts of food or drink did not much lighten the horror.

Once in their dungeons, prisoners were confronted with another dubious form of public attention. On feast and market days and during fairs, prisons were opened to the public and anyone who paid a sum could stare.[6] Prisoners often used these occasions to beg or to sell objects made in prison. From friends or family they received food, snacks, clothing, money and alcohol. This only partially took the sting out of being on show. 'For the pedestrians it was recreation, for the prisoners it was public exhibition', wrote one of the inmates.[7] In prisons possessing windows which looked out over public roads, begging and selling went on on other days as well, by lowering purses and wallets on a string. Prisoners climbed on chairs, benches or window ledges in order to establish outside contact.[8] In exchange for payment, warders were prepared to admit the curious, friends, family and even whores to the prison. This took place in spite of repeated calls to end a custom thought to go against 'the humane intention of government'.[9]

Even though the attention of the populace eased their daily burden a little, in the long run, it was that of the judges, politicians and philanthropists that prisoners needed, but until the beginning of the nineteenth century, it was from exactly these classes that such attention was not forthcoming. The prison system had not yet become 'the focus of attention and concern of the legal profession and the philanthropists', as was stated by the lawyer Domela Nieuwenhuis in 1859. 'The moment the dungeon doors were shut behind them', he added, 'social concern ended. They were consigned to suffer from the avarice of lesser functionaries and delivered up to plundering and maltreatment at the hands of their wretched fellow-prisoners.'[10]

Indifference of the Upper Classes

Every district, some large cities and even villages had their own prisons and their own rules. Those arrested and sentenced, those taken into custody for debts, adults and children, men and women, were all kept together in buildings that also served as shelters for beggars, prostitutes, the mentally handicapped, old people and the sick. The mayor of 's-Hertogenbosch, as late as 1818, wanted to set aside a section of the *tuchthuis* for 'infected public women, in order that they could recover'.[11] Often the black sheep of wealthier families could be found in prison, where they were shut up for a time to avoid the risk of scandal.[12]

Corporal and capital punishment, and banishing criminals outside the city walls, were still in use around 1800. There were hardly any rules for the implementation of the prison sentence and the length of any given sentence depended greatly on local and rather arbitrary remission customs. Most prisoners were not obliged to serve their time. Policy was aimed at making a prisoner earn his remission. Clemency played a role, in addition to earnings, and the prisoner had to hope for favours.[13]

Quite often not clemency but death ended the confinement. The Amsterdam lawyer, Henricus Calkoen, argued indeed that the fate of some confined criminals was so catastrophic that they should be longing for death. In 1777 he won the competition held by the *Floreant liberales Artes* society for 'the best Arrangements for the Punishment of Crimes in a well-to-do Society'. Among other topics in his *Verhandeling over het Voorkomen en Straffen der Misdaden* (Treatise Concerning the Prevention and Punishment of Crimes) he dealt in depth with the need for torture and capital punishment, but – typically of the indifferent – he mentioned the prison sentence in only a few short lines. He felt that, in order to adequately deter, deprivation of freedom had to be accompanied by bad food, severe discipline, corporal punishment, and by manual labour, carried out in public.[14]

Nowhere in his prize-winning treatise is there evidence of the slightest knowledge, let alone criticism, of prison life. He called the prison atmosphere 'mild'. Probably he, and many of his well-brought-up and educated fellow citizens, had never seen the inside of a prison. At public executions, magistrates, from their positions of privilege around the scaffold, minutely saw to it that rules were followed, whereas they left the treatment of criminals within the prisons to the judgement of warders bent on monetary profit.[15] Ironically, in The Netherlands, this indifference was fostered by the work of the man who earned a reputation in Europe by being the first to recommend improvements in prison life: John Howard.

John Howard

Howard was an ascetic non-conformist from the religious world of the Quakers and Baptists. During a trip to the continent, his ship was hijacked and, at the age of thirty, he ended up in a French prison. This experience was to greatly influence his later life and that of prisoners generally. Howard was a well-to-do and very devout man who, after the death of his wife in 1765, wished to give more meaning to his sinful life, and so he sought a philanthropic vocation. He found it as a county sheriff. During his prison inspections, he became both fascinated by the criminal underworld and impressed by the misery he saw. These experiences strengthened his vocation. He wanted, through systematic descriptions, to bring the prison problem to the attention of the public at large and the politicians.[16] In the 1770s he visited prisons in almost all western

European countries. He reported his tragic findings in a shocking book that appeared in 1777: *The State of the Prisons*. On his trips he was confronted with squalid prisoners who literally lay rotting in damp, cold and stinking hovels; they were dying of all sorts of infectious diseases, including the notorious prison fever,[17] and they surrendered themselves in the overcrowded sleeping places to betting, homosexuality, prostitution and assault and battery. Prisoners starved, were spiritually and physically maimed and became addicted to the abundant liquor. Howard worked out that in England more criminals died in prison than on the scaffold, and this in the days when capital punishment was frequently administered. His book was reprinted many times and led almost immediately to remedial measures in several countries. Howard contributed actively to the first Penitentiary Act of 1779 in his home country.

On the other hand, until well into the nineteenth century in The Netherlands, Howard's book was cited to show that the fatherland, in this regard as in others, was far more civilised than other nations.[18] Overcome by dismay at his experiences elsewhere in Europe, Howard could not believe his eyes in The Netherlands. 'Prisons in the United Provinces are so quiet, and most of them so clean, that a visitor can hardly believe he is in a Gaol', thus began his chapter on 'Holland'.[19] In a later edition, he added a very approving concluding sentence: 'I know not which I admire most, the *neatness* and *cleanliness* appearing in the prisons, the *industry* and *regular conduct* of the prisoners, or the *humanity* and *attention* of the magistrates and regents'.[20]

It is true that the Dutch prisons compared favourably to those elsewhere, but, in both his opening and concluding sentences, Howard seems to give too rosy a picture of how things actually were. A Dutch contemporary of Howard found the quarters for the accused 'most dismal'. He described the prisons as 'holes', 'the sight alone' of which filled him with 'horror'.[21] Prisoners lay there, without anything to do, months and sometimes years, waiting for their trial.

Howard's own reports also include passages which cast doubt on his favourable judgements. In the *rasphuis* in Amsterdam he saw ten to twelve men rasp wood in dust-ridden rooms that also served as their sleeping quarters. Later on he was informed that woodworking with saws that weighed seventy-seven to eighty-eight pounds 'had been the cause of frequent ruptures'. Lazy or defiant prisoners were flogged or relegated to bread and water in 'a dungeon under the ground'.[22] All he said about the underground dungeons in the Middelburg prison was that they were used as a less cruel alternative to torture on the *pijnbank* (rack).[23] A lawyer described these dungeons in 1777 as dark, unheated 'pits and holes'.[24]

Howard's favourable opinion of the prisons of Holland did not increase public concern for the fate of inmates. When scholars, during the

Batavian Republic (1795–1806),[25] began serious work on a Penal Code which would prevail nationally and was designed to replace all local statutes, edicts and warrants, the prison sentence was barely mentioned. These men took part in profound discussions about the pros and cons of corporal and capital punishment, but little more was said of the prison sentence than that criminals could also be held in confinement 'for a certain number of years'. They could be isolated if necessary and compelled to do manual labour.[26]

They did not concern themselves with the further implementation of the prison sentence. The *Crimineel Wetboek voor het Koningrijk Holland* (Penal Code for the Kingdom of Holland), finally brought into force in 1809 under the French vassal king, Lodewijk Napoleon (1806–10), added to this only that confinement could not last more than twenty years.[27] This law book remained in force only two years. The *Code Pénal* that was followed in The Netherlands even after the end of the French occupation (1810–13), defined two forms of imprisonment, *gevangenisstraf* (for correctional prisoners) and *tuchthuisstraf* (for criminal prisoners), but actual differences between the two did not exist in practice. The nature of the regime in either depended almost exclusively on the character and extent of the avarice of the warders.

During the Batavian Republic and the French occupation, reports were demanded and information requested about the condition of the prison system.[28] Lodewijk Napoleon visited prisons on his tours of The Netherlands and was sometimes so shocked that he ordered measures to be taken immediately. In Ravenstein, a small town between 's-Hertogenbosch and Nijmegen, the prison was a damp, pitch-black under-ground hole. 'He did away with this', wrote the king in his journal (he had formed the habit of writing in the third person singular).[29] Lodewijk was also against capital punishment. He removed the execution of criminals from his sight. When he took up residence in the palace on the Dam in Amsterdam, in the former city hall, the site for public capital punishment was transferred to the Nieuwmarkt at his insistence. Also 'De Boeijen', a prison located under the city hall, was partially moved to the Prinsenhof, the new city hall.[30]

Prison Life in Practice

The actions of the king are easy to understand when one examines reports. One from 1806, on the Gevangenpoort, in 's-Hertogenbosch, speaks of 'hovels' for the criminals with windows of barbed wire. Some of these hovels were so ramshackle and badly secured that prisoners were chained to heavy blocks and were 'doubly protected' at night with iron collars and handcuffs. In this same prison was 'the pit', an underground, black hole into which no light could penetrate and where even a straw bed was absent. The hovels stank, according to the observer Servaas van de Graaf, 'so purulently, so pestilentially' that he could not imagine 'how prisoners could survive even one night there without becoming deathly ill'. In spite of this, he wrote that prisoners in the district were dealt with 'decently and humanely' and were given good food. He was of the opinion that the abuses could not be traced to human error but to the bad physical state of the prisons.

In January 1809 provisional regents inspected the *tuchthuis* in Alkmaar at the request of the city council. In their report they state in no uncertain terms that the prison was in 'the poorest of states'. Everything pointed to disorder, unhealthiness and a 'nigh on to brutalizing negligence and indifference' of the warder. In order to spare the city councillors, they limited themselves to the main points in the 'tableau of human misery' to which they had been spectators. In the section for criminal prisoners, they found 'extensive filthiness and putrefaction', made even 'more horrific' by the snow which drifted in all over the place. The 'hovels' themselves were even filthier. In addition to this,'foul and tainted' air greeted them as they entered, which made going into the prison 'even in this cold season, deeply objectionable'.

Except for Sunday church visits, the prisoners were found to have been shut up for three uninterrupted months in their hovels. These places were cleaned in a slapdash fashion with water at most once or twice per year. The beds were full of vermin. Prisoners shared beds with the sick and the mentally ill and there were too few blankets even in the cold seasons. Clothing was filthy. Underclothing, stockings and caps were missing. What little food there was 'of the worst possible quality and wretchedly prepared'. A doctor was called for sick prisoners only after much insistence, but usually the warder reached haphazardly for some sort of medicine. At the end of this sad tale, the regents advised that the warder be sacked and that the house of detention be taken over by the city.[31]

It is difficult to say how exceptional the situation in Alkmaar was, even when judging by the criteria of those times. In the minutes of the Benevolent Society of Amsterdam prison conditions any better than those described in the Alkmaar report were seldom mentioned. Continuous complaints were registered about inadequate clothing and blankets, bad food, too few sleeping places and polluted water. Some prisoners attempted to provide for a few extras by selling their clothing to visitors. As a disciplinary measure, they could be shut away for days and weeks in a damp, dark cellar. More striking perhaps is a complaint that reached the members of the commission in the middle of the winter about prisoners held in 'De Boeijen' under the city hall, virtually without blankets or clothing. Two members went to look and found 'that prisoners of both sexes dared not to come forth on account of their nakedness'.[32] These descriptions make clear what Baron d'Alphonse, *Intendant de l'Interieur en Hollande*, had meant when he reported to Emperor Napoleon that Dutch prisons were badly deteriorated. In bygone days, one could have counted them as the best in Europe, but, the Baron wrote, 'il est impossible d'en avoir aujourd'hui la même opinion'. The majority of prisons at that moment were not thought to be more than, 'des cachots étroits, infectés, sans lumière, sans air'.[33]

In one way, the descriptions of Alkmaar and Amsterdam give a rather favourable impression of prison life at the beginning of the nineteenth century, especially since disciplinary measures are not mentioned. These measures, however, were severe. In 1815, for instance, the newly appointed *College van Regenten* (Board of Trustees) [34] of the *tuchthuis* in Gouda held out the prospect for insubordinate and insolent behavior of 'whipping with the *bullepees*, shutting away for days on end in the so-called "black hell" on bread and water and manacling with the body in a crooked position'. These new rules and regulations were brought in printed form to the attention of the inmates, who were also made aware that these measures could be increased or diminished 'as the worthy Trustees shall deem fit' at any given time.[35]

Lack of Rights

It is abundantly clear that prisoners had to reconcile themselves to their fate. They had no legal rights and their access to power was negligible. At most, they could complain to visiting regents, but only if they were prepared to listen and were not completely put off by the pestilential gust which greeted them as they opened the dungeon doors. In complaining, prisoners naturally ran the risk of being suspected of insubordination, and thus their chances for remission plummeted, causing them to justifiably fear revenge from the warder.

The prisoners' situation worsened significantly during the Batavian Republic and especially during the French occupation, even though, theoretically, the management of the prisons at that time had been taken out of the hands of the local authorities.[36] In practice, prisoners remained almost completely at the mercy of the warders. These warders lined their own pockets by keeping maintenance costs as low as possible; they invented their own methods for enforcing discipline and the profits from the canteen formed a welcome addition to their income. They did not shrink from selling liquor and went as far as to allow prostitutes into the cells. One warder in The Hague did not overlook his own comfort by treating his female prisoners as his personal harem.[37] In 1838, L. G. Bouricius, a member of the commission administering the Leeuwarden prison, wrote that everyone could still call to mind the *Cipiers-Koopmannen* (Merchant Guards) who had profited personally by skimping on clothing and food. 'There will be almost no one who has not heard repeatedly of the scourgings that were administered almost daily, completely at the discretion of coarse, uncivilized and alcoholic guards', he continued.[38]

Napoleon's passion for economy and that of the first governments under William I made better prison management even more difficult. Many small houses of detention were done away with by the French, leaving only heavily overpopulated large institutions. In these, prisoners went hungry, were ignored and maltreated. Just as in the case of public punishment, the prison sentence served a clear purpose, doubted neither by criminal experts, well-to-do citizens, nor by the decent working class: the deterrence of potential criminals. Only severe punishment would keep these depraved and wicked creatures of the lower classes from stealing, murdering and committing other violations. Much was expected of external constraint exercised by the state, and precious little of the internal constraint of the conscience of the people, always assuming that these common people were credited with a conscience at all. The common people were regarded by the nation's moneyed classes as dirty, uncultured, depraved and hopelessly undeveloped. Since criminals formed the dregs of this group, the dominant feelings of the upper classes were of vengeance and dread, and certainly not of compassion and understanding, let alone solidarity. For these reasons severed heads of criminals were exhibited on pegs even as late as 1800, while corpses of the executed lay rotting in the open air in gallows fields.[39] The idea of deterrence did not induce understanding or attention to the needs of prisoners; rather, they were considered very fortunate that they had not yet been put to death and, unlike many of the poor who were free, they got something to eat.

Deterrence and 'Civilizing Offensives'

In 1804 the leading experts in criminal law declared thus: 'the aim of all punishment is simply the safety of the civil state and its citizenry'. This aim could only be achieved by 'putting the criminal out of action' and by 'scaring off the criminal and others'.[40] When the *Crimineel Wetboek voor het Koningrijk Holland* (Penal Code for the Kingdom of Holland) was proffered in 1808, it was deemed imperative 'for the general welfare' to offer the citizenry a certain amount of protection against lawbreakers who threatened their personal safety and peace 'as well as the certainty of their possessions' by imposing 'well-earned punishment'.[41]

Moral improvement of criminals was scarcely pursued and, as long as deterrence was the only goal, the terrible standard of living of the 'free' poor blocked any improvement in the fate of prisoners. For, if the idea was to deter people, then life in a prison in which one was fed and where one had a roof over one's head had, at least, to be worse than the commoner's daily life of misery and dejection.

At the beginning of the nineteenth century, as the political and economic power of liberal citizens increased at the cost of that of the old élites, the social distance between the commoner and those in power diminished. These two groups began to encounter one another more frequently; this was connected to other social developments, such as the slow disappearance of home industry, the dissolution of family life and an increasing urbanization. Thus, the rich were in a position to confirm the image they had formed on the basis of indirect information concerning the low moral standards of the people at large. As a consequence, their anxiety increased.[42]

The extensive depravity of the common people in the nineteenth century was a favourite subject for speeches and documents. This depravity was not envied. *De Maatschappij tot Nut van 't Algemeen* (the Society for Public Welfare), *de Vereniging tot Zedelijke Beschaving van Arbeiders* (the Association for the Moral Refinement of Workers) and numerous charitable institutions attempted to improve public decency by education and material aid. The former society published a booklet in 1827 pointing out sources of 'domestic bliss' and warning against practices which could destroy this, such as 'domestic negligence, disorder and extravagance'.[43]

Criminals and prisoners were not spared this 'civilizing offensives', as the bourgois initiatives to lift the common people out of misery and depravity might be called.[44] The conservative Member of Parliament, Van Goltstein, pointed to 'the employment of correct preventative measures to forestall excesses of hotheaded passion in the common people' within the scope of crime prevention. The judicial civilizing offensive was meant to make the lower classes aware of their responsibilities and move them to religion and virtue.[45] In 1823, the philanthropists Suringar, Warnsinck and Nierstrasz, following similar initiatives elsewhere, founded *het Nederlandsch Genootschap tot Zedelijke Verbetering der Gevangenen* (the Dutch Society for the Moral Improvement of Prisoners). The value of this society was indisputable in the eyes of the founders. The 'moral situation' of prisoners was 'piteous': 'instead of being *better* at the moment of their release and having broken with the habit of wrong-doing, they often leave the prison *worse* than when they entered it'.[46]

Interest, Compassion and Frugality

Increased aversion to the physical violence accompanying corporal and capital punishment went hand in hand with the growth of attention paid to the fate of prisoners. The more enlightened and liberal citizens made use of this aversion to show up the conservative supporters of these punishments as barbarian and under-civilized.[47] This resulted, unintentionally, in the fact that both parties had to direct their attentions to the prison sentence, because this measure alone would remain if public punishments were dispensed with. This increased attention did not spring up overnight and remained very one-sided and limited for a long period, but it is certain that, from the second decade of the nineteenth century, prisoners in The Netherlands enjoyed the growing interest of Members of Parliament, scholars, lawyers, ministers, and even the King.

Legally, all that was then established with regard to the prison sentence was that the judge could sentence criminal law breakers to a maximum of twenty years' confinement in a *rasp-*, *tucht-* or *werkhuis* and correctional law breakers to a maximum of five years in a *verbeterhuis*.[48]

Many highly placed Dutchmen who had fallen from grace politically found to their cost, during the turbulent years of the Batavian Republic and the French occupation, just how severe prison life was. The anti-patriotic statesman Laurens Pieter van de Spiegel complained continuously about the abominable treatment he received when confined first in The Hague and later in Woerden in 1795–8.[49] The prison at Gouda became notorious under the monarchist Orangeists.[50]

Suffering is only properly realised when one has felt it personally. Because of this mechanism, many ordinary prisoners became objects of well-founded compassion after the French occupation from fellow-sufferers who had regained their political power. One of the first Royal Decrees (December 1813) after the liberation commissioned the president of the High Court to design proposals 'referring to the present state of the prisons and the most appropriate means of bringing to an end forthwith the inhuman neglect which, in this matter, has taken place in the last three years'.[51]

About a year later the Minister of Justice, Van Maanen, requested the Board of Regents to reflect upon an 'efficient' prison system that had to be 'economical' for the country and make 'the fate of prisoners as tolerable as possible'.[52] Philanthropic pursuit of improvement in the fate of prisoners had thus become linked to economic considerations. In every paragraph he emphasized that costs had to be kept as low, and profits from prisoners' work, as high as possible. Two years later, at government level, and particularly in the mind of William I, even less remained of the merciful intentions which had first accompanied the new interest shown in prisoners. The King found, for instance, that the food given to prisoners was too good and better than that of the free poor, so that the fate of criminals, in this respect, was better 'than that of citizens who must do their frugal best through honesty and hard work'.

As a consequence of these views, a commission was appointed in 1820 to determine to what extent public revenues could be increased if prison boards managed their own finances. This commission was instructed to focus its attention on means which, without hindering factories or other branches of national industry, would make prisoners' work 'more profit-able and beneficial' both for themselves and the kingdom.[53]

It is evident that the first interest shown at government level was intimately connected with the administrative expansion of the Kingdom of The Netherlands, established in 1815; this also led to increased government interference in areas other than the prison system. The government attempted to cut costs by leaving management to the regents, but it took over, once and for all, the responsibility for the prison system, at least on paper.

Prisoners' Health

Even though government paid only lip service to more philanthropic motives, public indifference and apathy began to change for the better. Interest in the prisons grew in wider society. The first area of concern was prisoners' health.

In 1818, *de Haarlemsche Maatschappij van Wetenschappen* (the Haarlem Society of the Sciences) offered a prize for the best 'scientific' answer to the question of how the prison system could be improved. One of the competitors, the lawyer Brand van Langerack en Cabauw, began his argument with a more general definition of his aim: how to focus the interest of 'compassionate' Dutchmen on the fate of prisoners. Because he wrote an essay that was more judicial than scientific, Brand van Langerack did not win any prizes, but his work did come to the attention of William I who adopted as his own work, many of his proposals for reform, virtually unchanged.

Typical of this new interest in prisoners – but also of its limited size in the 1820s – is that it took twenty years for van Langerack's work to be published under his own name. His book contains much exciting and unique information about the 10,000 Dutch prisoners[54] who, in the 1820s, were housed in more than 100 old cloisters or converted private dwellings. He describes in great detail the terrible conditions to be found in these converted prisons. Desease was common and work was absent. The sexes were confined in the same buildings as were prisoners of all ages, with the result that there was great overcrowding. Many of the rooms were so small that three rows of hammocks or cots were stacked against the wall. Hygiene was primitive, and van Langerack records how the authorities tried to limit the spread of infection by smoking the places with 'gaz oxigène muriatique'.[55] The bad air was thought to be the cause of gaol fever.[56] Van Langerack proposed measures to remedy all these ills. He wished to see sexual contacts ended by placing bars between prisoners and visitors. He argued for sleeping places to be separate from workplaces and for uniformed staff to be employed. He made a case for the organisa-tion of labour, larger prisons, and classification of criminals.

He defended himself in advance against accusations that he wanted to make the lot of prisoners 'too tolerable' by confronting these 'unfeeling criminalists' with the fact that a prisoner was 'also a human being', 'And moreover, a human being who has a considerable right to our compassion, because he most often came to have dealings with the law through poverty, youthful folly or fleeting passion'.[57]

Unhealthy Prison Life in Amsterdam

Between 1818 and 1820, the Amsterdam doctor Nieuwenhuys published in four large volumes his *Medical Topography of Amsterdam*. It might be an example of the growing public interest that in the plan of the book there was no mention of prisons, but that as the work progressed this changed. In the final volume, he presented a detailed and harrowing narrative of prison life in Amsterdam. The scant food, communal sleeping places, the rows of hammocks and cots filled with straw, the lack of work and also the disciplinary punishments ('placement in solitary confinement on bread and water, beatings with the *bullepees*, and sometimes fastening in heavy chains') are described by this doctor without emotion. However, he was moved in particular by the situation of prisoners who had yet to be tried, and he warned his fellow-citizens by stressing that 'you all, and even the most innocent among you, are potential victims'. The hovels disgraced a civilized country: 'Indeed, one would be justified in calling these prison hovels, even for the worst imaginable villain, inhumane.'

He found the accused in small, unheated, dark corners where the floors were sometimes completely blanketed 'with a crust of excrement'. These cells were 'so stuffy and slovenly' that, even in those uninhabited, he detected 'a most unpleasant smell'. Out of the inhabited ones 'an oppressive cloud' rose to meet him.

Compared to this, the situation of convicted criminals in the *huis van correctie* (men and women) and the *rasphuis* (men) was markedly better, although he also found prisoners packed together and noticed horrible odours, bad ventilation and even unheated sickbays. In the *rasphuis*, hard work was demanded and recalcitrant prisoners were punished by confinement in damp, underground cellars, as well as being physically punished. Nevertheless, Nieuwenhuys generally found very little fault with their treatment.

In the face of the criticism he directed at the extremely unhealthy conditions, Nieuwenhuys's rather mild judgement concerning the lot of convicted criminals demands some explanation. He had mentioned in passing and without expressing any anxiety that the death rate at the different prisons differed noticeably. In the *huis van correctie*, this rate was more than twice as high as that of the *spinhuis* for women. One has to assume that Nieuwenhuys found that this was a simple fact of life in prisons. In his report, he proposed a difference 'in staleness and cotamin-ation of the air' or 'idleness' and left it at that.[58] He did not even attempt a comparison with the death rate of the free poor. That was, of course, very difficult, and remains so to this day, but nevertheless, some remarks can be made. Nieuwenhuys's figures show that, between 1813 and 1819, an average of 190 prisoners inhabited the *huis van correctie*.[58] Every year an average of ten died. The average death rate over the given period was almost five per cent. Nieuwenhuys gave an approximate average of 160 prisoners for the *tuchthuis* or *rasphuis* for men, from 1800 to 1819. The average mortality rate was between three and four prisoners. Thus, the average death rate over that period was almost two per cent.[59] There were a few regrettable peak years in both prisons. In the *tuchthuis* the rate was 5.6 per cent in 1812 and 3.6 per cent in 1818, in the *huis van correctie* 14.9 per cent in 1813 and 9.7 per cent in 1817. The maximum *tuchthuis* mortality, then, was only just above the average for the *huis van correctie*.

In the province of Noord-Holland, the mortality rate among inhabit-ants in the first decade of the nineteenth century was 3 per cent.[61] In Amsterdam the figures were slightly higher.[62] The death rate in the *huis van correctie* thus far exceeded the norm. Mortality in the *tuchthuis* was less than provincial and city averages.

What can we learn from this? The general figures refer to the whole population, including the stillborn, infants, young children and the elderly who drove the average death rate up considerably. It is fair to assume that the prisons, on the other hand, were populated by people who were in the prime of their lives.[63] Inexact as it is, the conclusion must be that prison conditions were not only extremely unpleasant and bad for one's health but they also hastened one's death. Long-lasting confine-ment often resulted in nothing more than a delay of execution.

Sources of Power

The first signs of interest in and criticism of prison life thus did not arise from concern about the deterrent effect of the punishment. From this penal point of view, the abominable conditions in prison seemed to perform this function excellently, even though life as a free person was probably scarcely better. The first concern shown about prisoners had to do with the state of their health, and implicit in this is the admission that, in deterring wrong-doers, some measures were no longer permissible. The prison sentence might no longer cause visible physical deterioration. Brand van Langerack and Nieuwenhuys accounted for their aversion to the bad hygiene and the contagious living conditions of prisoners with the same arguments that their contemporaries used against corporal and capital punishment; it was shameful for a nation which called itself civilized. Departing from the opinions of their forebears, they saw physical punishment as a sign of uncivilized behaviour; it is difficult to see this as separate from the increasingly widespread rejection of physical violence, coupled with the monopolizing of violence by government, to which I referred in the introduction.

In this way, for the first time, prisoners gained a certain, albeit very limited, power over their punishers. *By suffering physically, they could bring into question the virtuous self-esteem of the punisher.* Paradoxically enough, the bad treatment they were subjected to increased their position of power, at least their potential power. While deterrence dominated as the penal objective, this power source was of little importance, but the first glimmer of interest shown in prisoners bore another hallmark. Brand van Langerack and especially the Society for the Moral Improvement of Prisoners were of the opinion that a prison sentence tended to make people worse and more depraved rather than better. This indirectly undermined the deterrent aspect of punishment because morally corrupt individuals would not, in their opinion, allow anyone or anything to restrain them from wrong-doing. Furthermore, tacitly and hesitantly, a secondary goal for punishment was added. The punishment had to *improve* prisoners as well.

Thus prisoners came into possession of a second source of power. *By remaining bad and persevering in wrong-doing, they gnawed away at the legitimation of the prison sentence.* From the further descriptions of their emancipation process, it will become apparent that both sources of power slowly grew and became more embracing. Not only did improvement of prisoners gain in importance as a secondary goal, but the belief in punishment's deterrent effect on prisoners and potential criminals was also increasingly undermined. In addition, as those responsible for punishment became more aware of the physical suffering of prisoners, their mental suffering also began to chafe; this followed, step by step, the recognition of a prisoner as *een evenmensch* (a fellow-man). This mental suffering, as we shall see, was markedly enhanced as a result of measures specifically designed to further the moral improvement of prisoners. The two power sources thus intensified each other in continuous reciprocity. *As the legitimation of the prison sentence – first deterrence, and then moral improvement – weakened because people remained criminals, it became more and more difficult to defend the inflicted suffering. And because, in the eyes of their punishers, prisoners continued to suffer, it was especially then that a convincing judicial legitimation was needed.* At the end of the century, insights into the causes of crime were developed which pointed to determining factors about which a criminal could actively do nothing. This made infliction of suffering even more difficult, if not impossible, to defend. In the long term, prisoners were to reap profit here.

At the beginning, increased attention and power worked only very partially to the prisoners' advantage and, indeed, often to their disadvantage. Opportunities to gain power remained only at the level of potential without, as yet, having a concrete impact. They had to suffer much more and commit many more sins before their increase in power could bear fruit. This can be attributed to their remaining only passive witnesses to improvements in their position of power until far into the twentieth century, and to their punishers contributing only unintentionally to this increasing power while intentionally pursuing completely different goals.

First Legal Precepts

One is struck by the way in which intentional and unintentional consequences were interwoven in the *Koninklijk Besluit* (Royal Decree) of 4 November 1821 'concerning the organization of prisons, in addition to the enacting and bringing into force of rules regarding food, clothing and bedding of prisoners'.[64] Explicitly, the goal of this decree was to reduce costs of the prison system by obliging prisoners to work on carefully specified projects. In separate work halls, they had to make -both their own clothing and that of the armed forces, among other things. Prisoners were used as underpaid forced labour in order to line the purse of the Exchequer. Implicitly, the Decree meant that, for the first time, concern for prisoners had been legally recorded; their emancipation process had been set in motion unintentionally. Food, clothing, bedding, lighting, heating, washing facilities and health care became attached to minimal rules, whereby the worst excesses, at least theoretically, were prevented. The cubicles and lock-ups had to be 'dry, airy and healthy' and might no longer be placed underground. By means of a classification of buildings, a better separation was aimed at between convicted and untried prisoners. Children, wherever possible, had to be held separately from adults. For moral reasons, prisoners were no longer permitted to sleep in the same bed, but this measure was partially defeated when prisoners had to climb over or duck under each other in order to reach their own hammocks.[65] By sharpening the supervision by uniformed personnel, sexual activity with spouses and prostitutes was also expected to diminish. An Appendix to the Decree laid down in detail what prisoners might eat each day, courtesy of the Crown.[66] This food contained, by present standards, too little protein, fat, calcium and vitamins A and B . The energy content of the food was also very low.[67] It is doubtful whether the food regulations were adhered to, because, even after 1821, prison life was still characterized by the old customs. To the dismal descriptions by well-to-do free citizens who chiefly learned of the facts which they recorded on the basis of a few visits, the following observations from the inside, by a confined debtor, add a melancholy supplement.

The evenings were, according to him, filled with cards, dominoes, draughts and dice. Much liquor loosened people's tongues. Around bedtime, the 'hovel boss' blew out the candle and the stench of an extinguished candle entangled itself with the 'ninety-nine other stenches' which already hung thickly in the crowded room. The chronicler managed to climb into his hammock with much difficulty:

> Now the night was master of this horrid hole, the night, dark and dejected as all the unfortunates no longer consoled by the slightest distraction. Now each and every one was forced to answer to himself and to an ever-present God. The gloomy night pressed down like lead in this condensed and contaminated atmosphere upon those sleeping, whose strained breathing was the origin of luke-warm drops which rained down from the attic upon their faces and hands. Heaving chests gasped for any relief, any fresh air that might cool the burning forehead: in vain! The atmosphere became even more oppressive and sleep would not descend on my eyelids, but an exhausting anaesthesia of both body and soul became my master, in the midst of all these exhalations. Here one heard, between waking and sleep, a frightful oath and there a name called in a plaintive tone, probably the name of a distressed mother, father or spouse. A scream, pressed out in terrible fear, echoed through the shadows and startled me. I thought I saw, shining, a pair of firey eyes gone wild, and started when suddenly a beseeching lamentation rose from another corner, in the shriek: 'Oh God, have mercy on me'. In the dungeon, a fearsome battle was waged at midnight between the good and the evil spirits of man, between the kingdoms of light and darkness; here the sufferer triumphed or sank deeper into the Slough of Despond. Oh, what a skirmish, what a macabre spectacle, surrounded by the close shroud of the night![68]

NOTES

1. From *Gezangen in den kerker (prison laments) (...)*, 1819, pp. 65–6 (*Treurzang*).
2 Jongh, 1846, I, Provisionele Instructie, no. 24, 20 Feb. 1814, p. 48; 20 Mar. 1815, 'Extract (...)', pp. 73–6; no. 69, missive 10 Nov. 1819, pp. 101–3.
3. Hamel (J. A. van), 1909, p. 37.
4. The Frenchman, Le Peletier, pleaded for this. See Foucault, 1979 (1975), p. 112.
5. Eggink, 1958, pp. 128–35.
6. Domela Nieuwenhuis, 1902, p. 22; also see Schama, 1987, p. 21.
7. *Kerkerleven*, 1870, 31.
8. See *MvhG*, 1966/67, pp. 54–6.
9. Jongh, 1846, I, no. 25, KB, 26 Feb. 1814, p. 52; missive no. 135, p. 217; also see *MvBR*, 1961, p. 241.
10. Domela Nieuwenhuis, 1859, p. 14.

11. *MVBR*, 1962, pp. 190–1.
12. Cf. Diederiks and Spierenburg, 1984 (in Petit et al., 1984); Hallema, 1958, pp. 181–2; from prison statistics, which were kept by government from 1837, it appears that, during the whole nineteenth century, small numbers of so-called *débauchées* were kept in houses of detention. Around 1910, the phenomenon fell into disuse and the feature disappeared from prison statistics, as well.
13. Faber, 1983, pp. 196, 198.
14. Calkoen, 1780, pp. 164, 179.
15. Cf. Bemmelen, 1923, pp. 19–21.
16. Ignatieff, 1978, pp. 47–57.
17. Probably a form of typhus. The fever was so contagious that, in 1750, almost all those present in the courtroom of the Old Bailey in London, including the judge, the jury and the lawyers, subsequently died of it, after two prisoners from the Newgate prison had been tried. The fever also decimated the crews of ships where prisoners were sent to work or on which they were transported. The last epidemic of prison fever in English prisons occurred in Newgate, as well, in 1802–3. Almost 100 prisoners died then from the disease. See Ignatieff, 1978, pp. 44–5, 155. Also see J. Domela Nieuwenhuis, 1884, pp. 13-14.
18. E.g. Pols, 1879, p. 27.
19. Howard, 1977 (1777, 1st edn), p. 119.
20. Howard, 1784 (3rd edn), p. 66, 1780 (Appendix, p. 22).
21. In *Liefde en Hoop*, 1827, part I, p. 209; also see pp. 351–6.
22. Howard, 1777 (1st edn), p. 126; 1784 (3rd edn), p. 58.
23. Howard, 1784 (3rd edn), pp. 47, 51.
24. Cited in Bemmelen, 1923, p. 21.
25. The Batavian Republic was strongly inspired by the ideas of the French Revolution.
26. Cf. Moorman van Kappen, 1982, p. 197 (draft of lawbook of corporal punishment, 1801, 1804).
27. Cf. Binsbergen, 1949, pp. 113–17.
28. Also see Faber, 1983, pp. 191 ff. (note 3).
29. Kikkert, 1981, p. 114, and Schama, 1989, p. 637.
30. Hallema, 1958, p. 200.
31. Municipal archives, Alkmaar.
32. Minutes of the Benevolent Society, p. 9. These minutes are in the archives of the 'Algemene Reclasseringsvereniging' (Probation Union) in 's-Hertogenbosch.
33. From the report *Aperçu sur l'état de la Hollande*. See J. A. van Hamel, 1909 (*De Gids*), p. 32.
34. As replacement for the French Benevolent Societies. Cf. Jongh, 1846, I, p. 49, Decree no. 25.
35. Hallema, 1958, pp. 236–9.
36. Bemmelen, 1923, pp. 22–4; Hallema, 1958, pp. 204–6.
37. Bemmelen, 1923, p. 21.
38. Bouricius, 1838, p. 13. In the *Code Criminelle d'Instruction*, warders were given the authority to administer corporal punishment; see Jongh, 1846, I, 13.
39. Cf. Jelgersma, 1978.

40. Moorman van Kappen, 1982 (draft 1804), pp. 57–8.
41. From a speech of Van Goltstein in 1847. See HdSG, 1846/47, Beraadslagingen, p. 324.
42. Cf. Regt, 1984, pp. 9–10.
43. *Gevolgen (...)* 1827, p. 3.
44. Cf. Kruithof, 1980.
45. HdSG, 1846/47, Tweede Kamer, Beraadslagingen, p. 324.
46. Bemmelen, 1923, p. 263.
47. Cf. Franke, 1985, pp. 87–173.
48. The *Code Pénal* distinguished between correctional and criminal offences. The criminal prison sentence consisted of incarceration in a *tuchthuis* and the correctional sentence was a maximum of five years in a *verbeterhuis* or *correctionele gevangenis*.
49. Bemmelen, 1923, p. 20.
50. Hallema, 1958, p. 199.
51. Jongh, 1846, I, p. 40, no. 19.
52. Jongh, 1846, I, pp. 81–3, no. 50, circular letter 30 Jan. 1816, no. 325.
53. Jongh, 1846, I, pp. 111–12, no. 77, KB, 12 Dec.1820, no. 97.
54. Including those in the part of present-day Belgium that then belonged to The Netherlands.
55. What is referred to here is a method of fumigating with chlorine gas, which was developed by the French lawyer and self-taught chemist Louis Bernard Guyton de Morveau (1737–1816). In 1772 he was called in to help with the control of prison fever in the detention centre at Dijon, effactually, as the reports would have it. See Corbin, 1986, pp. 139–40.
56. Brand van Langerack en Cabauw, 1819/1841, p. 24.
57. Ibid., pp. 13, 15, 16, 24, 38, 51.
58. Nieuwenhuys, 1820, part IV, pp. 173, 274, 287, 325.
59. Idem, pp. 286, 300. This refers to the average number of prisoners present on the first of January of the years involved. The actual average population can thus be slightly higher or lower.
60. Nieuwenhuys worked out the mortality using the *total prisoners present*, that is, all those imprisoned for any period at all during the year in question, no matter how short. While a comparison employing death rates of the population of a city, province or country can never be completely accurate, it seems to me that a comparison must be based on the *average population* of the prison. Nieuwenhuys, and many others after him who compared mortalities, came up with much more favourable percentages because the total number of prisoners per year always far exceeded the average population.
61. Cf. Hofstee, 1978, p. 198.
62. Cf. Jansen and De Meere, 1982, p. 187.
63. From an analysis of Reek and van Zutphen (1985, especially p. 183) it appears that the mortality among men aged between eighteen and fifty, also among lower class workers, accounted for one-third of the total deaths. See also Jansen and de Meere, 1982, 187.
64. Jongh, 1846, I, pp. 120–8.
65. Hallema, 1958, p. 223.
66. The decree contained detailed data about the composition of soups

and the nature of clothing and bedding: Jongh, 1846, I, pp. 127, 128. For measures and weights of those times, see the laws and decrees from 1816 (Sb 34), 1819 (Sb 8), 1869 (Sb 57) and 1874 (Sb 143).

67. See table about foods for prisoners in the period 1827–1957 in: Hartog et al., 1988 (3rd edn), p. 380.
68. From: Kerkerleven (...), 1870, pp. 27–31.

2

Death, Discipline and Depravity in Prison Factories, 1821–1850

Walk into our prisons, and see the general appearance of our youth: thin, pale and insipid, with sunken jaws, bulging, bleary eyes, scrawny legs, bent back and bashful look; see the portrait of by far the majority. Many enter the dungeon flourishing like roses; where is their blush? Ask it of them; no, never mind, they will not tell you: only a fearful sigh, a bleak staring eye, like that of one insane, will answer for them. Should you still wish to know, watch them as they eat their victuals, their daily ration, accompany them for days into the workshops filled with stifling air and follow them into the hidden nooks, into the secret places in the still of the night; watch as they gulp down the deadly poison with unnatural lust, and tremble; but ask no more![1]

During the nineteenth century, rational and increasingly scientific conceptions about man and society – according to Elias and Weber so characteristic of the civilizing process in western Europe – changed the thinking about crime and punishment. The ground for this change – was laid by French Enlightenment philosophers such as Voltaire, Montesquieu and Diderot, but it was embodied especially in the world-famous book *Dei delitti e delle pene* of the Italian Marquis Cesare Beccaria, that appeared in 1764.

To Beccaria, feelings of revenge and retaliation should not form the guidelines for punishment, but rather the extent of damage done to society by the criminal. He wanted to establish precisely, in proportion to the nature and seriousness of the crime, which punishment nullified this damage. In addition, he thought that the deterrent effect of punishment should not be sought in cruelty and the amount of suffering, but in heightening the certainty that punishment would follow a crime.[2] Beccaria's book was to influence the thinking of experts in criminal law in all western European countries. In case-law practice, his ideas contributed to hardly any account being taken of the person of the criminal, his place in society or psychological characteristics. The extent of the punishment depended mainly on the nature of the crime. Judges were not yet open to an appeal based on temporary insanity or extenuating circumstances and the penal code offered very few possibilities in this area. There was a tendency, much stronger than in our century, to view criminal activity as a consequence of a free and wicked act of the will.[3]

Monomania, phrenology and accountability

Outside the courts, criminals became the object of an increasing, albeit very one-sided, scientific interest. Esquirol and, later, Georget expanded the work of the Frenchman Pinel, whose ideas about the inaccountability of the insane were implanted in the *Code Pénal* by developing the 'doctrine of monomania'. They focused attention on intellectually perfectly normal people who committed crimes based on certain delusions (*idea fixa*) or an irresistible impulse or inclination. They thus took exception to the current opinion that only completely insane criminals could be deemed unaccountable.[4]

Almost at the same time, scholars such as Gall and Spurzheim were at work on the 'doctrine of phrenology' which assumed a connection between criminal characteristics and the growth of certain parts of the brain, manifest in the form of the cranium. In contrast to Esquirol and Georget, who undermined the foundation for moral judgement with their doctrine of monomania, and who deemed sufferers of monomania to be unaccountable for their deeds, Gall thought that criminal 'mounds', even when they pushed on the cranium wall in exceptionally developed bulges, did not reduce their possessors to apathetic victims of their own impulses. Moral freedom could not and should not be rationalized away. Instincts (*veilleitas*) had to be restrained by the will (*voluntas*) by training the extrinsic conscience through upbringing and religion. Threatening severe punishment was, of course, very appropriate to this end.[5]

The doctor, A. Moll, published his *Leerboek der Geregtelijke Geneeskunde* (Textbook of Forensic Medicine) in 1825 in The Netherlands. He agreed with the German scholar Henke in believing that sicknesses of the soul limited or eliminated free will and diminished the accountability of criminals. He rejected the doctrine of monomania. He did not believe in partial illnesses of an otherwise healthy spirit. He thought it very improbable that 'crazy people' could be 'reasonable as well'.[6] However, this doctrine was defended and expanded by countrymen such as the lawyer C. A. den Tex and the medical doctor H. F. Thijssen during the same period. By today's standards, their texts were filled with outdated connections between monomanias such as the craving to steal, kill or set on fire, and sex-related questions such as the size of the clitoris, masturbation, excessive gratification of impulses and menstrual upsets. In the courts, this new scientific knowledge usually left the judges cold. Outside the courts, experts resisted a doctrine which blurred the distinction between madness and wickedness. A French Solicitor-General called the views 'vain sophistry', and a professor put the question as to whether some doctors might not be suffering from monomania 'inasmuch as they imagine the insane everywhere'.[7]

Black Philanthropic Moralism

Whereas, in the texts of medical men with an interest in man's animal nature, criminals were considered bad because of a combination of mental and physical disorders, in the eyes of philanthropists, priests and pastors, they were primarily sinful and guilty, yet, with God's help, capable of reform. This ideal was held up to prisoners, starting in the 1820s, chiefly by members of the new Society for the Moral Improvement of Prisoners, who had implemented prison visiting duty. In the beginning, the male members made their reluctant way into the dungeons, but, very soon thereafter, in a number of places, so-called 'women's committees' were set up to visit female prisoners. From their reports, it is apparent that the well-to-do ladies and gentlemen were soundly shocked by the 'deeply depraved character of the prisoners' and 'the complete lack of refinement and any, even the most primitive, development'.[8] They had laid eyes on true barbarians, lacking any foundation at all for 'decency and intellectual civilization' and sunken 'into an abyss of moral corruption'. W. H. Warnsinck, co-founder of the Society, compared himself with 'a traveller in previously undiscovered regions of the world'. Until recently, this visiting was 'a completely unknown venture'. In spite of his appeal to recognize prisoners as unfortunate and pitiable 'fellow-men', he makes it obvious that the Society considered them primarily as sinful, guilty and deserving of punishment. He divided the prison population into four main classes: less guilty, guilty, more guilty and supremely guilty.[9]

Society members distinguished themselves from most of their contemporaries by believing that prisoner reform could be effected, trusting in the bible as the appropriate instrument. They saw themselves as explorers and behaved as missionaries bringing the Word to the savage interior of their own society. In this, the inspired founder and chairman, Willem Hendrik Suringar (1790–1872) went to extremes and quickly became famous at home and abroad as a 'philanthropist of stature'. Until his death, he would occupy a very influential position in the world of prison experts. Suringar had wanted to become a vicar, but ended up in commerce. His political career as local councillor and member of the Provinciale Staten (The Provincial States or County Council) of Friesland ended when he moved to Amsterdam in 1840. There he dedicated himself completely to charity and the prison system; one of his many roles was member of the administration commission of the Amsterdam prisons.

Shortly after the foundation of the Society for the Moral Improvement of Prisoners, the *Maatschappij tot Nut van 't Algemeen* (Society for Public Welfare) issued a prize for the writing of an elevating and sustaining book for prisoners on Sundays and feast-days. Suringar was the only contestant and won the 'Golden Prize of Honour' with his *Zedekundig Handboek* (Hand-book of Morals). He wrote stories based on prison life for all fifty-two Sundays which closely resembled sermons.

'Have insight into thy wrongdoing, thou cannot begin thy confinement better than with this straightforward declaration: I am guilty; because these three words are worth more than a thousand artificially invented excuses' was an example of Suringar's advice to new prisoners. To released prisoners, he gave the advice that they reconcile themselves to their fates and never forget 'that it is better to be poor than guilty'. In Suringar's opinion, a rebellious attitude was totally misplaced. Neither poverty nor social inequality, but avarice and a sinful character drove people to crime.[10]

Among prisoners themselves, according to a rehabilitated ex-prisoner, it had quickly become 'a generally prevailing feeling' that the Society was nothing more than a club of preachers who tried to 'hoodwink' the rabble by spreading 'bible tracts'. Suringar's *Zedekundig Handboek*, an example of which lay in every workplace and dormitory, was seldom consulted, according to an ex-prisoner. If a rookie leafed through it too long, the others made a laughing stock of him and promised some 'prettier' reading material. They alluded to pornographic and inflammatory prison pamphlets and poetry which circulated in the large prisons and from which someone read aloud on boring Sundays. According to the ex-prisoner this stirred the senses to indulgement 'in secret sins' and homosexual acts.[11]

Aside from the apparently not very successful reform and preaching, members of the Society did do especially profitable work for prisoners. They continually pointed out abuses and became the first link between prisons and outside.[12] They insisted on improved working and library facilities. They assisted ex-prisoners, who had often been out of circulation for years, in searching for work after release. Right away, in the first years of their existence, Society members stressed education in reading and writing.

Apart from this, the whole question of education was fraught with difficulties characteristic of the time. The prison governor, Bouricius, admitted that education was, indeed, necessary in forming the conscience and promoting a interest in religion, but it would be totally wrong to go so far that a prisoner 'considered himself too learned to pick up a spade or trowel'. Almost all prisoners belonged, according to him, to the rank of manual laborers and one had to guard against a desire, inspired by education 'to raise oneself above one's rank'.[13]

The emancipatory advantage that prisoners could gain from education was, thus, recognized by their punishers but still not entirely nullified. After about 1850, more and more criminals entered the prison gates illiterate to leave years later, admittedly physically weakened, but able to read and write. This did not prevent recidivism, though. And the education was minimal and sometimes only carried out by fellow prisoners. In some prisons, education never got off the ground.

Growing Interest

While present views might find the attention paid to prisoners in the 1820s of dubious value, this interest was, for prisoners, a tool for emancipation not present before that time. Or, as one member of the Society described it:

> The simple thought that people exist who are interested in them is for the prisoners comforting and encouraging; the fact that they are given something, for no reason at all, with which to fill their idle time, affects the majority deeply and they begin to see themselves no more as totally suspect, forlorn and forgotten.

The fact that interest for prisoners was growing is obvious as well from the reactions of people who found this attention exaggerated. In 1840, less than twenty years after the foundation of the Prisoners' Society, a fervent proponent of public corporal punishment complained in an anonymous brochure about the 'excessive, *exaggerated* interest' shown in prisoners. This 'inordinate interest' in 'the most infamous, abject and incorrigible villains' he thought to be 'exceedingly ridiculous'.[14]

Because of the growing interest, much more is known of prison life from after 1825 than before that time. Reports by Dutch and foreign visitors and a growing stream of laws, Royal Decrees, circulars and missives give a rather detailed reflection of daily life. It becomes clear that headway made with the guidelines in the Prison Decree of 1821 was very slow or non-existent in practice, but that reasonably far-reaching changes still took place in prison life. Numerous small prisons in the country were phased out to be replaced by a number of large institutions within about twenty years. There, 300–800 prisoners were crammed together in dormitories and workshops that were much too small. In every provincial capital, a *huis van bewaring* was set up for those awaiting trial and those very briefly punished. *Huizen van arrest* appeared in every city with a law court.[15] Apart from the distress of the transports which were part and parcel of these huge removals, this bringing together, especially of convicted criminals in a few huge institutions, meant that visiting by friends and family, not by chance in the neighbourhood, became difficult.

The new prisons in Leeuwarden, 's-Hertogenbosch, Woerden and Hoorn were populated exclusively by men, criminal and correctional convicts being separated.[16] Women, both criminal and correctional, were housed in Gouda. Boys spent their time in Rotterdam, girls in Amsterdam. In other prisons, for instance the Amsterdam *rasp-* and *spinhuis*, men, women and children were not yet separated.[17]

Mummies in a Sepulchre

Daily life in the large prisons is described by the Dutch prison expert, Bouricius, governor of the prison in Leeuwarden. In his opinion, the period of vengeance and deterrence had passed, but cost considerations and profit-making held sway over the running of the new prisons, which ostensibly were oriented to 'improving the convicts' spirits'. To save space in workshops and dormitories, only the height, breadth and girth of prisoners had been taken into account and not their moral or physical condition 'as if one wished to stack up mummies in a sepulchre'. The designers of the new prison system had forgotten, in Bouricius' opinion, to take into account 'the number of noxious fumes that could be emitted from all those bodies decaying because of former debauchery, bad food and filthiness'.

In the large prisons, dozens of prisoners had access to only two-and-a-half to four cubic yards of space per person. Hammocks hung in rows above each other, chairs and tables were absent and aisles were so narrow that those present could not even stand at the same time. In the 1830s, there was still no light to read or play cards by, unless prisoners themselves bought some oil and a lamp at the canteen. They had to spend from four in the afternoon to eight o'clock the next morning in these spaces in the winter months. This situation was so unhealthy, according to Bouricius, that many died of it or became permanently weakened, despite new sickbay arrangements.

Bouricius found that the overpopulation of workshops and dormitiories seriously undermined common decency. The massive lumping together of 'impure elements' was thought to infect the 'less depraved portion' with evil. He judged it impossible to either repent or 'reflect on God's word' in dormitories where tall tales were told, new crimes and escape attempts were planned, homosexuality was practised and where anyone who felt 'one better impulse' rising in himself must needs smother it to escape ill-treatment by his fellows.[18]

The dormitories, it is clear from his descriptions, were rooms in which people had to get through the evenings and nights in idleness. They were totally at one another's mercy, knew no privacy and were continually subjected to group pressure, maltreatment, mockery, intimidation and sexual approaches. Breathing space was not only absent figuratively but was also literally almost non-existent because of lack of fresh air. Outside the dormitories, they were forced to engage in factory work in equally over-populated workshops. Sentences of ten to twenty years were not uncommon.

Foreign Visitors: 'c'est au coeur qu'il faut aller'

Prisoners were no longer neglected and forgotten in dark hovels. They were now watched by experts with eagle eyes. The Frenchman, Moreau-Christophe, Inspector-General of prisons in his country, imitated his countryman, Appert, by describing the organization of Dutch prisons as 'very deficient'.[19] He thought that all the good intentions had broken down after 1830 because of the old and deteriorated buildings, laid out according to old-fashioned views. He was deeply surprised by the extensive implementation of factory work in prisons. In France, heavy forced labour was demanded in the *bagnes* and prisoners were deported to penal colonies, but there were no workshops where profit-making was all-important.

Moreau-Christophe was uncommonly satisfied with the cleanliness of the prisons. Whatever he inspected, he found it neat and clean, right down to the prisoners' ears. Despite unhealthy ventilation in workshops and dormitories, he sincerely doubted the deterrent working of the Dutch prison system. 'La bonté du coeur hollandais'(the decency of the Dutch soul) was thought to have led to laxness. He characterized the prisons as large factories where well-fed, well-dressed and well-paid labourers were obliged to stay the night and which they were not permitted to leave, for a shorter or longer period. 'La reste n'a rien de répressif ni d'intimidant' (for the rest, there is neither repression nor intimidation), he thought. Disciplinary measures were found lax. He was amazed that, even in that situation, a quarter of the calm and phlegmatic Dutch prisoners had to be given disciplinary punishment. He was against corporal punishment and wished to intimidate not the body, but the spirit: 'c'est au coeur qu'il faut aller' (it is the heart one must go after). The punishment had to affect the prisoner's self-love, his very soul.[20]

Almost at the same time, Ramon de la Sagra, a delegate of the Spanish *Cortez*, described much more extensively and with a good eye for detail the 'stacking up of people' in the large prisons. In Woerden there were dozens of straw beds so close to each other that they actually formed one giant one. Many were thought to have become ill by working for long periods in the stuffy rooms. In the prison at Gouda, an institution housing 350 women convicted of correctional or criminal deeds, he took umbrage especially at their coquetry. He noticed that they wore their uniform hat in a personal way 'to be pleasing and appear beautiful'. He wanted to do away with that hat and argued that their hair be closely cropped to force them to 'meekness and submissiveness'. The ladies ogled even during their airing and, on his tour of the building, they cast him 'shameless glances'. But, other sorts of details did not escape him either. Women were packed into the workshops. The dormitories, as everywhere, were much too small, so that the hammocks hung three rows high and right beside each other. The immorality offended him more than the bad ventilation: 'All those women sleep in that place in the dark, without any supervision, so that nothing exceeds the futility and indecency of the rounds made by the male employees through these places in the night'.[21]

Reverend Heldring had gone to Gouda in 1847 in connection with a fever epidemic which was barely over and had led to an unusually large mortality among the women. He could not even enter a room of seventy girls because of the 'infectious air'. In order not to faint, he had run outside.[22]

Between the visits of Ramon de la Sagra and Reverend Heldring, the women's prison was visited by a group of English philanthropists who had gained great repute not only in England but also in other parts of Europe for charitable work in prisons: William Allen, Samuel Gurney and, particularly, his sister Elizabeth Fry. This commission too took exception to the free access of male guards to any part of the building. Elizabeth Fry personally lodged a complaint about this with the Minister of Justice. The commission's general impression was particularly negative. Workplaces in the attic were too cold in the winter and, in the summer, 'frightfully warm'. They found the dormitories 'especially unhealthy' and conducive to immorality because women slept practically against each other without any supervision worth mentioning.[23]

The prisons in Leeuwarden, Woerden, Hoorn and Gouda were over-crowded and filled with pestilential air. This was not so in the prison for juveniles in Rotterdam. Ramon de la Sagra praised both the building and the strict regime. He also extolled the virtues of the girls' prison in Amsterdam and saw it more as a reformatory than a place of punishment. The Spanish delegate did not visit houses of detention, but he gained a very poor impression of them from talks with experts. Accused and convicts, children and adults, murderers and petty thieves, were all lumped together in institutions where complete idleness, chaos and immorality had the upper hand. He did not consider this situation to be typically Dutch; everywhere in Europe he had met with 'this abominable system'.[24]

Some of these houses of detention were visited in 1840 by the above-mentioned group. They formed a predominantly negative judgement. Cleanliness was usually adequate, dormitories overcrowded. The group found surveillance poor and inadequate, sickbays deficient, punishment cells damp and dark and the buildings old, unhealthy and badly ventilated. Immoral activities and perverse conversations were not prevented in any way at all, so that only 'l'amour du vice' (the love of vice) was kindled instead of 'sentiments du devoir et de la vertu' (sentiments of duty and virtue).[25]

Descriptions thus far of prisons in the 1830s and 1840s emanate from highly placed persons. We also know what an anonymous prisoner thought of the changes in the prison system after the Prison Decree of 1821. He was confined in various prisons for seven years. Generally, he found the situation worsened. The wage for work had been reduced, remission had become more difficult to obtain, visits from relatives had been reduced, correspondence had hardly become possible, food was worse, discipline stricter and the piling up of people in workshops and dormitories had got out of hand. Descriptions of life in the dormitories were gripping. Traffic in things to eat and gambling went on at a lively pace. During fights to preserve the internal hierarchy, a look-out was posted. Murderers, arsonists, rapists, street thieves and burglars were lumped together in one space. Many allowed sexual abuse in exchange for food:

> How many victims has this cancer already dragged to the grave! Those who sold their bread or mid-day meal for weeks and months on end in order to gamble, and then, faint with hunger, were so easily tempted to a wicked or unnatural deed.[26]

A 'rehabilitated prisoner' who had lived through twelve years in four different prisons delivered harsh criticism in 1843 about food, work, education, care and personel. There were many too few sickbays, which led to sick prisoners being sent back much too soon to the workshops, where they collapsed again, and, often, wound up paying with their lives. His 'dearly bought experiences' drove him to critical and moving descriptions of the social jungle in the large prisons. A pecking order based on strength determined both the relationships between guards and prisoners and those among prisoners themselves. In the course of daily affairs, guards acted as if they were equals, but, at the slightest dissention, they demonstrated their authority and handed out harsh punishment. In dormitories and workshops, informal leaders had the last word in an equally heavy-handed way. Sometimes fellow prisoners were formally appointed 'supervisors'. 'Woe to the unfortunate who has not learned to please the supervisor!' wrote the ex-prisoner. He mentioned 'silent stoolpigeons' who 'without the slightest consideration' blew the whistle on talkative fellow prisoners in order to earn several months' remission. In the workshops, prisoners attempted to outdo one another with 'depraved fairy stories' and tales of 'virtuoso villainy'. In the evening, after work, many threw themselves into their hammocks 'from sheer boredom and apathy', while others went on to tell smutty and subverting stories. Some tried to indulge 'their animal and unholy lusts' in homosexual contacts with young prisoners in exchange for money or provisions.

Many convicts also appear to have had 'a personal enterprise' in prison, which consisted of, for instance, usury or buying food to sell later at a profit. Logically, prisoners who had sold their bread were not immune to hunger in the long run. They subsequently committed an offence in order to get food in the lock-up or let themselves in for 'scandalous deeds' in exchange for something to eat.[27]

'Confinement thus claims the lives of many people'

This and practically all other descriptions of Dutch prisons stress how unhealthy they were. Both Bouricius and Ramon de la Sagra publicized death rates which confirm how harsh prison life was. These cover the years between 1830 and 1840. The differences from year to year and prison to prison are very conspicuous. Bouricius reported figures for Leeuwarden prison varying from four to eight per cent. De la Sagra's figures varied even more. In Woerden, the death rate seems to have been only 0.82 per cent in 1836 (5.85 per cent in 1833) while, at Leeuwarden, like Bouricius, he found a death rate of about 8 per cent (1833).[28]

General mortality in The Netherlands was on average 2.72 per cent in the same period.[29] Despite the changes which had been made since the turn of the century, prisoners' health had not improved. For many, conviction leading to confinement for a period of years, could still effectively mean a death sentence. The health situation deteriorated significantly in the 1840s. From prison statistics that began to be recorded yearly in 1837, it appears that huge numbers of casualties took place in the prison population between 1846 and 1849. In Table 2.1, the mortality in prisons and houses of detention can be compared with the national percentage.

TABLE 2.1 Mortality in prisons and houses of detention compared with the national percentage, 1837–50.[30]

Year	Average number of prisoners	Mortality rate in prisons for convicts (%)	Overall prison mortality rate number	%	National mortality rate (%)	National av. mortality rate for people over 5 years of age (%)
1837	3640	3.4	92	2.5	2.8	1.6
1838	3596	4.5	132	3.7	2.7	1.6
1839	3595	4.3	125	3.5	2.6	1.6
1840	3934	4.4	137	3.5	2.6	1.6
1841	4007	3.9	128	3.2	2.5	1.6
1842	4478	3.5	119	2.7	2.8	1.6
1843	4699	3.8	140	2.0	2.5	1.6
1844	4647	4.7	174	3.7	2.6	1.6
1845	4730	4.8	174	3.7	2.5	1.6
1846	5584	8.8	349	6.3	3.0	1.6
1847	6077	18.1	826	13.6	3.3	1.6
1848	5214	13.3	592	11.4	3.1	1.6
1849	4505	9.6	331	7.4	3.3	1.6
1850	4117	6.3	187	4.5	2.5	1.6

TABLE 2.2 Mortality rate of the average population in separate prisons, 1841–50.

Year	Leeuwarden (%)	Woerden (%)	Hoorn (%)	Gouda (%)	Leiden (%)
1841	5.9	3.0	3.7	4.2	2.6
1842	4.9	2.1	2.8	4.3	2.0
1843	4.2	2.7	4.0	5.6	2.7
1844	5.0	4.3	3.0	5.9	3.6
1845	7.0	3.3	4.5	4.7	3.3
1846	7.2	4.2	3.8	19.3	15.3
1847	11.9	10.5	12.8	29.4	33.2
1848	11.6	7.9	12.3	32.2	16.2
1849	9.5	11.4	6.8	12.5	9.2
1850	7.4	6.7	6.8	3.5	6.5

An important cause of the huge death rate in 1846–9 was certainly the increased number of prisoners crammed into already overcrowded prisons. This was connected to a significant scarcity of food and poor harvests which had greatly encouraged theft. In addition, the summer of 1846 was unseasonably hot, a fact which made a stay in prison totally unendurable. In 1847, the mortality rate was even higher, according to van Bemmelen, because of food scarcity and fever epidemics.[31] The consequences of this can be seen from the separate rates for the large prisons at Leeuwarden, Woerden, Hoorn, Gouda and Leiden (Table 2.2). The condition of female prisoners in Gouda and military prisoners in Leiden must have been infernal. Between 1846 and 1849, almost as many women died as could be accommodated in the prison.

These figures did not lead to agitation and worry among politicians and prison experts. In *Lobatto's Jaarboekje* (Lobatto's Yearbook), where the figures were published, the only comment to be found is that excessive heat in the summer of 1846 had 'a harmful influence' on conditions of health situation in prisons at Gouda and Haarlem. 'Many fevers' and 'uncommon sickness' had dominated. When the death rates rose again in 1847 and 1848, they were reported without comment. The psychiatrist, Schneevoogt, published an article in 1848 about prison systems in which he argued that, in every prison, there was a higher rate of mortality than in ordinary life. Poverty and deprivation suffered by prisoners before their confinement and 'their dissolute, profligate lifestyle' he took to be 'predisposing causes of illness'. The sudden change in lifestyle in prison, the lack of freedom and the 'often depressing emotional states' served only to hasten the appearance of illness.[32]

This apart, it is worth wondering whether Schneevoogt knew the actual mortality figures. He did not report them; neither did the Members of Parliament who were so vocal about the prison system in this period of drafting a new Penal Code. This illustrates just how limited interest in the fates of prisoners still was around 1850. Not until 1852 did the *Genees-kundige Courant* (Medical Journal) publish reactions to the tragic figures. The editors compared the figures in prisons in Leiden and Leeuwarden with the substantially lower figures for the free population in both places. They came to the only possible conclusion: 'Confinement thus claims the lives of many people'.

The editors did not only seek the causes in climatic conditions and scarcity of food. They also denounced the inadequate medical care given sick prisoners who dragged themselves through life 'in the most wretched way'.[33]

It is important to consider what the mortality figures meant. A total of roughly 4,000 prisoners died between 1837 and 1850 in all prisons taken together, approximately as many as the average locked up there per day in that period; in a few large prisons this was even worse. Ten to twenty years' confinement was imposed for a great number of offences. Those given long sentences stood, statistically, very little chance of leaving prison alive, especially if we assume that the unhealthy life increasingly weakened the physique as years went by. Additionally, many prisoners had to drag themselves through the rests of their lives in indifferent health after years of confinement. This cannot have gone unnoticed, but there were few allusions to it. During this very period, politicians even stressed that prisons did not deter sufficiently.

Factory Work

Visitors' descriptions show that not much had changed at all, in spite of government interference. Issuing directions was easier than their enforcement. The occasional inspections were announced ahead of time, giving warders and boards of regents every opportunity to prepare before the visit and to threaten prisoners, who hoped to vent their criticisms. 'The entire prison was in an uproar, as if His Majesty had arrived. Warders, doctors and guards appeared in fancy dress, and many prisoners were on the lookout to get a glimpse of the eminent man', said an eye-witness in sketching the atmosphere on days of inspection, which, he said, were often brought to an end with 'a delicious repast' at the home of the administration commission president.[34]

Articles in the 1821 Prison Decree dealing with work certainly were put into practice as quickly as possible, because prisons had to pay their way as far as possible with money and products resulting from work. This consisted primarily of manufacturing cloth for prisoners' use and for other government services, such as the War Ministry and the Marines. An important consideration here was that no 'legitimate grounds for complaint' be given 'to private individuals in the kingdom involved in industry'. 'Large mechanical devices' were also to be excluded from the workshops. Wages were determined in agreement with the usual 'trade' price. A portion could be kept by prisoners for purchases from the canteen, another portion went to their 'exit fund' (this they received at release) and the remainder went into the coffers of the institution. All this led to the supplanting of punishment objectives by profit motives and budget problems. Many prisons turned into real factories.

The length of the work day depended on daylight, varying from seven hours in the winter to thirteen-and-a-half in the summer. The advent of the longest days meant waking at five o'clock and ending work at half past eight in the evening. In their 'free time' prisoners were expected to clean as well. Only on Sunday was work laid aside. To encourage assiduousness, piecework was introduced and any remission partially depended on the diligence shown and the contents of the exit fund. This last condition was intended to prevent prisoners suddenly being freed without resources. The summer was considered the most appropriate time for release, because ex-prisoners could find seasonal work.[35]

The Changing Position of Power

The factory-like structuring of prison work meant a significant change in prison life, which, in the first two decades of the century, had consisted of loitering with nothing to do in dark spaces and hovels. Whether prisoners saw this as progress is another question. They had to do heavy work for low wages and practically had to give up the lucrative manufacture of lids for pipe-bowls, which they had formerly been able to sell. This new work did, however, change both their status and their position of power. From useless outcasts who only cost the government money, they became cheap labour which fed public revenues. Civilized and philanthropic feeling had formerly prevented their state of health from disintegrating to the point where it became visibly deplorable; now health became important for financial reasons too. High productivity could not be expected from badly-fed and sick prisoners. Healthy prisoners had something to offer, for the first time. In 1826, for instance, when permission was given to issue 'a warm drink' on winter mornings to invigorate them, this gesture was not exclusively merciful.[36] The same held for other initiatives concerning food, bedding, clothing and health care.

It is difficult to determine to what extent violent insurrections in prisons at Utrecht and Leeuwarden in 1822 and 1826 gave voice to the growing awareness by prisoners of their own power. Before this time, prisoners had, of course, shown resistance to their situation without the outside world being aware of it, but now, as a particular illustration of the increased interest, reports appeared in the papers. According to the *Utrechtse Courant*, the prisoners in Utrecht destroyed all the looms and other machines and broke open cell doors to free fellow prisoners because they were disappointed by the pardons announced annually on the King's birthday. The rebellion was quashed by a military show of strength, without leaving any victims. In Leeuwarden, 'a serious revolt' broke out in the new prison. Here too, hundreds of prisoners destroyed machines and equipment and broke through walls and roofs. Order could not be restored 'without severe measures'.[37] Prisoners clearly did not suffer their fate with complete resignation. And the general public was now ac-quainted with their situation too.

Disciplining

The quality of care for prisoners improved minimally but remained harsh. Not counting supplements from the canteen, meals consisted primarily of bread and soup, containing just enough nourishment for basic survival. In addition, they often were given spoiled food because guards let them-selves be bribed by suppliers.

Most wages paid out to the prisoners reappeared in the cashbox of the canteen, where Genever brandy and beer were available. After many complaints, restraints were imposed on the use of liquor in 1839.[38]

That prisons were still harsh places can be shown by the existence of institutions such as the *pistole*. Well-to-do prisoners could rent a *pistole*-room and choose meals at their own expense. They did not have to work and could continue to wear their own clothes. Just renting a *pistole*-room with a good bed cost more than the wages retained by most prisoners. *Pistole*-prisoners could also supply themselves with the best food and drink, including excellent wines.

An ex-prisoner had not one good word to say of the *quartier aristocratique*. 'The gentlemen pistoliers carouse and regale themselves as bacchants', he reported, after his 'rehabilitation'. Family and friends had free access the whole day long. Even whores appear to have been let in, while 'one poor devil' was not allowed to press a parting kiss onto 'the tear-stained cheek' of his legal wife, visiting from afar.[39]

The advantages of the *pistole* were out of reach of the majority of prisoners. It was often precisely bitter poverty and unemployment which had driven them to crime and landed them in prison in the first place. Once there, they were also subjected to growing restrictions relating to order, discipline and the enforcement of decency. This partially consisted in formalizing existing practices, but many new rules were introduced as well, almost all of which had to do with disciplining the previously deplorable, but also, undisciplined prison life. Incentives for diligence and hard work were already part of the system in 1821, as well as special punishments for those guilty of 'laziness, wilfulness and bad behaviour'. In 1828 boards of regents were given legal authority, when escape threatened, to put prisoners in handcuffs, but, where possible, this had to occur without 'causing pain or harassment'. In 1839 rebellious behavior by untried prisoners could be legally punished at a regent's order by solitary confinement for days on end. Convicted prisoners could additionally be put on bread and water 'combined, if necessary, with locking up in chains'.[40]

A series of stipulations for order influenced the disciplining of prison life even more than this mixture of old and new disciplinary measures. A circular from the conservative Minister of Internal Affairs, Baron H. J. van Doorn van Westkapelle, in 1836 had very important and far-reaching results; order and discipline in prisons were described in detail and extensively justified. Improvement in the lot of prisoners seemed to have reached its limit for the standards of that time. The minister thought that the great number of repeat offenders meant that, generally, the prison sentence was 'unsatisfactorily daunting' and did not sufficiently effect 'their moral improvement'. The circular appeared when corporal and capital punishment were being increasingly criticized and Members of Parliament had begun to press for their abolition. Thus, the deterrent effect of the prison sentence became even more important. On precisely this point, the minister harboured severe doubts.

First, he pointed to the improved accomodation and clothing, and to government-supplied food, which could even be supplemented by 'snacks' from the canteen. Prisoners enjoyed 'many pleasures of a sociable life' and it was, therefore, understandable that a sentence was 'unsatisfactorily daunting', because life outside, for the same person, was even more 'worrisome and wretched'. The minister appreciated that, without reasonable treatment, nothing would result from prison labour, but prisoners were treated better than the labour warranted, in his opinion. While order, rules and 'complete silence' were thought to dominate foreign prisons, the minister saw an unwholesome chaos with all its unwanted consequences in his country's prisons: 'dissipation too often deteriorating into lawlessness'. Prisoners appear to have slept, talked, hollered and sung on the promenade 'at will and whenever they chose'. In the evenings, especially winter evenings, prisoners were shut up in their dormitories without supervision, where, by the light of a candle or oil lamp, they surrendered themselves to smoking, games and 'the most licentious and perverse conversations'. While 'tasting this freedom and enjoyment' deterence was thought to be insufficient and moral improvement unrealizable.

Using this sort of reasoning, the minister found his second cause of recidivism. Instead of houses of reform, the prisons were 'training schools for roguery of all sorts', where 'the half-corrupted' was turned into 'a villain'. The chance for introspection was denied 'the good ones'. 'Good impressions' retained from religious education and schooling would be 'numbed'.

Now that the health essential for heavy work could not be impaired, an increase in deterrence was sought by order and discipline. The minister proposed seventeen regulations which were to form a strong foundation for disciplining prison life in the nineteenth century. Among other things, he wanted 'an appropriate silence' to be observed in the workshops, under the unflagging supervision of guards and work managers. For their airing, prisoners were supposed to 'be lined up in ranks' and, under supervision, march 'in fitting order' around the promenade. Within the building, he wished to see them walking 'in a like order' through the halls. In their free time, they were expected to keep busy with prescribed household chores, even when senseless activities had to be invented 'so as not to leave prisoners to their own devices, but obedient to the will of others and never idle'. They were not allowed to be anywhere in the building, not even in the dormitories, without supervision. An end had to be put to gaming, smoking and gatherings, as well as boisterousness and shouting. In their stead, the minister wanted the 'completely identically' clothed prisoners to keep themselves quietly busy writing, reading, making small crafts or being read to from edifying books by 'the most competent prisoners'. No one was allowed in their hammock before lights out. And a prayer had to be said first 'in a loud voice'.[41]

After three months, the minister requested a report on experiences with the new prescriptions for order. He was probably not satisfied, because, a year later, he warned once more against too many 'enjoyments' and too much philanthropy. Shortly thereafter, visits were reduced to one per week and visitors could only be received in a separate room, under supervision of the guards. Smoking, gambling, cards and liquor were forbidden. Only untried prisoners were allowed to receive gifts from acquaintances. Letters had to be read first by warders.[42]

The enjoyments prisoners had were thus systematically withdrawn. Additionally, measures were taken against homosexual contacts, 'immorality' as it was called. Complaints about this increased as visits were restricted, particularly those of prostitutes. The rule that henceforth all prisoners had to sleep in separate hammocks or cots was already part of the system in 1821. Afterwards, pressure was brought to bear to light the dormitories minimally at night and to enforce decency by nightly rounds of inspection. The hiring of female guards in female prisons made potential contact between female prisoners and male guards impossible.

The Minister of Justice pushed for obliging prisoners to sleep 'head to toe' in their hammocks so as to prevent, as far as possible, 'all conversation and immoral tendencies'.[43] This was in vain, as it again appears in complaints about 'far-reaching depravity' in dormitories. As Bouricius described it:

> In those dark hovels and spaces there is too much devotion to the most abominable abberations of natural instincts. Catching them red-handed is impossible. Rooting it out is even worse. They must clothe and unclothe themselves within inches of the other; they lie right next to the others, under, above or beside each other. They, yes, the women as well, must climb over each other to get into their hammocks.[44]

Not only the prisoners, but also the previously all-powerful *cipiers* (governors/warders) and their guards were affected by the new regulations for order. Instituting boards of regents had already seriously reduced their freedom of action, even though little of this was evident in practice. They were obliged to wear uniforms. The system brought into force in 1821 took away from them the lucrative canteen management; this was transferred to free operators. They could administer light punishment at their own initiative but not without registering it and informing the regents within twenty-four hours.[45] More serious punishment was only allowed to be imposed by regents. Guards were obliged to live within prison walls. In many respects the lives of these guards differed little from those of the prisoners.

This loss of power was clearly not accepted by warders without resistance because in 1827, the interim administrator of the prison system warned warders, guards and governors not to show enmity to each other in public. Prisoners could make use of this disagreement. Henceforth they, on pain of dismissal, had to act in a way that prevented the slightest doubt about 'the good harmony'.[46] The administration feared a 'spirit of insubordination and rebellion', perhaps in connection with the violent revolt in the Leeuwarden prison in 1826.

Disciplining and Foucault

The disciplining to which these rules and regulations formed but an introduction is related to the 'civilizing offensive' begun outside the walls, aimed at habituating the common folk to order, regularity and self-discipline. Prison experts used concepts such as 'deterrence' and 'the prevention of criminal contamination' as rationalizations, but one can only understand these developments fully in the context of the long-term changes of feelings and rules of conduct, outlined by Elias. Michel Foucault also saw discipline as a dominant characteristic of prison life in the nineteenth century. He views the disappearance of the scaffold as a component part of a process of extensive disciplining and dismisses scholars who typify this development as the humanization of criminal law.

The increased use of confinement as punishment meant, according to Foucault, that not the body of the criminal but his soul had been chosen as the objective, even though physical suffering went hand in hand with psychic penalties.

Certainly Foucault can be seen to have provided a poignant and practical characterization of changes in the punishment of criminals in the nineteenth century, but he wishes also to extend his argument. He does not see these developments as unintended and unplanned consequences of civilizing processes, but rather as a new 'power strategy' aimed at the criminal and rebellious sections of the population. This would be more effective within a society, where crime became increasingly experienced as an attack on society as a whole and less as a threat to powerful individuals (the sovereign). Manipulation of the soul and the attendant disciplining of behaviour was, simply, better for 'power' – Foucault seldom names concrete, flesh and blood possessors of power.

It is noticeable that Foucault describes the developments which I have called prisoners' emancipation as an intentional augmentation of the power of the punishing élite. I think that this contrast arises from the fact that Foucault does not distinguish between intended and unintended results of human endeavours and plans, and from his reified use of the concept of power. What Foucault calls strategic advantages of power were unintentional results of concrete goals, such as the promotion of crime prevention and moral improvement. Foucault, conversely, interprets these goals as elements of a power strategy. In his vision they mask the real goals of this strategy: subordination and a more efficient exercise of power.

Foucault's explanation fails to account for the evidence which points to the failure of this strategy in the long run. As an unintended result of the attention paid to prisoners, of the theories developed about crime and punishment, and of the research that was done on the effects of penal changes, it became increasingly clear that imprisonment was less effective against crime than had been thought or hoped. Thus, if there was a strategy of power, as Foucault suggests, then it must be stated that, *in spite of* this strategy, crime became more difficult to manage and the prison sentence became more difficult to justify. The growing sensitivity to the plight and pain of prisoners made it extra difficult to vindicate suffering in prison. Unintentionally this increased (at least, potentially) the power of prisoners.

It might be better not to speak of power strategies at all. Many social developments in the area of criminal justice, science, politics and economies were thus so intertwined that the changing treatment of prisoners unintentionally became embedded in a structure which I call an emancipation process. The balance of power between prisoners and their punishers shifted slowly, falteringly, to the prisoners' advantage. Not until after the Second World War did prisoners work actively and consciously for their own emancipation. At that point their emancipation process took on the character of an emancipation movement. This distinction between movement and process, even though artificial, and despite the inextricability of movement and process in social reality, is important. An emancipation movement implies an active organization with charismatic leaders who begin at the bottom to fight for a better position, less oppression and equal rights. Such a prisoners' movement certainly did not exist in the nineteenth century. Then, the emancipation of prisoners was fostered especially from above, and largely unintentionally. It was the beginning of the twentieth century before committed politicians and professionals, working with action groups of well-educated, political ex-prisoners, tried purposefully to accelerate this process. Without the preceding developments, the opportunity to actively contribute to prisoners' emancipation would not have been created and nothing would have come of it. The emancipation process of prisoners thus came into being through a reciprocity of unintentional results of penal and other social developments and active, consciously fought-for improvements in their position.

However unaware prisoners were, until far into the twentieth century, of their own emancipation process, their physical and mental suffering was not in vain. The sources of power which I have described – increased sensitivity to another's pain on the part of punishers and the demand for beneficial effects of sentencing – became more significant. Their suffering forced punishers to a stronger justification for sentencing, and prisoners, indeed, continued to suffer intensely. They suffered inside the walls and outside, during transports. Often they arrived ill, weakened and underfed at their destination. Many died during transports or shortly thereafter.[47]

Deterrence versus Improvement

In spite of the Society for Moral Improvement of Prisoners, many did not believe in reform or rehabilitation of prisoners and feared, above all, that every betterment in prison life brought with it decreased deterrence. The lawyer, C. Asser, for instance, had little patience in 1827 with all the 'beautiful theories' set down on paper 'in abstraction'. He found it laudable that the Society attempted to console prisoners 'by convincing them of the righteousness of the imposed sentence', but he thought bitterly little would come of improvement. Nothing could wipe out 'the disgrace' in society 'that forms the inheritance of malicious crime'. In addition, he was of the opinion that the 'bitter experience' had conclusively established that prisons actually encouraged moral depravity. And, nothing could be done about that, because, according to Asser, this evil was inherent to all prison life.[48]

Deterrence was the only objective of punishment and he therefore considered both capital and corporal punishment and banishment much more suitable than sentencing. At the same time, the former judge, Donker Curtius van Tienhoven, argued exactly the opposite. The public viewing of corporal and capital punishment would morally corrupt spectators, while crime was thought to have diminished with the increased use of the prison sentence. As counterpart for Asser's pessimism, Donker Curtius van Tienhoven asserted that even the 'greatest monster' could be receptive to remorse and reform. Additionally, he thought the prison sentence, with its obligation to heavy labour and severe discipline, sufficiently deterrent, particularly now improved investigation had heightened chances of capture.[49] Almost all prison experts saw imprisonment without severe discipline as insufficiently deterrent. That is hard to understand by present standards. No matter how hard one tries to imagine oneself in the society of those times, it remains difficult to find a trace of anything pleasant, let alone tempting, in prison life. Still, the prison expert, Bouricius, thought that the proposals of 1821 had removed 'much of the oppression of confinement'. It had become only 'a transfer' to another society, where one experienced 'less misery, destitution and worry' than in free society. For many, the prison sentence 'encouraged new crimes' and he even thought it was 'also a pleasure' to return to prison. The largest obstacle was 'the sociable interaction' and this brought him to his conclusion: 'As prisoners they had it too easy'.[50] Deterrence was thought to have decreased while crime increased.

Almost at the same time, around 1840, the Member of Parliament and prison expert D. T. Gevers van Endegeest wrote that stern disciplinary measures were needed 'to fill prisoners with aversion to prison life'. Recently, the rise in discipline and regimentation was thought to have put an end to 'revelry, festivities, music, yes, even comedies, unlimited import of money and goods, noisy pleasures, screaming and the pleasures of liquor'. But it was still necessary to oppose pleasures and familiar intercourse because there were, according to him, too many people to be found for whom shame and loss of freedom meant nothing compared to the poverty-stricken misery of a free life.[51]

Naturally, it should be realized that many of the sad circumstances found in prisons were also part of the daily life of the free poor, but, when doubting the deterrent power of confinement, the gentlemen seem to have detected acceptance and even pleasure too easily, when, at most, one could speak of getting used to misery. They did not think much of prisoners' feelings and did not or would not see that loss of freedom in itself constitutes a severe punishment. As far as that goes, they sometimes resembled fishermen of today who deny the fish experiences any sensation of pain. When they did speak of miserable circumstances, they must have been very miserable indeed.

There is more to add to this. Dutch prisons housed about 3,500 to 5,000 prisoners daily between 1837 and 1850. Taking into account population growth, that is approximately three times as many as at present and six times as many as in the 1970s. People were confined for less serious crimes and sentences were much longer than is now the case.[52] In addition, criminals were still mocked, whipped, branded and put to death in public. Everything points to the fact that released prisoners ran into many more social and employment difficulties than in the twentieth century.

On what grounds did penal experts base their opinion that the system of punishment was not daunting enough? Crime statistics were either minimal or non-existent. Judicial statistics were published only from 1847. No one knew the number of crimes which became known to the police. One was almost completely in the dark concerning the scope of crime and the effect of punishment. Common perception was strongly influenced by public executions of punishment and incidental reports about crime and punishment in the newspapers.[53] There was some limited knowledge of recidivism figures but these were even less trustworthy than at present because registration was inadequate. Indeed, dubious recidivism figures were boosted in order to prove that punishments did not deter, but this only makes it more convincing that punishment in the nineteenth century was determined by an insecurity that inspired fear and by an image of man, applied to the dangerous lower classes, that is now difficult to understand.

Those who punished (citizens from the upper and well-to-do classes) saw prisoners primarily as deeply sunken members of the lower classes. That which they abhorred in the conduct and feelings of lower-class people, was, as it were, displayed in concentrated form in the prisons. The volume of their voices, the loudness of their laughter, the uninhibited and violent way in which they interacted, all attested to a deep depravity and lack of civilization. While they themselves, externally at least, maintained a high sexual impeccability, prisoners, in the absence of anything better, shamelessly gave themselves over to the *crimen nefandum*. The prisoners got by, in their own vulgar way, under the many restrictions. They did not sit together, silent and depressed, but told each other wild stories while they gambled and played cards. And they seemed to enjoy it too, both men and women. Instead of chilling misery, they found just what they wanted in prison: immorality and sociability of the commonest sort.

The fact that they knew their families to be plunged into despair, that they themselves lacked freedom of any kind, that they were routinely seriously ill, that they had to work their fingers to the bone to earn extra visiting time or a pipe to smoke and that their uncouth laughter accompanied slow death in great numbers from suffocating air, bad food, work pressure, changes in temperature, prison fever and the trials of transports, could not deflect their cultured punishers from the conviction that they excessively enjoyed the depraved sociability. They went even further in thinking this crime-inducing depravity to be as contagious as cholera. In very short order, a simple but well-intentioned thief would be strolling about the prison with new or more serious criminal plans. Crime sprung from depravity which had taken root deep in the prisoners and anxiously sought new places to anchor itself. Criminals were not attempting to solve their material and emotional problems illegally or to satisfy their desires in forbidden ways; they pursued evil from a corrupt disposition. They preferred evil to good and took to prison as ducks to water. Recidivism was especially related to this and much less to the social and economic circumstances which compelled ex-prisoners to criminal action.

If we try to enter into this way of thinking, it becomes easier to understand why, in the 1830s and 1840s, prison managers, lawyers, Members of Parliament and ministers feverishly sought severe restrictions and disciplinary measures, while the deadly existence in overcrowded prisons probably deterred more than ever. Crime prevention demanded something more or something different. Or, as Gevers van Endegeest wrote, it was about:

> diverting those detained from evil by keeping their attention focussed, by preventing social intercourse, by getting them used to a life of work, by drilling them in obedience, by binding them to an iron will and thereby breaking their hearts and submitting their wills, so that, in this way, conditions conducive to moral improvement are created.[54]

To achieve this goal, physical means of coercion which only affected criminals externally were no longer thought sufficient. Corporal and capital punishment and physical suffering in prison were not thought capable of deterring prisoners so internally depraved. They enjoyed immorality, as devils do flames. Measures had to be found that touched them internally, so that they would once again be susceptible to good impressions. Gevers, who formulated the above goals in 1840, was not a voice crying in the wilderness. He had not invented these ideas. In the whole western world, especially in the United States, experiments had been carried out for decades with psychic coercion. These new forms of punishment found a response in The Netherlands rather late. But, after that, they were quickly found to possess great appeal, as will be clear from the next chapter. Until the end of the nineteenth century, penal experts and politicians spoke and wrote of little else. A period for prisoners had begun that only contributed to their emancipation retroactively and in the long run. In the here and now, nothing awaited them but unprecedented suffering and actual powerlessness. Branded and beaten no more, with the suffocating crowding in dormitories coming to an end, new psychic ordeals were waiting in the wings.

NOTES

1. Beknopt overzigt (...), 1843, p. 36.
2. Beccaria, 1764, pp. 365–8; Cf. Blok, 1925, pp. 4–6.
3. Cf. Wiersma, 1969, particularly pp. 162–74; Moll, 1825, pp. 302–5; Ruller, 1987, pp. 30–1, 165 and 273, note 93, and van Ruller, 1989. Though use was made of psychiatric expertise during trials a few times at the end of the eighteenth century, that happened only incidentally: cf. Faber and Krikke, 1977, and Querido, 1977.
4. See Moll, 1825, p. 305; Aletrino, 1902, pp. 2, 4–6; Ruller, 1987, pp. 164–82.
5. Gall, 1805, pp. 49, 74, 81.
6. Moll, 1825, pp. 300–1, 336, 359–60.
7. Tex, 1830; Thijssen, 1826, 1830; Wiersma, 1969.
8. Bemmelen, 1923, p. 58.
9. *Liefde en Hoop*, 1827, part I, pp. 11, 201; *Liefde en Hoop*, 1828, pp. 100, 109, 111, 113–14.
10. Suringar, 1828, pp. 35–6, 189–94, 344–5. See also Suringar, 1840.
11. Beknopt overzigt (...), 1843, pp. 34–5, 37–8; see also Hallema, 1933.
12. Cf. Bemmelen, 1954, pp. 112–13, 118.
13. Bouricius, 1838/40, pp. 81, 85, 88.
14. *Liefde en Hoop*, 1827, part 1, p. 200; *Iets over lijfstraffen* (...), 1840, pp. 20–3.
15. Cf. Hallema, 1958, pp. 207–95; Petersen, 1978, pp. 87–150; speech of J. Gevers van Endegeest, HdSG, 1845/46, Beraadslagingen Tweede Kamer, pp. 423–32; Bije, 1826.
16. In the *Code Pénal*, a distinction was made between the lighter 'correctional' and more severe 'criminal' offences. For correctional crimes, the (correctional) prison sentence was a maximum of five years.
17. Cf. Fliedner, 1831, pp. 248–51.
18. Bouricius, 1838/40.
19. Appert, 1836, pp. 371–94.
20. Moreau-Christophe, 1839, pp. 87–113.
21. Sagra, 1839, pp. 235–344.
22. Heldring, 1881, pp. 233–48.
23. Mollet, 1840.
24. Sagra, 1839, pp. 314, 320.
25. Mollet, 1840, pp. 14, 17, 24.
26. *Mijn verblijf* (...), 1858, pp. 4, 17.
27. Beknopt overzigt (...), 1843, pp. 19–20, 26–7, 30–5.
28. Bouricius, 1838/40, pp. 61ff.; Sagra, 1839, pp. 272, 290, 295. Death rates of de la Sagra have been recalculated for the population present on 1 January.
29. Hofstee, 1978, table on p. 198.
30. The first prison statistics were included in the *Lobatto's yearbooks*. They were published later by authority of the government. National death rates are taken from Hofstee, 1978, pp. 198, 213 (table 20), converted from permillage to percentage.
31. Bemmelen, 1923, pp. 90–1.
32. Schneevoogt, 1848, p. 215.
33. WvHR, no. 1363, 9 Sep. 1852, p. 3.
34. Kerkerleven, 1870, pp. 82, 85.

35. KB, 4 Nov. 1821, arts 32–6; Jongh, 1846, I, no. 166, missive no. 49, 22 Dec. 1824, pp. 245–52; no. 211, missive no. 49, 24 Dec. 1825, p. 327; no. 231 and 251, missive nos 10 and 21 from 28 July 1826 and 19 Dec. 1826, pp. 380–1 and 395–404; Jongh, II, no. 528, missive no. 75, 25 Sep. 1848, pp. 70–1.

36. Jongh, 1846, I, no. 400, missive no. 105, 7 Feb. 1839, p. 570; no. 243, missive 13 Nov. 1826, p. 389.

37. *MvHG*, 1967/68, pp. 122–3, and *OHC*, 25 Nov. 1826.

38. Hartog et al., 1988, p. 380 (the diets of prisoners 1821–1957); Vriesaard, 1840, pp. 253–5; De Jongh, I, 1846, no. 402, circular MVBZ, 26 July 1839, p. 571.

39. KB, 4 Nov. 1821, arts 54 and 55; missive 23 Jan. 1824, no. 47, and missive 25 Feb. 1825; see also Jongh, 1846, I, nos 127, 171, 309, missive 25 Jun. 1828, no. 12, pp. 456–7; Beknopt overzigt (...), 1843, p. 22.

40. KB, 4 Nov. 1821, arts 47 and 49; Jongh, 1846, I, no. 322, missive 28 Nov. 1828, nos 30, p. 474; no. 295, missive 1 Mar. 1828, nos 17, p. 445; no. 405, missive 16 Aug. 1839, no. 173, pp. 574–8.

41. Jongh, 1846, I, no. 380, circular 10 Jun. 1836, nos 118, pp. 541–4.

42. Jongh, 1846, I, no. 386, circular 24 May 1837, nos 126, pp. 548–549; no. 405, instruction to warders, missive 16 Aug. 1839, nos 173, pp. 574–8.

43. Jongh, 1846, I, no. 380, circular 10 Jun. 1836, no. 118, lines 16 and 17, pp. 541–4; no. 407, KB, 21 Oct. 1839, nos 78, p. 579; Jongh, 1846, II, no. 498, missive 13 Oct. 1846, nos 135, p. 33.

44. Bouricius, 1838/1840, pp. 20–8, 44.

45. KB, 4 Nov. 1821, arts 46, 51 and 61; Eggink, 1958, p. 75.

46. *Kerkerleven*, 1870, pp. 4–6; Jongh, 1846, I, no. 258, circular 24 Feb. 1827, no. 12, p. 407.

47. Jongh, 1846, I, no. 234, missive 28 Aug. 1826, nos 11, p. 382; Jongh, 1846, II, no. 547, circular 2 Oct. 1849, no. 143, pp. 101–2; no. 426, missive 12 Oct. 1841, no. 103, p. 594; no. 521, circular 27 May 1848, no. 51; no. 527, circular 13 Sep. 1848, no. 102; see Eggink, 1958, pp. 131–4, about transports.

48. Asser, 1827, pp. 28, 108.

49. Donker Curtius van Tienhoven, 1827, pp. 18–19, 88–9.

50. Bouricius, 1838/1840, pp. 20–8, 44.

51. *HdSG*, 1839/40, Tweede Kamer, Bijlagen, p. 40; Gevers van Endegeest, around 1838, pp. 27, 31.

52. Cf. Ruller, 1986, and Haastert, 1984.

53. Cf. Franke, 1981.

54. Gevers van Endegeest, around 1838, p. 27.

3

Socialization by Social Isolation: Experiments with Penitentiaries in England and the USA

Whether we build prisons to restore the morality and religion of the people; or churches, in which they are to worship God; the object is the same: but, to all appearance, the repentance and amendment, the sorrow for the past, and the resolution with regard to the future part of life, will be more sincere in the prison, than it usually is in the church. For Heaven's sake, let us try the experiment of solitary confinement![1]

Surrounded as he was by submissive subjects prepared to call his most trivial thought an intellectual tour de force, the German King Friedrich II von Hohenstaufen (1194–1250) could easily have thought that he owed his powerful position to his unusually brilliant personality. Whenever, however and wherever he might have been born, he would have become a great ruler. Possibly this is why it occurred to him to question which language children would begin to speak if they were taught nothing at all: Greek, Arabic, Hebrew, Latin, their parents' language? It is said that he went to work on this problem by tearing several babies from the mother's breast immediately after birth and giving them over to wet nurses who were forbidden to speak a word. Presumably it was impossible, under these conditions, to give the babies any warmth because they died before the King could record even one word from their tiny mouths.[2]

Friedrich II's hypothesis amuses us because we understand that people can only learn to speak a language through communication with others. A private language, created by the lonely speaker and understood only by him, is difficult to imagine for the same reason.[3] Still, his grotesque experiment illustrates a particular way of self-experience which would become more and more characteristic in European society from the Renaissance on. 'It leads people to believe,' writes the sociologist Norbert Elias, 'that their actual "selves" somehow exist "inside" them; and that an invisible barrier separates their "inside" from everything "outside" – the so-called "outside world"'.[4]

Man as Homo Clausus

This depiction of man as a kind of closed box, as *homo clausus*, is the basis, according to Elias, of the misleading opinion that an individual could exist outside society, or that society could exist without individuals. With just as much difficulty as one can imagine a private language, can one imagine a singular individual who exists on his/her own, without others. A person develops in interaction with others and personality, thoughts and feelings are determined in a major way by these interactions. The representation of a self that leads a life independent of others is still attractive to many but it stands in the way of a clear understanding of society and individuals.[5]

The image of man as *homo clausus*, with a confined interior, was negligibly corrected in the nineteenth century by the insight that the human personality is social to the core. This was certainly connected with the larger social distance between people. The concept of *homo clausus* was presumably held and was more cherished by the powerful than by those who possess less power. 'The less powerful think, perhaps from sheer necessity and in spite of themselves, more in sociological terms than the powerful', according to Lissenberg.[6] Until far into the nineteenth century, differences in power were so large that punishers could be extremely blind to their own social shaping and to that of those punished. Those taking a more sociological view were too few to prevent penal reformers from viewing their criminal fellows as outstanding examples of *homo clausus* and making plans based on this view.

This observation seems, at first sight, to contradict the fear described in the last chapter of mutual moral decay and social coercion in the communal dormitories and workshops. Yet, this is only true to a small extent. The term 'moral decay', as the words themselves indicate, was used not as much for the adoption of criminal behaviour patterns as for an evil corrosion of the inner person, of the *soul*. Once decayed – and certainly in the still strongly religious nineteenth century this additionally brought to mind the devil's imperialism – evil-doing became something they could not do without. People were not bad because they behaved badly; they behaved badly because they were internally bad and morally decayed. Thus, knowledge of extenuating circumstances hardly influenced moral judgement of the perpetrator in the nineteenth century. Someone internally good would have resisted the temptation.

The vision of good and evil rooted in Christianity said that evil attracted sinful man more than did good. One would have to possess a very strong leaning toward good to avoid becoming infected during one's confinement by the ubiquitous evil. Isolation of prisoners would therefore accomplish a great deal. The combating of moral decay then was an important goal of the new type of confinement. But, for the improvement of prisoners, a goal certainly just as important, the decayed interior had to be cleansed of all stains as well. Therefore, the decayed interior had to be put into a position to better itself, on its own, in a social vacuum as it were. The immaterial postulate of a person as *homo clausus* was concretized by shutting criminals up within four thick walls and leaving them alone to work on improving their souls, with the help of God.

Bentham's Panopticon *and Foucault*

In addition to moral improvement, cellular confinement lent itself well to a rigid enforcement of the much-desired regulations and discipline. In 1791 Jeremy Bentham published his thoughts on an architectonic discovery, the *panopticon,* in which one could subject people to a perfect system of order and discipline. He was not actually considering people but institutions where, no matter what the goal, supervision had to be carried out, as in factories, schools, hospitals, asylums, workhouses, houses of detention and penitentiaries.

The longer those observed were kept in the visual field of those supervisors, the better the supervision, he maintained. This led him to the felicitous idea that it would be enough if those concerned could never, for a single moment, be convinced that they were not being watched. This situation he saw materialized in a circular building, the outermost ring consisting of apartments or cells. Large windows were placed in the outside wall of these cells and, on the inside, they were shut off with only iron railings. The supervisor, who had his watch tower in the centre and could look into all the cells with one glance around. By means of sun shades (Venetian blinds) and light-dimming dividers in the watch tower, prisoners were prevented from discerning whether the tower was manned. Small lamps with reflectors directing the light toward the cells 'would extend to the night the security of the day'.[7]

Bentham attempted to perfect his system of 'seeing without being seen' with numerous accessory provisions and measures. His plans, for which he also extensively outlined the savings, met with both criticism and support. They were not considered appropriate for factories, schools, asylums and hospitals. In a comprehensive postscript, he then proceeded to develop them further, especially for prisons. Here he explicitly described the *panopticon* as 'a new mode of obtaining power, power of mind over mind, in a quantity hitherto without example'. Under pressure from philanthropic critics, he backed off from completely solitary confinement. As a temporary means of breaking the spirit and 'subduing the contumacy of the intractable', solitary remained very suitable indeed, but two, three or, at most, four persons per cell ought to be the rule. He now saw the solitary confinement that he had, at first, unhesitatingly advocated for the sick, students and workers as an exemplary substitute for the much-criticized corporal punishment. 'Solitude thus applied, especially, if accompanied with darkness and low diet, is torture in effect, without being obnoxious to the name.'[8]

It was Bentham's book in particular with its candid descriptions of the practice of supervision and power which influenced Michel Foucault to interpret the penal reforms in the eighteenth and nineteenth century in terms of power and disciplining. In *Discipline and Punish*, he cites Bentham extensively to lend support to his theory that the later cellular system, in spite of all the penal aims, was nothing more than a refined means of imposing power. Foucault does not mention that Bentham wanted to contract out 'all powers' to free enterprise. Other aspects of Bentham's *panopticon* are also incorporated into Foucault's analysis in a contrived way and sometimes, as De Wit expresses it, 'dragged in by the hair'.[9] Foucault presents Bentham's *panopticon* as the blueprint for the prison system to come, while it is really a strange by-product or 'a symbolic caricature'[10] of the reform-minded sentiment which had seized the imaginations of English prison experts in the last quarter of the eighteenth century.

Other objections can be voiced against Foucault's exaggerated emphasis on practices of power, even though it is true that many prisons where Bentham's principles can clearly be detected were built in western Europe and the United States in the course of the nineteenth century. Examples in The Netherlands, for instance, are the domed prisons still in use at Arnhem (1886), Breda (1886) and Haarlem (1901).[11] Penal reformers, philanthropists, politicians and prison experts hoped to achieve better crime suppression by introducing strict discipline, by reforming criminal souls, by deterrence and by prevention of criminal contagion. In The Netherlands as well, it was believed that cellular confinement was the perfect means to achieve these ends, and it meshed excellently with the civilizing offensive begun in other areas of social life by well-to-do citizens. But very soon after the general implementation of cellular confinement in the Penal Code of 1886, it became obvious that expectations had not been very realistic. The failure of solitary confinement in buildings of *panopticon* design rebounded on the legitimation of the prison sentence. Foucault alleges that the cellular system consisted of a refined form of power politics and does not see that it contributed in the long run to the increase in power of prisoners and criminals. Through the failure of cellular experiments the power balance between punishers and punished unintentionally changed in favour of the punished, as will become clear.

Another objection is that Foucault locates the commencement of the disciplining reform of confinement during the eighteenth century and wisely does not mention that Bentham's book first appeared in 1791. He also does not point out that the first experiments with solitary confinement took place before Bentham, both in England and the New World, where what the Quakers had in mind was simply salvation for serious sinners. Thus, Bentham and his *panopticon* were not as exemplary of the new prison sentence as Foucault would have us believe. The central issue of the cellular system, solitary confinement, was abandoned by Bentham without a backward glance as if it had been something thoughtless, created by hasty writing. He saw more persons per cell an alteration which did not change the plan as a whole and even brought new advantages with it.[12]

Bentham designed a perfect supervision system based on an architectonic discovery; the Quakers in Pennsylvania wanted to get criminals to repent by isolating them socially. Two per cell was thought to be more corrupt than communal dormitories. Ideas of Bentham's were incorporated into the later cellular system eclectically, but the system was not based on them,[13] as Foucault repeatedly alleges. Differently stated: the prison system, together with other social institutions, was strongly influenced by a tendency toward much disciplining of social life. At the same time, the cellular system took root, but solitary confinement was neither essential to disciplining prison life nor explained fully by the general disciplining trend. Seen sociologically, disciplining and the cellular system are better understood, as I shall demonstrate, in connection with the structure and characteristics of the western civilizing process, than when seen as a 'power strategy'.

Ideological Origin of the Penitentiary in England

Many authors situate the religious origin of prisons or penitentiaries in which moral improvement and solitary confinement formed the central issue in the Rome of Pope Clement XII. San Michele, a cloister-like prison for juveniles, was opened there in 1703. The more practical foundations of the cellular prisons are usually sought in the *Maison de Force* in Gent and the Dutch *rasp-* and *spinhuizen*. The question arises whether seventeenth and eighteenth-century prisons are interpreted too much in the light of nineteenth-century developments when looked at in this way. The prisons actually resembled cloisters or workhouses for antisocial persons more than penitentiaries. In Flanders and Holland, solitary confinement, if used at all, was seen as a means of coercion more than a pedagogical instrument.[14]

One recognizes the ideological and pedagogical origins of nineteenth-century penitentiaries more easily in the first prison experiments in England between 1780 and 1830.[15] Even before John Howard made his influential proposals for reform in 1777, religious philanthropists, prison experts, enlightened philosophers and Whig politicians had all expressed their wish that criminals be corrected and disciplined less through their bodies and more through their spirits. A diminishing belief in the salubrious effect of corporal and capital punishment and physical privation in prisons played an important role here, just as it would several decades later in The Netherlands. Ignatieff states that reformers thought these punishments undermined respect for the law, both in criminals and in the wider public, but he discerns that public protest against physical punishment was absolutely out of the question. 'It appears,' he adds, 'that the reformers took their own heightened sensitivity to physical cruelty as symptomatic of general social feelings.'

Howard and other philanthropists thought moral correction could be achieved primarily through religious awakening of the conscience. They hoped that a disciplined life and solitary confinement at night would lead to this awakening. Philosophers such as Bentham and Joseph Priestley had a more mechanical image of the process of reform. They hoped that prisoners would internalize self-control and discipline 'as moral duties' by means of 'routinization and repetition'.[16]

Plans for the building of two penitentiaries were included in the Penitentiary Act 1779 thanks to pressure from Howard and other reformers. Prisoners would be shut up alone at night and would have to work extremely hard during daytime. The building process stagnated in about 1785, after the resignation of Howard as a member of the building committee. Serious objections were raised to so much government interference. Another factor was the reluctance to abandon the banishment of serious offenders for a system of imprisonment. When treasurers of public funds also resisted, the plans faded quite quickly. Only at the end of the century did actual experiments begin in newly-built prisons with combinations of solitary and communal confinement. These experiments faltered due to the opposition of the warders and severe public protests against the hard regime. Millbank was opened in 1817, the largest penitentiary in Europe (a capacity of 1,200), but now prisoners themselves violently resist the regime of solitary confinement and forced labour. Still, as Ignatieff points out after his descriptions of the English experiments, 'there was a new generation of rigour yet to come'.[17] He was referring to the influence of American experiments with completely solitary confinement, day and night, which would lead to the opening in 1842 of the strictly cellular Pentonville prison in London.

The Philadelphian and Auburnian systems

Pentonville put into practice the beliefs of the English reformers of the late eighteenth century in a roundabout way, because John Howard and his friends were in close contact with the colonial Quaker society in Philadelphia, the point from which new beliefs about penitentiaries would spread to all of the United States and western Europe. On 8 May 1787 a group of Quakers founded the Philadelphia Society for Alleviating the Miseries of Public Prisons. Struck by the fate of criminals, members of the Society visited the local prison on Walnut Street, where they were met with an accumulation of men, women and children, 'one sordid mass of humanity'. The Society was of the opinion that solitary confinement with heavy manual labour could reform 'these unhappy creatures'. As early as March 1789 these petitions led to a law whereby the Walnut Street jail was set aside for serious criminals from the whole state of Pennsylvania. Only a year later it was legally established that they were to be separately locked up in cells 'to prevent all external communication'.[18]

From that point on, in the English reformers' terminology, a 'jail' became a 'penitentiary'. The Philadelphia experiment almost immediately caught the attention of prison experts and penal reformers the world over because it provided an alternative to much-criticized communal confinement.

Many experiments with solitary confinement were begun soon in other parts of the United States. The method of confinement differed sharply from state to state. Work and visiting were sometimes permitted and sometimes not. Almost right away, reports trickled out of prisoners who had gone insane or had committed suicide after having been left to their own devices from one day to the next in dark, silent cells with nothing to do and no one to talk to. Large doubts remained about the effects of solitary confinement because huge successes with criminals thought to be incorrigible were also reported. In order to establish, once and for all, how prisoners would react to completely solitary confinement, a decision was made in the prison at Auburn (New York) to proceed with a bizarre experiment that had an especially tragic end.

Eighty serious criminals were shut up in cells, without work or reading material, and, from that moment on, they never saw another person. Only the guards opened the door from time to time to push in the food. These prisoners very quickly became mentally and physically ill, tortured by anxieties, depressions, hallucinations and physical complaints. Within a year, five prisoners had died, one had become insane and one had attempted to kill himself by running out of his cell when the guard brought the food and jumping over the balustrade. Twenty-six surviving prisoners were pardoned as compensation for the suffering imposed on them, but a disappointingly large number repeated offences and were quickly behind bars again. Completely solitary confinement had brought about death and insanity but not moral improvement.[19]

Solitary confinement which lasted day and night was abandoned after that time at Auburn. A system was developed whereby prisoners were shut up in their cells at night and put to work communally during the day in workshops resembling factories. At work they were not allowed to speak to each other. Silence was enforced by caning and whipping. At night they were physically isolated from each other; during the day, this isolation was spiritual. Discipline and regimentation took on rigid proportions.

The Auburnian system was adopted almost everywhere in the United States, but in Pennsylvania authorities obstinately persisted with solitary confinement, twenty-four hours a day. There, a totally new cellular prison was opened in 1829 on the outskirts of Philadelphia, in Cherry Hill. Prisoners were shut up alone, but they did get work to do in their cells. Regular visits from prison personnel were instituted to prevent the punishment becoming unbearable. Cherry Hill developed into an attraction. Days of more than 100 visitors from all over the world were not unusual.

While the Auburnian system had clearly triumphed in the United States, the controversy between the Philadelphian and Auburnian systems was just erupting in circles of European penal experts and politicians. For many years, prisoners in Auburn and elsewhere had been forced into silence with lashes of the whip and corporal punishment, but their resourcefulness in establishing contact was repeatedly greater than their guards had expected. The same went for the Philadelphian system, in which it was a point of pride that physical cruelty was not necessary to enforce law and order. This system was called 'mild and humane', but an official inspection in 1834 showed that especially severe corporal punishment went hand in hand with the prevention of contact and the enforcement of order and discipline; this sometimes led to the death of prisoners. They were also locked up without work in dark cells, on water and bread, as punishment.

The report of the inspection commission includes the words of a man, who, after several days, called out 'For God's sake give me a book or I shall die'. He was freed only after three weeks. A sixteen-year-old boy was held even longer in this sort of cell. After forty-two days, he banged wildly on the door. The report tells of what the guard saw: 'On looking in at the cell, the convict exhibited every symptom of delirium produced by starvation; he was on his knees, his eyes rolling in phrensy, and his frame reduced to a skeleton by the severity of his punishment.' Even then, it was two days later that he was released.[20]

Insanity and Masturbation

Based on reports from that time, it is difficult to establish how often loneliness led to insanity and suicide. One important reason for this is that almost all mental and physical ailments, including death, were ascribed to that which quickly came to be seen as the most significant moral problem: masturbation.[21] Thus, Dr Darrach, the institutional doctor at Cherry Hill, diagnosed eighteen cases of insanity in 1838, twelve of which he ascribed to excessive masturbation, 'this terrible vice'. Many illnesses were also assumed to have been caused by the 'secret vice'. In 1839, he detected twenty-six cases of mental illness; the misery of fifteen of these he ascribed to 'self abuse'.[22]

Until well into the nineteenth century, masturbation was claimed to be the cause of sickness, death and mental illness, a concept which convinced penal experts and, without a doubt, prisoners themselves, that not loneliness but the only pleasure still available to a person surrounded by four walls led to physical and mental decline and even death. There is no doubt that excessive masturbation took place; the ex-convict Jack Henry Abbott wrote in his on-the-spot report one-and-a-half centuries later:

> You become so consumed with impotent hatred, so enraged at someone or something in prison, you must *masturbate* to the violence taking place in your mind, because if you cannot contain it *somehow*, if you loosen the grip on yourself a little, you may start by speaking out, loudly – and end your days in a screaming, raging froth from which there is no return.[23]

A long list of loathsome sicknesses caused by masturbation was still hung up in each cell in 1833. The effects of masturbation, as presented to the prisoners, were 'so terrible' that the directors considered it their responsibility to warn against them. Deadly lung illnesses, chronic disruptions of the digestion, serious heart palpitations, tumours, skin disorders, impairments of libido, nervous sicknesses and other 'insidious and fatal' ailments were included among the lighter consequences compared to the severe attacks on mental abilities and complete insanity upon which those 'who habituate themselves to this debasing vice' could count. Summarizing, the directors announced that 'He who continues this habit cannot have either a healthy body, a sound mind, or pure morals'. The list ended with this urgent appeal: 'Let all who have been addicted to this loathsome vice thus described, *Stop, at once Stop*.'[24]

It is possible that the outdated spectre of masturbation has blinded prison experts and criminal lawyers, right up to the present day, to the devastating effects of solitary confinement on prisoners, especially in the Pennsylvanian penitentiaries. Even the political commentator, Gustave de Beaumont, and the political philosopher, Alexis de Tocqueville, who in 1833 after several months of travel in the United States, wrote a precise and comprehensive report about the American systems, hardly mentioned the psychic horrors. The probable reason for this is that deleterious effects were attributed far more often to masturbation than to the form of confinement.

Reception of Solitary Confinement in Europe

The Frenchmen's trip was supposed to provide an answer to the question of a preferred prison system for France. They visited almost every prison in which one of the two systems was in force. Beaumont and De Tocqueville thought that the Philadelphian system better achieved its goals than the Auburnian. Nevertheless, after considering the lower costs, they advised the adoption of the latter system in France. They were, however, not as enthusiastic and optimistic as many American experts. They proved to be very sceptical about the Utopian high hopes believing that the conviction that every man could be converted to do good, that crime would one day disappear and that the system of penitentiaries was the perfect means to banish all social evil, betrayed an unrealistic view of man and society. The repression for years on end of savage passions and the complete estrangement of prisoners from the world would surely lead to the rapid collapse of all the good intentions after release. Improvement was difficult to measure in prison and many prisoners were well-behaved because they hoped for clemency. The authors saw benefits especially in the impossibility of moral contagion and in the chance, small as it was, of a *réforme radicale*. At the very least, prisoners learned obedience and became familiar with a strict work rhythm.[25]

The French report was often cited later in The Netherlands by lawyers and politicians wishing to temper sweeping optimism, but real opponents of solitary confinement referred with raised voices in debates and with exclamation marks in articles to the devastating report by Charles Dickens in 1842 of his visit to the Cherry Hill prison. Dickens was accused by contemporaries of having used his literary imagination to distort the reality in order to attract more readers, but the facts used in his report agree with those found in the sterile descriptions of the scientific observers. It was most likely his emotional position that alienated prison experts who could only see buildings, systems and figures for recidivism. Possibly they were upset by his condescending tone, in which he very convincingly, full of understanding for their ignorance, accused them of monstrous cruelty. 'The system here,' Dickens wrote in the introduction,

> is rigid, strict, and hopeless solitary confinement. I believe it, in its effect, to be cruel and wrong. In its intention, I am well convinced that it is kind, humane, and meant for reformation; but I am persuaded that those who devised this system of Prison Discipline, and those benevolent gentlemen who carry it into execution, do not know what it is that they are doing.

He followed this up by expounding upon those things which he could intuit but the well-intentioned gentlemen could not:

> I believe that very few men are capable of estimating the immense amount of torture and agony which this dreadful punishment, prolonged for years, inflicts upon the sufferers; and in guessing at it myself, and in reasoning from what I have seen written on their faces, and what to my certain knowledge they feel within, I am only the more convinced that there is a depth of terrible endurance in it which none but the sufferers themselves can fathom, and which no man has a right to inflict upon his fellow creature. I hold this slow

and daily tampering with the mysteries of the brain to be immeasurably worse than any torture of the body: and because its ghastly signs and tokens are not so palpable to the eye and sense of touch as scars upon the flesh, because its wounds are not open to the surface, and it extorts few cries that human ears can hear; therefore I the more denounce it, as a secret punishment which slumbering humanity is not roused up to stay.

Dickens tried to create for himself an image of the lonely life within four walls after his visits to Philadelphia and other cellular prisons. He described the feelings and experiences of an imaginary prisoner, commencing with his first moments in the cell. The loneliness, the delusions, the fear of the walls, the anxiety about the fate of wife and children outside, the aggression which gave way to apathy and, finally, the panic at the prospect of release. Solitary punishment, he concluded, 'wears the mind into a morbid state, which renders it unfit for the rough contact and busy action of the world'.[26] He declared himself openly in favour of the Auburnian system, also called the *Silent System*. Perhaps he hoped to avoid the worst by propagating the less severe alternative. He had little success in Europe (including The Netherlands) although there were those who had already condemned solitary confinement there in no uncertain terms.

In 1827 the English penal reformer William Roscoe already saw both systems 'as destined to contain the epitome and concentration of human misery, of which the Bastille of France, and the Inquisition of Spain, were only prototypes and humble models'. This new punishment was, according to him, 'the most inhuman, and unnatural, that a tyrant ever invented'. The famous French general and politician, Marquis de la Fayette, who himself had experienced three years of solitary in the Bastille and who had experienced the European battlefields, wrote of the Pennsylvanian system: 'I have been subjected to all of this: and of all the sufferings of my life, none have exceeded – none have equalled that single oppression of being, for three whole years – ... exposed to the view of two eyes, watching my every motion, taking from my very thoughts every idea of privacy.' He argued for the Auburnian system without the obligation to silence.[27]

The poet and essayist Heinrich Heine wrote in 1843, during his stay in Paris, that the Pennsylvanian separation in cells particularly in France, 'this country of sociability', constituted an 'unheard-of cruelty'. The French population was, in his opinion, too magnanimous to wish to buy social peace at such a price. He wrote of his conviction that the 'appalling, barbarous, even unnatural cellular prison system' would not be imported. He characterized the many millions that building these new prisons would cost as 'scandalously wasted money'. The 'dungeons of the new bourgeois feudalism' would be just as thoroughly destroyed by the populace as the Bastille.

> How devastating and miserable these might appear to be from
> outside, they were still, definitely, only a cheerful bower, a sunny
> garden-house, in comparison to those small, silent American hells,
> which only a stupid pietist could invent, which only a heartless
> merchant, who fears for his chattels, could sanction

said Heine. He asked himself why a loving God was not sufficient for the
pious citizens to enable them to sleep peacefully.[28]

When Heine wrote his article many experiments with solitary confinement were being carried out in Europe, Philadelphian style. In England,
Belgium, Sweden, Switzerland, Poland and Hungary these experiments
had already led to formal importation of the system. France and Prussia
followed in 1844, Denmark in 1846 and Norway in 1851.[29] Numerous
experts, including the famous penal reformer Julius and his English
colleague Crawford, had pushed for the importation of the Pennsylvanian
or Philadelphian system after their visits to the United States. To reassure
those who feared for the physical and mental health of those shut up in
solitary, a commission of the Medical Academy of Paris, of which the
illustrious psychiatrist Esquirol was a member, stated 'that the system of
solitary confinement, day and night, keeping in mind the contact with the
different personel of the institution, in now way shortens the life of
prisoners, nor confounds their sanity'.[30]

In 1846, a congress on penitentiaries was held in Frankfurt, attended
by famous and prominent criminal scientists from virtually all European
countries. The authorities, including the Dutch Society members
Suringar, Mollet, Lurasco and the professor of criminal law, den Tex,
pronounced themselves unanimously in favour of the 'solitary or individual prison', so arranged 'that no possibility of social intercourse exists
between solitary prisoners themselves or with other prisoners'. Each
prisoner had to be kept busy in his cell with meaningful work, permitted
to enjoy 'the pleasure of free air' daily and to share in 'the pleasure of
religious, moral and school education'. It was also decreed that each
prisoner had to be visited regularly by clergymen, governors, doctors,
members of the supervisory and management commission and by other
visitors determined by regulations. The cellular prisons had to be built in
such a way that every prisoner could attend religious services and 'that he
see the serving clergyman and be seen by him without compromising the
principle of separation from others'. Only a small minority of conference
guests thought that this punishment should be reserved for short sentences. The remainder had no scruples about long-lasting solitary confinement.[31]

Thus the Philadelphian system swept through Europe.[32] The concept
of man as *homo clausus* resulted in a desire to teach criminals to live better
socially by forbidding them any type of social life for years on end:

socialization by social isolation. If there were criminal lawyers or politicians who sought the causes of crime in poverty, unemployment, bad housing and class differences, they were outnumbered in discussions which, certainly in The Netherlands, were dominated by those expecting nothing less than salvation of solitary confinement. They could not or would not see the psychological cruelty of this punishment, or they did not object to it, hoping it would deter others. They patted themselves on the back for their philanthropy, because they also contributed to the abolishment of 'barbarian' corporal and capital punishment. In The Netherlands in the 1830s, a remarkable struggle, difficult to interpret sociologically, broke out between scholars and politicians, who, by turns, accused each other in righteous tones of barbarous cruelty. From the prisoners' point of view, all this revolved around a choice between two sorts of punishment rivalling each other in cruelty: communal confinement in overcrowded and unhealthy prisons with public corporal punishment, or a loneliness that martyred, between ashen walls. The only long-term contribution they themselves could make to the disappearance of both sorts of punishment was to continue to suffer visibly and to remain committed to evil.

NOTES

1. Statement of the Christian philanthropist Jonas Hanway, one of the very first advocates of reformatory prisons and solitary imprisonment, in his *Solitude in Imprisonment*, 1776, London, pp. 98-9. From Bender, 1987, p. 208.
2. The Scottish King James IV (1473–1513) carried out a similar experiment. He sent two newly-born children to the inhospitable Highlands with a dumb wet nurse. For both experiments see David Cryspel, *The Cambridge Encyclopedia of Language*, Cambridge, 1988, p. 288.
3. Cf. Kenny, 1974, about private languages by Wittgenstein, pp. 176–98.
4. Elias, 1978, pp. 119, 131. See also Elias, 1978 (1939), Introduction. In this connection, the question remains whether the development described by G. H. Mead, 1974, pp. 135–226 of 'the self' and his distinction between the 'I' and the 'Me', should be seen as well in the light of this historically developed experience of self as *homo clausus*.
5. Cf. Goudsblom, 1977, pp. 126–32.
6. Lissenberg, 1979, p. 190.
7. Bentham, 1791, pp. 3, 25.
8. Bentham, 1791, Postscript, pp. i, 23, 33, 35.
9. Foucault, 1979, pp. 200–9; Wit, 1981, pp. 318–19.
10. Ignatieff, 1978, p. 113.
11. For a Foucaultian analysis of these prisons, see Vollemans, 1978.
12. Bentham, 1791, postscript, pp. 21ff.
13. In their classic book about the cellular prison in Philadelphia, Teeters and Shearer (1957) refer to 'the bizarre plan of Jeremy Bentham' only in a note p. 35n.

14. The octagonal prison in Ghent was founded in 1772. The regime could be compared in some ways to the Auburn system, as described in this chapter, but without obligatory silence. Cf. HdSG, 1845/46, Beraadslagingen, p. 424. For the history preceding cellular imprisonment, see also Quintus, 1887, pp. 3–22.
15. The descriptions in this paragraph are mainly derived from Ignatieff, 1978, and Bender, 1987. See also Priestley, 1989, pp. 2–14.
16. Ignatieff, 1978, pp. 67, 73.
17. Ignatieff, 1978, pp. 95, 173.
18. Teeters and Shearer, 1957, pp. 6–10.
19. Beaumont and de Tocqueville, 1833, pp. 13–14; Teeters and Shearer, 1957, p. 202.
20. Teeters and Shearer, 1957, pp. 98, 100, 102, 169–71.
21. Hare, 1962. According to Hare it was a Philadelphian psychiatrist, of all people, who first directly associated masturbation with insanity (p. 133).
22. Teeters and Shearer, 1957, pp. 176–7.
23. Abbott, 1981, p. 78.
24. Teeters and Shearer, 1957, pp. 98, 100, 102, 169–71.
25. Beaumont and De Tocqueville, 1833, pp. 42-8, 60-2, 87, 416.
26. Dickens, 1842, pp. 131–5.
27. Teeters and Shearer, 1957, pp. 26–7.
28. Heine, 1964 (1843), p. 133. Translation by Kate Simms.
29. Teeters and Shearer, 1957, p. 206; see also 'Beknopt overzigt (…)', 1843, pp. 67–76.
30. 'Beknopt Overzigt (…)', 1843, pp. 69–70.
31. Juridical magazine *Themis*, 1846, pp. 641–2.
32. For a survey of the reception of the solitary system in Europe, see the speech of the Member of Parliament, Gevers van Endegeest, in 1846. HdSG, 1845/46, *Beraadslagingen Tweede Kamer*, pp. 423–6.

4

Barbarian Scaffold versus Civilized Solitude:
From External to Internal Constraint

Das strenge Philadelphische Pönitenziarsystem (Strafsystem) macht, mittelst Einsamkeit und Unthätigkeit, bloss die Langeweile zum Strafwerkzeug: und es ist ein so fürchterliches, dass es schon die Züchtlinge zum Selbstmord geführt hat. Wie die Noth die beständige Geisel des Volkes ist, so die Langeweile die der vornehmen Welt. Im bürgerlichen Leben ist sie durch den Sonntag, wie die Noth durch die sechs Wochentage repräsentirt.[1]

If any lesson at all can be learned from social history, then it is that no form of cruelty is foreign to man. Still, the word 'humanization' appears in almost every article written about the development of justice. The authors seem to think that the way in which criminals are punished has become more and more compatible with human nature: mild, friendly, understanding. Some also seem to believe that they have explained this development: it was altogether atrocious and cruel, but, little by little, repressed, friendly human nature surfaced and the torture disappeared, corporal and capital punishment were abolished, and, increasingly humanely, criminals were only locked up in prison.

One thus elevates oneself morally above one's ancestors, but, just as little as historical developments can be better understood by calling everything more justifiable which is presently perceived as normal, can these penal developments be better understood by seeing them as consequences of unfettered benevolence. In short, in using the term 'humanization' one implies a moral judgement, while what one really needs is sociological insight into the interconnections between penal and other social developments.

Sociological Interpretations

It is even more confusing and inaccurate to use the term 'humanization' when the facts also make this moral judgement very doubtful. Nevertheless, the argument is found in many judicial and historical studies that the abolishment of corporal and capital punishment and the institution of solitary confinement can be seen as an important phase in the humanizing of penal practice. However, in what decisive way is it crueller or less humane to whip, brand, and put to death than to shut someone up for years in a small, dark cell without any social contact worth mentioning? One would have to make very arbitrary decisions, indeed, to answer that question. Additionally, a judgement argued in this way would not add to the sociological understanding of these changes in punishment.

From discussions which took place in newspapers, in parliament and in circles of lawyers and prison experts in the first half of the nineteenth century, it is quite clear that advocates of the new solitary confinement realized perfectly well that this was an especially severe form of punishment, no less arduous than public punishment. Very simply, more was expected of this sort of punishment in the struggle against crime and recidivism. At best, it was found less severe because criminals would eventually have a cleansed soul to show for it, while corporal punishment was meant purely as a deterrent and could harden the offender and make him vengeful. Even spectators were thought to risk depravity in witnessing displays of corporal and capital punishment.

The establishment of these facts does strongly undermine the already dubious humanization theory but, nevertheless, does not throw much light on penal changes in the last century. Something more important and also very different was taking place, something which cannot be fathomed from the explicitly stated intentions and rationalizations of penal reformers. Solitary confinement, after all, presented a very welcome alternative to the punishment on the scaffold particularly detested by liberal modernists. These enlightened citizens elevated emotional rejection of the raw cruelty of justice to a sign of intrinsic civilization, thereby labelling politically conservative supporters of public punishment as barbarians harbouring medieval ideas. Public punishment thus gained political significance and became a tool in the struggle between liberals striving for more power and their conservative opponents, including many upper-class members of the old aristocracy, like the Minister of Justice, van Maanen.[2] Characteristically enough, five of the so-called 'nine men' – the nine Opposition Members of Parliament who, in 1844 under Thorbecke, introduced a motion advocating a radical, liberal alteration to the constitution – were very outspoken in debates against public executions of punishment. It was the strongly liberal Dirk Donker Curtius – charged by King Willem II in the year of revolutions all over Europe, 1848, with setting up a commission to make parliamentary democratic changes to the constitution – who as Minister of Justice, proposed, in that very same year to abolish public branding and whipping. The directly elected Lower House passed a Bill to this end; this was, however, defeated by the old, ultra-conservative senate just before the Upper House elections.

The fact that the civilization argument, especially on the issue of public corporal and capital punishment, could play such an important role fitted into a long-term development whereby everything to do with the human body became surrounded with feelings of shame, aversion and embarrassment and was thrust behind the scenes of social life. Norbert Elias described, analyzed and characterized this development in western Europe as a civilizing process. The barbarism of public displays of punishment lay not so much in the cruelty as in the public visibility of mutilated, bloody and dead bodies on squares upon which homes fronted. It was fitting for civilized persons to abhor these sights. At the very least, they were expected to wish such scenes removed from the public eye, as was the case in diverse west European countries. In this way, the sting was taken out of the abolition movement. Capital punishment disappeared out of sight and, consequently, out of mind. In those countries, though, non-public capital punishment was retained for a long time, while The Netherlands, steeped in democratic tradition, had stronger objections to the furtive putting to death of criminals, and abolished capital punishment in 1870. The loathing of public physical violence also makes it understandable how the psychological cruelty of solitary confinement could be admitted to an extent and yet not severely oppress the refined citizen's conscience. Solitary confinement was, after all, a preeminently civilized punishment. It left the body untouched and, even better, was rigorously hidden behind thick walls from almost everyone's eyes. Naturally, the proponents of public punishment – who were continuously accused of barbarian leanings – attempted, in turn, to accuse the advocates of solitary confinement of inhuman cruelty, but this sounded reasonably unconvincing coming from those attempting at all costs to retain such ignominious displays as public whipping and hanging. Defenders of solitary confinement could easily gloss over the cruelty of this invisible punishment by pointing to the goal of moral improvement, while dwelling on the gory details of immoral scaffold punishments. Because even the deterrent function of corporal and capital punishments could be doubted, they occupied a much stronger position in debates about both crime prevention and civilized emotion. Proponents of public punishment themselves emphasized that they felt a strong aversion before they advocated retaining it as an indispensible deterrent.

The debate in legal circles in the first half of the nineteenth century was, thus, not whether punishment should be less cruel, but whether psychological restraints were preferable to physical ones. Doubt had arisen in the trust, placed for centuries, in the deterrent effect of public judicial violence. From the image of man as *homo clausus*, the belief had grown that moral improvement could be effected by isolating prisoners socially. Instead of keeping them from committing crimes by externally imposed pressure, one wanted to bring criminals to the point where they refrained from evil deeds, spurred on by an awakened conscience. The emphasis shifted from *Fremdzwang* to *Selbstzwang* (external to internal constraint). In the sphere of criminal punishment, this was marked by a move from social constraint to self-constraint.

These changes in criminal justice fitted into a long-term development which was characterized by a similar shift in many other areas of social life. All sorts of rules for conduct in one's daily life, which originally had been thought to come from above or outside, became internalized. These included love-making and relieving oneself in rooms closed off from others, holding intestinal gases in, not belching after eating, and eating with knife and fork, but also compulsory school attendance for children, the forbidding of child labour, working at set times and, very recently indeed, the doing of household chores by husbands.[3]

Another point of view also deserves attention. As social life became more complex, differences in possession of power diminished and many social tasks were divided, individuals in western European societies came increasingly to depend upon others at a greater social distance from themselves and were forced to take these others into account more often. To operate in society, one was forced to try to empathize with the feelings and interests of one's fellow-being. It is very likely that this increased the ability to see others, including criminals, increasingly as like oneself, as *evenmenschen* (fellow-men). Lashings and whippings administered to criminals on the scaffold could also come to be felt as welts on one's own back.[4] The detachment with which one had witnessed the thrashing of a strange body in earlier days would gradually have given way to an identification with those punished, so that the pain, hypothetically at least, was inflicted on the observers as well. This psychological mechanism can – if reversed – be compared to the attitude of torturers who distance themselves from their fellow-man by seeing him as an object, an animal, a non-person.[5]

This is a very plausible idea and connects readily with contentions on earlier pages, although protesters against corporal and capital punishment gave evidence of suffering more from their own civilized feelings than the pain experienced by their fellows on the scaffold. It is certain that members of the cultured upper classes considered lonely solitary confinement less awful than communal confinement or corporal punishment. They themselves preferred reading good books and taking up new studies in solitary cells than dwelling in the midst of a crass and illiterate rabble or being dealt with painfully and shamefully on the scaffold. Solitary confinement coincided, in that sense, with the appeal to more and more people from the upper social classes toward the end of the eighteenth century of a new ideal: that of going into comfortable and undisturbed retreat. The stuffy rooms, filled to overflowing, in which the city's working class had to live during the majority of the nineteenth century, were the antithesis of this ideal. According to the sociologist Goudsblom, it was 'a horrifying experience' for those brought up to the standards of the 'better circles' to be confronted with these lower-class conditions.[6] It would be exactly when identifying oneself with this 'inferior' class, used to crowded rooms, that one could readily imagine solitary confinement being a much more grievous punishment. Thus, in the thoughts and hearts of the punishers, solitary confinement hit the people hardest who needed it most: wretches without an ounce of civilization. Or, as Professor den Tex, a Member of Parliament, put it in 1844:

> He in whom the tiniest traces of good can still be found feels happy in the solitary confinement which frees him from the contagious community of the most tainted individuals, whereas, it is precisely those evil creatures, in whom every decent feeling is stunted, who will experience this confinement as severe.[7]

Not everyone saw public executions of punishment and solitary confinement as mutually exclusive,[8] but the large majority was for one and against the other. The number of opponents of public punishment had begun to grow even before solitary confinement had gained any recognition as an alternative. There is evidence that public punishment by whipping was imposed less often in the second decade of the nineteenth century, while resistance to capital punishment had already increased at the end of the eighteenth century.[9] Cellular confinement thus accelerated the abolitionist movement.

The whole evolution, seen from the prisoners' perspective, meant that their sources of power were growing. They could confound the escalated hopes of their punishers for this new punishment by continued recidivism and by showing less moral improvement than predicted in the theories about solitary confinement. Within the context of increasing identification with one's fellow-man, prisoners could make the legitimation of the prison sentence difficult by continuing to suffer. But, before any of this could have emancipating effects, decades of talk and debate about prisoners passed. Doubts about the beneficial effects of the prison sentence were stifled by optimistic tales about solitary confinement. The extent of compassion felt for prisoners was only demonstrated by those who preferred whipping and branding them on the scaffold to enforcing loneliness in a cell, because they had more faith in deterrence than in moral improvement. Supporters of the new punishment were driven more by their own civilized feelings than compassion for fallen fellow men. However, judges, academics and politicians were no longer at all as indifferent to the lot of prisoners as they had been around 1800. The prison sentence had, indeed, become a centre of public interest by the 1840s. Newspaper readers were forced by articles about penal reform to engross themselves in criminals' souls. Prisoners did not become loved, but less unloved than when they had been unknown.

Attempts to Import the Auburnian System into The Netherlands

The very first reports about 'the prisons of Philadelphia' were accessible in 1796 in a translated booklet by the French Duke de la Rochefoucauld-Liancourt.[10] But it was only in the second quarter of the nineteenth century that Dutch lawyers and politicians fell under the spell of solitary confinement, even though little of its intended purpose was understood at the beginning. Some thought 'the torment of their own conscience' would deter criminals better than the 'most horrible torture'.[11] Conversely, J. S. Mollet, committee member of the Society for the Moral Improvement of Prisoners, spoke of 'moral medicine'. He saw the new prison as a sort of 'hospital' or *lazaretto* where one put criminals 'into quarantine'.[12]

After 1840, when the national excitement about the Belgian secession began to ebb, the possible implementation of a cellular system and the abolition of public corporal punishment stirred up deep sentiments. Conservative citizens used the penal developments to resist, using fierce law-and-order language, the increasing influence of liberal modernists with their so-called enlightened notions. Reciprocally, the weak philanthropists took advantage of the situation to depict their conservative opponents as miserable old men holding back the progress of civilization with barbarian whips and branding irons. Safely ignoring the densely-packed prisoners succumbing in great numbers to misery, the free and educated sector of the nation argued the pros and cons of corporal punishment and solitary confinement in drawing rooms and clubs, in books, brochures and newspapers, as if their lives depended upon the discussion.

At government level and in parliament, many diverse and far-reaching Bills came and went. The future fate of criminals depended, in this period, on fleeting convictions and ideas which were alternately supported and abandoned with an ease which made it seem that they concerned only minor changes in a police ordinance. Using arguments that sometimes seemed to have been thought up minutes before, these noble gentlemen opined about the benefits and drawbacks of twelve or even twenty years of solitary confinement for prisoners. Within less than a ten-year period, it was proposed by government that heavy, public, forced labour (chain gangs), the Auburnian system and the Philadelphian system be brought into force, as well as that public corporal punishment be totally abolished. A Bill to lock criminals up for a maximum of twenty years following the Auburnian system of nightly isolation and communal work with enforced silence was adopted in 1840 by both the Dutch Upper and Lower Houses. Seven years later, the Lower House voted for a maximum of fifteen years of solitary confinement according to the Philadelphian system (day and night in the cell). These far-reaching Bills were never actually enacted, for a diversity of reasons. Finally, in 1851, an experiment in solitary confinement not exceeding half a year was implemented very carefully with a select category of criminal.

This turbulent and, from the point of view of legal security, sordid period in Dutch penal history began in 1839 with the submission of a Bill by the conservative Minister of Justice, van Maanen, for a Penal Code. Solitary confinement did not, at first, appear in this Bill. Only after Lower House pressure did he include a variation of the Auburnian system. During at least a quarter and, at most, half of their term of confinement, those sentenced to 'long-lasting, heavy *tuchthuis* punishment' (fifteen to forty years) had to be 'gaoled in isolation in a secluded cell'. Only for a breath of air and communal work could they leave their cell, and this had to go hand in hand with the 'keeping of silence'. Those sentenced to 'heavy *tuchthuis* punishment' (seven to twenty years) were subject to the same rule.[13]

During the public deliberations over the Bill in June 1840, opinions about solitary confinement differed considerably. The conservative Member of Parliament, Ridder van Rappard, preferred whipping and branding to shackling a criminal 'like an animal' in a dungeon and 'to whom it is forbidden to share his experiences with others, and who, even when he is admitted to communal work, is regarded as dead among the living'.[14] On the contrary, the Member of Parliament Gevers van Endegeest, one of the first experts in the area of the new prison sentence, argued that prisoners be completely solitarily locked up with work to do in their cell for the first half of their sentence (a maximum of ten years). After that they would be allowed to work communally. He understood well what the point was of the new punishments. The criminal must not be restrained by 'force' but he must obey 'from respect' and submit 'from conviction'.[15]

Finally, a fundamental amendment to the prison system was accepted, by thirty-four votes to nineteen, which could forbid criminals virtually every social contact for a maximum of twenty years.

Some weeks after the Lower House, the Senate also adopted the new system of punishment following the Auburnian model by eight votes to seven. The Bill was printed in the *Staatsblad*[16] but actual implementation never took place.

The Philadelphian System and the Dilemma of Penal Reform

In 1842, parliament had fallen under the spell of the Philadelphian system in which prisoners stayed, day and night, in their cells. It wished the Bill revised. The conservative Minister of Justice, De Jonge van Campens

Nieuwland, showed great flexibility by replacing the adopted Auburnian system with a new Bill within a year, whereby both criminally and correctionally sentenced prisoners had to be locked away 'in solitary cells' during their entire sentence, a maximum of twenty years.[17] Except for 'putting on display', he wanted to abolish all public corporal punishments. The Auburnian system was rejected by the minister because silence was not enforceable with strokes of either cane or whip and 'the language of gestures' always remained possible. It was clear to what an extent he saw the criminal as *homo clausus*, who, completely alone, could attain good:

> The unbroken isolation of a criminal, removed from all opposition of the outside world, will give him the chance to reflect seriously, not only on the difficulties of his situation, but also on their causes. The incessant contemplation of these ideas will turn not every, but still, many a criminal in upon himself, and cause him to feel the moral necessity, when finally returned to social life, to improve his inner existence.

By way of diverse amendments he finally presented a Bill in 1845 in which the prison sentence in its entirety, that is, a maximum of fifteen years, had to be spent in solitary.[18]

This gave rise to a fundamental debate in parliament. Although the death rate among prisoners, as we have seen, reached a tragic high point in this period, the members were completely unanimous about one thing: the existing communal prisons hardly deterred at all, indeed, they were such pleasant places that they encouraged crime. The difference between life in freedom and that in prison, later called *the dilemma of penal reform*,[19] formed a leitmotiv in the debate.

The Minister of Justice set the tone on this issue. He felt that prisons had taken on the character of ordinary factories, the only difference being the question of freedom. Care, clothing, sleeping arrangements and food were better than in 'the lodgings left behind'. According to the minister, 'the distraction and diversion' provided by work and 'the company of members of their own crowd' made the lack of freedom easy to bear.[20]

The moderate, liberal Member of Parliament Uytwerf Sterling argued that the criminal missed only a freedom 'from disasters', a freedom of suffering from 'hunger and cold', a freedom from 'idleness and misery'. Compared with that freedom, a life in prison would be very comfortable. Gevers van Endegeest even spoke of this life in terms of pleasure. One was not meant to think that he mercilessly wished to hurt or torment his 'wretched fellow-men', but the dungeon, after all, had to function as punishment and 'not as pleasure; as deterrence, and not as enticement'.[21]

Most of the other speakers accentuated the insufficient deterrent power of the existing prisons. All this is difficult to understand. Using present-day standards and concepts, prison life at that time bore all the hallmarks of an unbearable existence. Did the Minister of Justice and parliament know nothing about sickness and the huge mortality in prisons? They did – despair, sickness, death and suicide were seen by Uytwerf Sterling as characterizing existing prison life even more than they would the proposed cellular system.[22] But they did not conclude from these facts that prison life deterred. Either they were of the opinion that people of the lower classes themselves thought that life and health were not important, or the daily life of these lower-class citizens was sometimes, indeed, much more miserable. Characteristic of relationships between social classes, which were seen as God-given, is that not one speaker came up with the idea of improving living conditions of the lower classes instead of making prison sentences more severe. Stealing to survive was understandable, but not, therefore, less evil and condemnable.

There was another class-determined way of thinking which made parliament see prison life as much more pleasant than it must have been for the prisoners. They expressed their indignation and horror at the immoral and morally corrupting contact between prisoners in the massive dormitories. The Minister of Justice said that he would have expostulated about this at length 'if my feeling for decency did not seal my lips'. In prison 'the last spark of shame was extinguished'. Prisons were, as Uytwerf Sterling saw it, 'training schools for crime'.[23]

It is clear that the prisoners, enormously crowded together, did everything in their power to lighten their physical and mental pain. They sought support from each other with their tales, they fought for work bonuses and remission, they justified their behavior and themselves in each others' eyes and they forced each other into sexual practices. This social intercourse, this 'infectious moral plague',[24] will not have fostered much good, but parliament was also convinced that most prisoners enjoyed it. Materially, prisoners fared better than in freedom, and the social contact offered them all their uncivilized, vulgar hearts could desire. Actually, parliament interpreted communal prison life in such a way that it became impossible to increase deterrence unless, as Gevers van Endegeest remarked, one let the prisoners starve by government authority.[25] The only way to reach them was to remove the pleasures of that social contact. This was precisely the gist of the proposed penitentiary system, that additionally offered chances of moral improvement. Still, by choosing the cellular system, one also relinquished deterrence as the sole principle of punishment. Crime could only be combatted by punishment explicitly aimed at moral improvement which implicitly still deterred in a civilized way: solitary confinement.[26]

In spite of much support in parliament for the new form of punishment, the Bill was not successful. Both those for and those against the penitentiary system objected to the fact that only the first book and not a whole Penal Code was offered.[27] The part dealing with punishment was rejected by thirty votes to twenty-six, and the minister retracted his Bill.

Enlightened Vanguard against Conservative Barbarians: An Uneven Battle

Meanwhile, the conflict over the new system and the connected abolition of corporal punishment had also flared up fiercely outside parliament. In the newspapers, conservative and progressive readers harassed each other with letters to the editor.[28] Suringar, chairman of the Society for the Moral Improvement of Prisoners, involved himself in the discussion with a passionate plea for the Philadelphian system. He argued that cellular punishment was especially severe and painful and did, indeed, sometimes lead to suicide and insanity, but he was prepared to pay this price for punishment that prevented communal depravity and aroused remorse, because

> it is better, no matter how awful, to lose one's senses than to keep them to smother remorse about wrongs done, to confirm oneself in wickedness, oh yes! to commit wickedness again.

The fact that loneliness encouraged the sin of masturbation he cancelled out against 'the ravages of body and soul' which homosexual contacts in communal prisons would bring about. Moreover, 'protective agents' and appropriate punishments were thought to exist against 'a too violent continuance' of masturbation.[29]

An article written at just about the same time by Professor den Tex was as startling and influential as Suringar's booklet. Den Tex was additionally a member of the Dutch Lower House where he presented himself as a very moderate liberal. He saw incisively what the gist was of the new punishment. It was aimed at 'taming and regulating passions and lusts'. Mind, will and time had to contribute to this in unison. 'Those convicted should *learn to see* the criminality of their actions, and thereafter to *wish* to refrain from them,' he wrote. Experience had not yet conclusively proven, as he saw it, what the results of solitary confinement were. He was able to see some drawbacks to the 'less favourable health situation' and 'greater incidence of insanity' among prisoners, but it did not yet follow that the system be rejected. 'But,' continued den Tex, 'I do not hesitate to go further,' and he quoted the German poet Mullner who 'not mistakenly' had written: *Das Leben is der Güter höchstes nicht* ('life is not the greatest good'). Worse than physical death was the moral death of prisoners in the existing prisons.[30]

There were those who had occasion to doubt the philanthropy of den Tex and Suringar when confronted with this sort of far-reaching statement, but they were usually found among upset citizens who imagined their lives and goods threatened by the imminent abolition of public corporal punishment and who themselves were accused routinely of merciless cruelty because they wanted to retain these sorts of punishment. This went on primarily in the *Weekblad van het Regt* which had appointed itself a keen opponent of public corporal punishment and defender against criticism of solitary confinement. The editorial board endorsed without criticism the ideas of den Tex, Suringar and other champions of the new punishment.

In 1842, S. P. Lipman, an Amsterdam lawyer, wrote a lengthy article in this weekly whereby he endorsed the 'clear ideas' of the Swedish Crown Prince Oscar who had argued that 'so-called physical-pain punishments' were so bad that the preferrence should be given to the 'psychic-pain punishments'. Lipman was very optimistic about the effect of the Philadel-phian system. He thought the danger to body and soul deemed inherent to this punishment to have been refuted clearly on 'historical grounds'. He believed that the punishment of long-term solitary confinement was com-pletely in keeping with the 'precepts for philanthropy' according to him.[31]

Proponents of cellular punishment congratulated themselves continu-ously for their high degree of civilization and compassion. Did they not see that solitary confinement lasting for years could be torture or would they not see this because, in their enlightenment, they had fixed upon this alternative in revulsion against public punishment, seen as barbarian and uncivilized? It is certain that disagreeable reports about the tragic results of solitary confinement were swept under the carpet. The *Algemeen Handelsblad* overtly refused to place letters to the editor which called for the retention of corporal punishment.[32] As a reaction to this, the Amster-dam publisher, Goossens, placed an advertisement in the *Opregte Haarlemsche Courant* in which he urged the letter writers to send the refused copy to him. He wanted to compile this in order to destroy the impression that, in The Netherlands, one desired 'only one-sided' infor-mation about affairs upon which 'the peace and safety of good civilians' depended.[33] Indeed, an anthology from this publisher appeared in 1843 in which cellular punishment was fiercely attacked and corporal punish-ments passionately defended. It was typical of the atmosphere surround-ing these discussions that no contribution was signed with a genuine name, probably for fear of being labelled barbarian and uncivilized. For that matter, the writers did not hesitate to depict supporters of solitary confinement as cruel 'torturers' using so-called philanthropic motives to ignore the pain of victims of crime and to aim solely at moral improve-ment of the criminals. Similarly, 'Philatethes' from Amsterdam attacked the sham compassion shown scaffolded criminals with opportunistic indignation about the cruel fate of prisoners in solitary:

> The lack of freedom is not enough for the theorists of today; they
> wish to inflict pain upon the souls of criminals in the prisons, this,
> they say, is even worse than corporal punishment. Yes! assuredly,

but it is barbarian, medieval, inhuman, cruel, loathsome (I shudder as I write), it is an unjustifiable, inefficient, and insufficient punish-ment. Still, solitary confinement is *barbarian, medieval* and grue-some, because it is similar to the inhuman practices followed in times of the barbarians and in the Middle Ages with regard to the accused and the sentenced.[34]

The tone of most contributions was scornful and aggressive. Much pent up anger was vented against the condescending attitude of the half-witted philanthropists who spouted enlightenment and civilization.

The booklet, which besides its law-and-order-language still contained serious objections to the implications of solitary confinement, was either ignored in press and parliament or referred to derisively. [35] The *Algemeen Handelsblad* tagged the articles as 'mystifications' and suggested that they were 'self-made pieces cobbled together' from one and the same writer whom it called a 'lover of castigation, instinctively and with all his heart'.[36] In an anonymous brochure from 1844 this reaction was judged characteris-tic of the predominating refusal to entertain arguments against cellular punishment. The anonymous writer bemoaned the fact that 'noble, respectable men' let themsleves be swept along by their feelings and did not listen to 'the voice of reason and judgement'.

In his own brochure, however, the writer had no idea how to control his own feelings. Tired of being accused of barbarism, he doubted the necessity to shut criminals away 'just as one shuts animals away in pens'. Was that consistent with man's nobility and civilization? And where must one seek civilization in the persons of Professor den Tex and Society chairman Suringar who had already written that the awakening of feelings of decency in solitude could well lead to insanity and deterioration of health, indeed, even to death:

> We quake at these ideas, and, one way or another, these feelings ought to be called medieval and barbarian. Well, tell us truely, which law justifies your ardour for improvement? What gives you the right to confound with self-torture the senses of your fellow-man or secondarily to undermine his physical powers? Is it Godly, is it human right? Pray, tell us, do.[37]

Opponents of cellular confinement were in a difficult position. All their verbal eloquence and their often pertinent protests faded in the light of their defence of corporal punishment, which provided crude displays on national market squares. They held forth, doubtlessly against their better judge-ment, that civilization meant rejection of both physical and psychological forms of cruelty, but proponents of cellular punishment were bothered by corporal punishment solely because of the public physical violence and the vulgar atmosphere of the village fair in which it officially took place. Precisely these uncivilized elements were lacking in solitary confinement.

Moreover, solitary confinement was surrounded by an aura of enlightenment and scientific progress, just as a progressive atmosphere with broad-
minded ideas about human self-determination and women's rights hangs
around the present movement for euthanasia and abortion. Advocates of
cellular punishment counted themselves an enlightened and civilized
vanguard, while its adversaries knew themselves to be regarded as conservative barbarians, no matter how fiercely they tried in word and writing
to resist this. Additionally, they wished to retain corporal punishment, not
from a preferrence for physical violence, but as a preventative measure.
They too abhorred violence, but the threats to person and goods which they
saw in society forbad them to give in to this. On this point, they were forced
to go against their own feelings when reasoning. This made their articles
less convincing. They did not argue self-assuredly, but defended themselves
from the start and without being asked against opponents who remained
condescendingly convinced that they were right and morally superior.
They lapsed into aggressive utterances arising from unadmitted impotence.

Also in 1844 an anonymous brochure appeared showing all the traces
of this uneven battle. The author presented alarming figures about
insanity in the cellular prison in Philadelphia and Lausanne in Switzerland. But, his businesslike account of this damaging material degenerated
quickly into scorn for the 'twaddle about enlightenment and civilization'
and the 'miserable outcry' of his opponents, 'young people lacking
adequate experience'. He proceeded to defend corporal punishment with
unavoidable shilly-shallying. One must not think that supporters of
corporal punishment 'found pleasure in the fear and pain of our fellow
men', but that they were convinced 'of the evil in the heart of man' and
that they knew that people existed who did not recoil from shame,
vilification or loss of freedom 'but did from pain and death'.[38]

The editorial board of the *Weekblad van het Regt* did not miss this
chance for a free shot. In a review of the brochure they spoke mockingly
of 'our flogging friends' and 'floggers'. The writer was dismissed for wishing
to retain the punishment of flogging but also for betraying his aversion to it:

> It seems, indeed, that one does not dare recommend one's scourges,
> but begs forgiveness and indulgence for them; as if one does not
> dare introduce them openly, but leaves them to crawl and skulk.[39]

The figures dealing with insanity were simply denied and shoved aside.
This battle was being fought on another level and on that level the
brochure writer lost helplessly.

Draft for the Penal Code of 1847

Government and parliament did not pay much attention to sounds of
protest. In 1847, Minister of Justice De Jonge van Campens Nieuwland
presented a draft for a complete Penal Code in which, of all the scaffold

punishments, only capital punishment was retained. Both correctional and criminal prison sentences comprised solitary confinement for the duration of the sentence with upper limits of five and fifteen years, respectively.[40] The minister wrote in his explanatory memorandum that 'the usefulness' of the system had already 'so frequently' been discussed that the government was of the opinion that it could 'confidently' refrain from defending itself. He did reiterate that, for the time being, 'no satisfactory insurance' existed that criminals could stand more than fifteen years in solitary 'without injury to their mental capacity or without damage to their health'.[41]

It would also have been impossible for the government to do more than vaguely trust in the outcome because nowhere in Europe was solitary confinement of criminals for such a long period legally allowed. In 1842, Pentonville prison began with a maximum of eighteen months' solitary confinement, but some years later, 'as the authorities became familiar with its effects', the maximum length was reduced to twelve and then to nine months.[42]

Parliament began again with many days of exhaustive debate about a new penal system. In the game of opinions on solitary confinement, it was obvious that the cards were already cut. The supporters were seemingly so convinced that they were right and that they formed the majority, that they hardly stirred during the debate. Thus, primarily opponents spoke. They were upset by the long term of confinement, but Baron van Goltstein posed the crucial question in casting doubt upon the reforming power of the punishment:

> Is it possible that a person will be able to undergo development toward either good or evil, when he is not brought into contact with his fellow-men and subjected to temptation, against which he is then obliged to struggle and emerge victorious?[43]

Of the members who spoke, a number were against the proposal because they wished to retain public corporal punishment. Others showed that they were for the new cellular system precisely because the country would thereby be freed of public corporal punishment.[44] The draft for the first book of a Penal Code was accepted with thirty-five votes to fifteen. Events came to a standstill during the discussions for a second book when a vast majority of Protestant members of parliament resisted the omission of established punishments for transgressions against right of *exequatur*.[45] After that, the House wanted to repeat the whole procedure with regard to the Penal Code.

This delay, due to the political events of 1848 during which The Netherlands received a new constitution and the Dutch Lower House came to consist of directly chosen representatives, led finally to cancellation. Thus, it was partly chance that decided that criminals could not be plucked from a full life to be shut up in a small cell for fifteen years on end, with their only social contact being short talks with men who inspected their every word and deed for signs of moral improvement.

There was little, if any, increase in compassion for prisoners, as was clear again and again from the discussions. Civilized feelings were at odds with themselves at the sight of corporal punishment, and upset by the vulgar, licentious and boisterous contact between prisoners in communal dormitories and workplaces. Consequently, based on completely short-sighted and unproven theories about human feelings and spiritual life, a new punishment was invoked which was thought to better match civilized tendencies and, most importantly, hide the suffering of criminals. Invisibility gave rise to doubts about deterrence, but, both those for and against were unanimous that cellular punishment was unusually severe.

The First Prison based on a Cellular Image of Man in Amsterdam

Even though attempts to institute it were frustrated many times, enthusiasm for solitary confinement hardly declined at all. After the national reforms of 1848 which mainly increased the political power of the liberal bourgeoisie it began to dawn on people, at least in parliament, that the human spirit could succumb to long-term solitude and that social functioning could be damaged. The changed make-up of the Lower House could have had much to do with this, all the more so because sentiment, much more than empirical knowledge, determined opinion-forming. Before 1848 approximately twenty-five of the fifty-eight 'Noble Well-to-do Gentlemen' were conservatives and just as many conservative-liberals. The liberal opposition was seriously in the minority with eight or nine men. After the first direct elections in November of 1848 the liberals occupied half of the sixty-eight seats. No more than eighteen members of the old House had been chosen. The extremely conservative Senate became somewhat more liberal when its thirty-nine members were appointed by the directly elected Dutch Provincial States, and the King could no longer interfere with the appointment, as he had frequently done before. Additionally, the radically liberal Donker Curtius succeeded the conservative De Jonge van Campens Nieuwland as Minister of Justice. From a 'distinguished dignitaries' club', chiefly made up of conservative 'political amateurs' who often allowed old school friendships to play a role in their political stand, the Lower House became a club of mainly liberal solicitors, lawyers, notaries public and judicial and administrative civil servants. Even though faction or party pressure was still minimal, Members of Parliament nevertheless had to take more account of the political consequences of their standpoints than before 1848, when, in considering important questions, almost every member was of the opinion 'that their political wisdom should not be withheld from the populace'.[46]

It is quite probable that their ideas about crime and punishment were slightly more social than those of their predecessors. Certainly the revolutionary events in Europe and at home will also have influenced these ideas. It is true that in The Netherlands popular uprisings were limited to a failed riot on the Dam in Amsterdam, but this must still have harmed the narrow, 'cellular' image of man (*homo clausus*)which Members of Parliament and penal reformers had adopted. The revolutionary events, according to a later Minister of Justice, Modderman, had served to shake the belief in moral improvement of commoners,[47] but that must have been short-lived. The fact that six years passed after the failure of the 1848 attempt to abolish branding and flogging before the liberal Donker Curtius again introduced such a motion will perhaps have been connected to fear of revolution, but, in 1851, while waiting for the new Penal Code, parliament was already working on a proposal to make solitary punishment possible on a small scale.

That was necessary because in various parts of the country many experiments with solitary confinement were taking place as a result of the debates in the Lower House. In some places, parts of prisons had been made suitable for solitary confinement. Amsterdam, in 1844, had already received permission to call for tenders for a completely new cellular prison (*huis van arrest en justitie* for 200 inmates) at the *bastion Schinkel* on the Weteringschans.[48] Little more than a year later building began.

For readers who had had occasion to take 'a curious and interested glance' at these activities, the *Algemeen Handelsblad* wrote in 1847 that the building consisted of three wings which were emitted like separate rays from a central hall. From this hall, guards could oversee the rows of cells in the wings 'at a glance'. All cells were alike and had small windows of frosted glass. In each cell could be found a closet pot made of baked brick, a wash basin, a gas lamp, a hammock, a three-legged stool, a table and a small storage cupboard. The wooden cell door was covered with steel on the inside, and had a food hatch and a spy hole through which the prisoner could be watched 'without knowing it'. 'Mutual communication between prisoners is an impossibility', the newspaper announced to its readers.

Around the prison site a circular wall was built. Between the wings and the circular wall were to be placed the walking areas; they had the form of a half (women) and a whole wagon wheel (men). These spaces were separated from each other by the 'spokes' so that prisoners could not make contact with each other during their airing. The *Algemeen Handelsblad* added:

> The prisoners walk, to and from the walking areas, fifteen steps from one another, and wear a sort of cap, from which the visor hangs downwards over the face, to beneath the nose. They can see through two holes in the visor, made at the height of the eyes, but are not able to distinguish another's face.[49]

Various authors seized the opportunity presented by the building of the first cellular prison to emphasize their standpoint on solitary confinement. 'What strange questions have been already been elicited by that eccentric building! What daring speculations and mistaken conceptions it has brought into being!' wrote the psychiatrist Voorhelm Schneevoogt in *De Gids*. Subsequently, he attempted to refute all objections to long-lasting solitude – he himself found twenty years acceptable – in order to establish that only when alone could 'the mind' of a prisoner be opened 'to the benevolent influence of morality and religion'.[50] The judge Vernée visited the newly-built prison with some of his friends. The building as a whole made 'a very deep and serious impression' on one of his friends but another thought it primarily a shame that so much money was being spent in order to 'dance attendance on such rogues'. Unanimously, they called reports of insanity and illness 'exaggerated, ungrounded, indeed, untrue'.[51]

The brand new prison was put into use on 1 October 1850. The rules urged the personnel to treat prisoners, above all, with 'leniency and compassion'. Dwellers in the cells were meant to receive on arrival 'a number plate' which always had to worn 'visibly, on their bodies'. This number replaced their name until the moment of release. They had to be addressed with this number. On reaching the cell, if prisoners could not read themselves, the rules and several proverbs, glued to cardboard, were read aloud. Then the solitude began. Smoking and chewing tobacco, as well as liquor, were 'strictly' prohibited. They had to take a foot-bath every month, and, every second month, 'a complete bath'.

Discipline was strict. Article 50 read that they must wash, comb and 'further clean' themselves 'sufficiently' every day after rising. Then they had to roll up their hammocks and put their cells in order. In the evenings, at the tolling of a clock, half an hour before bedtime, prisoners had to roll out their hammocks and prepare themselves for the night. At the next toll, they were expected to go to sleep 'at once'. During the day they were obliged to work long hours in their cells. In the summer this was fourteen hours (from 6am to noon, 1–6pm, and 7–9pm), and, in the winter, ten-and-a-half hours (from 8:30am to noon and 1–8pm). Only on Sundays and recognized Christian feast days was work replaced by reading, writing or drawing. Prisoners who, under these conditions, still managed to disturb the peace could be punished by withdrawal for eight days of work, reading material, visits and the reception or writing of letters. Even their exercise could be cancelled. Severe trespassers could be shut up for eight days 'in a dark cell, either on ordinary food or bread and water'.

The rules also provided for visits, four times a day, from either the governor, doctor, minister, committee members, teacher or cell visitors from the Society for Moral Improvement of Prisoners. Rules were unclear as far as visits of family or friends went. It is true that the possibility existed of receiving such visits in a special 'speaking place', under guard, but this was not a right and nothing was specified about frequency. Additionally, visitors had to be in possession of written permission.[52] Important practical limitations also came into play. For years, the prison in Amsterdam was the only cellular prison and convicts from the whole country were brought there. Visitors often had to travel far and they would seldom have had either the time nor money for such an endeavor.

Supplementary regulations for personnel and for departments give an even better idea of how punctiliously the theoretical views of solitary confinement were put into practice. The library, for example, had to contain primarily religious and moral works and, as a change from this 'more edifying reading material', only 'life histories, travel descriptions and printed sermons' were permitted. The prisoner would barely have taken up residence in his cell before the governor was obliged to pester him with questions 'with the object of uncovering as much as possible about his former life, disposition and character'. Possible depressed feelings had to be noted and combated 'in the most appropriate way'. He had to ensure that the light burned day and night in the cell for the first period of confinement, so that the prisoner could be watched every second of the day through the spyhole.

Any resistance gave the authorities the right to act 'more decisively'. Female guards in the prison for women were instructed in extra detail. In talks, they 'with singular diligence', had to 'make themselves acquainted with the chief proclivity which had led to the misery of the woman's fall, and then employ and profer the appropriate means by which to oppose or conquer this main imperfection'. They had to regularly change the proverb in every cell and thereby make clear 'the power and the sense' of each one. They were expected to urge the prisoners to learn the proverbs by heart and recite them aloud in their cells. The female guards were urged to work toward maintaining the prisoners' 'feeling of guilt and of the compassionate punishment', as well as the hope that they could be restored 'to the grace of God and man' by improved behaviour in their lives.[53]

Thus, the bourgeois civilizing offensive was launched powerfully within prison walls. Visitors from the Society for Moral Improvement of Prisoners, called 'moral instructors' by board member Lurasco, added their little extra to this.[54]

Experimental Introduction of Solitary Confinement: Torture or Blessing?

Not only untried prisoners but also law breakers sentenced to a correctional prison sentence of a year or less were shut up in the cellular prison in Amsterdam and in other *huizen van arrest and justitie*. This was in contradiction of the law, which, indeed, did not yet recognize the punishment of solitary confinement. The government therefore decided in 1851 'to end the controversy about the authority over solitary confinement by provisional law'. A Bill was drafted giving the judge the authority, where he found 'in the circumstances of the crime or the character of the guilty person' special cause for it, to impose the punishment of solitary confinement. The Bill prevailed only for correctional prison sentences of a year or less, and only half of the sentence could take place in solitary. In this way, the government implicitly established that solitary confinement was twice as severe as communal confinement. The maximum length of solitary confinement was then six months in this Bill. In his memorandum, the Minister of Justice Nedermeyer, ridder van Rosenthal, stressed that the Bill was directed at accomplishing 'a gradual implementation' of the cellular system.[55]

During the deliberations in the Lower House in 1851 very few speakers remarked that there was anything peculiar about the Bill and about penal practice in the country.[56] After all, up to and including 1847, the central question in discussions about solitary confinement had been whether it would serve to replace corporal punishment and communal prisons, described as pernicious houses of pleasure. Without the law having changed, penal practice, partly on account of these discussions, had undergone modifications. First and foremost, the number of reprieves for corporal punishment awarded increased dramatically and, after 1848, when the Senate reversed the abolition of flogging and branding, reprieve was invariably awarded. After this, criminals were only 'put on display' on the scaffold, but this punishment was seen as a diversion for both the public and the person punished.

At this same time, sections of *huizen van arrest and justitie* were made suitable for solitary confinement, an activity which was to culminate in the first use of the completely new cellular prison in Amsterdam. The Bill of 1851 thus bore out a penal practice in which corporal punishment was no longer inflicted and in which serious criminals sentenced to these corporal punishments remained in the detested communal prisons. Those not yet sentenced and those sentenced for less serious, correctional offences were, however, submitted to a type of confinement which just recently had been portrayed as more severe than corporal punishment. The Minister of Justice, Nedermeyer van Rosenthal, found a tactful solution to this problem by stressing the double character of cellular confinement: torture and blessing. A punishment which combined both elements was precisely what was wanted 'in the spirit of the times and the needs of this century'. The minister went even further:

> One shall have to agree, that that solitary confinement, that being left with one's own reflections, that threat of being left to one's own thoughts for a long time, everything, as it were, which can make solitude a spectre for the uncivilized person, for the serious criminal,

that the same lonely situation applies to the innocent and those briefly fallen, to him in whom all the principles of morality are not erased, it must have a salutary influence, and that, thus, in the view of science, the combination of both characteristics of the punishment, cannot be other than very desireable, most efficient and useful.

He continued to adjust his concept of cellular punishment to the intent of the Bill in the rest of his comprehensive argument. While as a member of parliament he had barely lifted a finger in 1847 against solitary confinement of very long duration and had gone so far as to want the punishment to be followed by deportation, he now made a case for the scientifically 'completely established insight' that solitary confinement could not last longer than twelve or eighteen months without danger to body and mind. He still suggested that negative effects of longer lasting confinement were perhaps due to an inadequate execution of the punishment. A good regulation for visits could prevent much calamity.[57]

The politically independent Member of Parliament Provó Kluit was able to see through the noticeable change which had taken place in debate about solitary confinement, compared with three or four years before. He pointed out that 'for several years' it had been feared that crime would increase with the disappearance of corporal punishment. Therefore, the replacement system, cellular punishment, had been portrayed in 'terrifying colours'. One had alluded to the 'lonely and bleak walls' of the cells, where often 'despair and suicide' could be found. Now, all of a sudden, one spoke 'of a *favour from the administrative authority*', and the favour consisted of being shut up 'in that which one until just recently saw as the most terrifying of prisons'. This blessing of solitary confinement, said Kluit mockingly, had to be bestowed preferentially on convicts who were the least depraved, and the most receptive to improvement! In his opinion, cellular punishment had to be brought to bear first, in all its harshness, upon the worst criminals.[58]

The Minister of Justice refuted both the practical and principal objections to his Bill[59] which was adopted by thirty-five votes to twenty. In June 1851, the Upper House passed the Bill unanimously.[60]

Thus the parliamentary discussion about the cellular system, whereby ten to fifteen years of solitary confinement for serious offenders had been strongly argued for continually, wound up leading to a Bill which managed only to deprive persons who had committed small offences of all essential social contact for no more than half a year.

The first step had been taken towards complete implementation of the cellular system. This was quickly followed by the abolition of all public scaffold punishments with the exception of the death sentence. In 1854 a Bill about this from the Minister of Justice, Donker Curtius, was accepted

practically without discussion. Corporal punishment had not been practised
for several years, because requests for reprieve were always granted.
According to the minister, experience had shown that these punishments
'which one used to deem indispensible' could now disappear without
danger from penal legislation. An overwhelming majority of MPs silently
agreed with this. In passing, the maximum length of solitary confinement
for correctional criminals was increased to a year. It became clear that
they had begun to think more carefully and critically about cellular
punishment. What had still been obscured in 1851 in order to at least
make a start, was now straightforwardly spoken about by the minister. It
was true, he said, that 'even very recently' it had been believed that
criminals could be sentenced to long-lasting solitary confinement. From
this point, one had now 'almost unanimously' backtracked, 'and one may
call it good fortune that it did not occur through a hasty final ruling that
long-lasting solitary confinement became part of our legislation'.

Slowly and with great caution it would now have to be established how
far one could go with the implementation of cellular punishment. 'The
dispute is not yet decided', Donker Curtius stated in his memorandum.[61]
The entire Bill was passed by forty-five votes to three. In the Upper
House, which voted for the Bill on 27 June 1854 by twenty-six votes to
three, the minister put his spirit of reflection into words. Shortly after
implementation in France of the cellular system, he said, it had been
abandoned and experiments were being done in England with all sorts of
hybrid forms of confinement. In such a time of transition, in the opinion
of the minister, it was expedient to look on attentively, to think it over and
not to learn by bitter experience.[61]

Cellular Hothouse Plants

The enthusiasm for solitary confinement had abated for a short period,
but would grow again slowly and lead to legal expansions in the second
half of the nineteenth century. In the meantime, the general public must
hardly have known any longer what to think of this punishment. Shortly
after the introduction of the new cellular prison in Amsterdam, Society
chairman Suringar refuted reports in daily papers that prisoners could, in
spite of everything, speak to each other in 'a common room'.[63] Not only
inside, but also outside the prison, strict watch was kept that the improvement cultivated in solitude not be ruined through sociability.

The first cellular convicts were fostered like hothouse plants and the
flower was eagerly awaited. The visits of Society members could be
compared to the circuit of their young plantings made by gardeners in the
first days of spring. Instead of curious visitors to the fair at the beginning
of the century, prisoners now received visits from experts, who were more
involved in observing them as legal guinea pigs than in cheering them up.

Complaints about loneliness were seen by visitors only as proof of a not yet improved spiritual life. In this way, cellular prisoners were not just confined within four walls; they were confined as well in the thoughts and patterns of expectation of their punishers who saw cries of despair as shrieks of the devil and who wanted to see prisoners' faces glowing with happiness from all the goodness they felt germinating inside them. The Amsterdam prison was also the first in The Netherlands based on a 'cellular' image of man.

After release, it could be of advantage to prisoners to sing the praises of the purifying effect of solitary confinement. One prisoner who put his experience of solitary confinement in France into words for a Dutch governor seems to have understood this advantage very well. At his entry into the cell, he had first recoiled, 'a cold shivering mastered my whole body, and I, who six weeks previously, in the defence of Vicenza, had been exposed for 36 hours to the destructive grapeshot of the Austrians, trembled here in the cell, solitarily confined, as a weak and helpless child'. But, little by little, he formed a bond with a parson who, to his great delight, lent him the collected works of Schiller. No average prisoner by a long shot! He also did not miss a beat when working out what his listener wished to hear:

> After fourteen days had passed, I began to be used to the loneliness, because, just as the worst affliction is slowly assuaged, the compunction of conscience makes place for remorse. And can anything more appropriate be thought of for this awakening than solitude? Left to himself with his conscience, fallen man must begin to reflect; at this point all self-deception ends! The frozen crust which has covered the conscience, as it were, begins slowly but surely to thaw, the moment approaches when speaking to the heart, one feels, realizes and attains the conviction of one's mistakes – and when that moment has arrived, then it sinks gradually into the deeply shocked soul, – reason triumphs over our abberations, remorse makes its appearance, increases hand over fist, and the affliction, the first-felt deep affliction, is altered into a wistful but calm mood.[64]

This will have been music to the ears of advocates of cellular confinement. They will not have doubted the truth of his words and there will certainly have been many prisoners who really believed as strongly as this in the fairness of the punishment. Making a virtue of necessity was the only choice available to them to lighten the torment of the cell. 'Loneliness makes man more Christian, and Christians more godlike,' wrote their fellow-sufferer in freedom. Pacing to and fro in a drab cell with windows of frosted glass, one could, indeed, find this a soothing thought in a society much more religious than ours.

NOTES

1. 'The strict penitentiary system of Philadelphia makes mere boredom an instrument of punishment through loneliness and idleness. It is so terrible an instrument, that it has brought convicts to suicide, Just as need and want are the constant scurge of the people, so is boredom that of the world of fashion. In middle-class life boredom is represented by the Sunday, just as want is represented by the six weekdays' (Schopenhauer, p. 313).
2. Cf. Franke, 1985.
3. Cf. Elias, 1978, 1982.
4. Cf. Spierenburg, 1984, pp. 184–5.
5. Cf. Michel Ignatieff in NRC *Handelsblad*, 'De dodelijke eenvoud van het martelen' (The fatal simplicity of torturing), 3 Oct. 85, p. 8. See also Christie, 1988.
6. Goudsblom, 1987, p. 202.
7. Tex, 1843, pp. 396–7.
8. Faber (1989) illustrates this aptly in his description of the public execution of a triple murderer against the walls of the first cellular prison in Amsterdam.
9. See Spierenburg, 1984, and Franke, 1985.
10. Rochefoucauld-Liancourt, 1796.
11. Donker Curtius van Tienhoven, 1827, pp. 87–8. See also Asser, 1827, pp. 85–7.
12. Mollet, 1828, pp. 250–1, 312, 252. Resistance to the dispacing of deterrence in favour of moral improvement was pronounced. Cf. Brueys, 1829, pp. 405–7.
13. HdSG, 1839/40, Bijlagen, pp. 24, 60, 64, arts 14 and 15.
14. HdSG, 1939/40, *Beraadslagingen Tweede Kamer*, p. 180.
15. HdSG, 1839/40, Bijlagen, pp. 38–40 (first amendment) and pp. 72–3 (second amendment), *Beraadslagingen Tweede Kamer*, pp. 184–5. See also Gevers van Endegeest, about 1838, p. 31.
16. Sb, 1840, nos 20–6, incl.
17. HdSG 1843/44, Bijlagen, pp. 19–20.
18. HdSG, 1843/44, Bijlagen, pp. 23–4; HdSG, 1845/46, Bijlage (appendix), letter 23 Apr. 1846, p. 408.
19. Mannheim, 1939.
20. HdSG, 1845/46, *Beraadslagingen Tweede Kamer*, pp. 415–16.
21. HdSG, 1845/46, *Beraadslagingen Tweede Kamer*, pp. 415, 418, 431.
22. Idem, pp. 417, 419, 429.
23. HdSG, 1845/46, *Beraadslagingen Tweede Kamer*, pp. 415, 418, 431.
24. Tex, 1843, p. 404.
25. HdSG, 1845/46, *Beraadslagingen Tweede Kamer*, p. 429.
26. Idem, pp. 416–17.
27. Idem, p. 445.
28. For example, in *De Avondbode*, 7, 21 and 27 Feb., 30 Mar., 1 Apr., 1840. *Iets over lijfstraffen (…)*, Amsterdam, 1840.
29. Suringar, 1842, pp. 19, 21–2, 27. See also WvhR, 5 Dec. 1842, no. 344, p. 4.
30. Tex, 1842, pp. 532, 550, 579, 581–7.
31. WvhR, 24 Dec. 1842, no. 350, pp. 3–4.
32. AH, 2 Dec. 1842. See also 22, 25 and 29 Nov. 1842, 12 Dec. 1842.

33. *OHC*, 27 Dec. 1842.

34. Goossens, 1843, pp. 74, 76–7.

35. E.g. *Nederlandsche Jaarboeken voor Regtsgeleerdheid en Wetgeving*, 1843, part V, pp. 549–54.

36. *AH*, 20 Feb. 1843.

37. *Pennsylvanisch of eenig ander gevangenisstelsel (…)*, 1844, pp. 17–48.

38. *Nieuwe Berigten (…)*, 1844, pp. 23–6.

39. *WvhR*, 18 Nov. 1844.

40. *HdSG*, 1846/47, Bijlagen, pp. 296–7.

41. Idem, Bijlagen, pp. 324–5.

42. Cf. Ignatieff, 1978, p. 4.

43. *HdSG*, 1846/47, Beraadslagingen Tweede Kamer, pp. 343, 345.

44. Idem, pp. 347, 350–1.

45. The right of a government to give or refuse permission for the proclamation of church precepts, given by foreign ecclesiastical authorities: cf. *Algemene Geschiedenis der Nederlanden* (General History of The Netherlands, encyclopedia), 1977, part 12, p. 330.

46. Idem, part 12, pp. 318–20, 345–6.

47. Modderman, 1861, pp. 15–16.

48. Cf. Faber, 1989, p. 73.

49. *AH*, 2 Aug. 1847.

50. Schneevoogt, 1848, pp. 182, 200.

51. Vernée, 1849, pp. 5–19.

52. *WvhR*, 11 Nov.1850, pp. 1–3; *AH*, 28 Oct. 1850.

53. Rules and instructions established between 1851 and 1868 by the Commission of the Administration, for personnel. Archives of the *Genootschap tot Zedelijke Verbetering der Gevangenen* (Society for the Moral Improvement of Prisoners) of the *Algemene Reclasserings-vereniging* (After-Care Society) in Den Bosch.

54. Lurasco, 1850, p. 16.

55. *HdSG*, 1850/51, *Memorie van Toelichting*, Bijlagen, pp. 433–5.

56. *HdSG*, 1850/51, Beraadslagingen, p. 695.

57. Idem, 698, pp. 1–2.

58. Idem, pp. 700–1.

59. Idem, p. 705.

60. *HdSG, Eerste Kamer*, 1850/51, *Memorie van Antwoord*, pp. 142–4.

61. *HdSG*, 1853/54, Bijlagen, p. 434.

62. *HdSG, Eerste Kamer*, 1853/54, Beraadslagingen, p. 204.

63. *AH*, 5 Nov. 1851.

64. *Mijn verblijf (…)*, 1858, p. 47–9.

5

Penal Reality for a Prison Inspector, 1850–1886: The Suffering behind the Death Rates

As we were going through some of the magnificent passages, I inquired of Mr. Creakle and his friends what were supposed to be the main advantages of this all-governing and universally overriding system? I found them to be a perfect isolation of prisoners – so that no one man in confinement there, knew anything about another; and the reduction of prisoners to a wholesome state of mind, leading to sincere contrition and repentance. Now, it struck me, when we began to visit individuals in their cells, and to traverse the passages in which those cells were, and to have the manner of the going to chapel and so forth, explained to us, that there was a strong probability of the prisoners knowing a good deal about each other, and of their carrying on a pretty complete system of intercourse. This, at the time I write, has been proved, I believe, to be the case; but, as it would have been flat blasphemy against the system to have hinted such a doubt then, I looked out for the penitence as diligently as I could. And here again, I had great misgivings. I found as prevalent a fashion in the form of penitence, as I had left outside in the forms of coats and waistcoats in the windows of the tailors' shops. I found a vast amount of profession, varying very little in character: varying very little (which I thought excessively suspicious), even in words.[1]

Life in prisons in the third quarter of the nineteenth century was very harsh, and could hardly have been made harsher without consciously endangering the lives of prisoners. But in newspapers journalists voiced the feelings of many well-to-do citizens in writing that punishment was no longer punishment but reward. Philanthropy had made 'an enticement' of prison, 'a temporary sanctuary and refuge to relax from the commitment of evil'.[2] Members of Parliament, time and again, denounced prison life as privileged. In 1864, reacting to the Budget of the Ministry of

Justice, they pushed for the avoidance of 'any unnecessary luxury and comfort in prison' in an attempt to prevent it imperceptibly losing 'the character of a place of punishment, in the view of the uncivilized rabble'.[3]

Because the life of misery of the lower classes was accepted as a God-given fact of life, a prison sentence had to exceed this misery in order to deter. But the difference between a prison sentence and a 'sentence' to daily life as a commoner was very small in the nineteenth century. Too small, obviously, to make the prison sentence, at least materially, appear sufficiently deterring in the eyes of well-to-do citizens, whose witnessing of the sufferings of needy fellow-men induced less sympathy than today[3], and also too small to sustain the opinion that life in prison should never be allowed to materially exceed that in freedom. The Minister of Justice, M. H. Godefroi, spoke out sharply in 1863 against this 'unfortunate image'. If prisoners could never be allowed to live a life materially better than 'the honest man', then, he said, government would have to furnish prisons as slum dwellings. Prisoners would also have to be fed 'bad, spoiled food' and wear rags instead of decent clothing.[5]

The liberal minister could also have fought this unfortunate image with a Copernican about-face by focusing his criticism on the miserable life of the mob, instead of on a relatively good prison life. However, this was not an acceptable political stand in the mid-nineteenth century. For many, there could not be moral improvement enough for the lower classes, but improvement in the material standard of living was thought much less expedient. Moreover, much poverty found among these people was thought to stem from their extreme depravity, which could be combatted by solitary confinement. Many thought this depravity to be precisely what was fostered by the good life in communal prisons. Thus, luxury inside prison continued to rankle well-to-do citizens much more than abject poverty outside.

At the same time rules and regulations for the *pistole*, giving wealthy prisoners the opportunity to supply themselves with all amenities for a certain price, were quietly revised by Royal Decree.[6] The *pistole* threw a very peculiar light on the nineteenth-century concern for too little deterrence. While the difference between prisoners and paupers was small, a gulf existed between the classes. While social awareness was virtually absent, class prejudice dominated all discussions about crime and punishment. It is sometimes difficult when reading all the treatises and deliberations to keep in mind the suffering in prisons, because it was trivialized in very civilized language according to the logic of that time, or even portrayed as a form of entertainment for the lower classes.

Prison Deaths

The businesslike circulars, missives, Royal Decrees and statistics give us only a very limited insight into the suffering of prisoners. For example,

Society chairman Suringar published figures in 1859 showing the limited number of inmates with very long sentences in the communal prisons at Leeuwarden and Woerden.[7] He used this data in his plea for uninterrupted solitary confinement of all convicts, even of those with long sentences, but did not enter into what was implicitly revealed by his statistics, that a huge number of those with long sentences must meanwhile have died in prison.[8] This was noticed by the lawyer J. Domela Nieuwenhuis, who was just as fanatical in supporting solitary confinement. Suringar's figures demonstrated, according to him, that 'whatever prison system one adopted' there would always be 'many more' who died in captivity than in freedom.[9] His conclusion was that there could be no objection to the full implementation of solitary confinement, because then at least 'moral death' would be combatted. The ex-prison regent in Woerden, C. J. N. Nieuwenhuis, mentioned that he had noticed that 'most' of those convicted of serious crimes 'pined away after several years of punishment and did not live to see the day of their discharge'.[10]

Prison statistics confirm the high death rate in the late nineteenth century, even though the figures no longer reach the outlandish extremes (except at Leeuwarden) of the 1840s. They reveal a gradual improvement in the health situation – see Table 5.1, which shows that the mortality rate, in an average prison population of about 3,500, fell below the national figure (including infant deaths) for the first time in 1865.

The health situation differed greatly in the large communal prisons, as is obvious from the death rates for the years 1851–70, shown in Table 5.2.

In the *Nederlandsch Tijdschrift voor Geneeskunde* (a Dutch medical journal), a doctor compared the mortality in Woerden and Leeuwarden in the 1850s with that of the local prisons. Only in the years in which cholera was rampant, 1859 in Woerden and 1855 in Leeuwarden, did a

TABLE 5.1 Mortality rates in the average prison, 1851–80 (five-yearly averages).[11]

Period	All prisons (%)	Penal prisons (%)	National mortality rate (%)	National average mortality rate for people over 5 years of age (%)
1851–5	4.1	5.4	2.6	1.5
1856–60	3.9	5.2	2.6	1.5
1861–5	2.8	3.7	2.5	1.5
1866–70	1.8	2.0	2.5	1.5
1871–5	1.4	1.5	2.5	1.5
1876–80	1.7	1.8	2.5	1.3

TABLE 5.2 Mortality, as percentages, of the average population in separate prisons, 1851–80.[12]

Year	Leeuwarden	Woerden	Hoorn	Gouda	's-Hertogenbosch
1851	13.5	6.6	5.7	1.2	–
1852	10.9	6.4	4.5	4.5	–
1853	4.8	6.3	4.8	2.9	–
1854	5.4	7.7	5.4	4.5	–
1855	3.4	4.0	6.6	4.5	–
1856	4.1	3.0	5.0	6.8	–
1857	4.2	1.9	3.3	5.8	–
1858	7.8	5.1	4.6	5.1	–
1859	8.6	1.8	4.1	6.5	–
1860	12.3	3.0	5.0	4.6	–
1861	6.5	2.8	2.7	5.6	–
1862	9.0	3.1	3.2	–	–
1863	5.5	1.3	4.3	–	–
1864	5.4	3.4	2.9	–	–
1865	3.4	2.3	2.7	–	–
1866	2.3	6.6	4.7	–	–
1867	3.8	1.3	1.5	–	–
1868	2.2	2.1	2.6	–	–
1869	1.6	3.4	0.8	–	–
1870	2.5	3.2	2.2	–	–
1871	1.5	4.0	2.4	–	–
1872	2.8	1.7	1.4	–	–
1873	1.2	1.6	2.1	–	–
1874	0.7	–	0.6	–	0.9
1875	2.9	–	2.6	–	1.7
1876	1.7	–	2.0	–	3.5
1877	4.2	–	2.4	–	2.6
1878	3.3	–	0.7	–	0.0
1879	1.0	–	2.4	–	2.0
1880	2.3	–	3.4	–	4.4

relatively greater number of people die in freedom than in prison, yet the mortality rate of those living in freedom never came within range of 10 per cent or more even during cholera epidemics. The doctor sought the causes of high mortality rates in prisons in tuberculosis, 'fevers' and the huge temperature differences (from -10 to more than 30°C!) Very few of the corpses he had autopsied were free of 'reasonably strong' signs of tuberculosis, but, in Woerden, convicts had also died of 'freezing'. He found the prison at Leeuwarden structurally inadequate, 'unless one values the health of those confined for their crimes less than that of those who enjoy their freedom in society'.[13] A number of years later, in the same journal, another doctor also commented on the high mortality rate in prisons. He did not seem upset about the magnitude of prison deaths in general, but about 'the excess of deaths' (from five to more than twelve per cent) and 'the horrible ratio' in Leeuwarden to those in other prisons.[14] Fevers prevailing in the whole province of Friesland were said to be the cause and not inadequate accommodation.

The Cell: Hell for the Incorrigible, Salutary for the Corrigible

If it were not for the documentation of a tour through The Netherlands made in 1857 by the prison inspector P. W. Alstorphius Grevelink, probably only statistics would have survived, providing cold evidence of suffering in prisons. His report provides a precise image of prison life.

The Minister of Justice, Donker Curtius, had appointed the ex-lawyer, Grevelink (1808–96), prison inspector in 1854. During his tour in 1857, he visited all the prisons and *huizen van bewaring* (*huizen van arrest en justitie* and *huizen voor militaire en burgerlijke verzekering*) and he spoke extensively with warders, governors, prison regents, educators and doctors. Again and again, they alluded to the extreme depravity in communal dormitories and the bad influence of communal confinement. Grevelink had heard several times of appeals to be allowed to sit out one's time alone, because one could no longer stand 'the blasphemous and sinful conversations'.[15] Scandalized stories about depravity were regularly supplemented with allegations about the pleasure with which prisoners wallowed in these cesspools of vice.

Grevelink's informants' views of solitary imprisonment were just as positive as their statements about communal imprisonment were negative. Some were able to support their views with experience, others based them purely on fantasy, but virtually everyone agreed that cellular confinement had salutary effects and that the dangers of suicide and insanity had been grossly exaggerated. Prisoners would learn to retain feelings of guilt and virtue and would turn to reflection and remorse.

In addition to governors and staff, Grevelink spoke to prisoners themselves. The majority were very positive about solitary confinement, but these statements should not be given too much weight. Prisoners, as much as their punishers, were groping in the dark when it came to understanding the agonies of this modern form of punishment. All they knew was that sentences were halved when carried out in the cell and this probably had a strong appeal. More important is that their attitude to the two forms of confinement was used as a trustworthy gauge of their moral condition. Incorrigible villains would be likely to choose the depraved company of other prisoners, while better convicts would choose salubrious solitude. Prisoners aiming at a possible remission of their sentence or at other favours and wanting to make a good impression were well served when they showed visitors that they approved of cellular confinement and denounced communal confinement. This bias also led to everything heard or seen by visitors coming out in favour of solitary confinement. Should convicts complain of the solitude, that was the voice of their extremely bad conscience, precisely the object of this system of punishment. Should they manage to show a brave face, then it had again been proved that the least depraved prisoners found the punishment salutary.

A committee member of the Society for the Moral Improvement of Prisoners, the parson E. Laurillard, unintentionally put this almost tautological consideration pithily into words: 'Never have I met someone better-disposed who longed for communality instead of the cell. The cell is a hell for villians, but communality a hell for the better-disposed'. Thus experience had had to teach him 'that all better-disposed prisoners prefer the cell to communality.'[16]

Neither was prison inspector Grevelink free of a similar bias. Many prisoners must have seen through this because they told him precisely what he wanted to hear. Some spoke highly of their own moral progress and assured him that they would only have become worse had they stayed in communal prisons. A large number of prisoners interviewed by Grevelink mentioned 'being their own boss' as a significant advantage of cellular confinement. They probably honestly meant this too, because communal dormitories were social jungles complete with mutual intimidations and power struggles often settled with violence, sometimes ending in death.[17]

Unheated Cells, Stench, Vermin and Overcrowding

When he made his tour in 1857, the prison situation in The Netherlands was very chaotic and would stay that way for many years to come. A number of cells had been constructed haphazardly in some, but certainly not all, prisons and remand-houses. These cells were often dark hovels which, even 'in the harshest cold of winter',[18] could be barely heated or not at all. Precepts for visits were ignored on a regular basis. Convicts to whom cellular sentences had not been given were often solitarily confined, even children.[19] In several prisons Grevelink came across fearful children under fourteen, crying continually.[20] In the half-cellular prison in Deventer, the warder said that children could be confined to cells without problems if they were handled kindly. Without any comment at all and, as far as we can tell, supportive of this opinion, Grevelink continued his report with the following 'metabletic' text:[21]

> I found here a boy of 12, who had been here a month and seemed to be good-humoured. When asked how long he still had to stay, he answered: 'six more nights'. He was most frightened of the nights. At the beginning of his sentence, he had done nothing but weep; this had lasted, however, only four days. Kindly dealt with, he soon began to sing, so that this had to be forbidden.[22]

Grevelink made observations and presented his findings coolly. Only seldom did he judge. He called the communal *huis van arrest* in Amersfoort 'one of the worst prisons', but, precisely for that reason, since cellular confinement was being discussed, it provided 'no topic for special remarks'. Young and old recidivists, those sentenced and those pending sentence, all were lodged in the same space. It was so cold in winter that prisoners had to remain, day and night, 'on their army cots because they could not otherwise stay warm'.[23]

Slowly but surely, Grevelink's report grew to an impressive survey of richly variegated misery: cold and heat, loneliness and overcrowding, violence and depravity. Topped with stench and vermin, life in solitary cells and especially in crowded rooms became even more unbearable.

All descriptions so far apply to prisons where the accused, those detained on remand or those convicted were confined for a short time. In some prisons, only a few were detained, in others, more than a hundred. These prisons accommodated almost half the total of 3,500–4,500 prisoners between the 1850s and 1870s. The large prisons at Woerden, Gouda, Hoorn and Leeuwarden housed 1,500–2,500 prisoners. These were old blockhouses, mansions, castles and cloisters, which had later been furnished as prisons and which were being rebuilt and enlarged at every turn.

Prison statistics show that in the 1860s and 1870s, in these large prisons including the cellular prisons, an average of 1,300 disciplinary punishments were meted out yearly. Around ten per cent consisted of 'bread and water' for several days or weeks. Almost half of those punished were shut up in the punishment cell for a period of time and a further twenty per cent in the punishment cell on bread and water. Sometimes they were additionally put in chains. The remaining punishments consisted of the deprivation of certain privileges or a ban on the buying of canteen articles. It is certain that, in one of the large prisons, order was still enforced with strokes of the pizzle whip. Prison statistics included no data about this. Corporal punishments were forbidden by the Minister of Justice, Smidt, close to the end of the 1870s.[24]

Prison inspector Grevelink visited the four large prisons in 1857. The prison for criminally sentenced men in Woerden, where, at the time of his visit 356 prisoners were housed, did not seem much changed since the 1830s and 40s. The sight of the overcrowded dormitories where each person could claim no more than three cubic metres of space, made him sigh that he had taken on 'no pleasant task'. In one of the corner towers of this old castle, there were eight punishment cells. These cells, which could not be heated, looked to Grevelink like 'vaulted cellars'. In these isolated cells prisoners were left completely to their fate. Should they call for help, no one could hear them. Grevelink spoke to three prisoners who had each been shut up there for a year, 'without once having been out in the air, and fed less than nowadays is the rule'. A prisoner had recently committed suicide in one of those cells. Because Grevelink was making his inspection tour primarily 'from the standpoint of cellular confinement', he immediately remarked : 'One would err seriously if this unfortunate occurrence were held against the cellular system'. The extreme deeds for which they had been punished provided 'evidence' of the 'most unheard-of depravity, dominating the communal halls'.[25]

When he made his tour in 1857, convicted women were still housed in the old, rickety prison at Gouda.[26] The building was apparently so severely overrun 'by vermin which could not be done away with' that staying there in the summer was 'well nigh unbearable'. A sewer close by spread an unhealthy stench. Grevelink learned from the health official that the women's health situation was 'very adverse', something very apparent from the high mortality rate.

Overcrowding certainly contributed to the unhealthiness. The 285 women slept 'with a number of small children' in dormitories where the layers of hammocks could be considered, in Grevelink's words, as 'one unending bed'. They had at their disposal three to five cubic metres of space. Thus, in Gouda as well, not much had changed since the 1830s and 1840s. Grevelink was most upset by the lack of cells, because he thought cellular confinement 'to be highly recommended', especially for immoral women.[27]

In the correctional prison at Hoorn, where 746 men were communally confined, he directed his attention particularly to the forty-seven recidivists who had been solitarily confined before. He did not attribute this recidivism to the cellular confinement but used it as an argument in favour of lengthening the maximum period of confinement; they had obviously not been kept long enough in the cell. Ten of these repeaters had been questioned by Grevelink without the reason for repeated offences coming up for discussion. According to the commandant, these were prisoners 'whose account could be trusted the most'. This preselection ensured that Grevelink was bound to hear exactly what he sought. Prisoners praised the health situation in the cells where they were free to be their 'own boss' at least. Fellows who were against solitary belonged 'to the lowliest type'. Prisoners said that they had quickly become used to solitude and that it had freed them from 'the frequently dangerous and harassing contact' in the communal rooms. Only one prisoner admitted preferring communality because he could not stand the loneliness. 'He had to acknowledge, however' wrote Grevelink, 'that one heard much that was wrong and almost never a good conversation there.'[28]

Reading his report, one is often tempted not to take Grevelink seriously and to doubt its truth. But he was chief inspector of the prison system in The Netherlands, and the Minister of Justice and Members of

Parliament were waiting impatiently for his report. His way of speaking and thinking really did not differ from that of Members of Parliament, members of the Society for Moral Improvement of Prisoners or other prison experts. His naive views and concepts are perhaps the more noticeable because he also provides factual descriptions. The value of his remarks can be, as it were, immediately checked. Without concentrating our attention on this naivety – and running the risk of being accused of prejudice, hodiecentredness and obtrusive moralism – it is, in my opinion, not possible to understand why one punished the way one did in the nineteenth century. The fact that Grevelink could look around and think so naively bears out the powerlessness of prisoners, in spite of the increased interest in them. They were not yet listened to with the desire to understand and no intellectuals or experts as yet stood ready in solidarity to use their expertise to defend prisoners' interests.

In the second half of the nineteenth century many wished to improve prisoners and, with that goal in mind, put them in surveyable cells. The cellular system was thought to be wholesome and necessarily based on strongly individualistic concepts of man and society. Subsequently, one could witness the wholesome effect of the system and its necessity by using one's programmed outlook, just as Grevelink did, to judge the result. Almost no one saw through this or wanted to as long as observation did not reflect disadvantageously on cellular confinement. Grevelink, of all people, had to learn this by bitter experience. He concluded his report with the moderate recommendation that a combination of solitary (a maximum of three years) and communal confinement (with alcoves instead of hammocks) would be most desirable. This bought him the harsh criticism of even more dogmatic proponents of solitary confinement and led finally, in 1872, to his 'honourable' discharge as prison inspector, as we shall see in the next chapter.[29]

Retrospectively, it is difficult to understand why Grevelink's report became the object of so much criticism because on practically every page he shows himself to be an exemplary defender of solitary confinement and he broadly enlarges upon the failings of communal confinement. He also unearthed a great deal of prison suffering, but, and this is characteristic of the one-sided interest, no words were wasted on this in press or parliament. Everything revolved around the choice of system. Suffering was only of importance if it bore upon this decision and that was seldom the case.

Higher Tolerances of Pain, Less Compassion and Selective Observation
Both experts and laymen were at a loss when it came to predicting the effects of long-term solitary confinement. Still, Grevelink's report reveals that, in the prison for around 500 criminally sentenced men at Leeuwarden, convicts had been solitarily confined for years under circumstances

reminiscent of the severely-criticised experiments in the United States at the beginning of the century. He does not report how these illegal practices were justified. According to the law journal *Themis*, the prison management had simply taken for granted that solitary confinement was 'better' and 'prohibited nowhere'.[30] House rules also permitted solitary confinement of convicts if an administrative commission found this 'advantageous'.

These prisoners were not permitted to attend religious services, but instead received 'from time to time' an address by a religious teacher, a preacher, a vicar or the commandant. When not confined in the cell for disciplinary punishment, they were allowed to go for a half-hour's walk on the inner court, alone. There were fourteen of these cells in total, varying from nineteen to forty cubic metres.[31]

Keeping in mind his commission, Grevelink did not waste time on the huge communal dormitories and workplaces. He did visit all cells and speak with the prisoners he found there. One of them had already been in prison for nine years. At the time he spoke to Grevelink, he had been solitarily confined for nineteen months, working as a spinner, because he had been guilty of assault on a fellow prisoner in the communal hall. He said he hoped to be able to sit out the remaining nine months of his sentence in the cell. No one bothered him in the cell, while in the large halls there were always bullies. 'Also, one hears nothing but bad mouthing; he who is good at the start there will finish bad', he said. Time passed much more quickly in the cell, he had not been sick at all and he felt healthier than in the communal hall because of 'the purer air'. He was greatly attached to his daily walk in the court.[32]

Grevelink wrote extensively of a prisoner who, after ten years of solitary confinement, with ten years to go, complained 'about nothing'. This man was allowed daily, only 'as a privilege', to speak for half an hour with fellow prisoners in the inner court, 'so that the solitude was not absolute'. Grevelink found that he did not look as if he were suffering. 'He also says he has always been healthy in the cell, except that he is a little thinner; but his mental potential has not decreased', he added. [33]

Thus Grevelink collected his evidence in favour of solitary confinement. If a prisoner, after sixteen months in the cell, frankly admitted not being able to stand the solitude and not being upset by 'the depraved topics of the hall' then Grevelink's comment was 'he did not appear to be sickly, but unprepossessing'. Still, he also met 'one of the most dangerous subjects', who did prefer the cell because 'he did not have to take account of anyone, except himself'. This was a thirty-four-year old man who had yet to sit out thirty-one years of his sentence, for diverse crimes. He had then spent about three years in the cell. The boredom, he said, was bearable and he killed time with spinning and reading. Grevelink reported, 'he had two pigeons who flew out through a half-open window'.

Was tolerance of not only physical, but also psychological pain, higher in the nineteenth century for those who grew up in hunger and misery than they are at present in western society? Or did people of position, like Grevelink, lack not only compassion but also the ability to recognize suffering in persons so distant from their own life situation, and who were villains to boot? Did they observe so selectively that trembling hands or dilated pupils really escaped them? Were prisoners so afraid of extra punishment that they were prepared to deny the most intense suffering? It is difficult to say. What we do know is that presently all sorts of psychological tensions and physical complaints are detected as a result of social and sensory deprivation in situations not even worthy of the name solitary when compared with cells in Leeuwarden at that time. And the disastrous effects of 'crowding' show up in situations which cannot even be compared to the overcrowded dormitories and workplaces of the nineteenth century.[34]

Recent experiments with solitary confinement show that people already begin to hallucinate after a few days. Volunteers completely shut off from the outside world showed severe reactions of physiological and emotional stress after two months. Complete solitude seemed to have a drastic effect on feeling, thinking and memory.[35]

There is no other answer possible than that prisoners from the last century had a far greater resilience, but it is just as certain that their punishers were often blind to their suffering and, when not blind, indifferent. This is clear from talks held by Grevelink with prisoners who did, indeed, stay in the communal halls, but who had before that time spent from one to nineteen years in solitary cells. Some had not been outside their cell for years on end because the privilege of walking in the courtyard had been withheld. Grevelink was imperturbable in subjecting these people, who had to sit out accumulated prison sentences from ten to fifty years so that they often were assured of dying in prison, to his obligatory questions. He meticulously wrote down the just as obligatory answers. He seems never to have forgotten his commission for a moment. A preference for the cell or for the communal hall, that was all he wanted to know from the prisoners.

Some prisoners could, of course, not choose between the devil and the deep blue sea. They came up with pathetic forced answers under pressure from Grevelink. Straight from the mouth of a fifty-year-old baker, who still had fifteen years to go in the communal hall after spending almost two years in complete solitude, Grevelink noted these words:

> This prisoner chose the hall, when the punishment was very long-lasting, but otherwise the cell, because one could be on one's own there and there was much argument and much that was wrong in the community. 'If I', he said, 'had to sit for ten years then I would

choose the cell; but for twenty years the hall, for the contact; though', he added, 'the hall also causes much sadness.'

Very few prisoners gave really unacceptable answers. If they did this very cautiously, Grevelink could still manage to suppress his prejudice, but one prisoner who had already put in eleven years, with sixteen to go, had spent thirty-four months in the cell, six of them without an airing, clearly went too far. He said he could not stand the solitude and preferred to stay in the hall 'experiencing more sadness from being alone than from his fellows, and not bothering at all whether he should hear something wrong in the group'. Plain talk. 'He seemed to me a depraved and dangerous prisoner,' wrote Grevelink.[36]

His report achieves a tragic climax with his rendering of a conversation with a fifty-nine-year old prisoner who had spent nineteen years in the cell. He had not been permitted out of the cell for the first nine years. After that he had been allowed to walk once or twice per week in the courtyard. Only in the last two years had this been permitted daily. This is the only conversation which reveals some of the misery which long-lasting solitude must have caused, according to the views of today:

> He could read and write when he entered prison, and his work consisted of fluffing wool, spinning and making clothes. In that nine-year period, he suffered two severe illnesses in his cell, one in cell no. 3, the other in cell no. 10. During both illnesses he had had the company of two other prisoners, but was always alone in the cell otherwise, and this lasted for 12 years in succession. He had now been out of the cell for 17 months and, when I visited, was working as an orderly; he was, however, not sick or sickly and complained only of rheumatism. During his very long period in the cell without being allowed a walk, reading was his only relaxation. Sundays the catechist came, but he received no other visitors than a member of the commission or the commandant, from time to time. Under more specific questioning, he answered that such long-lasting solitary confinement is stupefying; that he, after 17 months, still suffers from the results, as he has not recovered his old speech, he is of the opinion that if one makes it through such a period at all, one will at least lose the ability to speak and think. Furthermore, he thought that the cell was better for lighter punishments, because one is then free from temptations in the large halls, but that, for longer punishment, the cell was inappropriate. When asked how long he thought one could stand it in a good cell without detrimental effect, he answered: '8 to 10 years, and then with airings.' He had been in prison now for 24 years.

Why this improbably strong man had been so long in solitary was not mentioned by Grevelink. Here he saw only 'how long a person could stand to be solitarily confined'.[37]

It is not known how many prisoners were shut up unlawfully for decades in Leeuwarden. They fell outside the statistics, because they had not been sentenced to this punishment.

System of Coercion in 'Moral Hospitals'

The majority of prisoners sentenced to solitary confinement, when Grevelink made his tour, were in the strictly cellular prisons in Amsterdam, Utrecht, Gorinchem, Appingedam and Winschoten. After that time, many more of that sort were quickly built. In September 1872, the largest cellular prison in the country, with 300 cells, was put to use in Rotterdam. The cellular train (later to be used literally) was set on the rails in 1851 and could no longer be stopped. When the new Penal Code was instituted in 1886, more than eighty per cent of correctional convicts served their sentences in cellular prisons. The maximum length had by then been increased to two years. The cellular principle was gradually put into practice right down to the smallest detail. Cellular caps, cellular walking places, cellular churches, cellular coaches, cellular railway cars, cellular waiting rooms at stations, anything that could, did become cellular. All of this was meant to prevent prisoners recognizing each other or making contact with each other or with others.

Mortification, that is, the disappearance of individuality and autonomy so characteristic of total institutions,[38] was not then an unintentional result of cellular confinement. It was actually pursued by outlining the day's programme from minute to minute and unfailingly addressing the convicts with a number. A system of moral coercion was implemented that brought with it an unknown and probably seriously underestimated form of suffering. Solitude in these 'moral hospitals', as the cellular prisons were called,[39] lasted for much shorter periods than in Leeuwarden, and daily visits were better regulated. But walks with fellow prisoners were forbidden and a ghastly dimension was added by the enforced wearing of caps. Not all cellular prisons insisted on the legally prescribed wearing of cell caps and visitor regulations. Especially in the smaller prisons, rules were often loose and visits were often badly organized.[40]

In the large cellular prisons, regulations were complied more strictly. A reasonably precise description of events is possible, specifically in the cellular prison in Amsterdam, thanks to the reports of Grevelink and a few journalists, making it obvious that hardly anything changed in the period between the opening in 1850 and 1880. Each day was the same as every other, with the exception of Sundays, and that went on for decades. In February 1878 Sundays changed remarkably. Religious services could no longer be followed from behind half-open cell doors, but prisoners, wearing their caps, were marched single-file to the new cellular church. In this church, as reported by the *Algemeen Handelsblad,* there are 123 cells, planned as an amphitheatre, so that the one row protrudes above the others, and the prisoner placed there can see over the barrier without being able to work out who is sitting in front of him, while the barriers on the sides prevent him from seeing those sitting beside him. However, they can all see the vicars or priests, who stand on a gallery, reached by neat circular staircases. Next to the church a new cellular walking court had also been built.[41]

Grevelink visited the Amsterdam prison when it had only recently been opened. Among the 154 prisoners there were twenty-eight women. The prison comprised 208 cells which were not yet fully occupied. Grevelink immediately criticised the fact that several prisoners who were permitted to do household work did not always wear their cell cap as proscribed. Thus the cap did not always function as 'a complete hindrance to recognition'. He thought it better to do away with household chores outside the cells and recommended a separate walking place for each cell.

The daily visit had become a mere formality. The governor did his duty and faithfully visited every cell once a day. He delegated the visiting of the thirty-seven women's cells to a female warder. The governor admitted that not much more happened than an opening and shutting of cell doors. Not much had been realized either of the planned visits of educators, religious personnel, and members of commissions and of the Society. The daily visits (six of them), according to many necessary to prevent insanity, remained an ignored clause in the law of 1851.

Grevelink's report about Amsterdam is occupied chiefly with criticism about work, the canteen, ventilation, the white cell walls (he thought these would lead to eye problems), the walking places and the personnel. More importantly, he had heard and seen nothing that argued against an increase in the length of solitary confinement. 'No fear of suicide, nor insanity, nor physical weakness nor illness has been occasioned in me in the event of longer-lasting cellular punishment', he concluded. The recent years had produced no suicide attempts and only two instances of insanity 'one of whom was already insane and the other who had recovered in the cell'.[42]

Meticulous and extensive research in the archives might perhaps provide a decisive answer to the trustworthiness of these reports about suicide and insanity, but, one would thereby have to adopt the criterion for suffering used by lawyers and politicians of the nineteenth century. That criterion was very radical indeed; as long as prisoners did not become unmanageably insane or endanger themselves, then suffering from solitary confinement was not serious and cellular punishment fulfilled the objective of deterrence quite adequately. Very few emotional states between satisfaction and total despair were included by nineteenth-century cell supporters in the range they deemed important to decision making. Other descriptions stemming from the cellular prison in Amsterdam reinforce the impression that much psychological suffering was deemed acceptable.

A contributor to the *Weekblad van het Recht* visited this prison in 1872. A stay in a cell seemed to him 'a very severe punishment', but prisoners were, in his opinion, 'harassed' and 'humiliated' as little as possible. The sight of convicts in cell caps filled him with 'a definite horror'. The visit convinced him that the fate of prisoners was certainly not to be envied. But, he added, 'that is, of course, not why they are here'. Their fate had to remain 'horrible', no matter how bearable. Horrible it was, he assured his readers, 'believe me'.[43]

That judgements of solitary confinement extensively depended on subjective criteria is clear from the fact that, eight years later, in 1880, a journalist from *Nieuws van de Dag* had only positive impressions of his visit to the Amsterdam prison. At exactly the moment that he entered the prison, the midday meal was being brought around to the cells by prisoners 'whose face is covered with a mask, leaving only their eyes visible', something the journalist found only correct in connection with later recognition. It was said that many a prisoner, having rebuilt an honest life after release, had been black-mailed by fellows. The journalist praised the spy glass in each cell as 'again, a powerful means of control'. But despite the strict supervision, prisoners managed to break through the extremely well-enforced isolation. They lowered notes on strings through the ventilation pipes, threw stones covered with written messages over the walls of airing places and carried out whole conversations by tapping on walls. The journalist took it for granted that singing, whistling and humming were forbidden. Repeated transgressions meant being shut up 'in a dark cell'. His final judgement was positive. Definitely, one encountered 'suffering and atonement' in prison, but the treatment of prisoners from 'a physical and spiritual point of view', he thought 'practically unsurpassable'.

The secretary of the English Howard Association, William Tallack, who had visited the prison at Amsterdam in 1871, was even more enthusiastic. In *The Times* he reported: 'I can commend it in every way, except that it appears to me to be somewhat too pleasantly furnished to deter; in my opinion, a prison must serve both to punish and to improve'. Tallack spoke with the Society chairman, W. H. Suringar, who was also famous in England. The eighty-one-year old philanthropist seemed by then to be completely immersed in a cellular dream world. He considered solitary confinement of any length at all, even for those sentenced to life imprisonment, 'completely feasible'.[44]

Blind to Mental Suffering

Reading nineteenth-century documents concerned with solitary confinement, the question continually arises of whether punishers and those punished could, indeed, witness and stand much more suffering than we can today, used as we are to pain-killers and expert recognition of our own and others' psycho-social problems. The same question arises when one reads articles and debates from the first half of the nineteenth century in which public corporal punishment was trivialized and justified. But those sentenced to punishments on the scaffold at least screamed out in pain, and many witnesses showed a sensitivity to this suffering. Evidently, it was more difficult for people of the time to identify mental suffering, and those in solitary lacked the means and the words to express this psychological pain clearly.

The huge gap between punishers and those punished will have contributed largely to this. Each spoke a different language. Freudian vocabulary or the jargon of the welfare worker was not yet to hand, and the extent of the ignorance of psychological problems, judged by today's insights, becomes painfully clear in reading the booklet from 1876 of Vicar E. Laurillard, commissioner of the Society for Moral Improvement of Prisoners. There he reproduces a talk with a prisoner sentenced to the cell, under the title 'Together in solitude'.

'Do you not suffer from solitude?' asked Laurillard of the prisoner. 'Oh, I am never alone,' he answered. The vicar thought that he meant: 'God is with me, the all-present God'. But that was not the case. The prisoner told him that as soon as dusk fell he continuously saw images of himself. 'In short', he said, 'it is me, as if I have a double; I continuously see and hear myself; I sit beside myself and I walk next to myself. In the midst of others I was always alone; now that I am alone, I am usually together.'

Of course it is not justifiable to characterize this prisoner as schizophrenic based on these remarks, but we can be sure that he experienced things in his cell that he thought unusual and that we, using today's norms, would at least call alarming. Laurillard did not find this upsetting. On the contrary, he was reminded of a statement by the writer Jean Paul[45] about man, who through his self-awareness is never alone. The vicar thought 'this meeting with oneself' a good sign. 'Because he will also, especially in solitude, frequently encounter God. Because to forget oneself is a way of not thinking of God,' he preached. He ended his analysis with a maxim: 'Being shut off from the outside world leads to enclosing of the world inside'.

Thus psychological suffering was not only ignored, but also interpreted as a positive consequence of cellular confinement. Most other prisoners spoken to by Laurillard showed themselves to be grateful creatures who had nothing bad to say about solitary confinement. Occasionally one would emerge as less grateful. Under the heading of 'candour', for example, Laurillard lets a prisoner speak who complains of the preaching of Society members. He had had enough of the long sermons about 'my serious sin, my severe guilt, my weighty responsibility to the Everlasting Judge'. He was at least sensible enough to praise Laurillard for speaking, at least,'as an ordinary person'. He himself did that too:

> Sir! I have done evil, and therefore I bear my punishment; this punishment is measured out for me by judges; and it is good, I have earned it; but I do not know whether someone now has the right to make my legal punishment heavier, by repeatedly coming to me with accusations, and by misusing my powerlessness as prisoner in order to stone me in my sombre lodgings.

This prisoner saw the philanthropic meddling and pressure to convert more as an attack on his rights than as assistance toward emancipation.[46] One can easily understand this. Notes in secret codes, messages lowered on string through ventilation channels, signals tapped on walls, a pigeon or a canary, a household chore, the sin of masturbation, and, with luck, an incidental visit from a family member – those were the only pleasures in the second half of the nineteenth century to which cellular prisoners could look forward during the long, lonely days. In the communal prisons, the prime necessities were to get some fresh air and to survive in the social jungle where the weakest were assaulted, starved, humiliated and sexually misused. The many transports undermined both self-confidence and health, and often made contact with family impossible. From this sad and powerless position, nevertheless intensely observed by others, prisoners had to formulate their opinions of advantages and disadvantages of cell and community.

Sometimes they praised cellular confinement even more enthusiastically than their punishers; a few times because they really believed in its worth, but much more often 'as a lesson learned from outside', from fear of punishment and loss of favours or from hope that their sentence might be shortened.[47] Prisoners themselves proclaimed even more vigorously than lawyers, Members of Parliament and prison experts that the worst criminals enjoyed communal confinement. It is understandable that they tried to gain small advantages from their powerless position, but they unintentionally contributed to the eventual extension of the use of the cellular system to those with long sentences and the repeated lengthening of the maximum duration of solitary confinement. Given the choice between two forms of misery, they helped refine and enlarge one: cellular confinement. Grevelink's report, in which they were extensively cited, was thought 'striking' by the legal journal *Themis*, for example, because 'so many prisoners', even when the sentence length was identical, 'chose separation from each other' (the term 'solitary confinement' was thought 'unseemly' by the editorial board) and because only 'the most depraved and thus also precisely the most dangerous prisoners' chose communal confinement. The fear of suicide was thought to have been 'unfounded'.[48]

The vicar Laurillard wrote 'one does not whitewash with blacking', pointing to the communal prisons, convinced that cellular punishment was whitewash.[49] Only much later would emancipated prisoners, without fear, and their powerless punishers, stripped of illusions, declare that nothing could be whitewashed with a prison sentence anyway. Meanwhile, this insight had to wait until far in the future, as will be seen in the following chapter.

NOTES

1. From Charles Dickens, *David Copperfield* (The Penguin English Library), p. 923.
2. *AC*, 6 Aug. 1874, 10 Aug. 1874, 27 Oct. 1874 and 28 Oct. 1874.
3. Petersen, 1978, p. 83.
4. Cf. Swaan, 1983, p. 32.
5. Petersen, 1978, p. 82.
6. *Verzameling van wetten, (...)*, 1860–1905, KB, 29 Sep. 1875, no. 5.
7. Suringar, 1859, pp. 63–4.
8. Many fewer convicts with long sentences were housed in the prisons at Leeuwarden and Woerden than one had the right to expect on the basis of statistics for convictions.
9. Domela Nieuwenhuis, 1859, p. 160.
10. Nieuwenhuis, 1880, p. 507.
11. Prison statistics 1850–80. National mortality rate represents deaths per 100 male persons (averaged per decade). From Wever, 1940, p. 99. For the population over five years old, see Hofstee, 1978, pp. 213–14, Table 20.
12. Wever (1940, p. 97) arrived at slightly lower percentage for the prison at Leeuwarden because he started with a larger average population than that reported in the prison statistics. I have not been able to discover the reason for this.
13. Brauw, 1860, p. 569.
14. Zeeman, 1867.
15. Alstorphius Grevelink, 1857, p. 13.
16. Laurillard, 1876, pp. 3, 61.
17. Alstorphius Grevelink, 1857, p. 7.
18. Stuart, around 1870, p. 31.
19. For young offenders there were youth prisons at Montfort, Doetinchem and Alkmaar. But in the 1860s and 1870s hundreds (more than a quarter of whom were younger than thirteen) lived among the adults in communal prisons and *huizen van bewaring*. In 1874, almost 1,000 children (younger than sixteen) were confined (353 in penal prisons and 593 in remand-houses). About thirty-five per cent of them were younger than thirteen years old. (Prison statistics, 1850–80).

20. Alstorphius Grevelink, 1857, pp. 59–60.
21. 'Metabletics' is the name for a theory of societal change coined by Berg, (1968) 1956.
22. Alstorphius Grevelink, 1857, p. 63.
23. Idem, p. 46.
24. See prison statistics for the years 1861–80; Stuart, c. 1870, p. 34 and Stuart, 1869, p. 1; Alstorphius Grevelink, 1870, p. 48; for the ban by Minister Smidt, see Chapter 6; the nature of disciplinary punishments and the length of time they might last was only legally set down for the first time in the Prison Act 1886. Cf. Wöretshofer and Balkema, 1984, p. 15.
25. Alstorphius Grevelink, 1857, p. 17.
26. See also Stuart, 1865, pp. 3–4; Stuart, c. 1870, p. 40.
27. Alstorphius Grevelink, 1857, p. 17.
28. Idem, p. 37.
29. Cf. Eggink, 1958, p. 61; Petersen, 1978, p. 269.
30. *Themis,* 1857, p. 629.
31. Alstorphius Grevelink, 1857, p. 48.
32. Idem, pp. 49–50.
33. Idem, p. 51.
34. Cf. Jonge, 1980 (with literature references to *crowding* and sensory deprivation in foreign prisons). Kelk (1983, pp. 150–1) described two weeks(!) in a solitary cell as 'torture' approximately 125 years later.
35. Cf. Bloom et al., 1985, pp. 140–1.
36. Alstorphius Grevelink, 1857, p. 53.
37. Idem, pp. 54–6.
38. Cf. Goffman, 1984 (1961).
39. For example by Stuart, 1869, p. 3.
40. Alstorphius Grevelink, 1857, pp. 68–71.
41. *AH,* 26 Aug. 1877.
42. Alstorphius Grevelink, 1857, pp. 68–71.
43. *wvhR,* 1872, no. 3438, pp. 3–4.
44. *wvhR,* 1871, no. 3378, p. 4.
45. Jean Paul Friedrich Richter, a German writer, 1763–1825.
46. Laurillard, 1876, pp. 116–17.
47. Piccardt, 1866, p. 9.
48. Themis, 1857, pp. 628–9.
49. Laurillard, 1876, p. 61.

6

Cell Maniacs, Irish Sinners and Conservative Reactionaries: The System Controversy

Of course prisons and the system of forced labour do not reform the criminal; they only punish him and secure society against further encroachments on its tranquillity. In the criminal, prison and the most intense penal labour serve only to develop hatred, a thirst for forbidden pleasures and a terrible flippancy. But I am firmly convinced that the famous system of solitary confinement achieves only a spurious, deceptive, external goal. It sucks the vital sap from a man, enervates his soul, weakens it, intimidates it and then presents the withered mummy, the semi-lunatic as a model of reform and repentance.[1]

The passion and fervour with which penal experts and politicians discussed the punishment of criminals in the nineteenth century is understandable. Increasing resistance to flogging, branding and hanging of persons on crowded market squares was more a question of feeling than reason. 'You must see, see, see!' Reverend Laurillard urged supporters of the death sentence in his attempt to show how relative rational arguments could be.[2] We have also seen how these supporters, in turn, attempted to represent cellular confinement as especially gruesome and barbaric. In this way, differing emotions created friction, causing sparks.

It is much more difficult to understand why, in the second half of the nineteenth century, so much emotional engagement fired discussions about types of imprisonment. After all, the choice between corporal punishment and deprivation of freedom as punishment had already been settled in The Netherlands. But penal experts and politicians got wind of a new prison system being administered with success in England and, especially, Ireland. The origins of this system were totally different than those of cellular confinement. The basic principles had been developed in Australia, to which approximately 160,000 English criminals had been deported between 1787 and 1867. On Norfolk Island in the Pacific

Ocean, Captain Alexander Maconochie (1787–1860) had established a regime in which the central issues were no longer deprivation of freedom and infliction of pain, but work and moral improvement.[3]

Maconochie's *mark system* had ensured that he became wellknown. Prisoners were enabled to shorten their sentence by earning marks for hard work and exemplary behavior. Not solitude, but working *together* in a goal-oriented way with those who shared their fate was thought to more likely to equip criminals for a life of freedom.[4]

The Irish versus the Cellular System: Conflict between Concepts of Man and Society

In England and Ireland, in the middle of the nineteenth century, experiments were carried out with graduate systems into which elements of the Norfolk system had been incorporated. The Irish system, developed by the army captain Walter Crofton, is the best-known variant and could be described as release in phases. The first phase consisted of solitary confinement for a maximum of nine months for men and four for women. The solitude was much less absolute than that advocated in The Netherlands. 'Ridiculous extremes'[5] like cell caps, churches divided into cubicles and cellular airing places were not indulged in.

After the solitary phase, prisoners were transferred to communal prisons where they were separated at night into metal alcoves or sleeping cages. Prisoners were divided into five classes. In each class, sentence reductions and transfer to a higher class could be earned through good behaviour and hard work, using the *mark system*. Consistent good behaviour led to transfer to transition houses or *intermediate prisons*. This phase formed the essence of the Irish system. Prisoners enjoyed great freedom and were regularly sent into free society to shop or carry out a task. These excursions served to check whether or not sufficient internal resistence to the enticements of a free life had been built up in previous phases. During work, usually outside, there was little surveillance. Contact with the public was permitted and even encouraged. Prisoners who betrayed the trust placed in them were put back to a former phase. The most serious betrayal could even mean return to solitary confinement. Final release in the fourth phase was provisional. Prisoners received a *ticket of leave* which could be withdrawn due to bad behaviour. They were kept under strict police surveillance.[6]

The Irish system found little favour on the European continent.[7] In most places, and certainly in The Netherlands, resistance was strong enough to keep it from forming a serious threat to solitary confinement. It was seen as an extremely repugnant combination of communal and solitary confinement.[8] The vehement language used in articles and during debates to express both resistance to and enthusiasm for the Irish system leads us to suspect that combating crime had come to play a minor role in opinion forming. Moreover, in The Netherlands, crime statistics allowed a favourable interpretation between 1850 and 1880. The prison population decreased and numbers of those sentenced in the courts per 100,000 inhabitants remained relatively constant.[9]

Just as had been the case in the fierce discussion about corporal and capital punishment, the battle between the Irish and the purely solitary system was fought around issues divorced from crime prevention. Controversial concepts of man and society, differences in thinking or 'mentalities' were most important. 'Unfortunate factions' took up sides within this controversy, and, according to prison inspector Grevelink, challenged each other 'intemperately and hard-heartedly' in the House. What he meant was that liberals supported the cellular system and conservatives preferred a mixture of cellular and communal confinement, following the Irish model.[10] All these factors lent to the controversy a significance far exceeding the face value of the problem in question: how can prisoners be remodelled into responsible citizens?

The differing mentalities can perhaps best be characterized by comparing the writings of the most important representatives of the two systems: Jacob Domela Nieuwenhuis (1836–1924), who became professor of criminal law in Groningen and the 'anti-revolutionary' ex-Minister of Justice, Justinus J. L. van der Brugghen (1804–63). Domela Nieuwenhuis obtained his doctorate in 1859 with a thesis about 'separate confinement' and, two years later, a book of van der Brugghen's about the Irish system appeared. Actually, Nieuwenhuis's thesis contained everything that had been said or could be said about the cellular system. He portrayed and put into words widespread conceptions of crime and punishment. Many shared his opinions.

Van der Brugghen, on the other hand, was more a voice crying in the wilderness, even though he was able to count on support from lawyers for some time. Van der Brugghen's ideas, largely derived from famous German criminal scholars like von Holtzendorff and Mittermaier, enjoyed a brief popularity, but did not take root. His opinions were shared by only a few in The Netherlands and after his death in 1863, their number quickly declined.

The world of a 'Cellular Fanatic': Domela Nieuwenhuis[10]

Domela Nieuwenhuis saw 'moral suffering' through solitary confinement as a powerful means to improve criminals, because the 'evil predisposition' disappeared. 'Sensual suffering' on the scaffold or in communal prisons provoked only revenge and bitterness. He saw 'evil tendencies' as internal motives for criminal action. Whether evil tendencies arose from social deprivation or faulty character did not matter; they were evil and could spread like contagious diseases in communal prisons. Wickedness was, according to Domela Nieuwenhuis, just like liquor, possessed of 'something attractive, something contagious'. The conscience could be stilled – 'what a bliss'.

Thus, separation 'by walls', one from the other, remained the only meaningful prison sentence. 'Solitude' served as an appropriate force to move one to reflection 'about what one was and did, and to teach one what one must do'. In this way, Domela Nieuwenhuis arrived at an image of the criminal as *homo clausus*, who, in the absence of social contact, shut off from all previous social relationships, could be induced to improve his social behaviour. Uplifting visits from clergy and other do-gooders would hasten this process. Women were thought better able to stand solitary confinement because they already had a sedentary and solitary life and more easily adjusted 'to existing conditions'.[12]

Solitary confinement, at the very least, prevented criminal contamination and that was very important to Domela Nieuwenhuis. The cell system was a radical agent against 'moral death'. Even if an occasional prisoner weakened or lost his reason in his cell, he called attention to the fact that insanity could spring from 'the emotion at the source of the healing process for the internal person'. He questioned the meaning of insanity when compared with 'craziness' caused by 'the soul-annihilating poison of sociable contact', a poison which put the conscience to sleep.

Suicide too should not be taken too seriously, he thought. He referred to victims of violence in the huge dormitories and workplaces. Reasoning thus, there remained only the objection that the cell encouraged the offence 'that loves loneliness'. But masturbation, sinful as it was, was less awful than homosexual contacts in communal prisons and was 'if one does not yet know of it' at least not learned in the cell! So his assumption was that all that was good would come to the surface in the cell and that prisoners would not discover the sin of masturbation on their own.

Attention becomes focused here on a certain inconsistency within his argument, one characterizing all nineteenth-century considerations of prison sentences. Prisoners apparently allowed themselves to be completely moulded by their social surroundings in communal prisons, but their inherent strength was such that they could suddenly, when confined to a cell, grow into completely new personalities. This rational inconsistency was partly rooted in the fact that Domela Nieuwenhuis and many of his contemporaries emotionally preferred the image of powerless and pliable cell-bound loners to that of depraved, rebellious and insolent villains piled up in communal prisons. Such sentiments probably were instrumental in defining his opinions as were the colliding concepts of moral improvement and communal contagion. Still, the conceptual inconsistency, as we have seen earlier, permits another interpretation and even suggests a solution: good was inherent to man and all evil was introduced from outside by diabolical fellow-men. The cell was therefore salutary and the community depraved.

Domela Nieuwenhuis concluded that *fifteen years' solitary confinement* was not too severe 'because hope has not been destroyed, and, as long as that exists, man can endure suffering'. His aversion to communal confinement was so pronounced that he went so far as to condemn communal hospital wards. Just as Society chairman Suringar, he was of the opinion that 'he who is sick can die' and better to enter the hereafter 'well prepared' than 'badly prepared'.[13]

The World of an 'Irish Sinner': Ex-Minister van der Brugghen

How different were the thoughts and feelings of van der Brugghen![14] On the very first page, he pointed out the erroneous assumption that all prisoners were more depraved 'than those punishing and incarcerating them'. Many, in his opinion, had forgotten that government was not called upon to punish moral depravity but only the breaking of the law. These thoughts were definitely not widely entertained in The Netherlands. This was apparent as well from the almost complete silence surrounding the Irish ideas in newspapers and legal journals.[15]

The basic assumption of the ex-Minister was that crime resulted from 'too little will-power to follow the voice of one's conscience'. First the will had to be broken to be rebuilt into 'new moral power'. He judged the lonely life of the cell inadequate to this end. *Wanting* to do good differed totally, in his opinion, from *being able* to do good. 'An energetic act of conscience' had to proceed moral conviction. He distinguished himself from Domela Nieuwenhuis by considering moral improvement as something only to be achieved by *strong-willed* prisoners *by themselves*. Prison sentences were meant to help by creating amenable conditions and reintroducing prisoners by stages into free society. A sentence was primarily a preparation 'for their reentry into life in society' and here he formulated a principle that would have to wait until 1951 before it was laid down in Dutch penal law.[16]

Van der Brugghen undermined the image of man as *homo clausus*, step by step. He thought that prisoners would only develop their own moral potential if promised a reduced sentence which they could earn 'by drawing upon that potential' and 'by good behaviour in prison'. Meaningful work, religion, education and, above all, increasing freedom had to be concentrated on teaching 'practical moral principles' and developing 'a morality for real life'. Appearing to be filled with good intentions for the benefit of cell visitors had very little to do with the demands of a hard, realistic social life.

Solitary confinement was, of course, an *adequate* preventive remedy against spreading moral contagion, but it could not function as a *curative* for persons already depraved. He was not totally against solitary confinement but found that it must be functional and not last too long (a maximum of one year). He thought cell life unnatural and in conflict with the social or 'gregarious' nature of man. It was incorrect to see segregation *itself* as a means to moral improvement. Cellular isolation could lead to nothing more than awareness of guilt and sin, 'the condition *sine qua non* of all moral improvement'. He called it, additionally, 'a delicate tool', easily turned to the opposite purpose and leading to bitterness and hypocrisy. It was even worse should separation from 'evil in the outside world' lead to absolute separation from 'the outside world itself'. Separation of this sort blocked access to moral improvement. The harvest from solitarily improved prisoners was not much more than scrawny hot-house plants, which, once placed outside, washed away in the first gentle shower. Ethical weakness was the 'necessary psychological result' of long-lasting 'and therefore stupefying' solitary confinement.

He quoted from Von Holtzendorff:

> Would one not sometimes be tempted to imagine this separation fervour, carried to the extreme of futility, at some point erecting wood dividers between the graves of dead prisoners in order to perpetuate the cell system in infinity?

Van der Brugghen thought that the only solution could be a 'well worked-out coordination' between solitary and communal confinement with a 'step-by-step increase in freedom' playing the central role. He saw this already actualized in the Irish system with its *intermediate prisons* and *ticket of leave* system. The 'basic psychological concept' upon which it was based, was 'that one may expect a stronger awareness of *internal responsibility* with the granting of a more comprehensive *external freedom*'.[17]

Similar concepts of freedom and responsibility can presently be found in most pedagogical and penological articles, but a hundred years ago the Irish concepts were unusual and unwanted. Criminals had to be handled with strict discipline and punishment and not with freedom. Economical, political and other social connections between the classes were weaker and less widespread than at present. Members of upper circles then did not have to and could not strongly identify themselves with those socially beneath them. This made wanting to and being able to understand lower class feelings, lifestyle, misery and especially motivation to commit crime much more difficult. Religious convictions, socially much more deeply rooted than at present, facilitated the development of ideas of justice locating sources of criminal behaviour in individual sinfulness and evil tendencies. People decided of their own free will to do evil for their own advantage and because they lacked moral restraint. Solitary confinement was meant to alter these advantages into moral suffering and to build moral restraint. But van der Brugghen and his supporters wish to transform criminals, who lacked, in their view, not ethical awareness and good will, but will-power and social skills, into *social* beings.

Domela Nieuwenhuis wrote a critique of the 'little effort' of van der Brugghen.[18] Assuming he was refuting van der Brugghen's arguments, he revealed views which unintentionally made clear to what a great extent he saw man as *homo clausus*. Shut off from a sinful world and forced to reflect upon his past life, the criminal would become aware of 'what he is' and learn 'what he must do'. As soon as the internal conversion, 'the renewing of the heart by the criminal's becoming convinced of the wrongness of the sins of the crime', had taken place, the criminal would be gripped by 'an unconquerable revulsion against evil'.

While van der Brugghen wanted deeds, Domela Nieuwenhuis was satisfied with intentions. He dispatched will-power training in communal prisons and *intermediate prisons* with the rhetorical question: 'would one lead a person, beginning to recover from alcoholism, into pubs and public houses to practice his will-power?' Three decades later, in a reflective article about the systems' battle which he had won, Domela Nieuwenhuis was able to state triumphantly about van der Brugghen ('undoubtedly someone of noble character') that he was 'such an optimist that he thought he could harbour illusions about the forced togetherness of prisoners sentenced for crimes committed and their conversion or improvement by better influences in the midst of their communal association.'[19]

Battle between the 'Irish' and 'Cell Fanatics' In and Outside Parliament

After its experimental introduction in 1851, the cellular system continued to be praised and emotionally defended by members of the Society for the Moral Improvement of Prisoners. The objections against communal confinement were, to a great extent, of a sexual nature. They opposed immorality more readily than crime.[20] This helps to elucidate why Society members immediately attacked every attempt to mix cellular and communal confinement. 'We feel aversion, a most profound aversion to all and every social interaction of prisoners with each other,' wrote chairman Suringar.[21] Thus, when van der Brugghen became Minister of Justice in 1856, they drew their knives.

As Member of Parliament, Van der Brugghen had resisted frequently the cellular image 'of cleaning and improving a man as one would a tool, a machine, with mechanical energy'. As Minister, he made a case for building prisons which combined both cells and large halls for communal confinement (with separation at night into iron alcoves). His first budget immediately had to endure heavy criticism from the Lower House. He was accused of being of two minds, but he held to 'his feelings' that man could not be improved 'through a sort of mummification'.[22] Partially to appease a very distrustful Lower House, he commissioned inspector

Alstorphius Grevelink in 1857 to begin his tour of The Netherlands, discussed in the last chapter.

In addition to resistance from inflexible believers in cellular doctrine,[23] van der Brugghen also had to deal with opposition from within the penal system. A survey carried out among magistrates, commissions of administration and colleges of regents, on data and opinions concerning moral improvement, recidivism, insanity and suicide, taught him that the large majority stood strongly behind cellular confinement.[24]

In the Lower House, proponents of cellular punishment were subjected primarily to the retorts of the conservative Member of Parliament, W. Wintgens. As early as 1851, Wintgens told the House that the cellular system had managed to 'slip' into the law 'more because of actual building of prisons than sufficient discussion'.[25] Wintgens himself became Minister of Justice in 1868 and, during his short reign, the battle surrounding the Irish system flared up in full force. The liberal Member of Parliament, Godefroi, ex-Minister of Justice, called the Irish system 'a system of deception and hypocrisy' and allowed it to leak out that he saw prison inspector Grevelink as an evil genius.[26] In reaction to this, Grevelink wrote a vitriolic brochure in which he showed himself, more openly than ever, as a firey supporter of the Irish system. Deception and hypocrisy, he said, could be found especially in cellular prisons. He and others had often remarked that prisoners, at the opening of the cell door, could be found sitting with an open bible on their laps, 'but, alas, upside down'. He now recognized unhesitatingly the dangers of suicide and insanity, which he had trivialized ten years earlier. He admitted to having been silent about all of this 'for too long'.[27] This critical attitude cost him his job. In 1871, the liberal, J. A. Jolles, a convinced supporter of the cellular system, became Minister of Justice. He rid himself of the troublesome Grevelink by making the function of chief inspector of prison systems redundant under the pretext of reorganization.[28]

In parliament, the battle against the Irish system had already been decided by the stepping down of Minister Wintgens in 1868, even before the 'firing' of Grevelink. All succeeding Ministers worked with complete conviction, supported by a large majority in the House, on further expanding the cellular system. Circles of lawyers outside parliament included many supporters of the Irish system for several more years, according to debates of the Dutch Lawyers' Society in 1872. Proponents of the Irish system showed themselves, during discussions, to be motivated more by aversion to long-lasting cellular confinement than by concepts or penal principles. They spoke mockingly of 'cell maniacs' and 'moral and intellectual castration' but not one speaker appeared to have immersed himself in Irish concepts as deeply as van der Brugghen had eleven years earlier. The vote showed an overwhelming majority for cellular confinement to a maximum of three years, followed by communal confinement with classification and nightly separation into alcoves. A large majority likewise favoured the introduction of conditional release. Thus the lawyers did adopt Irish elements, but the Irish system as a whole was rejected by twenty-eight votes to twenty-one. This also broke Irish opposition outside parliament to further expansion of the cellular system.[29]

Legal Expansion of the Cellular System: Suicide and Insanity

In 1870, the year in which, after fierce discussions in press and parliament, the death penalty was abolished[30] in The Netherlands, the Minister of Justice, Jolles, proposed to extend the maximum length of a solitary sentence to two years. In his explanatory memorandum, he pointed out that the negative influence of solitude 'on one's mood' was not particularly significant. Seventeen years' experience of solitary confinement were supposed to have proved this. In the years 1866, 1867 and 1868, in respective populations of 3,914, 4,390 and 4,043 solitarily confined criminals (shorter or longer term), 'only' ten had committed suicide and six had become mentally ill. In the opinion of the Minister these figures were 'not unpropitious'. This illustrates how limited the criterion was that politicians and prison experts used to establish the suffering inflicted by solitary confinement. Seldom was a remark made revealing any awareness that psychic pain could be very intense without leading to suicide or visible insanity.

It must be admitted that the figures of Minister Jolles were and are difficult to interpret. Numerous factors having little or nothing to do with the nature of confinement can be influential. Figures are often incomplete and greatly dependent upon social definitions encompassing suicide and insanity.[31] This goes even more for the assumed causes. Prison governors preferred not to see solitary confinement itself as a cause. It is worth wondering whether prison doctors, in stating the cause of death, were always able to resist pressures from governors and whether they were not misled. It is important to bear in mind that, until 1880, civilians who became mentally ill were often placed in judicial houses of detention before eventually being transferred to an asylum.[32] Thus, psychic desperation was defined as a type of insanity only when a prisoner was completely out of control within his four walls, necessitating transfer to an asylum. Before a psychic disorder became a hindrance in a cellular prison, much time would certainly have passed. In free society, as well, the decision to commit someone to an asylum was made much later than it is presently; naturally this is connected with the professionalizing of psychiatry.[33]

All this makes Minister Jolles' figures especially difficult to interpret, but one is struck by the ease with which causes of insanity and suicide were sought outside the influence of cellular confinement or, as the Minister wrote, 'had already shown their influence before sentencing'. So, a confinement longer than a year would, according to the Minister, 'not harm' body or soul. He was assured 'almost unanimously' that periods of cellular confinement exceeding one year 'could do nothing but benefit the moral development of prisoners'.[34]

Data presented by the Minister to the House came from prison statistics. These show that he did not reveal that numbers of suicides and prisoners declared insane were systematically higher in cellular than in communal prisons. Inspector Grevelink had pointed this out in the report accompanying the prison statistics of 1861. He had added that the *absolute* figures were low, but that he feared an increase with longer periods of confinement and that he 'shuddered' at the thought of a maximum exceeding three years.[35]

This sort of comment marked the beginning of his slow fall from favour with the more dogmatic proponents of cellular punishment, leading, as we have seen, to his dismissal. From 1865 on, he added descriptions to the prison statistics of all the separate suicides and instances of insanity. Until far into the twentieth century, the government and then the *Centraal Bureau voor de Statistiek* (Central Bureau of Statistics) would continue to do this. Very little is known of the lives and feelings of prisoners in the nineteenth century, but these annual descriptions saved from oblivion the many hundreds who put an end to their suffering or escaped it in insanity.

Causes of insanity and suicide systematically were sought outside cellular confinement or in the mental illness itself. Grevelink received reports from the prison administrations. In their opinion insanity was for instance 'the result of hysteria', the person was 'already in a confused state on arrival in prison', 'became insane because of exaggerated alcohol misuse only a few days after being put in the cell' or 'had already been under care in the asylum before his arrival in prison'. About an insane prisoner in Sneek the administrator reported that he 'was known in his domicile as someone with mental problems. Regents are thus convinced that it was not the solitary confinement which made him ill.'[36]

Similar descriptions from the annually published prison statistics were, it appears, summed up rather one-sidedly for the House by Minister of Justice Jolles. If the report of the prison management had not explicitly stated that a prisoner who had committed suicide or become insane had been solitarily confined, the Minister assumed the opposite. Alcohol misuse, epilepsy, a 'dissolute' lifestyle or physical deformations were named often as explanations, but never solitary confinement. The Minister's summary was deemed 'exhaustive' by the commission of reporters and was thought to prove that the maximum period of confinement could 'safely' be extended to two years, just as proposed in the Bill. Some thought 'without hesitation' that the Minister could have asked for a longer period. Obviously egged on by these supportive sounds, the Minister called figures for suicide and mental collapse 'very slight' in his memorandum in reply.[37]

Disappointing Recidivism Figures

During the public discussion of the Bill, the suicide and insanity figures were not even mentioned. Some Members of Parliament asked for data about recidivism. The Minister's answer was that he had not provided this because it was too unreliable, but all the answers he gave make it patently clear that these figures did not reflect favourably on the cell system. This compelled him to very opportunistic arguments about the relationship of crime to prison sentences, which revealed that enthusiasm for cellular confinement rested on more than the assumed preventive effect. Cellular sentences appealed to the middle-class imagination because the depraved togetherness of communal prisons was thus radically prevented. For many of the champions of solitary confinement this depravity weighed more heavily than the crimes for which prisoners were initially being punished. Moreover, from the point of view of order, discipline and malleability, many would have valued the total powerlessness of evil loners. Solitude did not exclude improvement while it did do away with sexual vileness and criminal conspiracy or communal opposition. With only one dissenting vote, the Lower House voted in the Bill.

It is important to remember that solitary punishment already had, at this point, been in use in The Netherlands for twenty years. New prisons had been built to this end, designs were being made, many earned their living in this area and many had committed themselves to this system through their scholarly articles, their public utterances and parliamentary stands.[38] It was said that The Netherlands should not lag behind civilized countries world-wide in which the system had been adopted and, just as important, acceptable alternatives were not available except for the 'half-way measure' of the Irish system. Still, the recidivism figures would not cooperate. In order to expand the cellular system, in spite of unfavourable recidivism, Minister Jolles was prepared to doubt the preventive working of *every* prison sentence. Reports about recidivists, for instance, had 'completely' convinced him 'that living conditions exerted a great influence in that area'.[39] The nature and severity of punishment, he repeated later in the Upper House, had only a relative influence on the nature and severity of crime. 'Secondary conditions', he said, meaning social conditions and upbringing, were of 'very great influence' upon the committment of crimes.[40] The Minister was, admittedly, forced to these insights by unfavourable recidivism figures, but, the very fact that such figures could force him to this sort of realization illustrates the extent to which the introduction of solitary confinement unintentionally contributed to the emancipation process of prisoners. By committing crimes after release as well, they undermined again and again the legitimation of confinement, even more so because expectations concerning crime reduction were repeatedly coupled to prison reform. Little by little, the *structural* defects and inherent disadvantages of all forms of confinement became visible through the punishers' pursuit of improved forms of punishment. Knowledge of crime and punishment and relationships between them grew with the experience of and the continuous debate about new forms of imprisonment and their introduction. In the long run, this knowledge increased the power of the punished, rather than that of the punishers.

Now that the maximum duration of solitary confinement had been increased to two years, this sentence was more often imposed. Annual descriptions of incidents of suicide and insanity in prison statistics publicized only a portion of the misery brought to bear on many prisoners by solitude. That portion was too small to temper the enthusiasm of politicians and scholars of criminal law. Even disappointing recidivism figures could not do this. And, should even more misery have been visible, one would most likely still not have seen it. The many proponents of the system acted as socialists do who continue to believe in their ideals in spite of disastrous developments in countries who practiced socialistic ideas on a large scale.

Thus, in 1873, the Members of Parliament were offered a report by the liberal Minister of Justice, G. de Vries, about the operation of the cellular system, including a proposal to expand the period of confinement to three years. Experience with the system was supposed to have proven that 'the fruits' had not been expected in vain and that the frequently voiced grievances were, in reality, 'not to be feared'.

To prepare them for the disappointing figures, the Minister impressed upon the Members of Parliament that not moral improvement but 'complete, lasting separation of prisoners from each other' had been the main goal. He remarked that 'one second's acquaintance' served for further recognition and 'one immoral word' called up evil thoughts and could damn 'a moral existence'.

The Minister compared, over a period of ten years, numbers of those sentenced to solitary confinement per 100 convicts with the number of recidivists who already had been solitarily confined per 100 recidivists. According to him, there were always less recidivists than could be expected based on the numbers sentenced, but, in 1869, not even that was the case. Still, these figures were supposed to plead 'in favour of' the system. They were, of course, very tricky and did not really permit such a conclusion. The Minister appears to have understood this too, because he then postulated that solitary confinement would have been 'sufficiently effective' even if ex-prisoners had only been dissuaded from committing *more serious* crimes. In that case, they would not be leaving prison 'more depraved' than when they entered it. It appeared to him, from diminished numbers of long sentences, that numbers of serious crimes had diminished. Apparently he was not completely content with the persuasiveness of these figures and arguments. He concluded his interpretation of the recidivism figures with remarks which undermined the preventive aspect of every form of punishment even stronger than had been the case by his colleague Jolles. Other circumstances, such as alcoholism, were said to have strongly influenced recidivism. He added that the committing of petty theft appeared statistically to become 'a particular habit against which almost nothing can be done'. Then he pointed to the significant influence of 'education and enlightenment', because, in approximately eighty per cent of prisoners, the intellect appeared to be poorly developed. 'Great circumspection' thus was needed with regard to recidivism figures.

The Minister could not, of course, completely skirt the effects of solitary confinement on suicide, insanity and 'the mood' of prisoners in his report. Data that he had gathered were not very favourable. In the period from 1862 to 1872, according to him, there had been twenty-five incidents of insanity under all solitarily confined prisoners.[41] The Minister found the number high. Still, experience was supposed to have proven that the cell could not be seen as the cause of insanity. 'One can almost always find a probable cause outside the cell', he wrote, meaning alcohol abuse or a history of mental disease. The Minister remarked, concerning two cases of *mania religiosa* that:

> The one case occurred after five completely healthy months; the other contains complete proof that the cell exercised no influence; he was already occupying it for the third time.

To this reassuring explanation, he added that, in cellular prisons, abnormal mental functioning would be noticed much earlier than in communal prisons. The better medical supervision in cells would lead to a diagnosis of insanity for 'what in the communal prison, and in free society to an even greater extent, would be seen as excentricity or not noticed at all'. Given that prisoners in communal prisons were isolated in cells precisely 'because of insanity', the Minister could naturally just as easily have chosen for the less reassuring option that much insanity went unnoticed in cells. His remarks mainly illustrate the lengths to which one was prepared to go to reason away any negative effects of solitary confinement.

He deals in a similar way with the twenty-one cellular suicides and suicide attempts during this same period. In communal prisons, only twelve suicides had occurred in an average population four times as large as in the cellular prisons. According to the Minister, solitude did make the *carrying out* of suicidal longings easier, but did not give rise to these longings. In short, the cell provided more opportunity.

A public discussion of the Bill did not take place, though. The Members of Parliament and, consequently, the Minister as well, thought it better to wait for the new Penal Code, already being drawn up.[42]

The Cellular System in the Draft for the Penal Code

The House received the first draft of the new Penal Code in 1879. Numbers of sentences demanding solitary confinement had already increased significantly. In 1870, solitary confinement was the lot of more than forty-one per cent of all those correctionally sentenced.In 1877, the provincial courts of justice called for solitary confinement in seventy-two per cent, and the district courts in sixty-six per cent of cases.

In the draft, the old French differentiation between 'misdrijven' and 'wanbedrijven' (felonies and offenses), that is between criminal and correctional offences, was done away with. Punishable offences were divided into *misdrijven* (crimes) and *overtredingen* (transgressions). As far as detention was concerned, serious crimes were punished with life or provisional (maximum fifteen-year) *prison sentences*, while transgressions meant *custody*. Custody (also custody of defendants) could take place in communal halls. Those sentenced to prison who were older than sixteen and younger than sixty were destined for cellular confinement the first three years of their sentences. Exceptions were only possible on medical grounds. Those sentenced to a longer term would have to sit out any time remaining, above three years, in communal prisons, where they were to be divided into classes based on age, development and behaviour. They would be separated at night into iron alcoves.

The draft additionally included application of the *conditional leave* 'for good behaviour' after two-thirds and at least one year of the sentence had been completed. Minister Smidt saw the aim of this conditional leave as the dispelling of prejudice and mistrust in the outside world. It was thought that the 'Sword of Damocles' would ease prisoners' rehabilitation into free society because otherwise no one would be willing to contract an ex-prisoner. Employers would gain more power over released prisoners because, should they behave badly, 'a well-documented report to the police' was enough to land them in prison once more. The Minister deemed it of 'general societal importance' that terms of confinement could be shortened in practice without endangering the public order and safety.[43]

In a report to the King, the Minister called it 'an illusion' to imagine that a system could exist 'which would be able to redeliver prisoners to society as improved, let alone respectable, persons or even, for that matter, to protect them from all bad influences'. Overwhelming belief in the improvement possible through solitary confinement was, at about the time of its completed introduction, radically diminished.[44]

During the preliminary parliamentary treatment of the draft-Penal Code, Members of Parliament were offered a new report about the operation of the cellular system by the new Minister of Justice, A. E. J. Modderman. He remarked correctly, in his introduction, that since the last report in 1873, no important changes had taken place. Practically no expert remained who still preferred communal confinement or the Irish style to solitary confinement. 'The battle' still being fought concerned itself only with the question of how long cellular punishment could be imposed 'without damaging the convict's body or soul more than during communal confinement'. Precisely in this area many facts were contained in his report which were explained in the now familiar manner, favouring the cellular system and years of confinement. He even concluded that 'not a single case of insanity' had been 'a proven consequence' of solitary confinement.

This is not to say that the Minister knowingly interpreted the data in favour of the cellular system, but it is true that social and political pressure to introduce the system and deep-seated belief in its healing effect stood in the way of a critical analysis of the facts. It was true, for instance, that many more prisoners received disciplinary punishments in cells than in communal prisons, but this he deemed due only to the fact that much more was thought punishable in cells and chances of discovery were much higher. The majority of punishable 'transgressions' consisted of boister-ousness and especially of attempts to make contact with fellow-prisoners, often by means of new heating and ventilation systems. The Minister's concluding remark was that 'notwithstanding the disciplinary punish-ments', governors of the large cellular prisons had not hesitated 'to affirm their general satisfaction with prisoners' behaviour'.

This left the obstinate figures for recidivism. These still refused to align themselves with the beautiful theories, while the Minister understood that one 'rather generally' sought evidence in recidivism data 'for the more of less outstanding quality' of the cellular system. He began by remarking that recidivism was indeed 'a very weighty factor' but still not the only one to be kept in mind when one had to make up the balance. Consequently, he forged ahead, just as Jolles and de Vries before him, bringing the basis of every prison system into question in his attempt to explain disappoint-ing recidivism. There were persons, in his opinion, whom one could expect *a priori* to fall into 'repetition of crime, independent of the sort of prison sentence they were subjected to', such as 'habitual criminals' and 'indifferent persons, lacking in feeling for religion or morality, unmoved by good impressions'.

This reasoning was perilous. After all, huge numbers of this sort of criminal would have had to exist to neutralize the improving influence of solitary confinement on other prisoners. The Minister was sensible enough to refrain from drawing conclusions based on the existing data. To do this 'very complicated calculations' and other missing data would be needed. He admitted freely that 'here, in this country', for the time being, it was impossible to make 'direct comparisons' of recidivism following communal and solitary confinement. After this frank admission, he still managed a rationalization favouring solitary confinement. It would 'not have gone unnoticed' that solitary confinement then could only be imposed 'for a short time' and had, thus, only partially been able to exert its influence. 'And this is especially oppressive because more time is necessary, as a rule, for improvement than that spent by most convicts in the cell', according to the Minister. From the recidivism figures, which, disappointingly enough, could not really be seen as casting a favourable light on solitary confinement, he drew the rather paradoxical conclusion that confinement should last *longer*.[45]

Such argumentation convinced people like Foucault that the overt goals of prison sentences throughout time served only as a front for their real effect: improved exercise of power over groups in the population who threatened middle-class interests. Failure of the preventative and improving effect of a prison sentence would then actually constitute its *success*. The prison takes the most damaging elements of a threatening class under its wing and, at the same time, diverts attention from its own class-bound criminality. A manageable group of criminals is released from prison with the certainty that they will return. Increased recidivism would then be exactly what was aimed at by what Foucault preferentially calls 'the power'.

The prison sentence indeed had effects which in many ways corresponded with what Foucault saw as aims of 'power'. But it is clear that these effects were largely unintended. Should some scholars of criminal law or politicians have already discerned these effects, they had neither anticipated nor designed them in a moment of exceptional, sociological mental clarity. Nineteenth century scholars and politicians felt a great affinity to the cellular system based on historically developed leanings, interests and ideas of man which had both a lot and yet very little to do with overtly desired moral improvement and preventative effect. Above all, they had no alternative and would, in resisting, have risked estrangment from the whole Western world. They wanted to punish from a position of deep, moral injury and preferably to reform, they wanted to civilize the lower orders but keep them in their place, they wanted to prevent depravity and to fight crime, but, above all, they wanted to put into effect a system in which they had already invested much too much materially and immaterially to be able to relinquish it.[46] Unfavourable figures for recidivism could no longer move them to that point. Often

these figures could be doubted justifiably and too much official, public
and political pressure had been brought to bear on introduction of the
new punishment to be able to find the way back. This is quite different
from seeing recidivism as a desired result within a new power technique,
as Foucault does. His vision would have meant, and this is seldom
realized, that positive figures for recidivism would have had to work
against the introduction of the cellular system and other prison reforms.
We would even have to accept that Ministers and Members of Parliament, hugely resourceful, were interpreting unfavourable figures as favourable because the real aim of 'power' had to remain hidden: a paranoid
thought which is as incontestable as it is absurd.

Definitive Implementation of Solitary Confinement

The draft for a Penal Code was received positively but also critically by the
Members of Parliament, but the powerful Society for the Moral Improvement of Prisoners immediately protested against the proposed communal
confinement after three years in the cell. Moral improvement booked in
the cell would just be completely demolished. One would prefer to have
chosen for cellular confinement throughout a sentence, but all prisoners
should, in any case, be put into cells for the first *five* years. The Society
attempted to turn the tide on the coming calamity by succesfully
addressing the House and government.[47] The majority of Members of
Parliament, according to a report of the 'commissie van rapporteurs'
(commission of reporters) also found three years too short and pushed for
an extension to five years.

The powerless position of prisoners is well illustrated by protests
voiced by a majority of the commission against the proposed *right* to be
permitted to stay in the cell 'at their own request' after the cellular period.
Prisoners were allowed no rights at all. 'It conflicts with the character of
punishment in general that a prisoner, as opposed to the State, would be
given the right to undergo his punishment in the most pleasant way,'
according to the commission. For the same reason they rejected the idea
that a prisoner could be granted conditional leave only 'with his permission'. Every right and thus also 'the right to stay in prison' was deemed
absolutely forbidden. 'The State releases when *it*, and not the prisoner,
sees fit.' A little less than a century before prisoners gained the right to
complain formally about their treatment, the thought of *rights* for prisoners, even the right to refuse favours, put politicians in a bad mood.[48]

Under pressure from Members of Parliament and the Society for
Moral Improvement of Prisoners, Minister Modderman decided to
modify the draft. While his predecessor Smidt had stated with certainty
only a year earlier that more than three years in a cell could damage both
mind and body and make prisoners 'useless' in social life, Modderman

was able to add two years without compunction. He also lowered the minimum age from sixteen to fourteen years. The conclusion must be that the Minister and Members of Parliament decided to take the risk based on sentiment and pseudo-knowledge when, after thirty years of discussion and experience, a definitive decision about the cellular system had to be made. The continuously existing fear that the new cellular system would not be strict enough and would lead to outbreaks of crime must have gripped even supporters of the punishment. The pressure made Minister Modderman play safe, but deliberations in parliament about the new Penal Code show that many nevertheless feared chaos. An amendment which would have allowed reintroduction of the death sentence was narrowly rejected by a only a small majority of votes. The conservative-catholic Member of Parliament, Van Baar, contended vehemently that 'the safety of the State, of the innocent' had been lost sight of in the Penal Code. He found the system of punishment much too mild and spoke snearingly of the 'humanity system'.

Minister Modderman, one of the liberals in a conservatively tinted cabinet perceived that he would have to defend the cellular system against accusations of leniency. Using a didactic tone, he revealed his vision that the sentence had to cause *suffering* but not *harm*. In the cell, prisoners did not become more evil and the chance existed that they might improve. 'False shame' would get in the way of remorse in communal prisons and one received an upbringing in wrong-doing. 'Through the cell, thus, is not only the interest of the individual but also that of society served most potently; it is both stricter and more humane,' continued the Minister.

The excitement surrounding the idea of exaggerated laxity and the long prehistory of the cellular question were responsible for giving the separate issue of five years' solitary confinement the atmosphere of an anticlimax. Verbal and written opinions had been offered by dozens of criminal justice scholars over the years and politicians had spent days in debating the issue. Possible effects of five years' solitary confinement were still unexplored territory for everyone. Nevertheless, on 27 October 1880, this article was approved without deliberation and without vote. Tenders could be invited for new domed prisons, more cellular coaches and train carriages. While elsewhere in the world solitary confinement and its foundation in judicial ideology were being heavily criticized, the Dutch parliament silently committed the system to the books in a new Penal Code.

Silence did not however surround the adoption of conditional leave. Modderman's amended draft stated that this could not be granted until three-quarters and a minimum of three years of any sentence had been fulfilled. The liberal Member of Parliament, Patijn, proposed an amendment to remove the words 'with his permission' from the article. He deemed consent of the person concerned totally unnecessary. He reiter-

TABLE 6.1 Registered suicide and insanity in prisons, 1846–85 (five-year averages). The average prison population decreased between 1850 and 1885 from above 4,000 to less than 3,000.

Period	Certified insane	Suicide rate
1846–50	3.8	4.8
1851–5	8.0	5.6
1856–60	4.6	3.6
1861–5	6.4	2.4
1866–70	6.4	3.2
1871–5	8.0	2.6
1876–80	10.8	5.4
1881–5	12.6	2.8

ated that a prisoner did not even have the right to 'a stay in prison'. The change in the editing of the article was accepted by the Minister, but more criticism was expressed as well as to the content of this new institute. Conditional leave would make it more difficult rather than easier for an ex-prisoner. Police supervision would make a criminal past impossible to hide. Additionally, that a prisoner could be rearrested at any moment made his position on the labour market very weak indeed. It is worth remarking how thoroughly these arguments, which were also subscribed to by the Society for the Moral Improvement of Prisoners,[49] belie Foucault's power analysis. According to Foucault, expansion of supervision beyond the prison was precisely the aim of the 'carceral system'.

It is amazing that Members of Parliament spoke of conditional leave as if it were a revolutionary innovation, while countries like Germany, England (*ticket of leave system*) and Hungary had been using the system for a quarter of a century. Minister Modderman pointed this out and aired his impression that The Netherlands was not 'on a lower level' than these countries. 'One creates a period of transition, in which they are not smothered by philanthropy, but hardened under strict supervision,' according to the Minister. One could forbid prisoners to use up their 'exit' money in pubs and brothels. 'The conditionally released prisoner is stimulated to good behaviour,' was Minister's summary of the pedagogical concept underlying the new institute. Conditional leave was adopted, forty-six votes to twelve.[50] About four months later, the Upper House approved the new Penal Code as well.

It was at least five more years before the new Penal Code could be effected, particularly because of insufficient numbers of cells. That five year period was characterized by developments both in and outside prison walls warranting fear for the future, though from many different perspectives. The prison statistics show – remembering the caution necessary in relying on these – that in the period 1881–5, the average number of cases of insanity increased per year. In 1885, eighteen cases of insanity were observed and that is the highest number since 1846 when the registration of cases was begun. An average of three suicides per year was registered (see Table 6.1).

Of the eighteen suicides which, according to prison statistics, had been committed since 1880, thirteen had definitely taken place in cells and two in alcoves for nightly separation. Increasing numbers of the institutionalized insane can, of course, be connected with the law on mental illness, set down in 1884, and numerous other factors, but developments after 1886 point particularly to long-lasting solitude as a significant cause.

Conservative Reaction to 'Sickly Philanthropy'

Rebellion and communal resistance were made practically impossible by solitary confinement, but, outside prison walls, potential criminals threatened rebellion and revolution. The socialist movement and the movement for a general vote won sympathy from the 'dangerous class'. The *Sociaal Democratische Bond* (Social Democratic Union) was set up in 1882. Police, especially in Amsterdam, clashed continuously with gathered members of the union and canvassers for the socialistic weekly paper *Recht voor Allen* (Justice for Everyone), who were often surrounded by masses of people. The trials of these canvassers for breaking the peace, resisting the police or agitation regularly ended in disruption and riots.[51]

In short, authority was being challenged in a manner and based on concepts that filled many a citizen with revulsion and certainly unleashed a great longing for *law and order* among Members of Parliament and ministers. Just as authority was forced to bare its teeth, a Penal Code which was seen by many as much too mild, threatened to be brought into operation. No more bridewells, no death penalty, no corporal punishment, only confinement in brand new penitentiaries where many were better off in terms of food, drink, heating and lodgings than in free society.

Important developments were taking place at the same time at government level. The conservative Heemskerk Ministry took office in 1883 with baron M. C. Du Tour van Bellinchave (1835–1908) as the Minister of Justice, well-known for his extremely conservative leanings. Minister Du Tour, as he was usually called, swiftly became spokesman for the conservative forces in the Lower House. He appeared to have taken up the task of reversing the liberal policies of preceding cabinets. As far as criminal law went, the possibilities were limited. Not much could be changed in the new Penal Code, but it was legally established that a law must be drafted which stated the *principles* to which the practice of confinement must be answerable. Almost immediately after assuming office, Du Tour van Bellinchave went to work on this.

While his draft was still being worked out, he intimated something of its content to the Lower House. He spoke of 'sickly philanthropy' which 'presently and for many years' had dominated the prisons. He revealed that his draft proposed the reintroduction of corporal punishment in the prison at Leeuwarden and, as a disciplinary punishment, one could be locked, stooped, in chains. 'Stooped' was so severe that prisoners were chained with their noses practically touching their knees. He also wanted to put all convicts on bread and water for the first two days of their sentence.[52] With the reception by the Lower House of the draft of a Prison Act 'to set down the principles of the prison system' in March of 1884, it became obvious that he had included many more articles increasing the severity of punishment.

Minister Du Tour felt that 'the interests of society' demanded that prisons remain 'a feared place of punishment in the eyes of the people' and that an unimproved prisoner should, at the very least, get 'a nasty shock' from prison life. The Minister warned that one must always beware a shifting of the balance 'in favour of life *in* prison'.[53]

It looked as if conservative elements in The Netherlands wanted to get even about changes in criminal justice which they had experienced as misplaced philanthropy. The liberal *Weekblad van het Recht* fiercely opposed the draft. For example, the well-known scholar of criminal justice and chief editor of the weekly, A. A. de Pinto, called the bread-and-water article 'a sort of hunger-therapy'. To him the draft was 'a very dubious reaction' against 'the humane principles' which had dominated since the French period and against the new, progressive system of punishment. He spoke of 'torture' and of restoring to its 'ancient honour' the lash and rod.[54] The editors of the weekly stressed their civilized revulsion against corporal punishment. They did not protest against 'psychic suffering' but they did reject its enhancement through 'physical suffering'. They formulated a position from this point of view which clearly reveals how inaccurate it is to imagine purely philanthropic motives behind penal changes:

> Be strict, very strict in managing your prisons, deny the prisoner every pleasure, give him over to remorse of conscience, separate him from his fellow prisoners, shut him up, if he remains recalcitrant, in your black hole and often enough that he eventually develops an aversion to this, but do not hurt him and make him obstinate in his anger, do not uproot the good seed sown through education and religion with physical chastisements.[55]

The draft gave the champions of the cellular system the opportunity for an old-fashioned pat on the back for their humanity and progressiveness. And reactions were illicited from persons who felt themselves accused of cruelty. Little by little, the treatment of the Prison Act took on the character of a repeat exercise. During extensive deliberations in parliament, all facets of nineteenth-century thought about crime and punishment were formulated one more time, in order, so it seems, to be able to definitely renounce them afterwards. Members of Parliament, as de Wit remarks in his treatise about the debate, attempted 'to escape from the here and the now by using handed-down ways of thinking', but eventually had to make the switch.[56] This was also the last time that a very select group of highly placed gentlemen (a quarter of the eighty-six Members of Parliament belonged to the nobility) was able to decide the daily fate of thousands of unfortunates, because the revision of the constitution in 1887 substantially broadened the right to vote.

Memorable Debate about the First Prison Act

General deliberations on the Prison Act in March 1886 turned into a pitched parliamentary battle. Practically every article led to amendments and Minister Du Tour had to threaten continuously with withdrawal of his draft in order to gain a majority. It became clear very quickly that conservative and confessional Members of Parliament wanted increasing severity in prison life, while liberals fiercely resisted this and judged it a reactionary attack on liberal principles. Frontal collisions of opinions and emotions occurred, for instance in dealing with the proposal to put convicts on *bread and water* the first two days of their sentence. The 'menu Du Tour', as opponents mockingly called it, would make prisoners 'sensitive' to prison life right from the beginning and prevent the poor preferring custody as an alternative to paying their fines. Liberals called it 'a disgrace to the country' and saw in it a return to corporal punishment. But, after a debate lasting for hours, the proposal was accepted with a clear majority of votes. There was a heated discussion about the proposal to abolish *pistole*-rooms in penitentiaries and to keep them only in remand prisons. Some were afraid that if well-to-do citizens were deprived of the opportunity to distance themselves from 'the coarser prison routine', they would be pardoned more often. Thus, one form of class justice would preclude another. Others wanted to keep the *pistole* because they saw in it a means toward individualizing punishment, but the vote showed that a large majority thought differently.

Almost no one protested against expanding the minimum work period to ten hours per day. Then Minister Du Tour wanted to limit education to tuition in reading, writing and arithmetic for prisoners not older than thirty. The existing education consisted of more subjects and the age limit was forty-five. He hoped thus to make the punishment 'less eligible'. He had to back down after an emotional discussion, but the debate reached another climax almost immediately in the article about religious education, a sensitive topic in a pillarizing (Roman-Catholic and Calvinist pillars within society) and socialistically awakening country and also a topic which touched upon the legal status of prisoners. The Minister wanted attendance at religious services to be compulsory, 'except for explicit exemption'. He deemed religion 'such a strong means' of suppressing evil tendencies and prompting moral improvement that it had to be used even 'against the indifferent'. The keeping of order would also become endangered if prisoners gained 'free choice' in this area. Many Members of Parliament thought this proposal conflicted with the constitutionally specified freedom of religion. Van Gennep, Member of Parliament, thought the constitution not to have been written with prisoners in mind, because, should that have been the case, they would also have had to be given, for example, the right to amalgamate or to use the printing press. A century later these rights would, indeed, be given to prisoners, but in those days it was taken for granted that this was absurd. The concept of prisoners with rights, as we have seen already, formed a *contradictio in terminis* for many. A prisoner should not be permitted to absent himself 'on his own authority' from 'that which is judged desirable in the interests of his improvement'. The proposal to oblige prisoners to attend religious services, even when they had asked to be exempted, was eventually accepted by thirty-four to fifteen (predominantly liberal) votes.

Disciplinary Punishment

The last articles dealt with the enforcing of order and discipline. Disciplinary punishments were not legally regulated until 1886, but, it appears from prison statistics that a type of consensus existed in practice. Unruly, lazy, immoral, rebellious and violent prisoners were denied privileges like the use of the canteen and the daily airing; they were put on bread and water and shut up in dark punishment cells. There were additional corporal punishments, as we have seen in other chapters, but statistics do not include any data about these. Probably the use of corporal punishment began its decline in the middle of the century. It is certain that corporal punishments, in all the prisons, were abolished *de facto* in 1879 by Smidt, the Minister of Justice of that time. At that moment, corporal punishment was still in force only in the 'tuchthuis' at Leeuwarden, where the most dangerous criminals were housed.[57] To be clear, corporal punishment did not mean physical deprivations or painful forms of chaining (stooped) at that time. What was meant was purposeful infliction of blows upon a body.

Other disciplinary punishments were used frequently.[58] The Minister's proposals for punishments were no joking matter.[59] They varied from no airing to being chained, stooped, in an unheated, dark lock-up on bread and water. Despite all this, the Minister feared that enforcement of discipline in prison for those with a long sentence (who, after five years were returned to communal halls) in Leeuwarden would be threatened unless a separate article gave permission to impose corporal punishment there as well, consisting of a maximum of fifty lashes 'on the behind' with the bull's pizzle or cane.[60] The management of a prison should 'never', in his opinion, be 'absolutely powerless', confronted with an unwilling prisoner. And that could easily happen with the dangerous types in Leeuwarden. He cited the example of a prisoner who had recently told a member of the staff that one could do with him what one wished. But then, the Minister said, he, 'in other, less polite terms' had added: 'But you may not permit me to be beaten.' Truely an apt illustration of how the balance of power between punishers and those punished had shifted somewhat in favour of the prisoners through the prohibition of corporal punishment. As the twentieth century progressed, and psychic suffering as well became more and more difficult to justify, this power balance would shift gradually further. The growing sensitivity to the suffering imposed upon them constituted a power source for prisoners which grew in importance by degrees.

In the one prisoner's mild show of power, the Minister saw clear evidence of tolerance gone too far. He wondered whether one preferred 'total licentiousness and disorder' in prisons to making inveterate villains aware of their responsibilities 'by means of a chastisement'. The fact that several Members of Parliament insisted that corporal punishment was no longer used in prisons all over Europe cut no ice with him because the death penalty was still in effect almost everywhere. Only in The Netherlands could one end up practically powerless faced with 'most serious wrongdoers' because of the abolition of the death penalty and the ban on corporal punishment. Earlier governments had given away their best weapons 'from sheer dogmaticism'.

The Minister maintained that fear of roughness and cruelty was unnecessary. 'Really, anyone who fears misuse in that area, is certainly quite out of touch with the tendencies of the present day', he elaborated. It seems that he was right. Prison statistics indicate that, until its formal abolition in 1951, corporal punishment remained unused.[61]

Most disciplinary punishments received very little attention during the debate. They were approved, virtually in silence, while they certainly were not less painful than corporal punishment. Mental suffering caused by being locked in a completely dark cell clearly offended civilized feelings less than corporal punishment. But deliberations on this last point got out of hand and resulted in an extraordinary clash of opinions lasting a whole day. Liberal opponents of corporal punishment (including stooped chaining now) were particularly roused.

According to the liberal Kist discipline should never become 'torture'. 'Such cruelties' caused more bad effects than good. 'Torture' defiled whereas part of the purpose of a prison sentence was to 'elevate'. After other Members of Parliament had vented their feelings, Goeman Borgesius, the future chairman of the progressive *Liberale Unie* (Liberal Union) added a political note. He called the Minister 'a reactionary par excellence'. Chaining in a stooped position typified for him 'the spirit of reaction'. Van der Kaay pointed out that, should corporal punishments still be necessary to keep prisoners in line after five years in solitary, then the money used to build cellular prisons could better have been left in the state treasury. It would seem that the House gave a vote of non-confidence 'to that which it had brought into being'.

The Minister ignored the accusations of cruelty and reactionism. To him stooped chaining was not a corporal punishment. He admitted that it was 'harsh', 'very painful' and 'very severe' but, not 'an inhumane punishment'. Van Gennep disagreed. The punishment was, in his opinion, exclusively intended 'precisely and maliciously' to inflict pain 'on the body'. It was a way of misusing power against totally impotent persons 'to whom one can do anything one wishes'. He had very little respect for a 'moral influence' based purely on threats of physical violence.

Other Members pointed out that corporal punishment would affect not the worst but the most problematic prisoners. 'Management longs to have the last word; in the end prisoners must lie low and do what they are commanded,' the liberal Kist concluded. In contrast to the Minister's explanatory memorandum, Kist thought that not *all* means should be permitted to prevent loss of power to prison management. He hoped to rule out physical cruelty. Limits did exist, even if a prisoner himself pointed this out by saying: 'You may not beat us'. He did not see this as arguing against a prisoner's character. Rather, it would demonstrate 'that he still retained some concept of self-worth and justice'.

The Minister, of course, was not alone in his position against liberal opponents. Many Members listened in silence in the pleasant realization that they would show their censure in the voting process. Some showed their support for the Minister verbally. In between the arguments of supporters and opponents, the Minister often took the floor for long periods. Just before the casting of votes, he opened his conservative heart once more to the audience. In reaction to De Beaufort, who had spoken so feelingly of what one person might not inflict upon another, he admitted that administering corporal punishment did not produce 'a pleasant sensation'. Crime victims, however, did not retain pleasant sensations after their experiences, either. He continued: 'Gentlemen, I would ask you to recall the words of Alphonse Karr: "Que messieurs les assassins commencent!"' Should criminals stop murdering and stealing, indeed then prisons could be closed down.

On the issue of corporal punishment, the Minister got his way. The article was accepted, by forty-two votes to twenty-four. All those opposed were liberally oriented. Stooped chaining, however, was rejected, by fifty-four votes to twelve. Those who had voted affirmatively included only one liberal, who had gone astray.[62]

First Rights for Prisoners alongside many Obligations

Both the MPs and the Minister must have been so satisfied with this Salomon's judgement that they lacked the desire to begin a new, exhausting debate late in the evening. We know for certain that, just before the voting about the entire draft, the Minister uncomplainingly agreed to an amendment which has to be seen as a landmark in the emancipation process of prisoners. Disciplinary punishments could not be imposed 'before the offender is heard by the person giving the punishment'.[63] The 'commission of reporters' had already insisted on this in preparatory meetings about the draft. In order not to endanger the prestige of the directors, they hoped to avoid giving prisoners the right of appeal to the college of regents.

In his written answer to the commission, the Minister had said, of all things, that he had no objection to this embryonic form of right of appeal for convicts. Should the prestige of governors be threatened, the college would have 'even more reason' to band together to enforce the imposed punishment. The governor, knowing that the punishment could be changed or annulled 'in appeal' would be forced to work 'very justly'. Continued toleration of unjust treatment would, moreover, not be good for the prestige 'of public power'. The Minister was thus defining not so much a right for prisoners as one for the college of regents, admittedly without mentioning it at all in his memorandum. He deemed it 'undesirable' to make the hearing of prisoners obligatory. In practice, hearing was already the norm, but it would often occur that a prisoner did not take an interest in it 'because he had nothing at all to say "in his own defence".' This hearing would only provide opportunities 'for the utterance of new vulgarities'.[64]

The Member of Parliament introducing the amendment, De Vos van Steenwijk, called the hearing of those disciplinarily punished a principle underlying criminal proceedings 'of all civilized nations' that would have no bad effects if 'sensibly administered'. The Minister answered that he still did not care for it, but he thought the 'late hour' inappropriate to the expounding of his protests. He followed up 'on the nods received from different sides' by accepting the amendment.[65] Members of the House, already wearing their coats, approved the amendment without vote. The entire draft was finally accepted by forty-four votes to sixteen. About a month later, the draft was accepted by the Upper House as well, by twenty-four votes to five.

Prisoners had gained, for the first time, a right stated in law; it was, admittedly, a cynical right. They had to be heard before harsh punishments. Quickly thereafter, another right was granted. The 'Gevangenis Maatregel' (Prison Ruling), set down by Royal Decree on 31 August 1886, stated that they could lodge an appeal to the college of regents if their request to be exempted from obligatory religious exercises had been refused by the governor. This was not a cynical but a very limited right. Obligatory church visits, set down in the Prison Act, continued an uneasy existence alongside constitutionally established freedom of religion. Should the college of regents reject their appeal, prisoners remained obliged to attend church services. The article in the prison measure was aimed at preventing exaggerated religious coercion and not at answering emancipatory longings of prisoners. Alongside this a huge number of precepts, prohibitions and obligations existed. Grey prison clothing had to be worn, hair was 'cut short' and a beard was not allowed. 'As soon as' any chance existed of being seen by a fellow-prisoner, cell caps had to be worn in the penitentiaries. The use of 'tobacco and snuff' was no longer allowed. Newspapers were prohibited, but, given the tone of articles about criminals, clearly identified with first and last names, this was perhaps a blessing.[66]

Exchanges of letters were controlled by prison management. Letters with unpermissible contents had to be destroyed. Household rules defined the possibility of receiving visits from 'family relations', only at specified times. Penitentiaries had to offer less opportunity for such visits than remand prisons, *rijkswerkinrichtingen* and *rijksopvoedingsgestichten*. Only Sundays and feastdays were work-free. They had to be aired for a half-hour a day. Prisoners who did not wish to conform to this strict regime could, preliminary to imposition of potential disciplinary punishment, be separated or made 'non-dangerous' through the use of a straitjacket. According to the prison measure, a doctor and at least three members of the college of regents had to be present when corporal punishment was executed in Leeuwarden. The civilized gentlemen will have dreaded this, and perhaps corporal punishments were never dealt out for this reason.

The Prison Ruling further stated that male personnel could only visit the women's department accompanied by a female employee. The women's department included mothers with children. As soon as they could do without 'parental care', these children, even when they had been born in prison, were removed and cared for elsewhere at state cost.[67]

In spite of the implementation of conditional leave, the colleges of regents remained entitled to present a short list to the Minister of Justice, once a year, of prisoners entitled to remission and release, who had distinguished themselves 'by good behaviour and diligence'. This article applied only to convicts sentenced to more than two years. Remission was limited to three months or less per year. The article aimed to free prisoners in a season in which one could 'readily find a means of existence'.[68]

Even though the Prison Act and the Prison Ruling were filled with articles guaranteeing a strict regime, the fact remains that prison managements and colleges of regents no longer had full liberty to decide the fate of prisoners. New Ministers and Members of Parliament with other opinions could, moreover, change the rules. This happened, particularly after the First World War, in a way favourable to prisoners. The editors of the *Weekblad van het Recht* predicted, however, totally different developments now that the heavily criticized Prison Act had been adopted. The editors feared that corporal punishment would be reintroduced shortly in all prisons and even written into the Penal Code.[69] This did not happen, but the House did not retain the same make up either. After the revision of the constitution in 1887, which included the abolition of census enfranchisement, the socialist leader, Ferdinand Domela Nieuwenhuis, entered the House. Shortly before this, in July of 1886, the old Members of Parliament and Baron Du Tour van Bellinchave had seen confirmation outside parliament of their wise decisions. In 'de Jordaan' (a lower-class quarter in Amsterdam), people in the street climbed the barricades during the 'Palingoproer' (Eel Riots).[70] Police and army saw this as a socialist revolution of French dimensions. They shot with live ammunition at the roaring crowd, resulting in twenty-six dead and dozens severely wounded. A comment made in the House by the Minister of Internal Affairs, Heemskerk, about this appropriate, effective action earned him a standing ovation with cheers of bravo.[71]

Proprietary interests in The Netherlands entered upon a difficult period. The abolition of the pistole in penitentiaries was called a regrettable measure by the lawyer Quintus. The delicate gentlemen would become ill from the prison food, so that the state would have to pay for their care, whereas they formerly remained in good health and paid their own way. The pistole should, of course, be refused to those who, through 'low, animalistic passions' or 'with a contemptible objective', had committed serious crimes 'no matter how exalted their social position'.[72] When Quintus wrote this, socialist speakers were of the opinion that actually many highly-placed persons were committing serious crimes with contemptible objectives against the common folk.

NOTES

1. Dostoyevski, 1985 (1864), p. 36.
2. *wvhR*, 1864, no. 2554.
3. Hughes, 1987, p. 498.
4. Hughes, 1987, pp. 500–1; Rijksen et al., 1980, pp. 30–4; Rudé, 1985, pp. 111–12, 120–1.
5. A characterization by the German expert in criminal law Von Holtzendorff. From Brugghen, 1861, p. 39.

6. Data about the Irish system have been extracted from Brugghen, 1861, pp. 62–90; Rijksen et al., 1980, pp. 30–2; Duyl, 1881, pp. 60–102; Patijn, 1938, pp. 74–81.

7. In its pure form, the Irish system was adopted in only a limited way in both England and Ireland. A number of elements, such as the conditional release (*ticket of leave*), were put into practice. cf. Priestley, 1985.

8. E.g. Deinse, 1860, p. 455.

9. Prison statistics show that the average population in all prisons in the 1840s was above 4,400 and, in the 1870s, just under 3,400. Court statistics reflect a stabilizing of numbers of those sentenced. See also the information memorandum accompanying the proposal to abolish the death penalty in 1870, *HdSG*, 1869/70, Bijlagen, pp. 785–92.

10. Alstorphius Grevelink, 1868, p. 10.

11. The term 'cellular fanatics' was used by Alstorphius Grevelink when he landed in the Irish camp.

12. Later in the century there was a plea for a central cellular women's prison, even though women already lived in strictly separate departments. It was also feared that during 'communal singing' in the cellular churches 'passions' would be aroused, even though the two sexes could not see each other. See Nieuwenhuis, 1880, pp. 530–1, and Willeumier, 1881.

13. Domela Nieuwenhuis, 1859, pp. 3, 101, 110–13, 121, 122, 128, 129, 155, 159, 160, 175, 176, 183, 189, 192, 196.

14. One of the few who advocated combinations of cellular and communal incarceration before Van der Brugghen was the lawyer and philosopher Opzoomer. See Opzoomer, 1857.

15. Van der Brugghen himself had only found the article which contained evidence of 'lack of understanding' of the later Minister of Justice, Mr J. A. Jolles, in *Nieuwe Bijdragen voor Regtsgeleerdheid en Wetgeving*, 1860, part X, p. 471.

16. Article 26 of the Prison Act of 1951.

17. Brugghen, 1861, pp. 11–14, 18, 20, 23, 35–9, 41, 43, 45, 46, 49.

18. The System Controversy, 1861, nos 2323 and 2326.

19. Domela Nieuwenhuis, 1893, p. 283.

20. See, e.g., a series of articles in *AMC*, 31 Dec. 1853, pp. 5, 6, 12 and 19 Jan. 1854. See also Bemmelen, 1923, pp. 123–4, 130; Cool, 1856.

21. Suringar, 1859, p. 103.

22. Cf. Alstorphius Grevelink, 1857; Alstorphius Grevelink et al., 1858; also see Petersen, 1978, pp. 243–56.

23. See for instance *Penitentiair gevangenisstelsel (…)*, 1856.

24. Opzoomer, 1857, pp. 11–26; see also Petersen, 1978, pp. 250–1.

25. Alstorphius Grevelink, 1870, p. 14; 1868, p. 39.

26. Cf. Petersen, 1978, pp. 268–9; Domela Nieuwenhuis, 1893, pp. 285–6.

27. Alstorphius Grevelink, 1868, pp. 32, 45, 49–50. Later he distanced himself even further from the cellular system. See Alstorphius Grevelink, 1870, 1874.

28. Cf. Petersen, 1978, pp. 273–4, 284–5.

29. 'Handelingen' (proceedings) of the NJV, 1872.

30. See Franke, 1985, pp. 138–51.

31. Cf. Douglas, 1973.
32. Until 1870, numbers were an average of about twenty-five per year. After that, there were only a few per year, but it was not until 1880 that the houses of detention lost this function completely. See prison statistics for the years 1846–80.
33. On 1 January 1870, 3,375 people lived in Dutch insane asylums. That same year, 943 people were admitted. At present – in as far as the data can be compared – there are approximately 45,000 admissions per year and more than 60,000 persons institutionalized: psychiatric hospitals (approximately 23,000), institutions for the mentally handicapped (approximately 30,000) and psycho-geriatric hospitals (approximately 11,000). The total population has, meanwhile, risen from about 3.5 to almost 15 million. Figures for 1870 were found in a yearly report of the government survey of the insane and insane asylums, 1913 (See Table on p. 58). Present figures are derived from a CBS publication *Intramurale gezondheidszorg 1987* (Intramural health care), The Hague, 1987, p. 28.
34. *HdSG*, 1870/71, Bijlagen, p. 1807.
35. Report with prison statistics for 1861, p. 15.
36. See report with prison statistics for 1865.
37. *HdSG*, 1870/71, Bijlagen, pp. 1867–68.
38. Peter Young also points out how important bureaucratic and managerial particulars are to the understanding of penal developments, 1983, pp. 93–9.
39. *HdSG*, 1870/71, Beraadslagingen, pp. 1152–6.
40. Idem, Beraadslagingen Eerste Kamer, pp. 252–3.
41. Prison statistics show sixty-five prisoners declared insane in the same period (1862–71). Presumably the minister was using figures related only to 'huizen van verzekering'.
42. *HdSG*, 1873/74, Tweede Kamer, Bijlagen, A, pp. 3, 6 en Bijlagen, 105.3, pp. 1–6.
43. *HdSG*, 1878/79, Tweede Kamer, Bijlagen, 110.3, pp. 52, 55–6.
44. Idem, Bijlagen, 110.9, p. 194.
45. *HdSG*, 1878/79, Bijlagen, 47.24, pp. 69–71, 73, 76, 77.
46. Cohen, 1985, points out similar pressures of interest in later penal reforms.
47. Cf. Bemmelen, 1923, pp. 157–9.
48. *HdSG*, 1879/80, Bijlagen, 47.25, pp. 88–94.
49. Cf. Bemmelen, 1923, pp. 157–9.
50. *HdSG*, 1880/81, Beraadslagingen Tweede Kamer, pp. 108–9, 131, 133, 135, 138.
51. Rooy, 1971; Franke, 1981, pp. 66–9; Tijn, 1978, pp. 97–8; Oud, 1987, p. 131.
52. *wvhR*, 1884, no. 5011, p. 3.
53. *HdSG*, 1883/84, Bijlagen, 190.3, p. 3.
54. *wvhR*, 1884, no. 5011.
55. *wvhR*, 1884, no. 5013.
56. Wit, 1986, p. 88.
57. Art. 30, Title II of the draft-Penal Code of Minister Smidt (offered to the Lower House on 22 Dec. 1879) reads: 'No corporal punishments will be imposed to enforce discipline'. HdSG, 1878/79,

Bijlagen, 110.1.2. See also Schaaff, 1886, pp. 2, 20, 40, 75, 134–5, 150.

58. Prison statistics show that, in 1885, 2,000 disciplinary punishments were imposed. Almost 700 prisoners were shut up in punishment cells, often dark, for shorter and longer periods. An additional 650 prisoners suffered the same punishment, but they were restricted to bread and water as well.

59. The Minister proposed the following punishments:
   • 'Shutting up in a completely dark punishment cell or black hole.' A maximum of 48 hours. Unheated cells.
   • 'Shutting up in a normal punishment cell or lock-up.' A maximum of four weeks.
   • 'Solitary incarceration in a cell or space.' This was, of course, meant for communally incarcerated convicts.
   • 'Chaining, stooped, or normal chaining,' and 'Giving of bread and water instead of normal food.' A maximum of four weeks, interrupted every two days by the giving of normal food and temporary release from chains for one day.
   • 'Denial of work, the pleasure of fresh air, reading material, visits, the writing or receiving of letters, or the use of the canteen.'
   Airing could not be denied for longer than seven days at a stretch, with seven days in between. Of all these punishments 'many' could be imposed at one time. Cf. Schaaff, 1886, p. 15.

60. Cf. Schaaff, 1886, pp. 23–4 (note 2); see also the Prison Ruling from 1886, art. 116 (KB, 31–18–1886, Sb, 1886, no. 159).

61. *HdsG*, 1883/84, Bijlagen, 190.3, pp. 8–9; *HdsG*, 1885/86, Bijlagen, 27.1, pp. 16–19. Until 1951, it was separately recorded whether or not corporal punishment had been used in Leeuwarden.

62. *HdsG*, 1885/86, Beraadslagingen Tweede Kamer, pp. 1054, 1056–9, 1061–3, 1065–6, 1066–70.

63. *HdsG*, 1885/86, Beraadslagingen Tweede Kamer, p. 1069.

64. *HdsG*, 1885/86, Bijlagen, 27.1, p. 17.

65. Idem, Beraadslagingen Tweede Kamer, pp. 1069–70.

66. Cf. Franke, 1981.

67. In 1885, more than 300 mothers with childen were lodged in Dutch prisons, for shorter or longer periods (Prison statistics for 1885).

68. Prison Ruling, KB, 31 Aug. 1886, Sb, 1886, no. 159, arts. 6, 38, 41, 55, 58, 61, 64, 67, 69, 70, 71, 72, 73, 74, 78, 80, 92, 106, 109, 113, 116.

69. *WvhR*, 1886, no. 5254.

70. The game of eel-pulling was forbidden by police when the residents of 'de Jordaan' attempted to indulge in this sport. A riot resulted.

71. See Franke, 'Het palingoproer juli 1886', in *NRC Handelsblad*, 12 July 1986.

72. Quintus, 1887, pp. 175–6.

7

Misery and Insanity: The Reality of Cell Life, 1886–1914

After all, if we place the whole of present-day civilization opposite
that of the Middle Ages, which form of criminal justice is crueller?
There is such a thing as refined cruelty. Certainly cruelty is no longer
naive, but all the more hypocritical and sanctimonious.[1]

Shortly before the introduction of solitary confinement on a modest scale
in 1851, G. E. Voorhelm Schneevoogt, professor of psychiatry at Amsterdam, aggressively accused those opposing 'the *absolute* isolation of every
prisoner' of total lack of expertise in the area of the human soul. It
surpassed 'all imagining' that even experts maintained that prisoners
could become insane as a result of solitary confinement. He called
colleagues who thought other than he did 'shameless braggarts' who
'violently' twisted the facts. He thought no danger of insanity existed,
even after twenty years in the cell.[2]

Just over a half century later, when, in principle, *all* prisoners were
solitarily imprisoned, the *Bijzondere Strafgevangenis* (Special Penitentiary)
at 's-Hertogenbosch was largely populated by prisoners who had become
psychotic in the cell. The doctor at that prison, J. Casparie, thought it at
first 'incomprehensible' that cellular confinement caused such 'significant nervous disorders'. Only after he had allowed himself to be shut up
for a time and had experienced the oppressive solitude did he admit that
it was 'no wonder' that cellular punishment, in the long run, had a
disturbing effect on the human mind.[3]

Differences in Emotional Judgements of Solitary Confinement

That in those days it was impossible to intuitively grasp how very dismal
long-lasting incarceration in a bare cell with frosted windows could be is
remarkable when contrasted with today's views of solitary confinement.
When several hostages were released from Lebanon in 1991 after years of
partially solitary incarceration, the entire world press was astonished at

their mental health. In 1978, the Dutch psychiatrist, Frank Van Ree, entered voluntarily upon solitary incarceration lasting for fifty hours because he had been confronted in his work with the long-lasting 'isolation torture' of German RAF-prisoners and wanted to find out first-hand what these people had experienced. 'That those boys do not go crazy ...', he wondered, soon afterwards.[4] Van Ree meant months when he spoke of 'long-lasting', while Schneevoogt and Casparie were speaking of prisoners who lived in cells for years on end.

These huge discrepancies in emotional assessment of solitary confinement cannot be understood without realizing that both Schneevoogt and Casparie saw prisoners as fellow-men only in a very limited way. They were convinced that prisons contained mainly uncivilized, more or less degenerate individuals in whom 'higher or better feelings' were seldom developed. Casparie thought that especially the mentally degenerate, who, in his opinion, constituted a majority in prisons, could not stand solitude. He saw succumbing to solitude almost as a symptom of mental degeneration.[5]

Many articles provide evidence that, until far into the twentieth century, criminal activity and insanity were thought to go hand in hand. Mentally healthy persons with civilized or higher feelings were not criminal and would not become insane under a regime of solitude. All these preconceptions, sentiments and dated knowledge combined with the large social gap between punishers and those punished impeded an empathetic understanding of mental distress in cellular prisons. The large dimensions of this mental distress will become obvious from several passages in this chapter. A good understanding of the psychic effects of solitary confinement during the first twenty-five years after its general introduction necessitates a more complete knowledge of daily life in cellular prisons.

Cellular Prison Life in Practice, 1886–1914

At and just after the time of putting into operation of the cellular system and the Prison Act in 1886, more and more prisons were being completely or partially converted to cells. In Haarlem, Arnhem, Breda, Groningen, Zutphen, Alkmaar and The Hague new cellular prisons were built, the first three were dome-shaped, the others had the form of a cross. By the end of the century, there were ten cellular penitentiaries in The Netherlands, containing an average of about 2,000 prisoners. Almost every prisoner was sentenced to a term of five years or less so that the whole period of punishment was carried out in solitude, in accordance with the new Penal Code. Prisoners who had received longer sentences usually spent the first five years in the cellular section of the Special Penitentiary for men in Leeuwarden or in that of the Special Penitentiary for women in

Gorinchem. After that, they were transferred to the communal areas in those prisons and separated at night into iron alcoves. Convicts who proved 'after medical examination' not suited to cellular confinement or who were older than sixty went to the Special Penitentiary in 's-Hertogenbosch or, if female, to the communal area at Gorinchem. Many convicts with short sentences were cellularly imprisoned in one of the many remand prisons which possessed cells. Those in *custody* for transgressions and those not yet sentenced were housed in communal areas of these same prisons. Approximately 800 prisoners on average were held in remand prisons.

Based on the new Penal Code, drunks, vagrants and beggars could be sentenced to the concomitant punishment of placement in a *rijkswerkin-richting* (labour colony). These were located at Veenhuizen, Hoorn and Leiden(women). An average of just under 4,000 convicts lived in the communal areas of those colonies between 1886 and 1914. They had to do heavy work, accompanied by very strict enforcement of order and discipline. Finally, an average of 650 children were held in the *rijksopvoedingsgestichten* (youth custody centres, community homes) for boys in Alkmaar and Avereest and for girls in Montfoort.[6] The regime in these institutions was often just as harsh as that in the penitentiaries.[7]

From houses of detention or remand-prisons, where convicts were registered first, prisoners were transferred by cellular coach or cellular prison carriage to the penitentiaries. Each convict sat in a separate box so that even during transfer communication was practically impossible. And guards saw to it that there were no attempts at contact. Longer distances sometimes demanded the use of cellular train carriages. Special prisoners' compartments existed to prevent contact with fellow travellers. Once inside the gates of the prison, a cap was placed over their faces before they left the carriage. They were led one by one to the porter's lodge where they had to wait, face to the wall. First they were registered. From that moment on, their name was replaced by a number which was also the number of their cell, always to be worn visibly on their chests. A warder then called them up by number and brought them to a bathroom where they were thoroughly searched and washed. Their own clothing was exchanged for the grey prison suit. Often they were then immediately photographed in this impersonal state *en face* and *en profile*. Usually a thorough 'anthropometric description' had been made already, during their preventive custody, following the method of the Frenchman, Alphonse Bertillon. Practically every body part, including the phalanxes, would have been measured and, where necessary, described according to a detailed series of instructions.[8] After the photography, their beards were shaved and their hair 'cut short'. Only six weeks in advance of their release could they allow their beards and hair to grow again.

Once in the cell, the warder advised prisoners to read carefully the rules which hung on the wall. Then, 'normally with an encouraging word', he shut the cell door for the first time and the prisoner was abandoned to his feelings and thoughts. 'Usually he is then dazed and vacuous, he stares unceasingly at the door, he walks vacantly back and forth, until he eventually sinks onto his stool to burst into tears, or, what also happens, into a wild temper of ranting and raving', according to prison pastor, C. M. Dekker, who had obviously studied new prisoners through the spy hole in the cell door. 'Bit by bit' prisoners would grow calm and set about inspecting their cells.[9]

The head of the penitentiary at The Hague, H. G. Metz, also put the first seconds in a cell into words for prison personnel in his 'psychological manual':

> Alone with his thoughts; regret, remorse and despondency cause a state of despair to be born in him, and if later – and fortunately this does not happen often – this despair turns to desperation, then the seeds are often sown for insanity or a suicidal tendency develops.[10]

Prisoners received, their first two days in the cell, only the 'menu Du Tour' which was bread and water. Afterwards, three times a day, meagre prison food containing a bit of meat or bacon twice a week was shoved in to them through the food hole in the thick door with its iron mounting.

Cell Interior, Daily Rhythm, Work, Reading Material and Visits

The glass spy hole located in the cell door allowed warders, for example, to watch unnoticed as prisoners relieved themselves on the metal lavatory pail which was emptied two to three times a week. These pails often spread a strong stench through the badly ventilated cells, about 100 square feet in surface area. High in the outside wall was a frosted glass window which, even if opened, gave no view of the outside world. Because beds had to be folded up during the day, prisoners could only relax sitting down at a small folding table on a three-legged stool. Nothing more than a towel, an inventory list and a copy of household rules hung on the brick walls. Other furniture in the cells was very limited.

Dependent upon the type of work which they had to do ten hours per day, they also possessed a diversity of tools. Most prisoners made clothing for the army, navy and the prison system itself, but in many prisons, they also had to do numerous other sorts of manual work, such as sorting peas, glueing bags, picking oakum or plucking cotton. It was enormously stultifying and, because of the spreading dust, unhealthy work as well. Often it was unpleasantly cold, too, because the hot water heating system was usually only used between the first of November and the first of April. Moreover, it was accepted that a temperature of 55°F was 'sufficient'.[11]

They remained in these cells day and night. 'It is only a question of getting used to it', wrote pastor Dekker.

In most cases this happens relatively quickly. The first day is the worst, but thereafter one begins to live to the prison clock, because everything happens precisely on time.[12]

He was referring to the huge bell in the central hall which rang every section of the day in and out: waking in the early hours, work, breakfast, work, noonday meal, work, evening meal, work, rest, to bed at ten o'clock. In the short time that they had free in the evening, they sometimes were visited by a school master. All other evenings had to be spent in solitude. Books and other reading material 'with a moral purport' were dealt out from the prison library.[13]

Reading of newspapers was not permitted and prison papers did not exist. This made it possible that prisoners could be released during the First World War without being aware of its existence. At that point, the Minister of Justice was moved to send a circular urgently requesting that prisoners be told before their release what was happening in the world so that they would not arouse too much suspicion outside.[14]

From the circular one can infer that, during the short visits of warders, governors, teachers, pastors and members of the Society for the Moral Improvement of Prisoners, the topics of conversation were also limited to happenings within the four walls. It was, indeed, forbidden to have 'newspaper chats' – to provide information about public life outside the prison.[15] The circular also points out that certainly not all prisoners received visits or letters from family members. Visiting facilities were, furthermore, so limited that visitors perhaps forgot what they had wanted to say because of the emotion. Prisoners were allowed to receive visits for a quarter of an hour twice a month. This took place in a separate cell which consisted of three compartments separated from each other by bars and steel mesh. In the first compartment sat the visitor, in the second a warder and in the third the prisoner. Even shaking hands was impossible. The warder listened to everything and ended the visit if forbidden topics were broached. Both visitors and prisoners often refused to have anything to do with this frustrating contact. 'Many see it more as torture than pleasure, and there is actually much to be said for this,' stated pastor Dekker.[16]

In this visiting cell, a prisoner often had to learn that wife and children at home were suffering badly without the breadwinner. Any later show of sadness in their cell would undoubtedly have led to a reminder that they should have considered this before sinning.[17] The headmaster from The Hague, Metz, gave the warders moral advice based on 'empirical psychology'. Prisoners who had heard unfavorable family news or bad tidings had, for example, the 'right to compassion', but warders were not expected to do more than speak 'an encouraging word'. They were also expected to point out to prisoners 'the useful side' of their 'impotence' in that they would never again treat their freedom 'so rashly'.[18]

Airing, Disciplinary Punishments and Health

Once a day (in smaller prisons sometimes twice a day) prisoners were allowed to go outside into the cellular airing places. On their way, they had to remain a distance of fifteen paces from each other. They were obliged to wear their cell caps and often they had to bring the stinking lavatory pail with them. During their airing they were separated from each other by high walls. Heavily armed warders watched them minutely, as if they were 'guarding carnivorous animals from the zoo'.[19] Carrying their empty pail, the masked prisoners shuffled back to their cells once again. Once there, no contact of any kind was permitted with fellow prisoners. Singing, whistling, screaming, speaking loudly, beating or knocking on the wall, and ringing the bell in any situation other than 'by necessity' were forbidden. Nevertheless, a lot of knocking on walls took place and prisoners let notes dangle over the window sills on strings.[20]

Violations of the ban on communication were quickly punished by two days on bread and water or removal to a punishment cell or 'the cat cellar', sometimes in chains. Punishment cells, which contained only a wooden plank bed and a metal pail, were unheated. During 'severe cold' those punished got a woollen blanket. Books and visits were not permitted and prisoners were usually not aired.[21] One ex-prisoner, writing in a Rotterdam daily, called the punishment cell 'really terrible'. At five o'clock 'they' made it 'pitch black' by shoving a metal plate in front of the window. Every morning the doctor came to determine whether the punished prisoner could still stand it.

> Naturally they have also taken your tie, and if you are narrow-hipped, your suspenders, so that you will not do away with yourself from helpless vexation.[22]

Still, the urge to scream or contact a fellow prisoner must have been so strong that many were willing to pay with days or weeks in a punishment cell. Prison statistics show that, in 1900 in the cellular prisons, approximately twice as many disciplinary punishments were meted out as in 1886, while the average population grew by about fifty per cent. In remand prisons, the (much more limited) number of disciplinary punishments increased in this period by almost 400 per cent while the average population stayed practically the same. This development cannot be seen separately from the fact that more remand prisons became equipped with cells, so that an increasing number of prisoners could be and were found guilty of forbidden communication and other typically 'cellular' offences. Both in the penitentiaries and the remand prisons the situation seems to have become somewhat milder between 1900 and the First World War. The number of punishments imposed decreased about fifty per cent in this period; this was primarily due to less strict action in cases of 'forbidden contact'.

At about the turn of the century, approximately 1,500 prisoners per

year were put on bread and water for a period of time in cellular
penitentiaries. Approximately 250 prisoners wound up in the normal
punishment cell annually. About 100 prisoners were denied work, and
could not go to the canteen or the airing places for a period of time, severe
punishment in the context of solitary confinement. The completely dark
punishment cell saw only a handful of prisoners, but, in the first decade
after introduction of the system (1887–97), this still amounted to a total
of almost 300 prisoners. The punishment cell, made more severe by bread
and water and/or chains, saw an annual 500 prisoners for several days or
weeks. An ex-warder remembered that men 'tied down' there screamed
'sometimes for hours on end'.[23]

While the health of many a prisoner will have been injured by the stay
in punishment cells, the severe discipline and the long stay in the normal
cell, death rates were much lower than previously in the nineteenth century.
Table 7.1 shows that the death rate in penitentiaries and remand-prisons
(and houses of detention) between 1880 and 1910 more and more often
lay beneath the national death rates for men. One should remember that
prisoners were usually in the prime of their lives, while national death
rates include the large infant mortality and death from old age.

These death rates point to the fact that prison life still meant illness and
death in addition to mental suffering. Apart from this, death rates in labour
colonies were still well above two per cent at the beginning of the twentieth
century, a percentage which naturally partially reflects the unhealthy state
of many beggars, vagrants and drunks at the time of their arrest.

TABLE 7.1 Mortality rates in penitentiaries and houses of detention as a
          percentage of the average population, compared with the
          national mortality rate for men, 1880–1909.[24]

Period	National mortality rate	Prison mortality rate
1880–9	2.2	1.5
1890–9	1.9	1.2
1900–9	1.6	0.8

Religious Comfort and Sunday Boredom during 'Humane Treatment'

Prisoners were obliged to proceed 'except by special dispensation', every
Sunday to the cellular 'hokjeskerk' (box-church) wearing their cell cap.
They listened to uplifting sermons from behind chicken wire so that they
could not pass anything to one another. Pastor Dekker thought they most
enjoyed the singing, not so much because the text moved them deeply,
but because they were not even allowed to whistle in their cells and could
now sing 'at the tops of their voices'.[25]

Metz the teacher came up with a more psychological explanation for this enjoyment. After all, in the cell it was only 'by exception' that prisoners heard their own or another's voice. And voice and speaking were, in his opinion, 'important sources' of awareness.[26] A prisoner himself explained his longing for the church service completely differently. As they entered the church, the organ was being played and that sometimes gave them the opportunity to whisper something to another. 'Therefore, you look forward to Sundays.'[27]

Priests or pastors were intensely listened to. Sometimes prisoners cried but they also were known to laugh, like the time that pastor Dekker had a tickling cough and took a sip of water. 'Cheers', said one of the prisoners from his box. All his fellows burst into long-lasting, liberating laughter.[28] Singing together, laughing together, and the possibility of pestering the pastor must have provided a rare light moment in the darkness of cell life. Sundays were also special for another reason. Prisoners could write letters, admittedly heavily censured. Should letters contain complaints about the regime or treatment, they were returned or destroyed. On Sundays, prisoners were also allowed to have portraits with them of wife, husband, parents or children.

By present standards, cell life was harsh and excruciatingly lonely. The pastor seemed not to be aware that he had described something really awful, again evidence of how greatly the understanding of human misery differed from the present day, and of how relative those concepts are. Verbally, prison experts championed the 'humane' treatment of convicts just as their colleagues do today. 'In one word, the people are treated as *human beings*,' wrote pastor Dekker. He wrote that many people saw the solitude, in particular, as 'something awful'. But they had forgotten, in his opinion, that communal imprisonment was 'ten times worse'. The solitude was, admittedly, 'not the most pleasant', but experience had taught him that one got used to 'nothing more quickly' than that solitude.[29] Headmaster Metz showed a good eye for what we would now call 'sensory deprivation' and 'relational deprivation', but he did not find the punishment too harsh and he thought most prisoners had earned it. His most moving descriptions of cell life were written merely to promote in warders the habit of imagining what 'such a situation' was like. He thought they did this insufficiently. Naturally they entered cells daily, but 'habit' was thought to have made 'their souls' for the most part 'unfeeling'. His goals were primarily didactic, then, when he wrote:

> Imagine yourself solitarily imprisoned in a frightening cellar-like place, completely cut off from the outside world, provided only with necessities, everywhere brick: walls, ceiling, floor, nothing other than bare brick, thus, without the opportunity to observe things which catch the eye. Almost nothing which could make life interest-

ing has been introduced from outside. Bereft of acquaintances and family; beginning and ending the day like a machine; no one around you who takes your interests to heart, but others who by the nature of things can inspire fear.

Warders should thus be able to understand that it was no wonder that 'so many (became) insane, withdrawn, debilitated of spirit'.[30] We shall soon see that he demanded of warders that which politicians, doctors, prison directors and even many psychiatrists could not be moved to do, or only very reluctantly.

Psychic Experiences Related by Ex-prisoners

Prisoners themselves could often not understand why they did *not* become insane. In his series of articles in the *Nieuwe Rotterdamsche Courant*, the ex-prisoner cited earlier wrote that he had felt his brains 'swelling, swelling' and sat there waiting for the explosion of his 'bursting, overloaded head' but 'the break, which makes you crazy' did not come, to his surprise. He developed a fear for the empty corners of his cell. He felt again and again that something 'horrible' in a type of human form would come creeping out of these corners. [31]

Another ex-prisoner wrote a book, which included many passages about the psychic effects of cellular solitude. After his release, he landed in hospital, full of fears and hallucinating from fever. Two months later he was able to go home only to land in prison again shortly thereafter for theft. He decided to fake insanity, but very quickly this act became behaviour over which he no longer had any control at all. 'I was clear enough in my head, and still I had to pretend to be so crazy.' He tore his clothes to shreds, broke the window and lay on the floor 'kicking and hitting out like a madman'. Then he began to scream continuously that his head was on fire. He was shackled and put in a punishment cell for this behaviour. After this, he was placed in an observation cell where he refused to eat or drink and lay 'shrieking' the whole night. He continued to refuse food because he feared that he would be poisoned and he cursed the warders as murderers and mixers of poison. Only after two weeks of alternating punishment cell, bath tub and observation cell did he begin to take food again and show slightly less impossible behaviour. Until his release, he continued to have psychic problems. His head always remained 'somewhat hazy'. He suffered from lack of concentration, but could not let some thoughts go either.[32]

Publications by ex-prisoners were very rare at the turn of the century. Other facts show that the experiences they did manage to describe were not at all rare.

Psychological Effects of Solitary Confinement: Prison Statistics

Because, in principle, all those sentenced after 1886 were confined solitarily, psychological effects of solitude could be observed on a large scale. Until 1900, when the Central Bureau of Statistics (CBS) took over the responsibility for prison statistics, little more was reported than after how many months or years prisoners had become insane. Politicians and prison experts had often maintained, before the introduction of the cellular system, that such prisoners had already been more or less insane before their arrest and that cellular punishment could quickly be gotten used to after the first difficult weeks. The prison statistics do not support this theory. Usually prisoners had been in cells for months. Prison statistics for 1907 include a table which shows insanity appearing more often after a half year of imprisonment than after a couple of weeks. Of the 194 prisoners transferred to the state mental institution at Medemblik in the period 1902–7, almost half had been in prison longer than half a year and just over a third less than half a year. The others had been there an unspecified length of time.

For 64 of the 194 prisoners, a suspected cause of insanity was registered. For twenty-three, the stay in prison and 'specifically the *solitary* confinement' was thought to have played a causal role. All other causes fell under headings of masturbation, inherited tendency, family conditions or life style and earlier insanity. The compilers of the statistics remarked that the actual number of those insane was probably significantly higher. The short stay of most prisoners and the fact that the 'numerous borderline cases' were always difficult to diagnose, would often have made it difficult to ascertain psychical deviations.[33]

In the first year that the CBS registered data about insanity and suicide (1902), much was made of case histories. While in thirteen cases of insanity the cause remained 'unknown', the descriptions often pointed to a cellular influence. 'Solitary confinement' was not only explicitly mentioned, but also more closely described in seven cases.

> He appeared not to possess sufficient resistence to cellular punishment, so that he began to show all sorts of nervous symptoms under the influence of the cell; he had insomnia, he was afraid and expressed delusions of poisoning and persecution

was one example. It was added immediately that the number of cases was 'relatively limited' in proportion to the total prison population. Warnings were given against an all too obvious interpretation. Prison was not 'the only cause' of insanity. Earlier living conditions were important as well.[34] Later on, compilers almost never risked a thorough reflection of probable causes.

Even if one did not delve thoroughly into causes, the figures for insanity spoke quite clearly, as we shall soon see. This was less true of the figures for suicide, which were, in addition, very unreliable. No significance can be derived from the reported number of attempts, while precisely these attempts (including forms of serious self-mutilation) could have formed a good indicator of psychical suffering.[35] According to the statistics, there were, from the coming into force of the system in 1886 until 1900, in penitentiaries and houses of detention, an average of four suicides committed per year and an average of three prisoners having attempted suicide. In the period leading up to the First World War (1902–15), these averages increased to almost five successful suicides per year and six registered attempts. In an average population of approximately 3,000 prisoners, these are large numbers and the averages lay, certainly after 1900, above those for the preceding decade. It was remarked, in the prison statistics of 1907, that prisoners committed suicide relatively more often than did free citizens.[36] But the suicides and suicide attempts were certainly not only caused by solitary confinement. A substantial number of prisoners turned to these measures in preventive custody, where the social consequences of arrest and the prospect of long-lasting punishment undoubtedly played a role. Communal confinement could also, apparently, lead to despair.[37] In most cells, moreover, the practicalities of attempting suicide and succeeding were very difficult.[38]

Government Inspectorate Figures for Insanity in Prisons

The figures for insanity in prisons show a disturbing increase after the general introduction of the cellular system. For the years 1887 to 1890 the prison statistics indicate that an average of 12.5 prisoners were transferred to the insane asylum annually. After this period, prison management was faced with inspections from the government inspectorate of the care for the insane, as a result of the law on insanity of 1884. Beginning in 1891, annual reports of this inspectorate contained a section dealing with visits made to prisons and related institutions. In consultation with public prosecutors, governors and prison doctors, the inspectors defined what had to happen with prisoners who had become insane. The reports will be dealt with in detail, but it is important in this connection that management strongly resisted initiatives of the inspectorate. They refused to provide detailed information and protested against visits to disordered prisoners. Very few governors went of their own free will to the inspectorate for advice.

In prisons where inspectors were welcome, they found many insane prisoners of whom they had not been informed. The inspectors complained of this to the Minister of Justice. In circulars to prison managements, he insisted that the inspectorate be notified of each case of insanity 'straightaway'. According to the inspectors, reports did indeed begin to come in regularly.[39]

The actions of these inspectors thus strongly influenced both increasing numbers of prisoners declared insane and their treatment. They made partially visible what had largely remained hidden until 1890. However, this chapter will reveal that the increase in numbers of insane prisoners also had a lot to do with the cellular system. The increase was especially large, as one sees in Table 7.2. Reports show that, between 1891 and 1900, an average of almost thirty prisoners per year were transferred to insane asylums from penitentiaries and remand prisons. From 1900 to 1912, this average increased to more than forty-eight per year. In the last period, there was an additional average of seventeen to eighteen insane prisoners nursed in prisons and declared to be cured.

While these figures indicate that the number of the insane increased dramatically after the general introduction of the cellular system, the

TABLE 7.2 Increase in the numbers of insane prisoners, 1887–1912.[40]

Year	Total number of insane observed (and nursed) in prisons	Total number transfered to an asylum	Total number of insane observed (and nursed) in *rijkswerkinrichtingen*
1887	–	18	–
1888	–	12	–
1889	–	12	–
1890	–	8	–
1891	34		18
1892	26	78	22
1893	29		4
1894	30		17
1895	43	83	15
1896	40		22
1897	34		8
1898	45	108	16
1899	39		9
1900	50		16
1901	48	99	21
1902	32		29
1903	33		29
1904	65		13
1905	64		16
1906	81	279	20
1907	72		19
1908	112		24
1909	68	46	48
1910	78	60	50
1911	90	54	47
1912	103	89	32

interpretation of this development is not so simple. That figures began to rise only after a number of years is understandable, because the prisons only gradually filled with prisoners sentenced on the basis of the new Penal Code. Particularly the numbers of those with long sentences increased steadily in the first years. Moreover, the untried were more and more often solitarily confined as more and more cells appeared in the houses of detention and remand prisons. The fact that numbers of the insane continued to increase noticably even after 1890 could have a lot to do with the government inspectorate. The inspectors probably advised earlier transfer to an asylum and perhaps presumed malingering less often.

We do know that the number of free citizens admitted to a mental hospital noticeably increased as well. In 1880, 1,081 persons were admitted, in 1890, 1,366; in 1900, 1,779; and in 1910, 2,791 persons.[41] The sudden and dramatic increase in the numbers of insane prisoners around 1890 clearly did not run parallel to the tendency in these national figures, but the increase between 1890 and 1910 did, to some extent, although numbers admitted from prisons continued to increase more sharply. One should remember in considering this that, in the last period, the population of The Netherlands increased by almost fifty per cent while the average prison population remained almost the same. Certainly, if one keeps this in mind, the number of admissions from prisons increased considerably more than could be expected based on the national tendency.

However, the changing diagnostic which, in connection with a further professionalizing of psychiatric knowledge, influenced the national figures, might well have exerted an even stronger effect on the number of admissions from prisons. After all, prisons contained a large group of persons with psychic problems, sitting in cells, as it were, ready to be observed and diagnosed psychiatrically, while, in freedom, many persons had not yet been subjected to the psychiatric searchlight. Prisoners also lived in circumstances which, whether they were solitarily or communally confined, formed a substrate for the development of psychiatric problems. Also, many will have wound up in the justicial apparatus *through* their psychiatric problems. In any case, around the turn of the century *thirty to forty times* as many people, relatively speaking, were transferred to asylums from prisons as from free society. Nationally, in 1900, 1,779 free citizens were concerned from a population of approximately five million. From the prisons, remand prisons and houses of detention, between 1897 and 1903, an average of almost thirty-five persons per year were admitted from an average population of 3,000.[42]

Hard conclusions cannot yet be drawn about the psychic effects of solitary confinement, but, it is certain that in the Dutch prison system, at the end of the century, a huge, new problem was added: what to do with the many criminally insane or insane criminals.

The Problem of the Criminally Insane or Insane Criminals

In the many reports, books and articles written about this problem, an additional focus of concern was the many who were declared 'ontoerekenbaar' (not imputable), who thus were arrested but not further prosecuted. In reading these works, my attention was given primarily to *prisoners* who had become insane, even though it was often very arbitrary whether those awaiting trial would be sentenced after recovering or – if declared 'non-imputable' – would escape sentencing for good.[43]

While later opinion surrounding the problem of insane criminals at the end of the nineteenth and beginning of the twentieth century allocated it to the history of the TBR-measure (sentence to compulsory treatment in a secure clinic for an indeterminate period) and the psychopath laws, brought into operation in 1928,[44] the problem was seen in a much more diffuse way at the time. It had not yet been clearly divided up into the separate problems of insane prisoners, prisoners who had become insane, the dangerous or threatening insane and the 'non-imputables'. In prisons and psychiatric institutions these groups were still mixed, something which was increasingly experienced as an unacceptable situation. Specialized institutions and legal rules did not yet exist or were insufficient.[45] The question was whether separate asylums should be brought into being for insane prisoners or whether psychiatric departments in prisons would suffice.

It is, of course, important to distinguish whether the huge increase in numbers of prisoners declared insane had more to do with a growing conviction that the mentally ill did not belong in prison than with the implementation of solitary confinement. It was, however, precisely this growing conviction that led to many more mentally ill accused than before being placed immediately (before imprisonment) in insane asylums as 'non-imputable' and therefore escaping sentencing.[46] That made the increase in numbers of insane prisoners even more disturbing. How much did solitary confinement have to do with this?

This question was not often posed. A report in 1895 from a commission that investigated the desirability of prison-asylums did not once mention the influence of solitary confinement.[47] A year later, H. L. A. Visser, in his thesis dealing with psychiatric supervision in prisons, stated briefly that guilt for insanity could only partially be attributed to prison life. He concluded that 'in general' the cell only allowed illnesses to develop from which prisoners already suffered before detention.[48] The psychiatrist, L. S. Meijer, was much less reassuring in 1899. He made a convincing case for the number of insane prisoners being much larger than any figures had yet shown. Meijer was of the opinion that the general public, prison personnel, judges and others 'not psychiatrically educated' did not recognize many forms of mental illness because they primarily imagined them to consist of 'excessive boisterousness, profligacy and frenzy'. Many psychoses did not, however, manifest themselves so dramatically. The listlessness of the melancholic was seen as laziness, his silence as 'obduracy and obstinacy', the excitement of the manic as 'incorrigible impudence' and all sorts of 'deviations' as 'signs of a tendency to oppose and disturb the normal course of events'.

Meijer said that psychiatrists in prisons were repeatedly mistrusted. A 'smile of compassion' would greet the expert, someone so naive 'as to search for anything other than the recalcitrance of criminal personalities behind the bad behaviour of convicts'. He called the supposition of simulation in the prisoner and sentimentality in the psychiatrist 'a fatal tendency'. He himself assumed that twenty to twenty-five per cent of insane prisoners had not been insane before detention. This was partially explicable by a 'predisposition to psychosis', but, he admitted frankly that prison sentences, cellular and others, contributed to the breaking out of mental illness. Confinement in solitude aggravated the effect. He thought that the punishment 'itself' contained the germ of mental disturbances. In solitude, one could not unburden one's conscience by contact with fellows. The prisoner fought his battle alone against 'a conscience laden with guilt' and depressing thoughts. Meijer saw his analysis as proven by the fact that many recovered immediately upon removal from the cell. On the contrary, it was 'not seldom' that someone placed in a cell became quickly insane after years without problems in communal imprisonment.

Meijer closed his article with demands for safeguards against the frequent underestimation of mental illnesses and for more supervision by expert psychiatrists.[49] Understanding for cellular misery clearly went hand in hand with the promotion of the psychiatric profession around the turn of the century. Meanwhile, in Germany and France, scientific articles had already appeared in which psychiatrists debated the precise bases of 'Haftpsychosen', 'Gefängnispsychosen' or 'les psychoses pénitentaires'. Psychiatry had gained a new concept in illness: the prison psychosis.

Rise of a New Mental Illness: Prison Psychosis

In 1899, the German psychiatrist, Ganser, described pathological symptoms he had primarily observed in prisoners. Today 'Ganser's syndrome' is seen as an hysterical form of reaction to a situation which the patient cannot handle. The patient appears to 'pretend' in a primitive way that he is suffering from mental illness, stupidity or mental deterioration, but the reality is that he is trying to escape from an untenable situation.[50]

In 1901, the psychiatrist, Rüdin, was one of the first to formulate the question as to whether a psychosis characteristic for prisons existed. He left the question open but did establish the presence of catatonic symptoms in fifty-five per cent of prisoners who had become insane. Generally, the clinical picture was made up of simple hallucinations of hearing and sight, delusions of persecution, combined with fear and irritability. Terms like prison delusion, delusion of pardon, delusion of innocence and prison querulousness began to appear in prison jargon. The influence of congenital and degenerative factors was disputed but hallucinations, a paranoid delusion system and Ganser's symptoms were always named as characteristic of psychoses in those cellularly confined.[51]

The psychic consequences of cellular confinement, for so long and often still denied by Members of Parliament and prison experts, also became recognized in The Netherlands in textbooks of psychiatry. The psychiatrist, Jelgersma, wrote in his well-known textbook (around 1908) that when criminals – in his opinion often types who saw everything done to them as unfair and unjustified – landed in prison, they suffered from disturbances of digestion and weight loss in the first period. He thought these symptoms repeatedly gave rise to 'hypochondriac protests'. A 'not unimportant sector' then began to show symptoms of persecution delusion, according to Jelgersma:

> The strict discipline easily comes to be seen as persecution, and the prison governor and personnel as those effecting the persecution. An incidental comment, a conversation that is not understood, an innocent gesture becomes, in the solitude of the cell, an important happening that is brooded upon from all angles; far from enticing these deficient persons to fruitful meditation and working towards their improvement, as intended, it gives rise to bitterness and desire for revenge.

Under these conditions, it was Jelgersma's opinion that prisoners went on to develop a system of delusion. Paranoid delusions, became mixed with hallucinations. Prisoners thought their food was being poisoned and they heard threatening voices. This prison paranoia usually had a favourable prognosis. In another environment, symptoms generally disappeared. One could, in Jelgersma's opinion, therefore speak of 'making the patient mentally ill'. Should this be 'absolutely necessary' in order to guarantee the safety of honest persons, Jelgersma would have been able to accept it. But, should a different regime work just as well, he rejected solitary confinement because 'it cannot be permitted in any way at all to knowingly make someone mentally ill'.[52]

Jelgersma saw the theory that solitude led to remorse and improvement through 'reflections on the past' as an 'idealistic illusion'. At the time that he wrote this, between 2,000 and 3,000 persons were confined to cellular prisons based on this idealistic illusion.[53] Solitude led to bitterness and not remorse and predisposed one to hallucinations and delusions in his opinion. These symptoms were often accompanied by acute attacks of 'anxiety and depression'.[54]

Cellular Misery in Annual Reports of the Government Inspectorate

The awful, unintended results of the cellular philosophy were clearly to be seen in annual reports of the inspectors from the governmental inspectorate for the insane and insane asylums. The cellular misery so thoroughly described there, page upon page, is so varied that it is barely possible to summarize it. Inspectors travelled from prison to prison and found persons, refusing to eat, screaming, raging, weeping, dazed, hallucinating and severely paranoid, who destroyed their cell windows, covered themselves in their own faeces, wounded themselves or attempted suicide. Often they were heavily chained or restrained in a straitjacket, and if that did not help, cold water was poured over them.

Many of these unfortunates were continuously transferred back and forth between cellular prison, the Special Penitentiary for psychiatric problem cases in 's-Hertogenbosch and the state mental asylum in Medemblik. Should they be declared cured or 'unmasked' as malingerers they were sent back to their cells to immediately get into trouble again, so that they once again were transported to 's-Hertogenbosch or Medemblik. Additionally, symptoms of insanity were often not deemed severe enough to warrant sending prisoners to the Special Penitentiary or the state mental asylum, but, from descriptions of prisoners' complaints and inspectors' remarks, it is apparent that no reliable criteria for the severity of psychiatric disturbances existed. Sometimes prisoners were given work outside the cell or, as frequently happened in the penitentiary at Leeuwarden, were transferred for a time to the communal section of the prison until it could be established that they could again stand the solitude.

Serious dissention about diagnoses regularly occurred between prison doctors (almost always military doctors) and government inspectors. Practically every prisoner who showed signs of mental disturbance was first suspected of malingering. The assumption was made that prisoners preferred the government asylum where the regime was somewhat milder and life less lonely than in prison. Descriptions clearly show that prisoners inflicted great amounts of misery upon themselves in order to escape the cell. In spite of weeks in a punishment cell, they continued the assumed malingering and, if they stopped or 'confessed' to having feigned illness, it certainly remained dubious whether or not they were dissimulating (that is: showing normal behaviour and faking their confession) in order to avoid the punishment cell. Malingering was seen as tantamount to crime. The terminology fitted this view. In 's-Hertogenbosch the inspectors were confronted with 'a known malingerer'. This was 'a pale young man' who was also known 'as a malingerer' in Amsterdam, 'where he acted disgustingly and did not refrain from the most sordid behaviour in order to persist in his act'. Not until Medemblik was he 'unmasked'; there he 'admitted to malingering'.[55]

Sometimes inspectors had no idea what to make of it all. 'We found that he was mentally deranged and, at the same time, malingering,' they stated then.[56] Often suspicion of feigning was kept up for years. Sometimes complaints were finally recognized, as in the case of a prisoner in Utrecht. He had been sentenced to three years in the cell, had attempted suicide a number of times and smeared his naked body 'with his faeces'. He was therefore transferred to the Special Penitentiary at 's-Hertogenbosch. There he was thrice put in the black hole for a number of weeks and chained, because he continued to 'play the same role'. Only after that did he behave so calmly and orderly that the doctor deemed him again 'suited' for solitary confinement. Back in Utrecht, he was disciplinarily punished four times in one and a half years. He was again transferred to 's-Hertogenbosch where symptoms of a 'condition of stupor' were still visible that he had undergone 'under the influence of life in the cell'. These symptoms quickly disappeared 'under the influence of communal imprisonment'. 'Malingering could be ruled out. Due to expiration of the term of punishment, the convict was quickly released from that place,' concluded the inspectors in their report.[57]

Three-quarters of a century later, it is difficult to judge this stubbornly consistent suspicion of malingering. The inspectors themselves left clues showing that the assumption of malevolence was very easily made. In the same series of reports, written after 1911, in which the above-mentioned case is described, inspectors point out that one had to be 'cautious' in judging mental states. It had occurred to them that prisoners with characteristically degenerated faces, 'bird beak faces' or the appearances of idiots or imbeciles appeared 'after further research' to possess mental abilities not suspected from their appearances. Contrarily, prisoners showing no outward signs of disturbance appeared to be suffering, for instance, from melancholy. Especially in depressive disturbances, the existence of 'psychic aberration' was 'frequently' missed. While their inspection reports had overflowed for years with cases of suspected feigning, they now stated that 'feigning insanity' in the prison population occurred 'relatively seldom'. They stated that 'the aggravation of certain facets of symptom complexes' occurred 'more frequently'. Thus prisoners tended only to accentuate the problems which developed in solitude.[58]

Solitude, Masturbation and Prison Psychoses

In spite of the fear of being duped by malingerers, symptoms were often so marked that inspectors advised transfer to Medemblik or communal confinement. This points to the fact that it was openly admitted by the inspectors that cellular solitude caused many mental disturbances. Sometimes this was an implicit admission, but they also often explicitly pointed this out. After an inspection of a prison in Scheveningen where they had visited a 'striking' number of mentally deranged prisoners, the inspectors wrote frankly that, 'in many of these cases', they saw cellular confinement as 'fatal for the mind' and that they had advised, therefore, transfer to a prison with communal facilities.[59]

'Unsuited to solitary confinement', 'since solitary confinement is deemed disadvantageous for him' or 'solitary confinement was considered wrong for him' were the formulations with which the inspectors concluded many descriptions. Often the situation was watched for a further period of time, but a man in Utrecht earned immediate action. This was someone in a cell, 'weary of life' who had already spent three years in the cell and still had four-and-a-half years of his sentence to go. After that, extradition to Germany threatened. He threw himself 'from the second story'. The inspectors declared him 'mentally deranged' and he was transferred to Medemblik.[60]

In the years that the government inspectors did their sad work, the indication of the cell as the cause of psychic disturbances was made very difficult by what rightly can be called an 'intervening variable': masturbation.[61] Cellular confinement, instituted in part to prevent immorality in communal prisons, left prisoners with only themselves to fondle. Masturbation was abhorred by the inspectors. They saw it as 'a sad causal moment' in psychic disturbances and suicides and gave advice to combat 'this scourge of cellular prisons'.

In their first report about their visits to prisons, they had already remarked that masturbation appeared to be the cause 'in many cases' of 'nervous disorders' and 'disturbances having to do with the nerves'. Heavy work in fresh air and 'cold hip baths and washings' were thought to have led to improvement in some cases. They advised the use of 'closed gloves'. They wrote about 'a neurasthenic, physically and spiritually weakened by masturbation', about 'an individual weakened by masturbation' and about being 'severely addicted to masturbation'. Others had given themselves up 'shamefully to masturbation' and had thereby fallen into 'a state of stupor'.[62]

The inspectors never went so far, in spite of the misery that they witnessed, as to criticize the cellular system. But they did repeatedly point out the importance of psychiatric expertise, separate institutions for insane prisoners and especially observation cells in a special department. The inspectors proposed that these observation cells be so situated 'that the raving, singing and screaming of the prisoners can not penetrate to the rest of the building, that thereby the peace of others is seriously disturbed'. They wanted cells with their own tiny gardens, cells so built from the point of view of the spy hole that there were no blind spots in which a prisoner could hide. Warders had to be able to approach these cells so that the sound of their footsteps could not be heard by the person being observed.[63]

Most cellular prisons did not have separate observation cells. Screaming, howling and yelling must have formed a part of the noise which was taken for granted.[64] The term prison psychosis is first used in inspectors' reports for the years 1909–11, but, from their descriptions in older reports, it is clear that the characteristic symptoms of this psychosis were ascertained much earlier. Almost all prisoners who had psychic problems hallucinated. They heard voices and saw persons in their cells who frightened them or spoke threateningly to them. A man in Scheveningen slept badly and made a racket in his cell at night. He said he saw spirits, like 'the queen in mourning, Sequah and other people'.[65] Many hallucinating prisoners became paranoid, usually developing poisoning and persecution delusions.

The more comprehensive case histories illustrate that prison psychosis was not a theoretical invention, but hard practical experience. Powerless, prisoners tried to defend themselves against poisoning and persecution delusions by screaming, shrieking and breaking everything in sight. In Leeuwarden, a prisoner developed a 'secret antidote' for the poison that he thought the management was giving him. 'His arms and other body parts were covered with scars from abscesses and boils resulting from numerous auto-inoculations with the supposed anti-serum,' stated the inspectors. They characterized him as an 'untreatable chronic paranoiac' who 'again and again' had to be shut up in the punishment cell.[66]

Other prisoners tried more radical means of escaping the misery. They attempted suicide. Even then they were sometimes suspected of malingering. 'After application of the straitjacket he behaved well and began to work,' wrote the inspectors, for example, about a 'feigned attempted hanging'.[67] Prisoners could not reckon on being understood, even following a real, almost successful attempt. A twenty-year-old man barricaded his cell door, covered over the spy glass and hung himself from the little window with cloth binding from the tailor's work that he had to do. He was in a coma when the warders found him lying on the ground. Artificial respiration brought him back. When he revived, he immediately began to weep desperately. The man told the inspectors that he had felt 'so nervous' and had lacked the willpower to want to live further.[68] He was put to work weeding.

All of this sort of misery did not move the inspectors to emotional utterances. This is partially understandable from the aim of their reports (objective reflection of the psychiatric practice) and partially from their conviction that many prisoners with psychic problems could not be kept in check by any other means. Naturally, the inspectors protected themselves, as people often do whose daily profession confronts them with the misery of their fellow-man. Severe punishment was seen as an unavoidable method of coercion. Compassion could also be misused. About a

convict who 'under the influence of depressing conditions' had deteriorated both bodily and spiritually, the inspectors reported that he remained
'difficult and demanding' even on the hospital ward as often was the case
'in persons who have been treated to much compassion as a result of
bodily suffering and who have learned to exploit this compassion'.[69]

Treatment of Problem Cases in the Special Penitentiary in 's-Hertogenbosch

Until 1912, the Special Penitentiary in 's-Hertogenbosch was an intermediate and a terminal station for prisoners with mental problems. The
regime in that institution was especially strict. Disciplinary punishments
were imposed in great numbers. According to the institutional doctor, J.
Casparie, these punishments would give prisoners the feeling that they
were in the presence of 'their betters'. This inspired a healthy respect and
'even submission' and prisoners would feel best in such a position.
Casparie had become convinced that severe punishments, if imposed
after psychiatric observation, would work very therapeutically on prisoners, 'because they begin at last to feel the satisfaction that an orderly life
and regular work bring in the long run'. Should one not punish as
severely, he thought more room would be created for mutiny, vandalism
and assault on the guarding personnel and 'ourselves'.

Prisoners who developed psychic problems in the cell were first
brought to 's-Hertogenbosch and, when complaints continued, were
transferred to the government mental asylum in Medemblik. Most improved quickly, however, and were then transferred back to the cellular
prison. This is apparent from the figures which Casparie provided for the
years 1905 to 1910. In the six years, a total of 486 prisoners were
admitted. These included 228 old men who, on legal grounds, were
incarcerated in communal facilities. The remaining 258 younger men had
all developed serious psychic problems during their cellular confinement
in the penitentiaries.[70]

In 176 of these men, Casparie established that prison psychosis existed
and he went on to emphasize that this was a *cell* psychosis. Its lightest form
was 'a morbid irritability with symptoms of exhaustion', as he saw it. This
changed gradually 'into an as yet imprecisely circumscribed condition of
excitement combined with an urge to vandalism'. Finally there were the
prisoners with paranoid delusions and hallucinations whom he, taking
into account the course of the illness and the nature of the delusions,
included as well in 'the large group' of sufferers from 'prison psychoses'.
While Casparie saw many more connections between solitary confinement and psychic disturbances than had been assumed by politicians and
prison experts for a very long time, he did not contend that the cell alone
caused these psychoses. His idea was that 'the already so vulnerable mind
of the mentally deficient', influenced by emotions caused by punishment

and the monotonous cell life, was pulled 'out of its already not very stable balance'. Psychic disturbances came into being which could be compared to psychoneuroses and which developed a special character 'through the degenerative ground in which they had begun to grow, and the mental deficiency which had left its mark on the entirety of one's social life.'

The cell was, thus, not a sufficient, but a necessary condition, something which Casparie deemed proved by the fact that the psychoses quickly disappeared as soon as patients were placed in 'better surroundings'. He saw this as such an important characteristic of the psychosis that he spoke of it having 'diagnostic value'. Of the 176 prison psychotics admitted in the period from 1905–10, 84 recovered 'almost immediately' after arrival in 's-Hertogenbosch. Only a 'striking mental deficiency' remained in the prisoners. Others recovered more slowly, but the positive influence of communal imprisonment was also remarkable in these cases. Shortly before the period mentioned, cured prisoners were immediately returned to the cellular prison from which they had come. Casparie saw, however, that 'many of the patients' quickly returned again 'with the same clinical symptoms as before'. In order to prevent this, he first observed them in a cell in the detention centre in 's-Hertogenbosch. He witnessed this experiment's failure 'many times'. Right in front of his eyes, the 'completely grotesque picture' of the prison psychosis redeveloped:

> After a short period, the symptoms of exaggerated irritability appeared again, and I saw first the headaches, apathy, insomnia etc. make their appearance, then the excitability, raving, vandalism; then the hallucinations as well, the delusions, the attempted suicides, etc.

Only if the cell trial continued to go well for three or four weeks did he send prisoners back to a cellular penitentiary. Of the 176 psychotics, 38 were, indeed, returned to the cell. Only 13 of the 176 sufferers were transferred to the state mental hospital in Medemblik. No less than 125 psychotics remained in 's-Hertogenbosch; this reveals that the figures provided earlier for prisoners who had become insane (see Table 7.2) reflect the reality too favourably. An average of fifty prisoners were, according to those figures, transferred to an insane asylum between 1905 and 1910. In 's-Hertogenbosch there were an additional 125, that is a good twenty prison psychotics per year permanently committed. Additionally, approximately six psychotic prisoners per year (thirty-eight in the six-year period concerned) were brought back to prison as cured from 's-Hertogenbosch. It could be that a number of these later wound up directly in Medemblik and were counted twice, but, even then, certainly *more than seventy* prisoners per year had to deal with severe psychic problems. This results, within an average prison population (penitentiaries, remand prisons, and houses of detention) of 3,000, in a shocking two per cent. Nationally, in 1910, 2,791 free citizens were admitted to an insane asylum[71] (from a population of almost six million), that is 0.02 per cent, or one hundred times fewer.[72]

These figures and calculations give rise to many questions. It is important that Casparie, when discussing prison psychotics, did *not* mean the large group of 'non-imputables' and mentally disturbed who then, in contrast to today, still ended up in prison. He emphasized that, in the 176 prisoners mentioned, 'the cell was the provocation for the brief or more chronic mental disturbance'. These men were, admittedly, mentally deficient and degenerated, but that did not interfere with his conviction that 'one of the principal provocative moments for the *breaking out* of the mental disturbance' had to be sought in the 'unusual way of living' which these 'weakened personalities' had been thrown into through their placement in a cellular prison.[73]

Prisoners in the State Insane Asylum in Medemblik

Many prisoners, often after a long bout of suffering, came to be placed in the state insane asylum at Medemblik, that had been opened in 1884 as a consequence of the 'gestichtenwet' (institution law).[74] Until 1898, both men and women were admitted there. After that, first the calm ones and later all women were transferred to the insane asylum at Grave.

In 1907, the institution's doctor, J. Kat, wrote an article about the development of problems in Medemblik. Because of the large numbers of prisoners in the total population of the institution, it became apparent that the *no restraint* system (care without coercion, in as far as possible), long in use in Dutch institutions, could hardly be maintained. Prisoners were more aggressive, but primarily more likely to escape. Pressure on the direction to exert a more severe discipline was large, because the press, already at that time, thoroughly covered any escape of criminals.

For that matter, part of the institution then already resembled a heavily guarded prison with high walls, cells and military sentries. Should prisoners have feigned insanity to get to Medemblik, they certainly had a rude awakening after 1900. Kat called it a 'fallacy' that many healthy criminals had managed to avoid 'their rightful punishment' through malingering. Of all the convicts admitted since 1884, scarcely three per cent were thought to have feigned their illness. Kat also had no doubt that this percentage was too high and said that 'more than one of the earlier as malingerers treated, I would be more likely to say mistreated, would have been discerned as mentally abnormal by the present improved diagnostics'.[75]

From 1884 to 1891, a total of fifty-seven prisoners and sixteen declared non-imputable were admitted to Medemblik. From 1891 to 1901 this was already 234 prisoners and 163 'non-imputables'. From 1901 to 1911 the numbers grew further to 390 prisoners and 336 'non-imputables', thus an average of about forty prisoners and thirty 'non-imputables' annually. In 1911, 1912, 1913 and 1914, respectively forty-seven, forty-one, twenty-eight and seventeen prisoners and thirty-one, forty-three, forty-three and twenty-two 'non-imputables' were admitted.

The rather sudden decrease in numbers of prisoners in 1913 and 1914 was connected to the opening of the Special Penitentiary in Scheveningen. At the beginning *all* prisoners who developed mental problems were sent there. They could also, after recovery, stay there much longer than in 's-Hertogenbosch and the nursing facilities were much better, so that the sending on to an insane asylum was often no longer necessary.[76] The totals, then, were 823 prisoners and 654 declared non-imputable, admitted between 1884 and 1915.[77]

These figures are important. They show that, at the turn of the century, a development was taking place by which those arrested who were clearly mentally disturbed no longer were brought before a judge but were, instead, sent as 'ontoerekenbaar' (non-imputable) to the insane asylum at Medemblik. This development should have led, as I have said earlier, to a decrease in numbers of insane prisoners and not to the especially sharp increase which actually occurred.

Clinical Descriptions and Causes in Admissions Registers

Other figures exist which point in the direction of solitary confinement as greatly influencing the coming into being of serious mental disturbances. In both normal insane asylums and Medemblik the probable causes of insanity and the clinical picture presented by the patient upon admission were kept track of in pre-printed registers.[78] One could write a whole book just putting the value and the significance of some of the diagnoses into perspective, but within the psychiatric world of that time there was a clear consensus about clinical presentations and the accompanying symptoms. A structure based upon this consensus sufficed for the making of diagnoses. From year to year, the diagnoses show a great consistency.

In the tables printed in annual reports of the government inspectorate for mental health care from 1885 on, fourteen clinical representations can be distinguished until 1898 [79] and, from year to year, the percentage of those clinical representations (from the total number of diagnosis made) differed a few percent at most and often not more than one percent.

Until 1898, prisoners at Medemblik invariably showed two forms of *melancholica (agitans* and *attonita), hallucinationes* and *vecordia* far and away most often. Nationally, these clinical descriptions were used almost fifty per cent less often as diagnoses and, among the 'non-imputables' at Medemblik, even less often. From 1898 on, new psychiatric concepts and knowledge entailed a different classification of clinical descriptions. Then twelve clinical representations were distinguished.[80] Three differently named illnesses scored highest among prisoners: *amentia, insania neurotica*

TABLE 7.3 Clinical representations of insane prisoners, 1885–1915.

	National (%)	Prisoners (%)	'Non-imputables' (%)
1885–98			
Melancholica (agitans and attonica)	16.3	21.5	8.1
Hallucinations	6.1	13.0	8.1
Vecordia	14.8	28.7	12.5
TOTAL	37.2	63.2	26.7
1898–1915			
Melancholica	9.0	2.8	1.6
Amentia	6.3	15.5	8.9
Insania neurotica	5.8	24.4	11.2
Paranoia (vecordia)	10.3	29.5	13.2
TOTAL	31.4	72.2	34.9

and *paranoia*. Nationally, these illnesses again appeared much less often (22.4 per cent as opposed to 69.4 per cent). Table 7.3 shows the picture for *melancholica* in order to facilitate a comparison with the foregoing period.

As far as I have been able to determine, certain symptoms which, before 1898, were classed under the diagnosis vecordia usually came to be included under paranoia after 1898.[81] Often vecordia appeared between brackets after paranoia and vice versa. Melancholica, hallucinationes, paranoia (vecordia) and insania neurotica are all clinical representations which we could expect from cellular prisoners based on our ability to identify with them and on the descriptions of prison psychoses. The main symptoms of melancholica, as outlined by Jelgersma in his textbook of psychiatry, were, for example, impedance (the slowing down and hampering of mental processes), depressive ill feeling and indecisiveness.[82] After 1898, melancholica was diagnosed considerably less often in prisoners. One seems to have preferred amentia, which literally means 'confusion'. The first phase was characterized, according to Jelgersma, by agitation, anxiety and feeling oneself unwell. The patient became afraid that he would die or become insane. He became disoriented and found everything strange and unintelligible. He felt very happy and, at the same time, severely depressed and felt urges to suicide. Later, anger, wrath and distrust were added. He became suspicious and began to think that he was being poisoned. Fundamental forms of persecution delusion appeared, combined with depressive ideas of persecution. Apathy and hallucinations in the form of threats and voices made their appearance. Other delusions developed.[83] This clinical description seems almost tailor-made for cellular prisoners. Paranoia was probably ascertained if fear of poison-

TABLE 7.4 Grief as a cause of insanity, 1885–1908.

	National (%)	Prisoners (%)	'Non-imputables' (%)
Grief	13.0	44.7	4.6
Cause unknown	13.0	30.1	61.4
Grief as % of all causes (exclusively 'unknown')	14.9	64.8	11.9

ing and persecution anxieties had the upper hand.

The figures representing probable *causes* give an even stronger indication of the influence of cellular confinement on the development of insanity in prisoners. Twelve causes were distinguished in Medemblik.[84] Nationally, some subdivisions were made. But, both nationally and in Medemblik, 'grief' was seen as one of the possible causes. Whether or not the stated cause was also an actual cause is impossible to say with any certainty. It is not very likely, however. The government inspectors, in their comments on the national figures, also expressed serious doubts.

> Often something is given as cause which more rightfully can be seen as symptom; often it is guesswork and conjecture with only a mediocre chance that a guess is good'.[85]

After 1908, a number of physical causes were added in the national records and the cause 'grief' disappeared.

Grief is a broad concept, but it is not inconceivable that grief came to be associated with cellular life in the case of prisoners. It is certain, in any case, that, for many years grief was named almost *five times* as often for more than 800 admitted prisoners than was done nationally and even more often than was done with the 'non-imputables', as can be seen in Table 7.4. I have registered there how often 'grief' was named as causal and how large a proportion it formed of the totality of causes. 'Cause unknown' was filled in more often for prisoners than in the national records (and, even more often, for 'non-imputables'), something which also can be seen as significant.[86]

Of the more than 800 prisoners who were admitted to Medemblik, approximately ninety per cent had been sentenced to solitary confinement. The remainder had been under remand, awaiting trial. Of those sentenced, more than sixty per cent had committed a crime of property. The admissions register had an entry for the punishments to which prisoners had been sentenced. Approximately a third had received cellular confinement for a year or less, two-thirds had been sentenced to longer punishment. Almost fifteen per cent had had to endure four to six years of imprisonment in as far as mental problems had not led, in the meanwhile, to admission to Medemblik. The large majority of sentences in The Netherlands was short (less than one year). Those with long sentences ended up comparatively often in Medemblik, a fact which could again be said to point to a strong influence of solitary confinement on insanity.

Records of Admitted Prisoners

For practically every prisoner who had become insane and had been transferred to Medemblik, files have been kept as well.[87] These are folders in which admissions reports, observation reports of nurses, forms filled in by prison governors or doctors, letters from lawyers, public prosecutors, family members and the prisoners themselves, and loose notes from the doctor-director have been collected.

To gain an impression of what these records reveal, I investigated all those which had been kept for admissions of prisoners to Medemblik in 1900, a date I chose because, by then, the cellular system was through its growing pains. There were thirty-two records. Prisoners were brought into the institution confused, exhausted, rebellious, apathetic, and sometimes covered with wounds. They sometimes stayed stubbornly quiet, they sometimes told all about their delusions of poisoning, hallucinations, fears and neurotic complaints, and they sometimes could be found singing in the common rooms after a number of weeks. Men with red beards, black men with threatening voices, mothers who whispered their insistence that one slit one's wrists and police chiefs who unremittingly gave the order 'jerk off', populated the cells of these prisoners. In long letters to judges or doctors, they described their paranoid ideas in which conspiracies spread far over the country's borders by means of warders. They wrote letters filled with love and hope to family members and loved ones and received letters from mothers who continued to love them in spite of all the shame the family had felt as a result of their crimes and imprisonment.

Family members tried through letters to the doctor-director Frijlinck to reclaim the black but still beloved sheep. Some mothers begged for the freedom of their child. 'And his constitution can't stand it at all, he's much too nervous to be cooped up,' wrote a desperate mother to the doctor-director about her nineteen-year-old son.[88] The brother of a prisoner expressed, on behalf of his family, his surprise about the admission, in a lightly indignant tone. He placed the guilt with the cellular prison regime:

> Now that it has finally come this far, I must still lament even more deeply the fact that my brother is deprived of his freedom. It is obvious, in my opinion, that lack of freedom, continuously being lonely and alone, also in his thoughts, the lack of outside air which he was so used to, the interrogation from time to time, are so many causes for the worsening of the illness, if not the cause of its very existence.[89]

It was not only family members who saw a connection with solitary confinement. In almost every file, references are made to the bad influence of prison life. In the majority, 'grief' is filled in as the cause. He is 'suffering from an acute psychosis, probably under the influence of solitary confinement. At present, he is healthy. His resistance is still so low, however, that he would not be able to withstand the damaging influence of the cell', wrote doctor-director Frijlinck, for example, to the college of regents from the prison in Rotterdam which had asked for further information.[90]

These are general impressions which do not do justice to the rich but sad contents of the separate files. The more thorough description of some files does that a little better. The first prisoner admitted in 1900 was a seventeen-year-old boy. Paranoia was the diagnosis. The cause was thought to have to do with both 'grief' and 'heredity'. The boy had been guilty of theft along with others and had received a sentence of nine months in the cell. After a little more than a half year he had been transferred from the cellular prison in Rotterdam to Medemblik. 'Patient was brought here this afternoon. He has a very pale face and ill appearance. Speaks complainingly, says he feels very weak; and has suffered much from rotten and acid food; which he was offered by warders in the prison who were teasing him', was written down in the admissions report.

The young man thought he had been poisoned. He was continuously very sad and sunk in sombre thought. He complained of pain in his stomach and legs. He was afraid to be murdered by fellow-patients in Medemblik. For fear that his head would be cut off, he tried to escape. Fear of poisoning moved him to refuse to eat in Medemblik. Before his admission, the young man had gone through hell in prison. The doctor of the prison reported that the boy was irritable and nervous. As idiosyncrasy he mentioned masturbation. Drunkenness, heredity and shutting away in prison were thought to lie at the root of his insanity. Isolation had been tried as a 'remedy'. During his stay in the cellular prison at Rotterdam, disciplinary punishments had been imposed eight times. In half a year he had spent fifty-seven days in the punishment cell, first every other day on bread and water and later 'in chains' as well. Twice he was placed in an unheated punishment cell for two weeks at a stretch. The punishments were imposed because he screamed through the ventilation flaps, was subordinate to a warder and called him a liar, screamed through the cell door, beat upon the cell door, continuously sought contact with fellows by tapping, disturbed the peace and order, spoke out in the cellular church, broke the windows in his cell and refused to appear before the governor. Right before his admission he had spent eight days in the punishment cell.[91]

This prisoner's delusions were rather mild. Others were more comprehensive and grew into a prison psychosis. A thirty-four-year-old man was transferred to Medemblik after almost five months in the cellular prison at Arnhem. He had been sentenced to one year in the cell because of culpable bankrupcy. He had always been mentally healthy, as far as anyone knew. As the cause of his illness, which was called paranoia hallucinatoria, the prison doctor stated 'probably the stay in the cell'.

One week before his admission, the man announced that the warders snapped at him, again and again: 'he's going to Leeuwarden' (the penitentiary for those with long sentences). Everywhere where he went, he heard this. Then he said he was being spied upon by two men who mocked him and 'repeated everything that he said'. He could not move his face lest they say that he was laughing. He could not read lest they repeated everything. He could not even read 'silently' because they still repeated everything. The two sat up in a corner of his cell where the wires for the electricity were. 'He had already broken the window. Finally, he refused all food and drink because they were poisoned (mercury). In the evening, he screamed for fear of his stool pigeons, as he calls them,' wrote the doctor.

At his admission to Medemblik, he had an 'ill, suffering appearance'. He said little and did not understand why he had been transferred. He was dejected. He did complain a lot about the treatment in Arnhem. The warders 'bullied' and teased him. He did not trust the food in Medemblik either. He thought snails had been mixed into it to make him sick. He was comparatively calm but would not eat and suffered from hallucinations of hearing. There were 'stool pigeons' in his mouth and ears who told his thoughts to others. According to one of the first observation reports, he heard voices of the warders from the prison at Arnhem:

> They say everything that he does and that he thinks. 'Now he's laughing again, now he's looking to that side, now he wants to start reading again, he's not reading, now he is, etc. etc.' This goading keeps him from sleeping and when he asks if they won't stop they say yes, but they hoodwink him, they don't stop at all. They accuse him, 'you have struck at a glass window and broken it'. He hears them say, 'we can see you'. They work on him with a whistle, a whistle like those used in steam merry-go-rounds.

He was visibly improved even after a week. The fear of poisoning disappeared completely and the hallucinations of his hearing appeared less often. After two weeks it was stated that his condition continued to improve. 'His appetite remains good, his sleep is calm as well.' Quite quickly the man himself expressed his surprise about the delusions of poisoning and hallucinations. The observation report says, after one month, 'we are dealing here with a simple prison psychosis whereby discontinuance of the solitude has removed the cause and made way for quick recovery'. Doctor-director Frijlinck succeeded in preventing the return of this man to prison. At his intercession, he was pardoned.[92]

Most files from 1900 show evidence of long suffering with a less happy ending. Three prisoners died at Medemblik and some were placed in a normal insane asylum after the end of their term of punishment. I studied only thirty-two files of prisoners who ended up at Medemblik while approximately 800 are available in archives.[93] A study of all the files would, doubtlessly, give a more detailed image, but the data in this chapter sufficiently show how ignorant and unenlightened nineteenth century politicians and prison experts were in their judgements of the psychic effects of cellular punishment.

Power and Impotence behind Bars

This chapter has been concerned with the psychic effects of solitary confinement. The book in its entirety is concerned with power and impotence behind bars. As far as prisoners were concerned, power was slight and impotence huge. The necessity of severe punishment and harsh disciplinary measures was still generally recognized, but, both within criminology and the science of criminal justice, views that made the legitimizing of severe punishment more difficult gained ground. Gradually, the personalities of prisoners began to be given more attention than their crimes. The reports of the government inspectorate for mental health show that this shift from crime to criminal began to undermine the justification of disciplinary punishments in particular. In the report for the years 1909–11, the inspectors point out that from the outset 'the personality of the prisoner' must be taken into account as much as possible. 'Systematic insubordination and action undertaken against house rules appears in many cases to arise from not have taken this into account,' they wrote. By immediately adding as their 'second principle' that a prisoner must be given the feeling 'that the direction can see him off, has the superior power, that the warders are not afraid of him', they also indicated the tension that existed between emancipatory developments and the exercise of power. That this tension could be felt was, at the same time, an *aspect* of the shifting balance of power between those punished and their punishers.[94]

In practice, the second principle was paid strict attention to for the time being. In 1897, the 'Boonenoproer' (the bean riots) broke out in the cellular prison at Amsterdam. The whole of one night prisoners expressed their discontent with the bad heating and ventilation and the poor food by screaming, beating on the cell doors and 'making short work of everything in their cells which could in any way be broken'. The direct cause of the riot was the presence of stones and sand in their brown beans. Right in the middle of the riot, a new director, who instituted severe measures, was appointed. A large number of rebels were put into punishment cells for two to four weeks, on bread and water and in chains. They were also prosecuted for damage to government property, so that their sentences were extended by several months. During the riot, government constables stood at the ready in the wings and on the grounds with rifles 'to shoot anyone dead who would manage to leave his cell'.[95]

Attacks upon authority were dealt with harshly in other places as well, as can be seen from one annual report of the inspectorate. In November 1910, the communally confined prisoners at Leeuwarden rebelled against the firing of a presumably quite flexible servant in the work area. This servant had been fired, in their opinion, because an emotionally labile fellow convict had squealed on him. They no longer tolerated this stool pigeon on the work floor. A prisoner who acted as spokesman against the director was immediately placed in a punishment cell. Five other prisoners were successively brought to punishment cells because they came into action in the same way. The dispute seemed to have been settled for a moment, but shortly thereafter a convict threw a pail of water over the head of the stool pigeon and was removed to a punishment cell. During lunch in the common room, the fourteen remaining prisoners protested once again against the presence of the stool pigeon. Three of them were consequently brought to a punishment cell. 'Thereafter the meal took place without further disturbance,' noted the inspectors in their report.

In the evening it appeared that the rebellion had not left the stool pigeon unaffected. In his alcove he made quite a racket, 'he moaned and groaned, swore and screamed' and sang hymns. With broken glass from a bottle he attempted suicide, but this was seen as a feigned attempt. The stool pigeon was allowed to recover from his wounds for three weeks on the hospital ward and was then placed in a punishment cell 'because he had wounded himself'. Peace had already returned to the prison by this time, 'very certainly thanks to policy, the tact of the director and the functionaries who stood by him'. First in the presence of two policemen and later without guarding the stool pigeon was finally returned to the communal hall 'without this provoking any further difficulties'.[96]

NOTES

1. Statement of the German scholar of criminal justice, Temme. Quoted (in German) in Modderman, 1861, p. 151.
2. Schneevoogt, 1848, pp. 199, 218–9, 223–4, 230–3.
3. Casparie, 1912, p. 209.
4. Veldhoen and Van Ree, 1980, pp. 93, 110.
5. Casparie, 1912, pp. 228–9, 233.
6. See CBS-prison statistics, 1886–1914.
7. See, for example, the articles in *De Jonge Gids* by Herman Heyermans, 1898/99, and Maür, 1898/99. See also Olnon, 1986, pp. 94–9.
8. Concerning the implementation of the Bertillon system, see: KB, 22 Feb. 1896, Sb., 1896, no. 32; circular MvJ, 21 Jan. 1897, no. 121; circular MvJ, 29 Apr. 1898, no. 155, in *Verzameling van wetten (...)*,

1860–1905. See also: *Bertillonage (…)*, around 1895.

9. Dekker, 1910, pp. 195–6.
10. Metz, 1904/05, pp. 25–7.
11. *Stelsel, (…)*, around 1905, p. 12.
12. Dekker, 1910, p. 197.
13. *OHC*, 8 Feb. 1911, p. 5. See also J. J. Janssen, s.a.
14. Cf. *AC*, 24 Sep. 1914, p. 3.
15. Cf. *Enquête over (…)*, 1897/98, pp. 707–8.
16. Dekker, 1910, p. 200; cf. Elst, 1899, p. 150.
17. Cf. Dekker, 1910, pp. 101, 104.
18. Metz, 1904/05, pp. 39–44.
19. Elst, 1899, p. 149.
20 In The Netherlands, secret notes were destroyed, but in Italy, Lombroso came into possession of a large number of secret messages from prisoners. He published these (and texts which he found on cell walls, furniture, plates and in books) unabridged. See Lomboso, s.a., p. 7.
21. *Stelsel (…)*, around 1905, p. 12.
22. *NRC*, 18 Feb. 1906. See also editions from 22, 25 and 27 Feb. 1906 (feature 'Onder de menschen').
23. *Balans*, 1981, no. 6/7, pp. 26–8. All numerical data is derived from prison statistics which were produced by CBS after 1900.
24. From prison statistics 1880–1910. National mortality percentages for men come from Wever, 1940, p. 99.
25. Dekker, 1910, p. 205.
26. Metz, 1904/05, p. 47.
27. *NRC*, 22 Feb. 1906.
28. Dekker, 1910, pp. 205–6.
29. Dekker, 1910, pp. 192–4.
30. Metz, 1904/05, pp. 12, 55.
31. *NRC*, 18 Feb. 1906.
32. Feith, 1909, pp. 173, 197–8, 207. See also *NRC*,, 25 Feb. 1906.
33. CBS prison statistics for 1907, pp. xxxv–xxxvi.
34. CBS prison statistics for 1902, p. xxiii.
35. In prison statistics, appreciable differences existed between the number of explicitly reported suicides and the number that could be deduced from the also reported list of causes of death. It was regularly noted as well that medical men did not report as suicides incidents of suicide or 'sudden death' with which they had not been called to help. Apparently, doctors also existed who thought they could not report suicide as a cause of death and instead filled in 'heart attack' or 'suffocation' on the CBS tally cards. (Prison statistics for 1909, p. xxxii, and for 1917, pp. xxxviii and xxxix.) In 1903, a state commission asked prison directors to report the number of suicides and attempted suicides in the last two years. They reported fewer suicides than were registered in the prison statistics, but the number of attempts (forty-three) was much higher.(*Rapport van de Staatscommissee (…)*, 1904, pp. 203–4). An external control on these numbers did not exist. It will have occurred, therefore, that suicides were glossed over in order to save face for the prison. This held even more for attempted suicides.

36. CBS prison statistics for 1907, p. xxxvi.
37. *De Telegraaf*, 10 Dec. 1903.
38. Cf. Circular 21 Mar. 1905, no. 392, in *Verzameling van wetten (...)*, 1860–1905; Eggink, 1958, p. 123.
39. Circular 21 Dec. 1891, no. 144; circular 16 Mar. 1893, no. 190; KB, 31 May 1893, no. 55. In the report of government inspectorate for the years 1891–3, inclusive, 27–9. The annual reports can be perused at the Library of the University of Amsterdam.
40. Data for the years 1887–91 were derived from prison statistics. Thereafter, I used the more trustworthy data from the 'Reports of the government inspectorate on the insane and insane asylums and over the state of the asylums'. These reports appeared periodically and therefore contain many cumulative figures for periods of three to six years. After 1912, the figures were no longer specified as to institution (penitentiary, house of detention, borstal or government work institution).
41. From the annual reports of the government inspectorate. See, for instance, the report for 1913, pp. 58–9.
42. All these data come from the annual reports of the government inspectorate.
43. Cf. *Rapport van de commissie (...)*, 1895, p. 1010.
44. See Haffmans, 1986 and 1989, and Hofstee, 1987. This TBR-measure of the government for convicts, aimed at compulsory treatment in a psychiatric institution, is still an important component of the Dutch administration of criminal justice. Only the name has been changed in the meantime from TBR to TBS.
45. Cf. Geuns, 1899, p. 406. See also Roos, 1900, pp. 135–45.
46. Cf. Pouw, 1988, pp. 86–7.
47. *Rapport van de commissie (...)*, 1895, pp. 1003, 1006.
48. Visser, 1896, pp. 57–9.
49. Meijer, 1899, pp. 401–7, 410–11. See also Meijer, 1899 ['Staatszorg(...)']; Winkler, 1905, and Geuns, 1899.
50. *Winkler Prins Encyclopedie*, 7th ed, part VIII, p. 50. See also Amir, 1932, pp. 926–7.
51. Theunissen, 1916, pp. 409–16; see also Amir, 1932, pp. 926–7.
52. Jelgersma, around 1908, part II, pp. 1, 143, 145.
53. In 1916, the psychiatrist Theunissen explained that it was particularly the 'special aetiology' that distinguished prison psychosis. Just as particular life occurrences associated with a strong affect lent a certain direction to the delusions of psychosis, so too experiences of prisoners – prosecution, trial and punishment – expressed themselves in the nature of their delusions. Theunissen, 1916, pp. 416–31.
54. Jelgersma, about 1908, part I, pp. 271–2; part II, pp. 1, 372.
55. Annual government inspection reports for 1894–6, p. 47.
56. Annual government inspection reports for 1894–6, p. 44.
57. Annual government inspection reports for 1903–8, pp. 129–30.
58. Annual government inspection reports for 1909–11, pp. 105, 138.
59. Annual government inspection reports for 1894–6, p. 43.
60. Annual government inspection reports for 1894–6, p. 55.
61. See Hare, 1962, for the history of ideas about relationships between masturbation and insanity.

62. Annual government inspection reports for 1891–3, p. 34; 1894–6, pp. 41, 43, 44, 45, 55; 1897–9, pp. 42, 43, 45.
63. Annual government inspection reports for the years 1909–11, p. 138; 1899–1901, pp. 36–7.
64. A horrible description of the 'startling cries' that reverberated through the night as 'a brain surrendered to the weight of black emptiness', is included in Boeke and Van Mierop, 1920, pp. 53–6.
65. What is meant here is probably Sequoyah (around 1770–1843), a famous Cherokee chief. Annual reports for 1894–6, p. 43.
66. Annual government inspection reports for 1909–11, p. 124.
67. Annual government inspection reports for 1903–8, p. 126.
68. Annual government inspection reports for 1903–8, p. 156.
69. Annual government inspection reports for 1903–8, p. 142.
70. Casparie, 1912, quotes on pp. 192–5, 212, 221, 225–6.
71. Annual government inspection report for 1912, table on p. 58.
72. Casparie, 1912, pp. 202–5.
73. Idem, pp. 208–9.
74. Cf. Pouw, 1988.
75. Kat, 1907, p. 224.
76. Annual government inspection report for 1913, p. 21; 1914, p. 37; see also Deknatel, 1913.
77. Over and above this, between 1884 and 1906 an extra 249 people were transferred to Medemblik from the government work institution. I could not discover how many these accounted for after 1906. Figures come from the admissions registers of the government insane asylum at Medemblik, which are available for perusal in the government archives for Noord-Holland in Haarlem. See also Kat, 1907, p. 219.
78. I derived yearly figures about this from annual reports of the government inspectorate for the insane and insane asylums. Those from Medemblik come from the admissions registers.
79. Mania acuta, mania chronica, melancholica attonita, stupiditas post maniam, hallucinationes, insania cyclica, insania epileptica, insania hysterica, insania moralis, vecordia, paralysis cerebri, dementia, imbecillitas idiotia hydrocephalica, imbecillitas idiotia atrophica.
80. Mania, melancholica, amentia, insania periodica, insania epileptica, insania neurotica, insania toxica, paranoia, paralitica, dementia, imbecillitas, idiotia.
81. Jelgersma, about 1908; Wijsman, about 1890; Vijselaar, 1985.
82. Jelgersma, about 1908, part II, pp. 1, 23–4.
83. Jelgersma, about 1908, part II, pp. 2, 23–36.
84. Acute sicknesses, chronic sicknesses, heredity, critical period for a woman, excesses in one's sexual life, misuse of alcohol, hardship, old age, excessive work with one's mind, exaggerated religious zeal, grief, shock-anxiety-wrath.
85. Annual government inspection reports for 1909–11, p. 313.
86. Because more than one cause was sometimes reported, the total number of causes named (923 for prisoners and 685 for 'non-imputables'), including 'unknown', exceeds the numbers of prisoners and 'non-imputables' who were lodged at Medemblik.

87. These records are open to perusal in the Government archives of Noord-Holland in Haarlem.
88. Record no. 2418.
89. Record no. 2482.
90. Record no. 2477.
91. Record no. 2349.
92. Record no. 2389.
93. With thanks to Frans Koenraadt (Rijksuniversiteit Utrecht), who made me aware of the important contents of these files.
94. Annual government inspection reports for 1909–11, p. 105.
95. Noordhof, 1922, pp. 149–50; NRC, 13 Oct. 1928 (interview with the director who put down the insurrection); Feith, 1909, pp. 91–2.
96. Annual government inspection reports for 1909–11, pp. 125–6.

8

Wilful Sinners or Born Criminals: The Cell System Under Attack

Modern criminology is deterministic. … It searches, therefore, for the foundations of expressions of the will that we call crimes. It searches for these foundations not in the free will, but in the organism of the criminal, and in the circumstances which can influence either this organism or his deeds directly. It searches for these foundations in real life, builds on the obtained results means to combat crime and works out whether these answer to the double goal: reducing crime and protecting society against it.[1]

In 1909, the lawyer, J. A. van Hamel, was surprised about the cruelty of penal practice of a century ago. He asked himself 'with some shock' what might be said in another hundred years 'reproaching what we uphold in penal practice'.[2] Van Hamel could not know that diverse beliefs from his time would be taken over by the *Kriminalbiologen* in Nazi Germany. This, indeed, makes it difficult to look back on his time without 'reproach'. This looking back is made even more difficult by the unusual complexity of the penal and criminological domain at the turn of the century. New theories which were both passionately welcomed and contested, were developed about the foundations of criminal law, causes of crime, systems of punishment, indeed, about everything having to do with crime and punishment.[3]

At the beginning of the twentieth century, The Netherlands and the Western world viewed punishment, crime, criminals, prisons and prisoners differently than in the nineteenth century. A new science, *criminal anthropology*, had unsettled conventional thinking about crime and punishment. Lawyers translated the new scientific insights into far-reaching proposals for the reform of penal practice. They gave form to what quickly came to be called the *Nieuwe Richting* (New Direction) in penal law. In the United States at almost the same time *reformatories* were set up. They were, in numerous ways, diametrically opposed to the cellular system that, in The Netherlands, had been put into practice more rigidly than in

any other European country. Finally, socialists began to involve themselves with the prison system.

It now becomes a matter of extracting from the mass of new insights
and proposals those which came to have a lasting influence on penal
practice, particularly on the life of prisoners. As far as life went *within*
prison walls, this influence was very limited for some time to come, but
particularly the newly instituted 'voorwaardelijke veroordeling' (suspended
sentence) would lead to more convicts remaining *outside* prison. Only
after the war, much began to change within the walls as well. Without
some knowledge of what politicians, scholars and penal experts thought,
felt and proposed around 1900, these changes cannot be understood.

The Influence of Darwin

The origin of the most important development in the penal area lay in
Darwin's theory of evolution, which was expanded upon by the Italian
psychiatrist Cesare Lombroso in a book which became very well-known:
L'uomo delinquente. Shortly after its appearance in 1876, this book came to
be seen as a revolutionary breakthrough in what was then still called
criminalistics. Lombroso seemed to have established with scientific exacti-
tude that many criminals had been born with physical and mental
characteristics which predestined them to a criminal life. The *delinquente
nato*, the born criminal, made his entry into considerations about crime
and punishment. Lombroso described the born criminal as a creature
who had become stalled in the evolution of the human species. This
phenomenon, which also was thought to occur in animals, was called
atavism by Darwin.

In 1890 the atavism-hypothesis was defended by J. M. A. Kramps. He
explored the necessity for protection against born criminals and other
'anti-social creatures'. The 'microbes of crime' had to be handled with
'the same prophylactic methods' as the microbes of pathogenic bacteriol-
ogy. He wanted to lock born criminals up in prisons 'sans le nom', as
Lombroso also had characterized the places in which atavists should be
confined, but he admitted that this did not agree 'with our concepts'. But
he still felt he had to 'confess' that this would be the only radical way 'of
being delivered of that irredeemable race'. He compared this to the
destruction of sick animals in livestock.[4]

Building on Darwin's theories of natural selection, the Italian baron,
R. Garofalo, a disciple of Lombroso, made a plea for capital punishment
and the banning of criminals to uninhabited islands as a form of 'artificial
selection by the state'. He spoke of 'elimination of the elements least
suited to social life'. Because this would also ensure that reproduction of
these elements did not take place, he expected 'a moral improvement of
the species'.[5]

In the opinion of the Dutch criminal lawyer, J. R. B. de Roos, feelings of solidarity with one's fellow-man and more humane concepts would led to resistance to such proposals in The Netherlands. Moreover, he thought the selection theory to be very dangerous. Carried to its extreme, it would necessitate 'spontaneous butchery' of all those who were defective, incurably ill, idiotic, mentally deranged, sick, alcoholic, degenerate and living as prostitutes. A criterion which selected only criminals was lacking and few dead criminals would not improve the species. De Roos called the pleas for the death penalty 'a miscarriage of the positive school' of Lombroso.[6]

In spite of stubborn resistance by Lombroso, the atavistic criminal was rather generally rejected. It was, however, replaced by new characterizations of criminals corrupt to the core as degenerates, *fous morales*, inferiors, defectives, ethical defectives and the unbalanced. These were not thought to result from evolutionary regression, but from criminal predisposition augmented from generation to generation. They came into the world hereditarily burdened. The criminal behaviour of their ancestors, perhaps caused by unfavourable external circumstances, had gradually become fixed in the hereditary material. In 1892, the psychiatrist, Jelgersma, thought all degenerates to have been 'abnormal persons' from the outset and their whole psyches to be sick 'to their very foundations'. 'Criminals are a separate breed of the mentally ill', stated Jelgersma.[7]

J. G. Patijn, Solicitor General of the Supreme Court (of The Netherlands) criticized the atavism concept more fundamentally. He pointed to changes in social concepts of good and bad. He said that stories of cruelty in earlier times should only be seen as evidence that people in those times had had 'totally different ideas' from 'us, children of the nineteenth century'.[9] Attention paid to physical and mental characteristics dominated everything and distracted attention away from social causes, which were seen as very important by Patijn. He was not alone in this, because, coincident with the theoretical movement inspired by Darwin, a sociological movement was developing which was just as revolutionary.

Sociological Explanations of Crime

Interest in social causes of crime was partially a reevaluation of insights developed by the Belgians, Adolphe Quetelet and Edouard Ducpétiaux, and the Frenchman, A. M. Guerry, in the 1830s and 1840s.[9] These moral statisticians analysed statistics covering several years and discovered much regularity in total amount of crime. They concluded from this that crime reflected socioeconomic characteristics of society as a whole. Their work did not have much influence at first, but when the German, Georg (von) Mayr, very concretely showed in 1867 that the number of sentences for theft rose and fell with increases and decreases in prices of grain, interest was rekindled. The sociological school of thought within the criminal anthropology gained most of its influence, however, through its criticism of the work of Lombroso.

When Lombroso defended his opinions at the first congress for Criminal Anthropology in Rome in 1885, he was subjected to harsh criticism from the French scholars Lacassagne, Manouvrier and Tarde, among others. They thought that particularly the social *environment* made people commit crimes and they pointed to factors such as climate, seasons, temperature, the cost of housing and foodstuffs, legal status, living conditions and opportunities for crime. They did not yet propagate a truely sociological vision. It is true that Lacassagne had expressed his view in Rome which later became a classic, that societies 'have the criminals that they deserve', but, in another statement, which became almost as famous, he appeared only to want to place a different emphasis on causes of crime than Lombroso had done. He called the social environment 'le bouillon de culture de la criminalité' (the hotbed of crime). He compared criminals to microbes that only began to multiply in specific breeding-conditions.[10] That insight is still far from sociological notions of social constructions and definitions of crime and its social functions.

After Rome and Paris, criminological anthropological congresses followed in Brussels (1892), Geneva (1896) and Amsterdam (1901), during which the Italian and the French school came closer and closer to each other. The Italian, Enrico Ferri, in particular, made a case for a multi-causal theory. The book *Sociologie Criminelle,* in which he worked out that vision, became thicker with every reprinting, because he continued to discover new causal factors. Baron Garofalo described the fusion between the two schools aptly when he said: 'Circumstances do not make the thief, but circumstances make the thief steal'. Even Lombroso included more and more climatic and social circumstances in his later work, but he still passionately defended his *delinquente nato* at the congress in Amsterdam.[11]

The fusion between the two schools, also called *biosociology,* led more to a watering-down than a deepening of the sociological perspective. It was especially outside the community of criminal-anthropologists that sociological insights were developed which did go further than searching for causes in social conditions. Just before the end of the century, the sociologist, Emile Durkheim, wrote that a society without crime was unimaginable. He called crime a normal phenomenon, bound to the fundamental conditions of every social life. Criminals made obvious where the boundaries of public morality lay. They promoted the feeling of solidarity between persons and thus the level of integration of society as well.[12] These are not insights happily embraced by those fighting crime and perhaps, because of this, Durkheim played an almost negligible role in the thinking about crime and punishment in the beginning of the twentieth century.

The socialists were much more influential. Within and outside parliament, they painted criminals as victims of a criminal society within which owners of the means of production became rich at the cost of non-owners. The socialist view was written down, in a scientific tone with the use of many statistics, in 1905, by the Dutch sociologist and socialist, W. A. Bonger, in his famous Ph.D. thesis *Criminalité et conditions économiques.* Bonger showed, in contrast to the French environment-school, a good eye for the social construction of crime, but his thesis focussed attention especially on the considerable influence of economic conditions, by which, it is important to remember, he meant much more than the quantity of material ownership.[13]

The fact that it was no longer possible to speak of crime and punishment at the turn of the century without also speaking of society was clearly expressed by the lawyer de Roos. He called the distinction between anthropological and social factors much too simple. 'He who studies the individual, studies the group as well, because, reflected within one individual are the idiosyncrasies of group and society,' de Roos wrote.[14]

The Nieuwe Richting *(New Direction) in Criminal Law*

Though representatives of the anthropological and sociological schools of thought fought each other tooth and nail at congresses and in articles, they were unanimous on one important point: the behavior of criminals was determined by causes upon which criminals themselves could not have exerted an influence. This deterministic view of criminal behaviour, together with the dominant interest in the personality of criminals, pulled the rug out from familiar concepts of criminal law. Sin, guilt, responsibility, culpability and free will lost all meaning within the deterministic way of thinking. And, if criminals had no culpable guilt for their crimes, on what foundations could one continue to punish?

In 1883, the Austrian, Franz von Liszt, taking up his post as professor at the University of Marburg, translated the pressure to adapt penal concepts into an oration which would enter criminal law history as the *Marburger Programm.* His revolutionary speech was titled 'The goal concept in penal law'. In a determined tone, von Liszt held forth that punishment had historically developed from a 'blind, instinctive, vehement reaction' to crime, into a form of 'purposive protection of legal interests'. Punishment was supposed to satisfy a future goal, and only if this occurred, was it legitimate. Punishment is a means to an end, said von Liszt. He rejected punishment directed at the past as retribution and revenge. Von Liszt distinguished three ways in which the intended goal could be reached: improvement (that is to say, through instilling and strengthening altruistic, social motives), deterrence and incapacitation or 'the sequestering of socially defective individuals'. These three methods of punishing were thought to correspond to three groups of criminals, which had be proven to exist by criminal anthropology: *Gelegenheitsverbrecher, Besserungsbedürftigen* and *Unverbesserlichen* (opportunistic criminals, corrigibles and incorrigibles).

Opportunistic criminals who had been driven to their deeds by external factors had only to be deterred by deprivation of freedom. He wanted to confine criminals with hereditary and acquired tendencies to crime and needing improvement for one to five years in a house of correction. Only the first period would have to be carried out in solitude. Each year a check had to take place as to whether or not they were sufficiently improved to be freed under police supervision. The incorrigible habitual criminals, among whom he included beggars, vagabonds, prostitutes, alcoholics, thieves, the degenerate and the demi-monde, who were seen as threatening the social order, did not have to look to von Liszt for mercy. He spoke of letting predators loose on the public. Society had to protect itself from these incorrigibles. He rejected the solutions of cutting off their heads, hanging them or deportation, thus there remains only imprisonment for life or for an indeterminate period.

At the end of his speech, von Liszt powerfully summarized the goal-oriented nature of his system. Not the crime did determine the punishment, but the question of what was most appropriate for 'this' criminal or 'this' thief, with an eye to the future and societal protection. 'Not the concept but the perpetrator is punished'. He maintained that only with the help of criminal anthropology could the battle against criminal sickness lead to victory.[15]

Von Liszt's speech became the program of principles for the *New Direction* in criminal law. Everything said or written by representatives of the new politics of criminal law after this speech until far into the twentieth century showed clear traces of the *Marburger Programm*. The Belgian lawyer, Adolphe Prins, and the Dutch lawyer, G. A. van Hamel, very quickly set themselves up as disseminators of the new principles. Together with von Liszt, they founded the International Society for Criminal Law in 1889. Van Hamel showed himself to be a powerful and extremely active spokesman of the *New Direction*. In numerous speeches and articles, he again and again defended separate punishment of opportunistic criminals and habitual criminals, corrigible or not, as a form of *défense sociale* or 'criminal politics'. Most of his attention was focussed on habitual criminals, whom he alternatively called degenerates, the 'morally insane' or 'instinctive criminals'. He thought they had to be *treated* by doctors or rendered '*harmless*'. He even thought that forbidding marriage to prevent their reproduction was justified.[16] In 1890, he said they 'contained a threat of degeneration for a future descendents'.[17]

Van Hamel never carried out any criminal-anthropological research himself. He particularly favoured such innovations in criminal law as indeterminate sentences, *prison-asiles* for 'the mentally deficient', suspended sentences, different treatment for neglected children and a differentiated treatment for recidivists. Presently, most references to van Hamel and the *New Direction* are full of praise, the influence upon later 'humanizing' reforms being mentioned in particular.[18] The fact that the *New Direction*, in order to deal with a vaguely described group of degenerates, advocated a dubiously based rock-hard policy of incapacitate persons and of far-reaching medical treatment, which evokes associations with Nazi *Kriminalbiologie*, is usually forgotten or glossed over with an appeal to the spirit of the times. But, characteristic of the *New Direction* as it developed in The Netherlands, was precisely the partial mitigation and partial harshening of the practice of criminal law that was advocated. This led to members of the *New Direction* sometimes being accused of sickly philanthropy as well as inhuman harshness by conservative opponents.

Resistance to the New Concepts

For the legal profession based in Christian ideology, the so-called scientifically proven indefensibility of concepts such as sin, free will, guilt, revenge, responsibility and culpability was tantamount to heresy. J. Domela Nieuwenhuis, professor of criminal law, believed that the criminal anthropologists wanted to smooth away punishment and guilt, so that only 'measures for social defence' remained to combat 'anti-social deeds'. He felt that the *New Direction* saw crime as 'simply a natural phenomenon' that occurred according to unchangeable natural laws. What would then be left of retribution 'to all of those determined victims who could not help what they did?' Magistrates were no longer the arms of 'punishing justice' but members of 'the preventive police'.[19] The professor of criminal law, D. P. D. Fabius, spoke of 'the terrorism of unbelief'. Punishment, in his opinion, could never be anything other than 'earned and imposed suffering for culpable evil'. He thought that if the criterion of danger were used, all that was punishable could be enormously expanded or contracted. Penal law would be 'dissolved':

> Justice disappears more and more. Guilt is denied; the tenet of responsibility for one's actions pushed aside; moral responsibility banned from criminal law; the idea of retribution declared dead; punishment replaced by preventive measures; and justice swallowed up in the omnipotence of society. Pray, is this progress in penal science or its downfall?[20]

Domela Nieuwenhuis and Fabius were not real *spiritualists*, that is, declared adherents to the concept that the increase in unbelief led to more crime. They primarily attacked the lack of an ethical-religious groundwork to the new penal law. The Jesuit, F. Tummers, professor in ethical philosophy, added to this the spiritualist notion that religious training was the best means against crime. He thought that in denying an absolute, godly and ethical order, an important guarantee against arbitrary rule of the State was neglected. The public interest became, thereby, purely a political question. He felt that there would be nothing left to prevent the deterministic psychiatrists, the species biologists and the sociologists from using criminal law for their ideals 'whereby they act against crime in a way weaned of every ethical notion and judgement'.[21]

Confessional critics of the new concepts were primarily concerned that it would be every man for himself if the religious-ethical bases of penal law were let go. Traditional liberals were mainly upset by the huge confusion of concepts. The dangerous emphasis on psychiatry within penal law, the threat to individual freedom and the far-reaching leniency within the *New Direction* were thought to be built upon legal-philosophical quicksand. The lawyer, J. A. Nederburgh, member of the Supreme Court in the Dutch East Indies, showed that the denial of free will by the *New Direction* actually did not affect penal law. The chain of causes preceding an act of the will, he argued, did not count in penal law. Only evil will counted and, should this arise from bad character, even more severe punishment would be warranted. To preserve society it was necessary that people encounter resistance in punishable deeds. Nederburgh tried in this way to reinstate their old meaning to eroded concepts of deterrence and retribution. Improvement, protection and elimination of causes belonged to criminal anthropology and not to penal law.[22]

Feelings as well as ideas were at issue here. Representatives of the *New Direction* like van Hamel and the criminal anthropologist Aletrino allied their opinions to increased humanity. But the humane feelings of the *New Direction* were attacked by pointing out the inhuman cruelty of 'treatment' for an indeterminate period and the long term incapacitation of habitual criminals. It was specifically the lawyer Reinhart van der Meij, who made much of this. He stated that penal law was concerned with punishable deeds and not with personalities of the perpetrators. Penal law was not set up to consider motives. Improvement could then never be a goal of punishment.[23] Punishment which was not retribution and had nothing to do with guilt was, in van der Meij's opinion, absurd. If deprivation of freedom were to be purely aimed at protecting society, every reason for the imposition of suffering became invalid. And every criminal could easily say that 'a little trip South' would be more beneficial for his improvement than a couple of years inside.

Van der Meij lashed out viciously at the wish to shut mental defectives, the degenerate, the morally defective, the unbalanced and the incorrigibles up for an indeterminate period. He was of the opinion that these appellations were 'so vague and open to interpretation' that *all* criminals could easily be included. He called the indeterminate sentences 'a travesty of justice'. Criminals were robbed of their freedom 'until they have the good fortune that warders or psychiatrists feel like declaring them "cured", or they have become "non-dangerous" through stupefaction'. All this was thought to lead to more and more responsible persons being 'tried' by psychiatrists 'as if they were insane or under the legal age'. Now that proposals were being made to shut away 'dangerous' persons *before* they had done anything, van der Meij thought that everyone would run the risk of being shut away. 'The fact that we might *possibly* once commit an offense, makes us all dangerous until we are six feet under the sod,' was his opinion.[24]

All these penal and religious critics of the *New Direction* arrived at a defense of threatened concepts such as retribution, guilt, sin, responsibility and imputability. They rejected the perilous characterizations of perpetrators, goal-directed thinking in penal law, the emphasis on treatment and incapacitation and the displacement from deed to perpetrator as the criterion for the sentence. Their stance was mainly reactionary. The *scientific* criticism of the new concepts was not at all reactionary and even supported the concrete forms of criminal control and punishment which the *New Direction* stood for. The socialist and sociologist, W. A. Bonger, for instance, attacked biological explanations of crime and supported sociological explanations but, as the criminologist, van Weringh, remarked, he thought just as deterministically as the Lombrosian, Aletrino.[25] It was precisely this *determinism* which was the scientific heart of the *New Direction*. All the new criminological theories fixed their attention on the person of the perpetrator and social factors conducive to crime. They all put the familiar concepts of penal law such as punishment, guilt and retribution to the question. In doing this, they gave to the *New Direction* precisely the scientific status that supporters had hoped for and in which they believed strongly. Science was seen as capable of solving the problem of crime. Criminology was dominated by the 'diagnosis-therapy model'.[26]

An article of the psychologist G. Heymans, meaningfully entitled 'Excrescences of criminal anthropology' shows that even a scientific defense of the retribution principle certainly did not lead to a frontal collision with the *New Direction* in penal law. Heymans criticized the compilation of articles by Aletrino, published in 1898, which mainly furnished the lenient tendency within the *New Direction* with criminal-anthropological arguments.[27] Aletrino contended that the behaviour of criminals was completely determined, that free will did not exist, that nothing could be imputed to criminals and that they had to be dealt with as mentally ill. Heymans thoroughly attacked Aletrino's scientific argumentation in particular.[28] He himself proposed a concept of the will which left room for a 'moral awareness'. His idea was that this eliminated the objection against legitimacy of retribution, at least in as far as this rested upon denying a free will. But his conclusion was that 'the immoral will' had no right to exist and earned even the death penalty. Heymans also thought that in the 'treatment' of criminals it was right to take into account a degenerative predisposition. He supported suspended sentences, the abolishment of fixed sentences and harder proceedings against recidivists. The criminal anthropology, wrote Heymans, 'has at last brought to light the hereditary character of criminal tendencies and characteristics which predispose one to crime and thereby has justified the question of whether the transmission of crime could and should not be combatted by forbidding marriage or imprisoning for life.'[29] He said that the criminal anthropology had also proven that much criminals were 'once and for all unreceptive' to improvement. It is clear how Heymans, with his scientific defense of individual responsibility and guilt, arrived at similar *practical* conclusions to those of proponents of the *New Direction*.

Influence on Solitary Confinement

The practice of solitary confinement was changed hardly at all by these proposals up to the First World War. The Netherlands had just been filled with expensive, new prisons in which prisoners sat out sentences according to a brand new Penal Code. In an equally new Prison Act, the details had been established. Much had been expected of this in 1886. The disappointments had come to be felt relatively quickly. Numbers sentenced did not decrease and recidivism figures rose. And, while many prisoners suffered mentally without improving, outside prison walls at congresses and meetings, in books and articles, practically every concept which formed the bases upon which they had been imprisoned was being undermined. More and more experts began to say that criminals were actually mentally ill or mentally defective and that the imposition of suffering without any goal was thus not allowed, because they had committed crimes through hereditary tendencies or social conditions, both of which lay outside their own free will. Socialists even found, within the existing capitalistic society, every punishment of 'the victims' unjustified.

Other scholars divided prisoners into opportunistic criminals and habitual criminals. Solitary confinement could perhaps deter opportunistic criminals to some extent, but the shame of a prison record made it practically impossible for them to earn an honest living after their release. Furthermore, it was argued that many who were sentenced for short periods were not at all shocked by the prison and were thus delivered forever from their fear of punishment. It was, thus, important to search for alternatives for short sentences at the very least. Habitual criminals were not deterred at all. If the punishment were to be efficacious in their case, then they had to be improved, but the cell was judged unsuited for this goal. Improvement could only be achieved by treating them individually in reformatories, for as long as that took. Criminals who clearly could no longer be improved because their characters were corrupted by hereditary defects, could only be rendered 'harmless' by removing them from society, for life if necessary. But, they did not have to sit this time out in a cell.

Little was left to plead in favour of solitary confinement in the light of these new insights. Those who defended cellular confinement invited the suspicion that they wanted to impose suffering purely from feelings of revenge and retaliation. At the congress for criminal anthropology in Amsterdam (1901), Enrico Ferri spoke to them of the *esprit de vengeance* that dominated the system of punishment. He made a comparison between the mentally ill and criminals. Until Pinel took it upon himself to protect them in the Salpêtrière-hospital in Paris, the mentally ill were martyred, tortured and burnt. Pinel had shown that their deeds were determined and did not rest upon decisions of a free will. Ferri maintained that this was also true of criminals. Their deeds were the result of causes which had to be eliminated. The bolts and shackles would at some point end up in 'the museum of antiquities alongside the instruments of torture for the insane' where future generations 'would shrug their shoulders' thinking of us.[30] Ferri was rewarded with enthusiastic applause.

Solitary confinement was attacked in another way as well. Its salutary effect was thought to be rooted in the classical and strongly religious concept that criminals were sinners who had given in to evil tendencies of their own free will. But, new scholars with their deterministic vision did not see crime as resulting from free will, and thus concepts like guilt and sin disappeared like snow in summer. The process thought to take place in the soul of the prisoner in the cell did not even exist! The long chain of causes which had led prisoners into crime was only frustrated in its effect for the confinement period. Should these be causes of a social sort, they became even worse in the cell: marriages were strained and chances of legal bread-winning decreased further. Should these causes result from mental problems, the stultifying cell bred a couple of extras. Physically, the stay in a cell only made one weaker. Criminal talent remained untouched.

Proponents of cellular confinement thought that social functioning could be improved by isolating people socially. The belief that prisoners, in complete solitude, without meaningful social contacts, could become other and better persons, rested upon an image of man as *homo clausus*. It is obvious that this concept of man came to be undermined by the sociological movement within the criminal anthropology, the emergence of sociology as a science and socialism. Society was no longer to be understood as the sum of random individual deeds and, on the other hand, individual deeds could no longer be interpreted outside their social context. The deeds of most prisoners were no longer seen as crimes at all by socialists, whereas they saw the respectable behaviour of stock market speculators and directors of factories as severely criminal. Solitary confinement came to be seen by many as preposterous cruelty; the salvation by improvement that was expected of it a *contradictio in terminis*. Enrico Ferri could have scored very highly on a *citation-index* with his statement that solitary confinement was 'one of the greatest fallacies' of the nineteenth century. It also becomes understandable why this same Ferri was given genuine ovations at the criminal-anthropological congress in Amsterdam with his criticism of the cellular system.[31] Calls of 'bravo' were heard as a response to statements that the cell was 'inhuman' and 'apt to blow out the last flicker of social feeling still alive in the criminal'. Ferri was of the opinion that the thoughts of criminals in the cell went around in circles which invariably came out at the same point: crime. 'Where should better thoughts come from in these empty heads, when one shuts out with four frightening walls everything that could seed humanity and social feeling within this individual, poor in emotion?' Ferri asked. His opinion was that the criminal emerged from the cell just as empty as he entered it.[32]

Elmira: Reform as a Social Learning Process

One may conclude that, through the new concepts, the cellular system had changed from a showpiece into a millstone around the neck. In this atmosphere of crisis, reports reached The Netherlands from the United States about a new prison system that did seem to reduce figures for recidivism and that was founded on opinions which tallied with the new way of seeing criminals. The prison expert, Zebulon R. Brockway, had set up a *reformatory* in Elmira in which convicts could earn their freedom based on a *mark system*. Murderers who behaved themselves could be released after a short time, while burglars, if they did not watch out, might have to sit out their maximum sentence of several years. In fact, their punishment actually amounted to an indeterminate sentence.

In Elmira, each prisoner was subjected to a personalized educational program in which intellectual schooling, the learning of a trade and character-forming were the central themes. Prisoners had a lot of freedom. Disciplinary punishments were not imposed, in principle. When they had almost collected enough *marks* to be freed, work was sought for them. Only after a livelihood had been organized were they freed *on parole* and placed under supervision of a *transfer-officer*. Through continued good behaviour in freedom, definitive release could follow. After Elmira, similar reformatories were set up in other American states.

In contrast to the solitude of the cell, Elmira aspired to a far-reaching imitation of social life in freedom. The *homo clausus* idea thus, was not only opposed by sociological concept but also practical example. In

Elmira and other reformatories, one still hoped to effect a change in the interior of prisoners. Prisoners had to, and here lay the downfall of the cell, be given the chance to do good by means of a *social learning process* but they also had to *want* to do good from internalized moral conviction. With much more freedom and less external pressure than in the cell, one aimed at inculcating increased self-control and control over drives and impulses in prisoners. By making the length of a sentence dependent upon behaviour, one hoped to strengthen the will to self-management. Internal improvement in reformatories was exacted by the offer of an important *reward*: freedom. And a freedom wherein one could hold up one's head socially. In Elmira one wanted to be able to say of improved prisoners: 'they carry the barbed wire within them'.[33]

The Elmira experiment was was only brought to public attention in a comprehensive way in the late 1890s in The Netherlands by Aletrino and the lawyer, A. de Graaf. Aletrino thought that Elmira, with its system of treatment and education, had 'proved' that reform in physical, mental and moral areas was 'very feasible' and had even delivered 'wonderful results'.[34] In England, enthusiasm for the new education model led to the Borstal system that strongly resembled the Elmira system. The English system restricted itself, however, to youth between sixteen and twenty-one.[35] The Children Act, introduced in The Netherlands in 1905, meant that youths could also be shut up in government reformatories for an indeterminate period until their twenty-first year.[36] Except for after-care by such agencies as *Pro Juventute*, Dutch institutions did not much resemble Borstals with their *mark systems* and instruction in trades.[37]

Elmira-like reformatories were not tried in The Netherlands, although continuous proposals were made to this end. People who were somewhat conservative feared that reformatories would not sufficiently intimidate and deter.[38] But now that concepts like guilt and accountability had been undermined and the goal of punishment had gained priority, it had become more difficult to rationally justify pure imposition of pain. And furthermore, feelings having to do with the pain that one could impose on a criminal had shifted. Increasing interest in the personality of prisoners and criminals went hand in hand with compassion and enlarged awareness that criminals were human beings too, who could not help it either that they were 'not useful citizens'. J. R. B. de Roos thought that hate for criminals would disappear just as hate against the sick and the insane had disappeared. 'A feeling of solidarity exists, then, that becomes more comprehensive with a better understanding of the meaning of one person's life for that of another,' he stated. 'Civilization and solidarity' were thought to make all arguments for reinstitution of the death penalty 'inferior in importance'. 'Utility and feeling come into conflict here; I have no doubt that feeling will turn out to be the strongest,' said de

Roos.[39] He described, as one involved, in words of that time, that which sociologists like Norbert Elias and Johan Goudsblom later, with more distance, have decribed as the connection between *increasing interdependence* and people's affective life, which gave direction to the Western European *civilizing process*. As people became more dependent upon each other and upon more others, it became more difficult to see and treat some fellow-men as monsters. Connected to this, individuals developed a better eye for and sensitivity to the suffering of prisoners. The new concepts thus provided a new rational argumentation for feelings which had been growing for a longer period of time. We shall see in this chapter how this and many other developments made themselves felt in The Netherlands and how they, hand in hand with a significantly increasing interest, very concretely contributed to the emancipation process of prisoners.

Socialist Fight against Solitary Confinement

The new concepts in penal law and criminology theoretically supported very lenient and extremely harsh forms of crime prevention. It was, therefore, possible that both socialists and later, fascists used the concepts to gain scientific legitimation for their views on crime and punishment and to translate them into deeds. Until the Second World War, power was gained by schools of thought which, on the one hand, conceded that criminals were underpriviledged fellow-men and, on the other, saw them as monsters who had to be eliminated by eugenics. In the 1880s, socialists from the Sociaal Democratische Bond (Social Democratic Union) began to demonstrate powerfully how they represented the former school of thought. That is understandable. The union of social-democrats gradually became a union of ex-prisoners. Many members had gained experience inside a cell because they were too boisterous in attacking social injustice by hawking seditious magazines, disturbing the peace and insulting highly placed Dutchmen. This verbal stance did not disappear in the cell. Socialists had seen how bad conditions were for prisoners. They associated this knowledge with the oppressive nature of capitalistic society and they were vociferous in announcing their findings.[40]

Many socialists were the first prisoners who did not passively allow the misery to engulf them. The emancipation process of prisoners became active in character for the first time in history because of the socialists. In 1888, a socialist ex-convict was even made a member of the Lower House: Ferdinand Domela Nieuwenhuis. He had, because of a written insult to King Willem III in *Recht voor Allen*, lese majesty in other words, spent almost a year 'glueing bags' in the cellular prison at Utrecht. He was put on a transport on 18 January 1887, but on 31 August, the birthday of Princess Wilhelmina, he received three months' pardon under pressure of protests from a broad sector of society and because his becoming ill in the cell had served only to augment his status as martyr. His release led to massive enthusiasm in the Hague and Amsterdam, but in Rotterdam he was almost lynched by furious monarchists. From the cell, he arrived in the Lower House, a truely unparallelled form of rehabilitation. Some thought that he was as tortured by solitude in parliament as in the cell,[41] but sitting on plush seats did not make him forget his fellows from the penitentiary and neither did this occur after his membership in the Lower House. What John Howard had meant for prisoners in earlier days, Domela Nieuwenhuis came to mean for Dutch prisoners even more emphatically. He not only shed light on their misery for a large audience, but he also untiringly challenged the legitimizing of this imposition of punishment.

Ferdinand Domela Nieuwenhuis was, incredibly, a *brother* of the often referred-to cellular fanatic and professor of criminal law, Jacob Domela Nieuwenhuis.[42] Until he was very old, Jacob defended, almost without compromise and in a never-ending stream of publications, the cellular system which Ferdinand just as uncompromisingly depicted as inhuman cruelty in the Lower House and in articles. Shortly before the learned Jacob, looking back at 'the battle' for the cellular system, once more severely trivialized physical and mental suffering in the cell, Ferdinand joined battle with the Minister of Justice, Ruijs de Beerenbrouck, to attack the 'faulty foundations' of the penal system. During the general deliberations about the budget for Justice for 1889, Ferdinand said that the prison system took no account of 'the position of science'. People were removed from society because they had been guilty of anti-social deeds. He found that definitely no scientific answer to the causes of these deeds. Filled with admiration, the *socialist* Member of Parliament pointed to the work of Lombroso and Garofalo! 'They have put solid ground under my feet,' said Domela Nieuwenhuis. Still, he thought a few causes to be missing in the Darwinistic notions of crime. He said that Quetelet, in particular, had pointed out that society prepares crime. 'And the guilty person is only the instrument that carries it out,' he added. The guilty in prisons confirmed nothing more than the faulty organization of the state. 'They are actually *not the guilty*, but simply *the victims of Society*.' He described the prisons as 'huge poorhouses' populated for ninety per cent by 'poor bastards' who had violated property laws. Laws, however, were made by property owners. Thus Domela Nieuwenhuis arrived at an exposition of the Marxist analysis of society. Its correctness he thought to be confirmed by 'the population of the prisons themselves'. He saw theft due to need or as a result of unemployment as 'the most natural deed in the world'. He thought it 'a deed of self-preservation'. The same went, in his opinion, for the murder of foremen who advised rebellious workers to eat grass. He thought infanticide often took place purely in desperation. Solitary confinement was, according to him, not only 'extremely cruel' but also 'based on a very bad assessment of human character' because it was aimed at socializing people by 'completely isolating them from all others'. Domela Nieuwenhuis could not understand either why they 'who fought tooth and nail against equality in society were such proponents of equality in prisons'. He pointed to the uniform clothing, shaving of hair and lack of newspapers, which were 'a necessity of life' for many. 'I call it simple teasing, through which we disgrace ourselves,' he said to the Members of Parliament. The German delegate, Liebknecht, appears once to have said to him of Dutch cellular confinement: 'but that is sheer barbarism'.[43]

After this statement of principle, Domela Nieuwenhuis would continue in provoking fundamental discussions, but members of government only answered him when it concerned concrete questions.[44] He set himself up once more as candidate in 1891, but when he was not reelected, he turned away from parliament for good to move even further in an anarchistic direction. He was, however, not able to forget criminal law and prisons. He played an active role in 1897 in a survey by the *De Jonge Gids* (a socialist periodical), instituted by the play-writer Herman Heijermans, about the treatment of 'political criminals' in Dutch prisons. The editors wanted to bring into the open the 'atrocious treatment' of social-ists who were being 'tortured' for political offences. They also wanted to find out their opinions of 'the present cellular system' in general.

Thus, for the first time in history, Dutch prisoners were asked publically and freely to give an opinion. These were not average prisoners and their *opinions* were heavily politically biased. But, so too were the opinions of all experts who found that prisoners were still treated much too well. The survey offered some compensation for all the biased opinions and was now, for once, really directed at improving the prisoners' position. The bias of their actual observations was rather less than expected. Almost everything that the ex-prisoners wrote tallied exactly with descriptions in the preceding chapter. Critics of the survey indeed endorsed remarks about stench in the cells, too little light and the cold, filthy beds, bad food, restricted reading material, monotonous and meaningless work, the degrading shaving of heads, grey, uniform prison clothing, the solitude, visiting-conditions, the shame of transports and the sin of masturbation. But the critics took offence of the *general* judgements, and, it must be admitted, those surveyed gave a somewhat less neutral description of psychic misery than was usual in circles of prison experts. 'It is horrible', 'a continual torture', 'everything equally bare, dismal and dead', 'a most abject invention', 'intolerable', 'inhuman', 'spiritually and physically deadening', 'extremely cruel and inhumane', 'scandalous mistreatment', 'horrendous, murderous', 'a grave that kills the mind', 'no meaner, no more refined, no more dastardly-scientific violation of man than our present cell system', 'to understate it, a mixture of fanaticism, insensitivity and brutishness', these were some of the qualifications of the cellular system by known socialists.

Domela Nieuwenhuis put a lot of work into his answers. His general judgement implied complete rejection of the cellular system: it was cruel and served no purpose. It seemed to have been designed to 'render' persons 'idiots' and to make them 'mean hypocrites' unsuited to return to society. The cell was, in his opinion, a hovel in which 'the victim of our present society's lust for revenge and punishment' had to spend a long time 'paying for his resistance to the state's power'.

Prisoners were victims and solitude served no purpose. Thus, in the eyes of socialists, nothing remained but extreme cruelty. The fact that they could accuse precisely those men who thought themselves so civilized of purposeless, barbaric atrocities must have pleased them. These men could hardly defend themselves against this accusation without providing new ammunition for attacks. This was what made the role of the socialists so influential. They emphasized the cruelty of cellular confinement right at the moment that its justification had been undermined in numerous ways. Many scholars of criminal law, psychiatrists and other experts who had been asked for an opinion about solitary confinement as a result of the survey chose to remain silent. Those who did respond showed themselves to be very moderate or even added their little extras to the story. The fact that Pieter Jelles Troelstra, a socialist leader, wrote an approving letter in which he spoke of answering 'crime with crime' did not make much of an impression. But that respectable experts also reacted seriously prevented the survey being ignored as socialist propaganda.[45]

During the debate in 1898 about money for the new domeshaped prison in Haarlem, the socialist, van der Zwaag, had caused a commotion in the Lower House with his remark that one could better shoot those receiving long sentences dead, then they would at least be spared their cellular misery. He made a plea for agricultural colonies so that prisoners would no longer be 'tortured in a barbarian way'. The liberal Minister of Justice, Cort van der Linden, protested fiercely. He could 'categorically' guarantee that nothing of the kind took place, no 'torturing of prisoners' and certainly no torturing 'in a barbarian way'. Treatment in the cell was 'in spite of the strictness, as humane as possible, and perhaps one might even say: much too humane'. Van der Zwaag was invited to produce evidence.[46]

This vitriolic exchange illustrates how important the argument based on feelings had become now that rational justification of cellular confinement could hardly be provided any longer under pressure of the new concepts and recidivism figures. The socialist leader, Troelstra, who himself would soon receive a month's cellular confinement,[47] played upon feelings as well in 1898 in the Lower House. The 'greatest evil' in his opinion was that judges, when they were dealing out 'all sorts of horribly long prison sentences' were not aware of 'their significance'. They themselves should spend a few weeks in prison. Troelstra was especially upset about the severe punishments for crimes against property which, after all, were rooted 'in the social situation'. He called those punishments 'barbarian and criminal'.[48]

Although criticism on the cellular system was widespread, in parliament most of the criticism came from the socialist side. They continualy pressed for mitigation of the solitude, individualization of cellular confinement and introduction of the Elmira system.[49] The first promises for mitigation of the solitude were made to socialist Members of Parliament.[50] Through their tireless hammering away at its senseless cruelty, they forced proponents of cellular confinement, even outside parliament, into a defensive role which could only be sustained by making many concessions. In 1905, the socialist opposition to cellular confinement was given support once again at a scientific level by the socialist and sociologist, W. A. Bonger, in his famous dissertation about the connections between crime and economic conditions. Bonger did not find it difficult to understand why figures for recidivism showed that cellular confinement improved criminals just as little as the former communal confinement. Based on the 'mistaken theory' that man had a free will, the non-determinists 'alas' still believed that the criminal, left to himself and his own thoughts, would arrive at remorse. Bonger stated that man was a social animal, and asked how he could, thus, ever improve in solitude. His opinion was that confinement did not reduce crime, but was precisely one of the *causes* of increasing crime.[51]

Cellular Confinement with its Back to the Wall

The frequency of discussions about cellular confinement in parliament before the establishment of the Penal Code formed a strong contrast to the silence in years following. Now and then a Minister of Justice gave a reassuring answer to questions about recidivism, insanity or suicide, but a real evaluation was not forthcoming.[52] Outside parliament emotional criticism was expressed in newspapers.[53] And at the criminal-anthropological congress in Paris (1889), van Hamel contended that cellular confinement could still only be used for opportunistic criminals and a certain group of corrigible habitual criminals (those who had too much 'd'énergie criminelle'). For all other criminals, cellular confinement was at most suited only for their observation or in combination with communal confinement.[54] Not until ten years later serious objections had been voiced to the system in parliament. Long-lasting cellular confinement did not seem to improve prisoners and, baron van Welderen Rengers even called it a deciding factor in the Upper House, prisoners suffered too much physically and mentally from it.[55]

Soon more criticism was expressed. The prison expert, A. van der Elst, contended that, witness the uniform regime, nothing had come of individualizing cellular confinement. *Separate* confinement appeared in practice to be *solitary* confinement. Visits were sparse. Governors did not make their rounds, warders said only 'hello' and Society members had begun to let their visits slip. Cellular confinement was, in his opinion, cruel and 'evil in itself'. 'Should the practice, organized thus, not arouse rancour, despondency, despair or hate, dependent upon the temperament of the individual?' he asked.[56]

Van der Elst pointed also to the drafts for 'Kinderwetten' (Children Act) in which upbringing and not punishment was the core. Cellular confinement, in these drafts, had already been rejected as admissible for children up to sixteen. For children up to eighteen, its imposition was severely limited. The judge was thought to have to choose among a reprimand, placement in a house of correction or compulsory upbringing in a 'rijksopvoedingsgesticht' or in a foster home. The Children Act was accepted by parliament in 1901 and put into operation in 1905. They represented the first concrete success of the *New Direction* and, particularly, of van Hamel.[57] These laws brought the end of the annual shutting up of hundreds of fourteen- and fifteen-year-olds in cellular prisons.[58] Van der Elst thought that this had made 'a breach in our so fundamentally and so consistently enforced cellular system'. He hoped that one would now begin to realize that long-lasting solitude was, for normal constitutions, 'actually an overly severe trial of body and soul'. For the weak, it could even mean torture and 'a slow death sentence'.[59]

Critics were of the opinion that nothing much more remained of cellular confinement than a cruel aberration in criminal law. In spite of this, proponents and opponents of cellular confinement did not become irreconcilable enemies. They managed to meet each other in a realistic compromise: *individualization*. They thought the cell system to have failed because of a faulty, much too uniform implementation. Assigning to classes and groups and making distinctions in cell interiors, bedding, food, visits, clothing and reading material were thought to be able to negate many of the protests against cellular confinement.[60] The aspiration toward individualization became a very efficacious compromise because it was so vaguely described. The most conservative pleas for individualization aimed at a flower in the cell or a portrait on the wall while more radical arguments included thoughts of communal confinement and

Elmira-like institutions. J. Domela Nieuwenhuis, who hoped to save the cellular system with conservative forms of individualization, characterized the like treatment of prisoners as 'the *unequal* treatment of *unequal* individuals'.[61] Opponents of cellular confinement such as Aletrino, de Roos and van der Elst thought that individualization meant primarily the permitting of social contact. Both parties agreed on a reassessment of the abolished institution of the *pistole*. They thought it should be made possible once again for civilized persons to individualize their own punishment at their own cost. Socialists saw the *pistole* as a chance to improve the fate of political prisoners. Even in those circles, it was thought that a civilized stomach would have more difficulty than that of a vagrant in digesting prison food.

It transpired thus, at the turn of the century, that both friend and foe of cellular confinement could imagine improvements through individualization. In the Bill for amending the Penal Code in 1900, Minister of Justice, Cort van der Linden, showed himself to be abreast of the new consensus. He wanted to clear the way for a special law which would regulate classification and a 'certain mitigation' of cellular solitude. One was dealing only with 'labour pains' in the Minister's view. The correct principles had not yet come into their own because of 'a faulty application'.[62] This Bill, just as the almost identical one from 1904, was not processed for practical reasons. The discussion about the cellular system was stirred up rather than toned down by this. Opponents sawe their chance and proponents became fearful.

On 29 June, 1901, the Nederlandsche Juristen-Vereeniging (Dutch Lawyers' Society) arrived at decisions which would have been impossible fifteen years earlier. It was stated unanimously that changes in the penal system were wanted. Voting was almost unanimous for 'as much individualization as possible' and 'as much classification as possible on psychological and physiological bases'. And it was unanimously accepted that improvements were needed in long-lasting confinement, so that the separation would no longer take place 'in practically complete solitude'. It was also no longer permissible to 'systematically' exclude everything 'that brought the prisoner into contact with the outside world or reminded him of it'.[63]

In the knowledge that considerations about changes to cellular confinement were rife at ministerial level and that a large majority of Dutch lawyers longed for change, the doctor, criminal anthropologist and writer, Arnold Aletrino, thought the time ripe in 1906 to dedicate a whole book to the question: 'Is cellular confinement still acceptable and desirable?' Using an impressive number of quotations from Dutch and foreign experts, he arrived at a negative answer. Doing this, he attached a lot of value to the opinions of the prisoners themselves. He said he was surprised that 'until recent times' only the opinions of non-prisoners had counted and that only 'very recently' had interest for those of prisoners grown. His book also contained many quotations from the survey in *De Jonge Gids*, from 'written revelations' which prisoners had sent him and from (primarily foreign) articles by ex-prisoners. Cellular confinement had, in Aletrino's view, no longer any right to exist. First, he contended, had come the edifying speeches, and now, once more, individualizing measures which were supposed to save the cell. Aletrino did not trust these, and recidivism figures supported his mistrust. He had worked out that, in 1896, 29.6 per cent of those sentenced were recidivists and, in 1903, that this figure had already reached 41.3 per cent. He saw a fine future in indeterminate sentences and educational institutions like the American *reformatories*. The Elmira system would be the best possible 'in which the interests of the person-criminal and society came to the foreground and not the desire for revenge, restitution and infliction of punishment'.[64]

The book was influential but even more characteristic of the changed attitude to cellular confinement was the meeting of the Society for the Moral Improvement of Prisoners in 1907, dedicated to 'the administration of cellular confinement and its effect' in the presence of the socialist leader Domela Nieuwenhuis and known prison-experts. The speakers managed to put an end to the trivializing of cellular misery by the Society which had gone on for such a long time. Different speakers also showed that they thought the opinions of prisoners to be very important. Pastor Boeke had even presented a self-made questionnaire to twenty-five prisoners. He concluded that the cell 'blunts and confounds the mind'.

Almost all the speakers called the lack of social life in cellular prisons as the largest drawback and proposed the introduction of social intercourse in some form or another. Prison psychiatrists, van Mesdag and Casparie, made very clear that the period of dogmatic adherence to cellular confinement within the Society was over. They provided numerical data concerning health and insanity which corroborated that which had recently been called severely exaggerated. Without restraint, they called the depressing influence of the cell an important cause of insanity and severe nervousness. Casparie was to work his findings out later in an article, described in the preceeding chapter. For Society members in 1907, these were new, shocking reports. The socialists who were present rubbed salt in the wound with their emotional tirades against cellular confinement. The chairman, Simons' concluding statement was that only a few voices had recalled to mind the time when the cellular system had been seen 'as the panacea for all complaints'. He thought that practically everyone would now agree that the system needed change 'in many facets'.

As Deputy Minister of Justice and chief of the prison department, Dresselhuys, had followed the discussion with mixed feelings. He had naturally heard much that was interesting but he was forced to ask himself if Society members had any idea how much things cost at present! One spoke of more daylight in cells, but one had obviously 'no idea' how much money would disappear from the treasury if all prison windows were to be enlarged. Dresselhuys pointed out the hard reality to the animated speakers. One was stuck with a new and costly cellular system that caused much misery and little good. For the time being, there was no money to really do anything about it.[65]

This fact puts the importance of that being discussed into perspective. There were fierce arguments for and against changes which far exceeded the financial resources of the country. Many thought that much too much had already been invested in building new cellular prisons. And if new windows would break the budget, there was no point at all in hoping for an Elmira system. This made the fate of prisoners at that time more dismal still. They were being punished in a way that had meanwhile come to be seen by very many as a cruel aberration of penal law. The psychiatrist, H. van der Hoeven, thought the denunciation of *enforced* cellular confinement had occurred 'across-the-board'. He said that no one could any longer repress their horror and bewilderment upon experiencing 'the dismal, oppressive grave-like silence behind the bleak doors'.[66]

Cellular confinement whose theoretical foundations and practical implementation had been struck by devastating criticism, alterations and revolutionary alternatives which could not be financed – that was the balance made up in The Netherlands a quarter of a century after the general introduction of the system in 1886. Nevertheless, the prison system would still be subjected to drastic changes before the First World War: the introduction of conditional sentences and expansion of the conditional release program. Changes to life within the four walls could not be financed. Thus, it became even more attractive to keep as many as possible outside these walls and yet still make them prisoners to some degree within a full social life. It was not possible to effect a more radical break with the criticized solitary confinement in a way both economical and in agreement with the new concepts. The disappointing results of the cellular system unintentionally contributed to the introduction of conditional sentencing.

The Sword of Damocles

'Should the world perish tomorrow, then the last murderer must be hung today.' This pithy saying of Kant about the retaliatory principle was used in 1900 to show to what an extent conditional sentencing was directed toward the future and *not* at retaliation for evil committed in the past.[67] Should the world perish tomorrow, conditional sentencing would make no sense at all. Just before this new measure was brought into operation in 1915, the professor, Fabius, a declared proponent of the retaliation principle, wrote a thick book as well,[68] in which he tried to avert this disaster. Conditional sentencing was not a punishment in his opinion, not an imposition of suffering for sins committed. The new measure would degrade criminal law to a type of *Kriminalpolitik*.

Other than in the United States and England where the *sentence*, after a declaration of guilt, was conditionally put off, a conditional putting off of the *execution* of the sentence took place in The Netherlands; this was also called the Belgian-French system. This conditional sentencing meant, indeed, a revolutionary break with traditional conceptions of crime and punishment. But it was also an answer to the criticism that cellular confinement did not take the social nature of man into account. Improvement and education would, according to the critics of cellular confinement, only be possible through social contacts which made demands on the improved spirit. And which social contacts would make more severe demands on people than those of a life of freedom? The increasing understanding of social factors and social determination directed the attention furthermore at the disadvantageous effects of short prison sentences in particular. People who actually only through poverty, misery and opportunity had gone so far as to commit a petty crime were wrenched out of social life for a short period and overburdened with shame which lasted a lifetime. Should they be brought to remorse in the cell, society made it impossible for them after that point to translate their good will into deeds. Their families were disrupted and their jobs were taken by others. Also, it was argued, they often lost their fear of the cell through their experience of prison, a fear they still had had before they committed the opportunistic crime.

Recidivism figures lent support to the aptness of this line of reasoning. Those who had received short sentences reappeared relatively often in prison. Furthermore, this was not a minority of the prison population. Penal experts worked out that more than ninety-six per cent of prison sentences consisted of short-term detention or a prison sentence of six months or less.[69] These were facts which offered perspective. If one were to be able to permanently keep a portion of those with short sentences on the straight and narrow, much meaningless misery would disappear and much money would be saved.

The introduction of conditional sentencing is usually accounted for by the break with the retaliation principle, the rise in probation and after-care services and the admitted meaninglessness of short prison sentences. The fact that the fundamental idea behind the new measure fitted well into a long-term shift from external to internal constraint was, however, just as important and perhaps even decisive for the trust placed in it. A psychological mechanism was in operation. The concrete threat of punishment would compel the conditionally sentenced to refrain from evil for a long time at a stretch. Habit could, in this case, come to the aid of a second nature, 'just as, in the case of "habitual criminals", it tends to aid the cause of evil.'[70] From becoming hardened in evil to being mollified in good, all of this had to occur through habit. In his preliminary advice to the Dutch Lawyers' Union in 1890, L. U. de Sitter put forward the fact that punishment would continuously hang over the head of the sentenced like the sword of Damocles. This would ensure that the sentenced, in his opinion, had a 'continuous restraint' with which to curb his desires.

> Should he manage to practice this self-control during his probation, one can almost surely say that he will have won a victory over himself, that he has been saved for society.[71]

Conditional sentencing seems to have connected closely to conditional release, even though there were many who saw essential differences between them as far as penal law went. At the time of its very limited introduction in 1886, conditional release was defended primarily as a gradual transition from prison to full freedom and as a means to keep order within prison walls. Still, D. Z. van Duyl had already remarked, in 1881, that conditional release would offer 'the *real* evil-doer the most tempting stimulus to self-discipline, which will further lead to remorse and finally to improvement'.[72] Later on, J. H. Patijn described even more saliently and very precisely the pedagogical principle which formed its basis:

> Reward-directed effort towards good behaviour and work results can indeed also work educationally; even though in the beginning this effort does not result from noble motives and good intentions. Orderly behaviour and work can, almost without noticing, become habit which has a chance of being retained, even when supervision is gradually reduced and there is less punishment and finally none at all. Born of the what is often called hypocrisy, social adjustment can give satisfaction and be continued from higher motives. Even an enforced attitude can become habit and thus appear afterwards to have had effect educationally.[73]

It was certainly not all proponents of conditional sentencing and conditional release who placed so much emphasis on the educational foundations, but they did always speak of the 'stimulus' or the 'compulsion to self-control' which was thought to be the result. In the terminology of the sociologist, Elias, conditional sentencing and release meant a further shift from *Fremdzwang* to *Selbstzwang*, with the understanding, of course, that Elias invests his concepts with a much more comprehensive sociological content. He refers to the slow internalizing, which lasts centuries, of 'civilized' standards of behaviour which originally are experienced as strange and obtrusive; this was a long-term process in Western societies that took place largely unintentionally and without being planned. In the domain of criminal law and seen in the short term, internalizing of a specific external constraint was thus indeed aimed at and planned by some, even though, in addition to the educational objectives, pragmatic and purely judicial considerations played an important role. The imminent introduction of conditional sentencing was a *penal civilizing offensive*, comparable to the citizens' civilizing offensives which were carried out at the same time in the lower social classes by compassionate Societies.[74]

Introduction of Conditional Sentencing in 1915

In 1912, the Minister of Justice, Regout, presented a Bill to introduce conditional sentencing.[75] In the same Bill conditional release was made possible after nine months instead of three years.[76] This considerably expanded form of conditional release resembled the last phase in the Irish system that had almost unanimously been rejected a few decades earlier. The existing ruling for conditional release was, as it were, pulled along in the wake of a completely new form of punishment – conditional sentencing – which was based on a totally different concept of man and of criminal law than the Penal Code of 1886 with its strict cellular basis.

The Bill was defended in 1915 in parliament by the Minister of Justice, B. Ort, from the left-liberal cabinet of Cort van der Linden. In his explanatory memorandum, he placed a lot of emphasis on avoidance of unnecessary suffering. Speaking to the Upper House, he called 'reduction of the *unnecessarily* huge amount of suffering' actually 'the basic concept' of the new ruling.[77] These words indicate to some extent how strongly the new concepts had made the imposition of suffering on prisoners problematic. Now that retaliation had been rejected as a guideline and deterrence had been pushed to the background, suffering had to have *meaning* and be *necessary* in fighting crime and specific prevention. The suffering involved in confinement for a short period could no longer be justified. Several Members of Parliament had even pushed for a considerable expansion of the proposed applications mentioned in the first draft. Ort amended the Bill such that conditional sentencing became possible for prison sentences of one year or less.

The public debate in March of 1915 that lasted a good three days showed even more decisively how drastically the national penal climate had changed in thirty years. It was no longer argued that prisoners had it too good, whereas in 1886, a majority in the house had deemed harsh disciplinary punishments to be indispensable for that reason. In 1915, it was evident that many Members of Parliament were very aware of the profundity of prison suffering. The liberal, Rink, for instance, brought his 'personal opinion' to the fore to say that it was especially the tenor of the Bill 'to diminish the total of the human suffering and societal misery' that had pleased him. He found it remarkable 'how few people fully realize the vast suffering that accompanies confinement in a prison'. Prison brought with it physical, moral, financial and economic suffering by which innocent family members were also heavily affected. In his opinion, the influence of social conditions was so strong that the criminal deserved 'primarily commiseration'.

A fellow party-member in the 'Liberale Unie' (Liberal Union), Van Raalte, expressed, even more strongly than Rink, feelings which had grown in the changing penal climate. He called cellular confinement 'a terribly cruel punishment'. Looking to the future, he expressed his opinion that there would come a time in which a 'reaction' would take place against the practice of prison sentencing 'as immense as that against all sorts of other punishments since the days of Beccaria'. Minister Ort was receptive to this sort of expression. He added his own little extra by assuring the House that the new measure would 'first and fore-most' spare the delinquent 'the sharper forms of repression under penal law'. 'It will bring back to strictly necessary the quantities of intentional and unintentional suffering inflicted by the repression under penal law,' said the Minister. He added to this that 'at present' the suffering inflicted in the name of the state was 'much larger than can be deemed necessary'.[78]

That which was said by Minister Ort and diverse Members of Parliament had until just recently before that only been heard from the mouths of a few socialist Members. Now there were eighteen socialists in the House and they could leave criticism of cruel solitary confinement to the other Members. The article in which conditional sentencing was set down was carried without a division. The new measure was also accepted with a large majority in the Upper House.[79]

Thus, on 30 December 1915, a law was brought into operation which could keep thousands of *first offenders* and even recidivists out of prison should the judge deem them not yet totally depraved. Besides the *general* condition of not committing a new offense during their trial period of a maximum of three years, all sorts of *specific* conditions could be attached to the sentence. The condition of compensating for damages was named in the law, but the judge could make up other conditions himself, as long as they did not limit 'religious or political freedom'. Options were a ban on pubs, obligation to move house, forbidden access to certain persons or to certain places, abstinence from alcohol or the readiness to put oneself under supervision of one's family. Premature release was also dependent on the same ruling of general and specific conditions. Prisoners could come into consideration for this if two-thirds and at least nine months of their sentence had elapsed. Police supervision, customary in other countries, was not recognized by the law. The Prosecution Counsel was responsible for supervising compliance with the conditions, but could delegate this supervision to institutions for probation and after-care.[80] The introduction of the new institute went hand in hand, thus, with increasing government involvement in areas of probation and after-care. This involvement had been set down legally for the first time in 1910 in the 'reclasseringsregeling' (probation and after-care ruling).[81]

The First Wave of Emancipation

The new concepts of crime and punishment focussed attention sharply on the person of the criminal. What criminals had done wrong could only be understood by knowing their inner being, their biological characteristics and their special situations. Scholars spoke with prisoners, measured their skulls,[82] like the psychiatrist, Winkler, in the Leeuwarden prison, and read books about them. This concrete interest in prisoners was not entirely new. At the beginning of the nineteenth century, scholars, politicians and philanthropists had already descended into their awful abodes. At first they had been driven by curiosity but quite soon they had begun to have special intentions for their visits. With edifying speeches, they had tried to inculcate in prisoners an awareness of sin and guilt, hoping that remorse and repentance would make them better people. Somewhat later, visitors also wanted to see what the effects of cellular solitude were on prisoners.

Towards the end of the century, interest in prisoners not only increased sharply but also changed in nature. Firstly, it gained – in connection with the increasing professionalizing and state interference in the care for prisoners – a stronger supervisory character. The implementation of the new cellular system was organized in detail in a Prison Act and a Prison Ruling. Supervision of their enforcement formed part of the new rules. State inspection was expanded. Additionally, it was no longer so that inspections always had to be announced.[83] Inspectors wrote down many of their findings annually in commentaries to the prison statistics which everyone could peruse. In addition to this, government inspection of care for the insane was expanded to include the prisons. The inspecting psychiatrists periodically published a thorough report of their visits which, in principle, could be read by everyone.[84] Thus politicians and scholars of criminal law could, if they wished, learn more and more about prisoners.

Secondly, the increasing interest gained a strongly scientific character. Much differently than half way through the nineteenth century, this interest arose from a deterministic view of crime in which concepts such as guilt, sin and remorse had little substance. Instead of making prisoners aware of guilt and sin, they now heard that they were victims of their own temperament and of the environment in which they lived. The punishments which they underwent had to be meaningful in terms of the future. The past that had been so central to the retaliation theme was no longer important. The scientific interest was almost completely focussed on *specific* prevention. Punishment had to have a salutary effect on those undergoing it. The *general* prevention, that is, the difficult to measure deterrent effect on persons who had not yet committed a crime, disappeared completely into the background. This was important because the specific prevention could, indeed, be measured with recidivism figures. By repeating the offense, prisoners themselves could, as it were, attack the punishment which they had undergone. And they did just that. By making a case for the *general* preventive effect, much prison suffering would have still been defensible. But the new concepts were purely directed at why persons committed crimes and not at why so many did *not*. Most prisoners will not have been aware that they had thus come into an important means to power, but a certain group of prisoners was well aware of this and made use of it. The socialist ex-convicts let it sound out, loud and clear, even in parliament, that cellular confinement did not in any way answer to the goals set for it and was, thus, purely cruel and inhuman. During a survey conducted amoung ex-convicts, they vigorously denounced cellular misery.

Thirdly, socialist involvement in the fate of prisoners gave to the increasing interest, which was part of the emancipation *process*, the character of an emancipation *movement*. The socialists were the first convicts to make *active* use of the slowly grown sources of power for prisoners and to explicitly push to diminish prison suffering. They presented themselves, on the basis of their experience, as pre-eminent experts. This moved other experts to refer in their arguments to the opinions of prisoners with whom they had spoken. They were forced by the socialists to justify prison suffering, but, because of the new concepts of crime and punishment, these experts were only very partially successful. Much suffering was also unnecessary in their view and therefore unacceptable. The dismal aspects of cell life had also reached the public at large through articles by ex-convicts in dailies. Opinions of prisoners were published and taken seriously. The life story of a repeat offender, that appeared in 1909 in serial form in the *Algemeen Handelsblad* and contained many sorry passages about cell life, led to public excitement and even to the taking up of a collection in The Hague by 'young ladies who had been touched by the story'.[85] Practical and financial factors still made it difficult for the time being to change life within prison walls. A new law, however, attempted to keep people out of prison by sentencing them conditionally and granting them early release.

Up to this point, developments at the beginning of this century considerably strengthened chances for prisoner power, but this went primarily for the chances of prisoners deemed corrigible. Based on the new concepts, very severe treatment, indeed, was advocated for incorrigibles and recidivists. They had to be rendered harmless by confining them for life or giving them over to treatment by psychiatrists for a long time, preferably an indeterminate period. Many wanted to withhold from them all say about their own lives. They belonged to those incapable of self-government: the degenerate, the mentally inferior, the born criminals, the morally ill and the irresponsible. Self-improvement could not be expected of them. Society had to protect itself against them. Until the First World War, these concepts had, at most, practical consequences because of the harsher punishments which those deemed incorrigible received. A legal rule was not instituted but, in 1906, the Dutch Lawyers'Union called for special measures against criminals who balanced 'on the borderline between insanity and mental health'. Van Hamel wanted, as is evident from his preliminary advice, to sentence them to compulsory treatment in a secure clinic for an indeterminate period and possibly incapacitate them for life.[86]

Van Hamel's proposals formed a blueprint for the later introduced (in 1925 and 1928) Psychopath Laws on the basis of which mentally 'inferior' criminals would be shut away in special asylums. There they had to wait until the doctors found that they could again be freed without society having to fear them. There is certainly no cause to speak of increasing power for this group. Instead of in prison, they landed for an indeterminate period in asylums for psychopaths where they, like willless victims of their own minds which had been called ill, were completely at the mercy of the power of psychiatrists. Only recently has their position, powerless and without rights, been strongly criticized with the same arguments as were already being used by van der Meij around the turn of the century. The criteria upon whose foundations they were and remained confined were thought to be invalid and completely arbitrary. They were much more harshly punished than other criminals, without sufficient justification. In the 1988 amendment to the law concerning compulsory treatment in a secure clinic (TBR/TBS-measure), these protests are only partially met.[87]

The psychopath laws did, however, contribute considerably to the emancipation of prisoners. After all, precisely those criminals who were thought to be incapable of self-government, irresponsible and mentally disturbed disappeared from prisons. Because of this it became almost impossible to portray the population of prisons as a collection of the degenerate and moral defectives as had often happened around the turn of the century. Such persons did not have to be taken seriously or allowed rights. The psychopath laws freed ordinary prisoners of fellow-prisoners to whom, on grounds of their mental and physical condition, almost no power was due or was ascribed.[88] This made it easier to see prisoners as equal fellow-men who felt and thought just as other people did. We shall see that prisoners, after the First World War, expressed their repugnance at communal confinement in the Special Penitentiary at Scheveningen for this reason. 'Half-wits and 'crazies' with whom no one wanted any contact were confined there as well. They themselves had *done something wrong* but they were not crazy. The new, hard concepts about born criminals, mental defectives and incorrigible recidivists prepared the way for the making of psychopath laws which would make it possible to see the remaining prisoners as corrigible victims of circumstance and too much opportunity. The extent of mild feeling in the meanwhile about this remaining group was made clear in the new law for conditional sentencing and release. The fact that their lives would be improved, even inside the prison, had already been announced in 1917 in a thorough report by the Society for the Moral Improvement of Prisoners concerning 'the application of cellular confinement'. This report and the consequent public discussion corroborated how little legal room there was for change. The reporters, for instance, brought forward, not as a proposal but as a suggestion, that it was perhaps 'no longer so necessary' to 'completely thwart' attempts to make contact with each other by tapping. One wished to let prisoners in whom 'all fear of mutual moral infection' had been ruled out, walk 'in each other's presence'. The reporters 'even' wished to offer the possibility to 'some prisoners' to speak to each other. They, just as the Ministers, Members of Parliament and scholars who had spoken of 'mitigation' of solitude, seemed to imagine little more than this social contact during the airing when they spoke of 'very desirable moderation of the strict system of separation'. The reporters proposed all sorts of small, practical modifications of cell life. To the reader of today it will seem as if one was aiming from sheer necessity only at marginal improvements, but, from the perspective of prisoners at that time, all the proposals did, indeed, concern far-reaching interruptions of the monotonous solitude. That the reporters continually pressed for much circumspection during possible applications of their proposals and repeatedly denied being moved by 'sickly compassion' indicates that they themselves found their proposals not marginal but, rather, far-reaching. The critical report unintentionally confirmed how extremely strictly and rigidly the cell system was being administered. These reporters had, to some extent, even placed themselves outside legal delimitations with their proposals. For the intended mitigation of solitude, in particular, amendments to the law would be necessary.[89]

While Society members peacefully sat speaking of cellular confinement in a small hall, the world was on fire. The First World War would not leave the prison system untouched. It led rather quickly to changes which went much further than what the commission had thought possible, but not as far as the German, Neckeben, in *Ein Vorblick auf das Jahr 2000* (a preview of the year 2000) in 1891 fearfully predicted. Instead of a century earlier, as the lawyer, J. A. van Hamel, had done, Neckeben looked a century ahead. In his 'penological dream of the future', he found himself in an Elmira-like reformatory. Prisoners read prison journals in which they might even express themselves freely. Comfortable toilets, carpets on the floor and cozy recreation rooms. Anxiously, he received one surprise after the other. In his epilogue, he addressed the reader who perhaps had been upset by all the exaggeration. But, in America it was almost that extreme already and many Germans spoke sympathetically about the American institutions. Neckeben was satisfied if he had succeeded with his writing in 'highlighting the ridiculous aspects of some of the exotic institutions'.[90]

NOTES

1. Roos, 1900, p. 1.
2. Hamel (J. A. van), 1909 (*De Gids*), pp. 17–18.
3. Cf. Weringh, 1986, pp. 20–79, and Garland, 1985, 'The criminal (...)'.
4. Kramps, 1891, pp. 194, 207.
5. See Roos, 1900, pp. 37–9.
6. Idem, pp. 34–65.
7. Jelgersma, 1892, pp. 101–14.
8. Patijn, 1891, pp. 228, 232.
9. Cf. Weringh, 1986, pp. 20–7. See also Bemmelen, 1948, pp. 117–19, and Kempe, 1967, pp. 13–16.
10. Cf. Rijksen et al., 1980, p. 41.
11. Simons, 1901, p. 11; *Het congres (...)*, p. 493. See further Roos, 1902, and report of this congress in the *OHC*, 10, 11, 13 and 14 September 1901.
12. Durkheim, 1973 (1895), p. 70.
13. Cf. Heerikhuizen, 1987, and Bonger, 1916 (1905).
14. Roos, 1900, p. 5, and Roos, 1902, p. 295.
15. Liszt, 1968 (1883), quotes on pp. 27, 29–30, 32–6, 39.
16. Cf. Vries, 1986, pp. 94–5.
17. Hamel, 1912 (1890), V. O. vol. I, p. 548.
18. For instance, see Fokkens, 1981, 1.3, and Binsbergen, 1986, pp. 139–50. Weringh, 1986, p. 75, makes a connection with the German *Kriminalbiologie*. See also Fijnaut, 1986.
19. Domela Nieuwenhuis, 1899, pp. 8–9, 29–31. See also Domela Nieuwenhuis, 1912, p. 306.
20. Fabius, 1900, p. 72.
21. Vries, 1986, pp. 105–6.
22. Nederburgh, 1909, p. 79.

23. Vries, 1986, pp. 98–100.
24. Meij, 1908, quotes on pp. 281, 290–1, 299, 314–15; Meij, 1909, quotes on pp. 213–16, 222–3, 227.
25. Weringh, 1986, p. 47.
26. Weringh, 1986, p. 77.
27. Aletrino, 1898, 'Twee opstellen (...)'.
28. Cf. Weringh, 1986, pp. 55–60.
29. Heymans, 1901, quotes on p. 86.
30. Roos, 1902, p. 307.
31. Cf. Simons, 1901, *Het Congres (...)*.
32. Roos, 1902, pp. 308–10.
33. As a matter of fact, it later became known that things were less friendly in Elmira than had been thought at the time, something which in retrospect gives the discussion an unusual character. Governor Brockway, who had so emphatically pointed to the lack of disciplinary punishment, appears to have personally mistreated his prisoners if they refused to be improved. He had to defend himself in front of special commissions against hundreds of serious complaints and was even brought to the point of resigning (cf. Eriksson, 1976, p. 104). It was only in 1983 that Alexander Pisciotta brought the originally severely glossed-over treatment of complaints about mistreatment to light, in a detailed and convincing way (Pisciotta, 1983).
34. Aletrino, 1898, 'Over de (...)', p. 489. See also Graaf, 1899.
35. Cf. Hamel (J. A. van), 1909.
36. See Sb., 1901, no. 63, articles X and XI.
37. Cf. Olnon, 1986, pp. 99–106.
38. Engelen, 1900, pp. 279–83; see also Laurillard, 1899, 'Bedenkingen tegen (...)', and Laurillard, 1899, 'Een en ander (...)'.
39. Roos, 1900, quotes on pp. 42, 55, 57, 58.
40. Cf. Vlaming, 1989, and Rooy, 1971.
41. Romein, 1976 (1938), pp. 804–6.
42. Cf. Pompe, 1956, part II, 313.
43. HdSG, 1888/89, Beraadslagingen Tweede Kamer, pp. 534–7.
44. Cf. Petersen, 1978, p. 471.
45. 'Enquête (...), 1897/98, (I), quotes on pp. 693–6 and, 1898/99, (II), quotes on pp. 28, 108.
46. HdSG, 1897/98, Beraadslagingen Tweede Kamer, pp. 953–6.
47. In 1900 Troelstra was sentenced to a month's cellular confinement for insulting the public prosecutor; cf. Frieswijk and Sleurink, 1984.
48. HdSG, 1898/99, Beraadslagingen Tweede Kamer, pp. 359–63.
49. HdSG, 1900/1901, Beraadslagingen Tweede Kamer, pp. 404–9; cf. Petersen, 1978, pp. 473–7. See also Eggink, 1958, p. 176.
50. HdSG, 1898/99, Beraadslagingen Tweede Kamer, p. 374.
51. Bonger, 1916 (1905), pp. 526–8.
52. See HdSG, 1892/93, Beraadslagingen Tweede Kamer, pp. 225, 227; HdSG,1897/98, Beraadslagingen Tweede Kamer, pp. 112, 134; cf. Petersen, 1978, p. 471.
53. E.g. Ranitz, 1898.
54. Hamel, 1912 (1889), pp. 503–10 (V. O. vol. I). See also Hamel, 1913, p. 546.

55. *HdSG*, 1898/99, Beraadslagingen Tweede Kamer, pp. 116–17, 160. Cf. Vries, 1901.
56. Elst, 1899, II, p. 244.
57. See Kinderwetten (Children Act) in Sb., 12 February 1901, nos 63 and 64. Cf. Petersen, 1978, pp. 465–7, and Olnon, 1986, pp. 99–106.
58. The Children Act was responsible for annually saving more than a thousand children from the cellular misery, as is apparent from prison statistics from before 1900.
59. Elst, 1899, II, pp. 261–2. See also Roos, 1900, p. 131.
60. Cf. Simons, 1901, 'Nieuwe (...)', pp. 295–6; Simons, 1901, *De Beginselen(...)*, p. 552.
61. Domela Nieuwenhuis, 1891, p. 402; see also Domela Nieuwenhuis, 1884; 1886/87; 1902, p. 25.
62. *HdSG*, Bijlagen, 2, 100.3, p. 11.
63. Handelingen NJV, 1901 (II), pp. 202–7.
64. Aletrino, 1906, quotes on pp. 4, 43, 145, 170. D. Simons thoroughly criticized Aletrino in *WvhR*, 25 Jan. 1907, no. 8475, and in *De Gids*, Simons, 1907.
65. *Celstraf (...)*, 1907, quotes on pp. 15, 44–54, 55–8, 66–7.
66. Hoeven, 1908, pp. 17–19.
67. Drooge, 1900.
68. Fabius, 1914.
69. Lammers, 1889, pp. 62–3; Sitter, 1890, p. 43.
70. Nederburgh, 1909, p. 97.
71. Sitter, 1890, pp. 63–4.
72. Duyl, 1881, p. 224.
73. Patijn, 1938, p. 428.
74. Cf. Regt, 1984.
75. With the 'Kinderwetten' (Children Act), the conditional deferment of the 'tuchtschoolstraf'(roughly the same as 'Borstal punishment') was already effected in 1905. Cf. Slingenberg, 1916, and Fabius, 1914.
76. *HdSG*, 1911/12, Tweede Kamer, Bijlagen, 304.3.
77. *HdSG*, 1914/15, Tweede Kamer, Bijlagen, 32.1, pp. 2–4.
78. *HdSG*, 1914/15, Beraadslagingen Tweede Kamer, pp. 874–5, 890, 912.
79. *HdSG*, 1914/15, Beraadslagingen Eerste Kamer, p. 339.
80. Cf. Slingenberg, 1916.
81. Cf. Hallema, 1958, pp. 317–20; Fleers, 1976, pp. 18–19 and Fokkens, 1981, 1.1.
82. Cf. Weringh, 1986, p. 38.
83. Cf. Eggink, 1958, p. 62–4.
84. See the preceding chapter.
85. These articles were collected by Feith (1909), who writes in his introduction about the public excitement.
86. Cf. Vries, 1986, pp. 94–5.
87. Cf. Derks, 1987; Drost, 1980; Haffmans 1989; Winkels, 1991; Drost, 1991.
88. Even earlier, minors had disappeared from the penitentiaries. The 'kinderwetten'(Children Act) can also be said to have freed prisoners of a group deemed incapable of self-government.

89. *Celstraf, (...)*, 1917, pp. 1–15, 28–30, 38–9; *Verslag van de vergadering (...)*, 1917, p. 44.
90. Neckeben, 1891, quotations on pp. 6, 18–19, 64. Translation by Kate Simms.

9

Toughness and Leniency, 1918–1940: 'Deviations', Education, Incapacitation and Minimum Rules

The cell of today is a telling monument for a Christian government, which gets up and goes to bed with the bible in its luxury binding, carefully closed with golden hinges, for Pharisees, speaking always of God but having souls of straw and hearts of cork.[1]

Shut away for years with no other company than the toilet pail, its separate, rickety seat, the folding table, the three-legged stool on a jangling chain, the drinking crock and wooden eating utensils. At eye level, sanded into sightlessness, a barred window. Across from a window cursed with cataracts, an armoured door with spy hole, humiliating invention of a furtive genius! Three times a day, feed is distributed through a flap in the door, the metal lip falling to like the jaw of a taunting crocodile who has broken his fast. Every week the same menu, year in and year out, as monotonous as the clicking of beads of a rosary, as vitamine-poor as a sand storm in the Sahara, and not as decorously served as the sentences are, in bands and gown.[2]

In the neutral Netherlands, the First World War convincingly established the connection between crime and socio-economic conditions. So many Dutchmen became rich by smuggling goods and transgressing against the distribution laws that the number of sentences rose by almost 400 per cent within a few years. This led to a huge shortage of room, first in the remand prisons and later in the penitentiaries.[3] The Minister of Justice, Th. Heemskerk, introduced an emergency law which stated that the prison sentence, at his indication, could be served communally.[4] This special legislation quickly resulted in a well-reasoned breach with cellular confinement. The Minister also wanted to use one of the labour colonies in Veenhuizen to communally imprison the smugglers.[5] The World War was also responsible for initiating other developments which came to influence the prison system.

Clara Wichmann and the 'Action Committee'

Right after the war, substantial increases in crime led to public alarm and a short-lived call for harsh measures. Some members of the Lower House even argued for reinstatement of corporal punishment.[6] Articles in daily papers insisted upon more prisons and harsh measures to prevent escapes. The anarchist-socialist lawyer, Clara Wichmann, made use of these harsh sounds emitted by the press to point at the irrational nature of the call for more prisons. Lack of room in the prisons had, after all, come into being because of increased crime and had, thus, not caused it. Her opinion was that the significant increase in crime during the war 'resulting from the general upheaval, within a few years' time, thus, among the very same people as before' should have been able to convince everyone of the importance of socio-economic conditions in determining crime.

From this incontestable position, she unfolded her anarchistic-socialist vision of crime and punishment in a series of articles.[7] An emotional engagement also kindled by the First World War added conviction. Many of the more than a thousand young men who had spent at least ten months in prison for conscientious objection belonged to the socialist movement. Clara Wichmann's future husband, Jo Meijer, and her intellectual soul mate, Bart de Ligt, knew from this experience how harsh prison life was. Together with several revolutionaries, social-democrats, Christian-socialists and anarchists, Wichmann founded the Action Committee against the Existing Opinions concerning Crime and Punishment in March of 1920. Ten thousand copies of her manifesto were distributed. At the first meeting, she gave a speech about 'Crime, punishment and society'.

Both the manifesto and the speech read as a powerful overture to developments in penal law in the interbellum period. Clara's sudden death in 1922 prevented her from taking part actively, but what she would have thought was already clear then. She turned fiercely against the proponents of eugenic measures and the 'rendering harmless' of recidivists who were to become the focus of attention in the 1930s. The mild developments in the interbellum period would undoubtedly have not gone far enough for her. Her idea was that the whole prison system was geared to making 'people small, submissive, lacklustre, to breaking their pride and impairing them'. Punishment did not have any place in her thoughts. Punishment could only lead to 'external' improvement in her opinion. She characterized real improvement or 'purifying' as the 'deepest internal process' by which threats of punishment or punishment would most likely be counterproductive. This 'internal growth' had to originate within themselves.

As far as education was concerned, she had ideals for which the practice of criminal law was not yet ready. In the area of prisoners' power and their emancipation, however, she underestimated the possiblities.

She thought that interest in prisoners was very limited and that no one cared about their fate. 'The criminals,' she wrote, 'are unorganized; they have no representatives; they exercise no economic power; they are not able to explain their points of view, their motives to all the others, the honest citizens.' Apparently she was not aware that she herself and the existence of her action committee already refuted this argument to a certain extent. After all, with their meetings and brochures, her action committee actively and committedly brought the interests of prisoners and prisoners' right into the public limelight.[8]

I. SOCIAL INTERCOURSE AND CONTACTS WITH THE OUTSIDE WORLD

The cellular system can rightly be seen as the 'antithesis' of non-differentiated communal confinement. Shortly after the war, the 'synthesis' began to take shape. The new prison reformers argued for the saving of what was good in *both* systems.[9] This development can certainly be interpreted dialectically, but the synthesis was sought primarily in improved community and not as much in an improved cell system. This has much to do with the gradual nature of the development. Social causes for crime came to the foreground because of the First World War, but scientific and political awareness of the social formation of criminals had begun to grow even earlier, as we have seen. The image of man as *homo clausus* made way for that of man as social product. Criminals were no longer, according to A. J. Blok, seen as persons 'under a glass bell, dissociated from the conditions of their own physical and social environment'.[10] That the sinful prisoner under pressure of years of solitude could grow into a better and socially adjusted fellow-citizen was now widely seen as absurd. 'How could one have been so unpsychological!' exclaimed the psychiatrist, P. Bierens de Haan, and many others too.[11]

Actual change went much less far, but practically everything that did change can be characterized as a gradual (re)entry of social life. At first very careful experiments were done with readings, lectures and the showing of transparencies whereby contact among prisoners remained impossible. Wall decorations were permitted too, so that the outside world, at least as 'city-and landscapes' and family portraits, could enter the cells.[12]

The Open-air Prison in Veenhuizen

While the outside world hesitatingly crept into the cellular prisons, prisoners in the open-air prison in Veenhuizen had already formed a true community. They were put to work outside during the day and separated into alcoves for the night. The total population had very quickly decreased to less than a hundred selected prisoners from the more than a thousand (primarily smugglers) of 1918. The Minister of Justice, Heemskerk, decided in 1923 to continue the experiment on a limited basis (not more than 120 men) with persons sentenced to not more than one-and-a-half years. Restrictions on spending meant that the prison had to function 'almost without surveillance'. Governor H. C. C. Franck made virtue of necessity by presenting the large degree of freedom as an experiment. He extracted from prisoners at their entry a promise not to escape, using, of course, the threat of transfer to a cellular prison as a motivating factor.[13]

The emphasis he placed upon trust and responsibility showed that governor Franck had been influenced by the 'honour system' that had been introduced on an experimental scale in the American state of Arizona. The regime in Veenhuizen also showed characteristics of the American systems of 'self-management' or 'self-government'.[14] Convicts had to pass through three 'Reward Classes' and could earn all sorts of privileges. Franck thought that the system would support prisoners in their attempts 'to become good and to discard bad habits'. Some warders and the room guards, who were responsible for keeping the communal hall clean and who served the food, were chosen by prisoners themselves. Franck speculated that prisoners would not wish to disappoint this trust, once given.[15]

The new system was closely discussed and praised in the daily papers. In Veenhuizen the journalists did not see, as they did in cellular prisons, 'unhealthy, pale, shy, nervous smooth talkers and hothouse plants' but men 'in whom the light of freedom had been lit and who were beginning to feel grateful for that light'.[16] In spite of the small scale of the experiment, the open-air prison came to play an important role by providing empirical evidence of how things could be done better and differently in the battle against strictly cellular confinement and it came to influence the forming of opinions significantly.

The System of 'Deviations'

The fact that cellular solitude in The Netherlands had been carried through to greater extremes than elsewhere in Europe was apparent not only from the stringent implementation of cell cap and bans on speaking but certainly also from the lack of printed news. The process of improvement could not be interrupted by worldly information. This often led to absurd ignorance. The pressure to allow news of the outside world into the cells, at least in printed form, was so large that in 1925 the prison paper from Veenhuizen was made available to all prisoners.[17]

The 'New Spirit' also was expressed in the increasing criticism of the disrupting effects of short sentences, something which led in 1925 to a new 'Geldboetewet' (Fining Law). The judge could impose a fine, if he would otherwise have imposed a sentence of at most three months detention or confinement.[18] The Fining Law kept many out of prison and, thus, in a free social life. Almost at the same moment, life within cell walls changed substantially, even though this was not truely a radical break with cellular solitude. In 1923, pointing to the experiment in Veenhuizen, the Minister of Justice, Heemskerk, called it 'very important' that 'under the circumstances' solitude be mitigated 'to some extent' in cellular penitentiaries as well.[19] However, changes in the law were necessary to effectuate this. While waiting for these, he made it possible to grant prisoners certain privileges for good behaviour. The Prison Ruling of 1886 was amended in 1925 for this reason.[20] The changes in the Prison Ruling were thenceforth referred to as 'the system of deviations'. Here the uniform and strict implementation of the cellular system was not dismantled but 'deviated' from. After thirty days, 'general deviations' could be considered. These included: 'a somewhat more favourable' access to the canteen, 'a more acceptable rule' for visits, 'broader use' of the library and permission to attend readings or lectures. After four months, and thereafter monthly, 'special deviations' could be permitted, like reading a 'public newspaper', writing letters more often, transfer to 'a cell with transparent windows', letting one's hair or beard grow 'as one wished', longer periods in the open air, smoking on the promenade, permission to put 'some decoration' on the walls and to keep flowers, birds or fish in the cell.[21]

The ban on sociability was broken, but the break consisted of no more than a few cracks. The pedagogical side of the system of deviations, the motivation to good behaviour, grew more or less unintentionally into an alternative system of keeping order which consisted of the deferring or denying of privileges as punishment.[22]

Prison Life on the Inside

Shortly after the introduction of the deviation system, a prison teacher made clear just how extensive the loneliness of cellular life still was in a stirring series of newspaper articles about life in prison. His feeling for subtle details were obvious in his description of the often occurring religious fanaticism, the run-away fantasies and dreams, the all-dominating fixation upon the passage of time and the function of animals in the cell. There were prisoners who tamed sparrows and taught them tricks, who amused themselves for long periods by dissecting a dead bird or who had become so attached to a couple of flies that they stiffened with shock when the teacher unsuspectingly reached out to hit them. 'In their eerie, restricted little world, the proportions "of trifles" swell in front of their eyes and tiny things seem huge and important to them,' concluded the teacher – a contemporary description of what is still characteristic for life in prison.[23]

The research report of several years later, written by the ex-prison regent, H. van der Voo, in which he tried to definitively solve the problem of 'cell versus community' showed much less talent for putting oneself in another's shoes. His research resembled that of prison inspector, Alstorphius Grevelink, in the previous century. He asked a good thousand convicts in the cellular prisons what form of confinement they preferred: cellular or communal. Of all those questioned, 35.4 per cent preferred the cell and 64.6 per cent the community.

Van der Voo summarized answers of all convicts, but still reproduced their own words, wherever possible. Although Van der Voo concluded differently, the report shows how harsh the cell was for many. The 'preference' chosen by prisoners was rather theoretical. They were confined in cells and there was nothing they could do about it. Still, they had to wonder whether the misery of communal confinement was perhaps even worse. Approximately 350 prisoners said that they, contrasting their fate to that, had not got such a raw deal, and all the rest found anything an improvement on the oppressive and nerve-racking solitude. Their 'preferences' were not often very clear. A fifty-year-old farmer chose the cell 'because then you can cry once in a while and that's not possible in a community'. The wish of a twenty-one-year-old chauffeur was that others would not be witnesses 'to his sorrow and emotion'.

The great majority consisted of virtually uneducated persons who had committed a crime against property. In solitude, they attempted to come to some realization of their situation, but usually their thoughts endlessly circled in concerns about family left behind and how their lives could have taken such a disasterous turn. By reading and working hard they tried, often without success, to divert their train of thought. 'The cell is too lonely and that continuous "being on your own" makes you so unhappy. I am not used to that and have never experienced such a thing,' Van der Voo wrote down directly from the mouth of a thirty-three-year-old florist's helper. Almost everyone complained of 'nervousness', 'worrying', 'brooding' and 'beating their brains'. Many also thought that they were becoming 'shy' and 'reclusive'. They saw the solitude as 'stultifying', 'stupefying' and 'crazy-making'.

Solitude was rejected because social contact was lacking and the chance of suicide grew, but communal confinement, which they had often undergone in a remand prison or in the Special Penitentiary at Scheveningen, brought with it too much social pressure. Moreover, one came to share space with the mentally ill, boorish persons and incorrigible recidivists. The chance of moral infection was large, in their opinion. Fear of recognition in free society after release existed. One was no longer one's own boss and had to adjust to the will of the strongest. There were fights, challenges, and prisoners attempted to get others confined to a punishment cell. The weakest had no life at all. The strongest carried out a reign of terror. During meals, people burped next to you or pooped on the pail, and homosexual contacts occurred openly. Expressions of religious interest were mocked.[24]

In solitude, dangers of unlimited masturbation or endless sexual fantasies threatened, continuous thoughts of 'the girl' or 'the wife'. Some prisoners let their fellows know when they had come by knocking on walls or pipes. One prisoner thought that only shame could prevent him from masturbating. He wanted to be communally imprisoned for that reason. 'He works with pleasure but he reads not at all because he is always thinking "of his masturbation",' noted Van der Voo, who, even after all these talks, did not seem able to realize how harsh cellular punishment actually was. His analysis of the talks grew slowly into a fierce tirade against the lenient times in which he felt a sickly sentiment dominated. He printed his final conclusion in bold letters: **Keep the cell and do not expand the community.** His book was primarily used, then, to prevent the growth of too much enthusiasm for communal confinement. Members of Parliament and even the Minister of Justice pointed to it in connection with the moral dangers of 'the community'.[25]

First Breach in the Cellular Principle

The introduction of social intercourse in cellular prisons was not prevented by the report. A Bill of the Minister of Justice, J. Donner, was accepted by parliament in 1929; it implied a cautious breach of the cellular system. The law created the possibility of permitting prisoners who were eligible 'in connection with their personality and the offense' to be brought into the community 'for certain goals'.[26] Communal work was considered ('albeit at a certain distance from each other') for selected prisoners, communal instruction and the communal doing of physical exercises. Soon, the Minister added communal religious exercises and song. Communal activities had already been permitted in the past, but one was confronted with 'the rigid principle of solitude' again and again, while the 'moveable cells', as the socialist, A. B. Kleerekoper, called the cell caps, remained obligatory in doing these activities.[27] Tragicomical scenes created by this obligation to wear the cell cap are suggested in a report about the communal gymnastic and song exercises in a corridor of the Rotterdam prison:

> On the coconut fiber runner, numbers have been sewn, each man stands on his number. The men have the usual cap on, in which a small triangle has been cut underneath to make unrestricted breathing possible through the nose. The cap is, thus, not taken off; the jackets are removed, however, and the men usually are in stocking feet.'[28]

Meanwhile the Wall Street stock market crash had taken place and government policy was more and more determined by massive cut-backs. Again and again, the putting into operation of the law and an amended version of the Prison Ruling were put off. It finally happened on 1 January, 1934. Six months after beginning their sentence, prisoners would, from then on, be eligible for communal activities, recidivists only after a year.[29] Here and there cell walls were removed to create little areas for 'real' communal contact. In some, but not by far in all prisons, selected prisoners were brought together now and then in small groups, without being allowed to freely speak to each other. Reading of real papers was more and more often allowed. In Amsterdam, for instance, all prisoners 'in view of favourable experience' were permitted to read newspapers some months before their release and often this already took place after they had served four months.[30] Technical developments came to the aid of prisoners around 1930 when the radio made its appearance. One immediately saw in this an important means to moral improvement. The radio was expected to prevent 'fretting' and 'brooding' and to direct thoughts 'to the ideals of normal societal life'. A broader introduction of the radio occurred only after the war.[31]

In July 1937, the prison for young men was opened in Zutphen. The building, meant for approximately one hundred convicts, had been ready for years, but there had been no money for its further development. The prison statistics spoke rightfully of a 'historical development'. The Prison Act of 1886 was expanded with an article in which it was stated that the prison for young men was 'especially' aimed at 'their improvement'. More than three-quarters of a century after van der Brugghen had argued in its favour, The Netherlands got a prison with a progressive regime. At their entry into the new prison, the young men were first given a month of solitary confinement in the observation class. A plan was made for 'the further penal-educational treatment'. Then they entered the second class. During work, instruction, religious obligations and gymnastics lessons they were allowed to see and speak to each other, but the rest of their time was spent in the cell. The treatment aimed at imparting 'civilization and education'. Good behaviour led to transfer after six months to the third class. Here meals were also communal. Even in the evenings, these young men could leave their cells 'for recreational purposes' for a few hours. If they had been sentenced to less than a half year, they could become eligible for conditional leave after six months. Those with longer sentences were eligible for this after a year.[32]

As a contrast to the optimism surrounding improvement of young persons, a growing pessimism existed about the usefulness of prisons for adults. The generally recognized failure of the cellular system moved influential prison experts to plead for the most far-reaching form of communal confinement: that in free, social life itself. Scholars of criminal law and prison experts unfolded penological dreams which actually amounted to the demolishing of prison walls. The psychiatrist, van Mesdag, for instance, foresaw work institutions whereby the sentenced could just go home at night or work in free society and be confined to an institution at night. Prison would then possibly be seen as 'an old-fashioned measure from the grey past'. The professor of criminal law, Pompe, was of the opinion that, in the future, moral improvement would be carried out as much as possible 'outside institutions, in free society', under the supervision of probation and after-care agencies. Others pushed for experimental weekend sentences and nightly confinement. 'The punishment of deprivation of freedom', wrote the professor of criminal law, Röling, 'was a necessary phase in the development of means of punishment; the belief in deprivation of freedom is one of the fallacies of a period that has passed.'[33] He made this utterance a little too prematurely. It indicated the progressive attitude in circles of prison experts which also expressed itself in a new penal optimism: 'de opvoedingsgedachte' (the educational view).

2. THE EDUCATIONAL VIEW: A PENAL CIVILIZING OFFENSIVE

Improvement of prisoners was understood as something quite different after the First World War than in the nineteenth century. An increasing social awareness which was expressed, among other things, in more social and sociological explanations of crime, gradually gave new meaning to the pursued improvement. It was not so much disposition as social functioning which had to be improved. After the First World War, prison experts usually no longer spoke of moral improvement but of education. Factual and desired changes to the prison sentence were judged and defended from the point of view of this 'opvoedingsgedachte' (educational view). Many seemed to think of education as no more than learning a trade, receiving lessons, getting used to order and routine and learning to take account of fellow-men. Others went much further. Education was, in their view, meant to train the will, to teach control of temper and passion and to increase 'self-management' or 'self-regulation'. In contrast to the cellular improvers, the new educators thought that precisely broad social contact and a large measure of freedom were necessary in order to cultivate that self-restraint in confinement. Psychic inhibitions could only become second nature through practical exercises. The educators did not want self-restraint which was purely fed by good intentions, like that formed in cellular solitude, but a self-restraint which was based on 'will- and habit-forming'.[34]

This is the appropriate place to take a closer look at the relationship between this penal civilizing offensive and the civilizing process. According to Norbert Elias this process did not take place according to a plan or 'through any purposive education of individual people or groups', but was the unintentional result of shifting balances of power, advancing differentiation of social functions, and the lengthening of the chains of interdependence.[35] The penal educators, however, did purposefully attempt to impart to prisoners forms of self-restraint, regulations of affective life and control of conduct which they considered to be civilized. But, the very fact that they considered these forms civilized is characteristic for the phase of the civilizing process in which they found themselves. Criminal behaviour was, in their view, also uncivilized. After all, criminals gave in to their impulses too quickly, they weighed up the advantages and disadvantages of their actions insufficiently against each other and let themselves be led by feelings and passions.

The educational view was lent scientific support by new insights from psychology which were, again, characteristic of the phase of the civilizing process in which they were developed. In his *temperamentenleer* (theory of temperaments) the psychologist, G. Heymans built further upon the distinction which the German, Otto Gross, had made in 1902 between *primary* and *secondary* functions.[36] In his famous 'cube' he adds emotion and activity as psychic basic characteristics. He himself and prison experts did research based on the science of temperaments among criminals, vagrants and beggars. It is important that they repeatedly thought they had proven that a weak secondary function predisposed one to crime and anti-social behaviour.[37]

Heymans included 'the after-effects' of earlier impresssions or emotions in the secondary function. When he thought of persons with a strongly developed secondary function he saw 'the more thoughtful types, in whom all that once has been consciously registered remains, so that it, even without coming up in memory, continues to deliver its proportional contribution in all further thinking, feeling and acting'. In contrast to these were the primary types, 'persons of the moment', in whom every impression, independent of its impact, 'immediately was not only erased by the next but also made useless'.[38] It is clear that a strongly developed secondary function was associated with civilized persons, sensitive to punishment, who possessed powerful self-restraint and self-control. Primary types, contrarily, could not keep themselves in line. Experiences with punishment were forgotten the moment they walked out through the prison gates.[39] Here the resemblance to the Lombrosian account of criminal activity in terms of atavism catches the eye. The criminal psychologist, G. H. A. Feber, thus also compared primarily functioning criminals, just as Lombroso did, to primitive folk and children. The temperament psychologists did explicitly what critics of Elias accuse him of doing implicitly: placing people on a lower rung of the ladder of civilization and attaching a moral judgement to this.[40]

Training of the will and encouragement of self-restraint: the theoretical foundations of the educational view were clearly formulated in The Netherlands, but in prison practice very little came of this. Possibilities to put the theories into practice with adult prisoners were lacking. When Minister Heemskerk produced his circular in 1924 about the system of 'deviations', immediate extensive and intense consideration was given to it. The psychiatrist, van Mesdag, for instance, gave his opinion, in a speech about the deviation system, that the privileges were pedagogical means to arrouse the interest of the prisoner, to provide him with new motives, to open up to him new worlds of thinking and feeling, to slowly lift him 'out of the situation of impotent lowness to that of greater power' and, finally, to 'work him up' to the level 'of the intellectual, moral and esthetic normally thinking and feeling person'.[41] Even the prison directors thought that they had ascertained educative effects. In yearly reports they wrote of how prisoners had made a real effort 'to check the up to now often uninhibited operation of evil tendencies'. Prisoners 'managed' themselves better, kept themselves better 'under control', took their fates once more 'in their own hands' and trained their wills.[42] The portraits on the wall, the little birds, the cigarette now and then and the other 'deviations' seemed to have made of a cellular failure a sudden pedagogical success. Some even said that they had scientifically proven that the prison sentence augmented the secondary function.[43]

The optimism surrounding the educational view could possibly have something to do with what the professor of criminal law, Röling, in 1933, called 'the bad conscience of the community'. When, at about the turn of the century, the insight came to the fore that society itself was guilty of causing crime, he feels that the 'good conscience with which one had punished' also disappeared. 'One found salvation in the educational view. Education is doing good for the delinquent. And one stilled thereby the question of whether it was actually justifiable to inflict suffering on a criminal,' Röling said in his public lesson about 'the educational view in criminal law'. That was in 1933, right before a remarkable harshening of the penal climate pushed the educational view temporarily into a strongly defensive position.[44]

3. THE EMANCIPATION OF PRISONERS

Even though the greatly increased interest in psychic and social characteristics of prisoners had a lot to do with scientific curiosity and with the refining of their punishment, that interest made it more difficult to see them as inhuman rabble. In many reports and articles prisoners were portrayed as persons of flesh and blood, just like everyone else. This, intentioned or not, fostered understanding for the psychic and social characteristics of prisoners and their miserable existences.

Journalistic Compassion, Conscientious Objectors and the Imprisoned Fellow-man

Articles about prison life in dailies attracted many readers. Prisoners were described in these with much psychological insight and empathy. Much emphasis was placed on social conditions which had led them into crime.

A serie of articles in *Het Volk* were written by the socialist writer Maurits Dekker, who, as innocent suspect of a double robbery with murder had spent four months in custody.[45] Very emotionally, Dekker described prison as hell on earth. 'Outwardly and in actuality a city of the living dead', was his characterization of prison. He described the cell door as 'a gravestone' of a 'cave-like mortuary'. Behind every cell door, however, lived a person, 'one who loves, one who suffers, one who has done evil, one who has tripped in the battle for survival: a criminal. But a human being, one who is as I am, as we all are.'[46]

A critic for the *Algemeen Handelsblad* reviewed the book *Wij achter tralies* (We behind bars) of the German political prisoner, Georg Fuchs. He saw Fuchs as a 'loudspeaker' for the voice of his fellow-prisoners 'making it known world-wide how it actually is in prison, and questioning whether mankind can justify this any longer'. He thought that the 'increasingly bitter' feeling about prisons in all countries was that they were 'shameful to our culture'. 'May many read this book', he concluded. Thus the critic functioned too as a loudspeaker for the voice of prisoners.[47]

The very concerned interest in prisoners and their unfree existence was, both in The Netherlands and other Western European countries, partially an unintended result of the First World War and political disturbances. Indignation caused by the experiences of prisoners of war and political prisoners spilled over into normal prison life. They suffered from psychic problems which were described as 'barbed wire illness' and which strongly resembled normal prison psychoses. 'It is to be hoped that the symptoms of barbed wire illness at last will be able to open some eyes to the irrationality of the prison sentence, by which we weaken the nervous system, make the people unsuited for society and thus, cultivate recidivists,' wrote the psychologist, Kohlbrugge, in his influential book about the inner life of the criminal.[48]

The Netherlands remained neutral in the war, but many conscientious objectors were given a prison sentence. Precisely these politically aware prisoners pushed, after the war, for the founding of the Action Committee against Existing Opinions concerning Crime and Punishment. Connected with this, members of the founding committee, put together a volume of letters and articles from political and ordinary ex-prisoners under the title *De Vergetenen* (The Forgotten). They thought the time ripe for a 'protest from the common people' against the 'unnatural and inhuman' prison system, but then the common people must first know something of 'the harmful barbarianism' with which prisoners were treated. The intended purpose of the book was, 'to form a gate, an open gate, which provides an entry into the other's shut-off world'. The Action Committee organized, into the 1930s, lectures and meetings at which they insisted upon far-reaching reforms. The editorial staff of *De Jonge*

Gids (The Young Guide) pressed for a 'battle for more humanity' in areas of crime and punishment.[49]

Increasing Sensitivity to Prison Suffering

The penological, scientific and public interest in prisoners arose from and stimulated the awareness that prisoners were also humans 'not always so very much worse' than free citizens.[50] That awareness was never totally absent of course, but much points to the fact that it penetrated more deeply after the war into the feelings of people who had something to do with the prison system. The already so problematic justification of judicial infliction of suffering caused by the deterministic concept of man became even more so when more elements of prison life came to be seen and felt as suffering. Anyone who still placed an element of retribution in the punishment was set the task of accounting for 'the expressly intended suffering' and 'making the necessity of the treatment to which he will be subjected sound credible to the delinquent'.[51] This put the emancipation process of prisoners into high gear, improved their chances of power, increased understanding for their needs and had consequences for the ways in which they were treated.

A warder told of how, in 1928, at the beginning of his career, it was very usual to drag an unruly prisoner to the dark punishment cell and, if ordered, put him in chains. Now he would be ashamed 'to treat a fellow-man in this way for a few hundred guilders a year'. His opinion was that he and his colleagues would refuse to do that at present. 'Times have, as far as that is concerned, changed colossally,' he said.[52] This increased sensitivity to the suffering inflicted upon prisoners expressed itself as well in the criticism of the rule to give them only bread and water for the first two days of their detention. A lawyer denounced especially the 'mentality' upon which this was based. Resistance to a life-long prison sentence grew forcibly too. One opponent saw it as nothing more than 'brutal revenge'.[53] The increasing sensitivity came through even more strongly in the extremely emotional tone with which various authors went to battle against cellular confinement. The known solicitor and poet, François Pauwels, wrote in 1926, that the system in The Netherlands belonged to the 'most miserable and backward' in Europe. People languished like animals in dark hovels. He compared the wild appearance of 'imprisoned cell-beasts' in the courtroom to that of exhausted draught animals. Others wrote of a 'slowly destructive killing hell'. A prisoner came to have a 'death mask' and was left all alone 'with his guilt and his faeces'.[54]

The new cell critics were not any less fierce than some of the opponents of the cellular system half way through the preceding century. Sometimes they even used the same arguments.[55] However, it was now progressive to be against cellular confinement and for prison reform, whereas opponents of cellular confinement in the preceding century had, on the contrary, been labelled as conservative because they usually also supported the retention of public corporal and capital punishment. Now proponents of cellular confinement had to defend themselves against allegations of barbarism and cruelty. There are also indications that political controversy played a role here. Mainly socialists and left-liberals made use of cellular confinement in order to put the sentiments of conservative and conventional people in an unfavourable light.[56] That these also felt the critique to be of this nature was apparent from the petulant tone in which they offered resistance. It was not so bad as the 'cellular confinement antagonists' so 'assiduously' proclaimed, wrote the judge, A. A. Cnopius, in defense of cellular confinement.[57] In a Catholic weekly an expert defended cellular confinement and himself:

> It is possible that the reader will be surprised to hear this opinion being expressed. The cell is so maligned at present that one seems all but barbarian when one dares to defend it. Still, I shall take the risk.[58]

This is the tone of people who feel they are being attacked. In defending cellular confinement, one had to take into account the 'shudder' that overcame 'the average reader' when solitary confinement was brought up.[59]

Even though it was certainly attempted from the socialist and left-liberal quarter, opinion forming surrounding cellular confinement was not totally determined by political dividing lines. That was clearly obvious in two articles in the Catholic daily *De Maasbode* about cellular confinement. Instead of allowing itself to be pushed into a conservative corner, the editorial staff made a sort of foot-race in abhorrence of it. Referring to cellular confinement, they spoke of 'untold amounts of human misery' and 'terror'. They greedily cited the Calvinist ex-minister Heemskerk, who had addressed the left opposition in the Lower House thus:

> I do not need to learn from the gentlemen not to have much sympathy for cellular confinement. Perhaps they have even learned that from me and have forgotten this fact and now they tell it to me again as if it were something new that they have discovered themselves!

The editorial staff, agreeing fully, went on to cite the Roman Catholic senator, Heerkens Thijssen, who had called cellular confinement 'indecent' and a 'torment'. They felt that they thus prevented 'persons from the left' taking over 'the issue'. 'In a rightist government, it has undivided attention.'[60]

Public aversion to cellular confinement, especially in the 1920s, was so widespread that no single party could afford to throw itself into the breach to defend it. In the previous century, during the battle about public punishment and cellular confinement, relatively little compassion for prisoners could be perceived, but now people appeared to be driven by genuine sympathy. Distances between social classes had become much smaller and criminals were seen by many as victims of social injustice. 'Understanding all does not absolve everything, yet it does absolve a lot,' wrote even such a moderate reformer as the emeritus professor of criminal law, Simons, in 1929. He had concluded his parting address two years earlier with the words: 'We must have a humane penal law, or nothing'. His colleague, A. J. Blok, found that feelings of retribution had become weaker 'with the deepening of the roots of love for one's fellow-man'.[61] One was able to see prisoners more easily as 'fellow-men' than had been possible in the previous century.[62]

This contributed to the increased recognition. of the thought that prisoners had feelings and rights. The 'entire populace', the psychiatrist, van Mesdag, said, 'is beginning to take an interest in our penal practice and the way in which our prisoners are treated.' 'Our prisoners' was also the title given to a newspaper article about solitary confinement.[63] The editors of another daily even put 'Our fellow-criminals' above an article about probation. The ostracized were at least verbally reinstated to society. The writer, M. J. Brusse, deemed it necessary in this climate to apologize in a newspaper article for the fact that he had interviewed a prison governor, while his sympathies lay with the poor prisoners.[64]

Ex-prison regent, Van der Voo, looked with disfavour upon these developments. Sneeringly, he remarked that 'the so-called democracy' felt itself called upon 'to take an interest in the fate of the prisoner; the press attempts to point out how a dignified existence for convicts can be achieved'. He thought 'this ultramodern appreciation' of prisoners had to do with 'a sentimental, sickly philanthropic tendency'.[65]

Power, Opinions and Prisoners' Rights

The fact that even prisoners had rights was at first primarily felt. Precisely the people who noticed this most keenly had objections. 'All that is lacking is that they have a say in prison-management!', wrote the prison regent from Alkmaar, C. D. Donath, in his criticism of the system of 'deviations'.[66] Pompe, indeed, pushed for something as unbelievable as 'democracy in the prison' five years later. He wanted to let prisoners choose 'their own leaders' from among themselves. That would give prisoners what they 'very urgently' needed: self-confidence.[67] Others were convinced that prisoners had too much of this already. The prison governor, M. Noordhoff, found criticism of the miserable life in cells heavily exaggerated. He found that prisoners often applied to the visiting commissioners and authorities 'about trivialities'. 'How then could they ever resign themselves to the experience of brutal treatment?'[68]

These remarks point to the fact that prisoners themselves had become aware that the balance of power was shifting in their favour. Governor Noordhoff gave his opinion of how that had come about. The prison had become, 'as it were, a glass house'. Police and probation officers wandered in and out every day. Inspection was actually not even necessary any more because, of all the civil servants connected to a prison, there would 'most probably' be one with a relationship with a daily paper, who would be 'eager' to 'bring to light a bestial treatment of a poor prisoner by a hard-hearted and coarsened governor'. His opinion was that 'irresponsible action taken against a prisoner' would not remain hidden 'and this would cost a governor dearly'. The strenghtening position of power of prisoners cannot be illustrated more aptly, even more so because Noordhoff also indicated that he, if need be, would try to settle the power struggle to his own advantage with hard measures. Very hard means were no longer at his disposal, however, because, as he was very keenly aware, he was being watched:

> Should it pass the Lower House without interpellation, then there would still be at least a half-dozen questions addressed to the Minister of Justice.[69]

Such questions were, indeed, posed about suspect situations. In 1935, socialist Members of Parliament even proposed a motion, albeit unsuccessfully, whereby they pressed for a parliamentary investigation of applications of the prison rules.[70] Prisoners also gained the opportunity to address themselves directly to the outside world. The *Maandblad voor Berechting en Reclasseering* (a monthly for probation officers and after-care agents) introduced, in 1922, the regular feature 'From the cell and from life'. The editorial board hoped for reports from prisoners and ex-prisoners. They expected the column to produce 'echos' of 'the misery of the cell' and 'the happiness' about conditional sentencing. The column was open for the 'opinions of convicts about crime and punishment and about justice'. Admittedly, one could not yet speak of really free expressions of opinions, keeping in mind the censorship by prison staff and the editorial board, but, in the light of the process of emancipation, this possibility to publish must still be seen as an important breakthrough. In the very first column, an ex-prisoner complained of extensive filthiness and bad hygiene. Two years later, a complaint about insufficient clothing during their airing in the winter led to almost immediate ministerial action. He allowed military overcoats to be distributed to prisoners.[71]

Recognition of Sexual Problems

Various contributions in the column were concerned with sexual need and the problem of masturbation. Apparently, some prisoners did little else than battle against masturbation. 'I wanted, at any cost, to preserve my freshness and resilience', wrote a released prisoner. One can only guess at the intensity of guilt feelings provoked in prisoners when they gave in to their lust. Keeping this in mind, the distribution of mirrors was recommended. The prisoners would then be able to see how pale and thin they had become. The author saw in this 'a powerful motivation' to 'protect themselves against certain vices'.[72]

In contrast to this unpleasant proposition, there was a real recognition of sexual need. In 1928, the psychiatrist, van Mesdag, asked emphatically for attention to this huge problem during a meeting of the Dutch Lawyers' Union. Van Mesdag knew that he was dealing with a serious taboo. He had never read anything about it in books or articles. 'One is silent about this because one feels at a loss about how to deal with it,' he said. He did not have a solution either, but he did at least want to establish, once and for all, that prison was incapable of paying attention to 'a very important function of the body, which is also significant in psychic health'. Considering that sexual intercourse was 'a normal right' of married persons, he asked if there were reasons why this right was denied prisoners, especially as their wives also suffered from this. Government would, in his opinion, at least have to recognize this right. Then solutions could be sought. In the Soviet Union and in America, he asserted, sexual contacts were already being permitted on an experimental basis. Van Mesdag could not imagine such experiments taking place in The Netherlands for the time being. He made a case, thus, for more sport, work, recreation and moral education, 'through which the power of the sexual drive over the person could be broken to some extent'.[73]

Van Mesdag had started a ball rolling. Other lawyers endorsed the importance of the sexual question and extended it to cover female prisoners as well. How new this all was appeared from an article in a lawyers' journal about 'The sexual life of prisoners'. After a long period kept under wraps, sexual need had now been 'openly' confronted, according to the author. A 'satisfactory solution' had not yet been found, 'that is obvious', but he pointed to experiments in Mexico where married prisoners could receive their wives in separate rooms and where 'for a few hours, the illusion of homely happiness' was offered.[74]

First Minimum Rules for the Treatment of Prisoners

Prisoners were considered more and more to be persons with *rights*. This was usually formulated somewhat globally by speaking of the right to a decent existence or a humane treatment, but others wrote very exactly about, for instance, 'the right to protest' or 'the right' to appeal negative decisions about conditional release.[75] With this cautious zeal for prisoners' rights, Dutch experts were ahead of attempts by the League of Nations to arrive at a convention which would set down rules and regulations for the treatment of prisoners 'to alleviate the inhuman fate of many prisoners'. The English Howard League had already pressed for just such a convention in 1925. Since that time, one spoke repeatedly in the League of

Nations about the extremely bad treatment and torture of prisoners in many countries. However, things had not come so far yet that rules for treatment had been issued. 'But, continuous publicizing of abuses in this area, informing of the public about inhumane treaments suffered by prisoners in various countries, will finally have to lead to such barbarianisms becoming impossible,' judged a leading Dutch newspaper.[76]

Within another international organization, more successful work was being done to establish a system of rules for the treatment of prisoners. At the penitentiary congress in London in 1925, the Commission Pénitentiaire Internationale was charged with investigating whether it was possible to formulate 'general rules' which would guarantee all those deprived of their freedon by judicial authority 'a decent treatment'. At the congress in Prague (1928), yet another new commission, upon which the Dutch ex-prison inspector and professor of criminal law, Simon van der Aa, served, was assigned the same task. In 1929, he published the results of the activities of the commission in the *Bulletin de la Commission Pénitentiaire Internationale*: a system of minimum conditions for the treatment of prisoners. The emancipation process of prisoners had, for the first time in history, led to a formal establishment of minimum conditions to which 'from humanitary and social viewpoints' the treatment had to answer. The ruling did not yet have much status. It was offered to governments and they could do with it what they wished. But, the commission rightly pointed out that prison managements could use these conditions as an argument in their attempts to raise money for improvements to the prison system. The commission hoped that the conditions would lead to significant improvements in the situation of prisoners and would be stimulating to the 'massive modern movement' of penal reform. On 26 September 1934, the commission realized a great success. The minimum rules were accepted in the General Meeting of the League of Nations. A year later, the same meeting pressed for a widespread publication of the rules in countries where they had been accepted.[77]

The ruling included fifty-five articles about housing, treatment, visits, correspondence, discipline and personnel which can be seen as just as many seeds of the rights of prisoners. Confinement was not allowed to damage their mental or physical health and had to be directed at improvement and rehabilitation. In article 41, it was stated that prisoners had to have the opportunity 'every day' to address their appeals or complaints to higher authorities outside the prison.

A Dutch translation of the ruling was distributed by the Minister of Justice by circular in 1937. The editorial board of the probation monthly did not deem it necessary to print all fifty-five articles because the contents could be 'taken for granted' for Dutch concepts. The rules were thought to be especially designed for 'countries backward in penal law'. In

The Netherlands and many other countries, it was said, one only went ahead with the publication 'for reasons of international courtesy'.[78] In some important areas, the rules could not be taken for granted nearly as much as the editors of the monthly had wished to suggest. On the contrary, damage done by the prison sentence and especially the stringently applied cellular confinement to the mental and physical health of prisoners was practically unanimously recognized.

Figures for suicides and insanity continued to affirm the damaging influence upon mental health.[79] A possible influence of mitigation of cellular life cannot be constituted from these figures and other research data,[80] but the institutional doctor, B. P. Westerhuis, from the Special Penitentiary in Leeuwarden, thought that he had clearly ascertained a strong influence exerted by the permitted 'deviations' and social activities. The previous ten years had led to many fewer prisoners (nine) being transferred to an asylum than in the decade before (twenty-nine). 'The distraction and the will to remain in control of oneself prevented the restlessness which we so often had seen playing a role in the past and after which a cell psychosis frequently came into being,' he explained. Cell psychoses still occurred. He thought, moreover, that it had 'seldom' been apparent that the psychosis already existed before the sentence. Malingering also occurred 'very rarely'. He argued for more mitigation, as punishment causing many to be restless and 'even insane' could 'scarcely' be called efficient.[81]

As far as damage to physical health was concerned, the Dutch prison system did not fulfill the minimum conditions either. The doctor, J. A. Putto, thought that the chance of death from tuberculosis in the prisons was greater than in free society. In 1940, the doctor, H. Wever, arrived at even more disquieting conclusions in his Ph.D. thesis about the health situation in the Leeuwarden penitentiary. He had established an 'upsettingly' low content of vitamin C in convicts. He had even found the first signs of scurvy in a few convicts, a feeling of tiredness and painful limbs. Wever assumed an influence of cell life upon the existence of tuberculosis.[82]

Wever also compared death rates with those of men in free society since 1830. These had continuously decreased, that is to say that the health situation in prisons had become less and less unfavourable relative to that in free society. That is an emancipatory development of great importance. It is, however, true that death rates in prisons decreased more slowly after the war than those of free men. For example, the death rate of the average prison population was the same in 1939 and 1940 as it had been in 1919 (0.49 per cent).[83] The absolute figures were seventeen (1939) and fourteen (1940) deaths in average populations of 3,496 and 2,872. In these years, proportionately about twice as many men died in free society as in the prisons. Presently, more than three times as many men die in free society.[84]

Influences Outside and Inside Prison Walls

Apart from their physical and mental condition, the question arises whether the developments in the interbellum period had a substantial effect on the subjective experience by prisoners. Could prison life be better endured? What is certain is that the number of prisoners decreased significantly and prison suffering thus decreased *quantitatively*. The institute of conditional sentencing and the extended opportunities to impose a fine had resulted, in the 1920s and 1930s, in a reduction by almost a half of the number of unconditionally imposed prison sentences. Both the number of short sentences and the number of sentences for five years or more were noticeably reduced. In comparison to the first decade of the century, the number of unconditional prison sentences of five years or more per 100,000 inhabitants was more than halved. Moreover, prisoners were more often released after two-thirds of their sentence had elapsed.[85] In connection with all these developments, the average population of all prisons decreased from 3,179 in 1910 to the post-war low of 2,394 prisoners (30.6 per 100,000 inhabitants) in 1930.

Many saw the decreasing population as but the beginning of an ongoing emptying of prisons. The prison sentence was put, in the opinion of the psychiatrist, Bierens de Haan, 'in a posture of defence', which was 'a weak position'. That was, indeed, true to all appearances. Several prisons were closed because they were underpopulated.[86] In the period from 1933 to 1939, the prison population increased significantly because of the so-called 'crisis-crime' and a sudden harshening of the penal climate. But in 1940 the numbers again reached the level of 1932 with 32.5 prisoners per 100,000 inhabitants.[87]

Much changed within prison walls as well from the perspective of prisoners. Prison suffering thereby probably decreased somewhat *qualitatively*. The law of 1929 had made communal activities possible. Misconduct was more often seen as a symptom of illness than an expression of bad will, through the increased involvement of psychiatrists. The system of 'deviations', additionally, offered the possibility of keeping order and enforcing discipline less by means of heavy punishments and more by withholding or denying privileges.[88] Privileges were also new. The solicitor, De Vrieze, wrote in *De Telegraaf*, after having visited the Amsterdam cellular prison, of 'a colossal turn-about' and a 'revolution'.[89] Most likely he exaggerated, but, the solitarily confined who lacked other experiences often strongly blew small happenings out of proportion; for them the 'deviations' must, indeed, have meant a lot. Above all, they gained some influence over their own existence, something which must have decreased, to some extent, their feelings of complete powerlessness. One prisoner saw a real break with the 'miserable situation' of the past. 'Upon my word, this was a great gesture,' he wrote. Ex-convict, Van Iependaal, saw in the 'deviations' likewise an important alleviation of cellular exist-ence. 'Small changes, whose effect, nevertheless, was large and allowed hope of more and better.'[90]

More important in the light of their emancipation process is that the privileges gradually began to be seen by prisoners as *rights*. The Minister of Justice himself, Donner, had pointed this out already in 1925, when he denied the danger of dissimilar applications of the privileges in different prisons. He thought prisoners would have 'the feeling that they also had a sort of legal position'. 'Arriving in another prison, they complain that things are absent which were present in the former prison,' said the Minister.[91] In the 1928 yearly report for a penitentiary, it was remarked 'that the fear is not imaginary that some of the deviations, at first permitted as privileges, could later come to be seen and desired as rights, whereby the character of encouragement and reward will fade and, finally, disappear'. Patijn predicted the same thing with regard to condi-tional release.[92] These remarks showed a vision of the future and socio-logical insight because, after the Second World War, that which had been feared would, indeed, happen: privileges became rights.

Emancipation of Female Prisoners

It was more and more often asked, in and outside parliament, that attention be focussed on the position of female prisoners. This had to do with both the emancipation of prisoners and that of the women. Members of Parliament pushed for an open-air prison for women so that they too could profit from 'the healthy, educative work in the open-air'.[93] In the international ruling for the treatment of prisoners, a separate article (50) about women was included. They were allowed to be guarded only by other women. Male functionaries were expected to be forbidden entrance to the women's prisons or women's departments. If, as exception to the rule, men were allowed entrance, they were expected to be accompanied by a female functionary. The lawyer, E. C. Lekkerkerker, who had written a Ph.D. thesis about American *reformatories* for female prisoners, untiringly promoted the interests of women prisoners. Many rules which only made sense and only were possible when there were large numbers, turned out to be senseless and incapable of implementation for the just over fifty Dutch female prisoners.[94] The women's departments of cellular prisons were gradually discontinued. Practically all the women were housed, around 1930, in the penitentiary at Rotterdam, which was also a 'Bijzondere Strafgevangenis' (Special Penitentiary), and in a number of 'hulpstrafgevangenissen' (auxilliary penitentiaries). Differentiation, thus, according to age, crime or psychic condition was out of the question. Experiments with limited communality were hardly possible.

This problem, which, as a matter of fact, is not yet solved even today, was fundamentally addressed by a commission in a voluminous report 'about government, punishment and educational institutions for women and girls'. Lekkerkerker was the secretary. 'The most serious objection is that women's institutions are all, without exception, subdivisions of men's without once the question having been raised of whether this is suitable for the female group,' she wrote as introduction. The more detailed criticism, by today's standards for women's emancipation, had a conservative character which confirmed existing role patterns, but Lekkerkerker still had to defend herself against accusations of 'ultra-feminism' and 'exaggerated feminism' in the face of male reactions to the report. This happened because the report argued for separate facilities for women.

The reporters said that the opportunity did not exist for 'a household education' and 'even' the cooking was done by men. Nor was there anywhere 'even the slightest hint of hominess, which could form the object of female interest and serve as an exercise in household competence'. They thought the sombre cells and monotonous prison life insufficient to meet the strong emotional needs and fantasy of women. The report contained a large number of proposals for making punishment more fitting to these female needs, but the practice of cut-backs ensured that none of these came to be practiced. Moreover, within a penal climate which was becoming severely harsher, totally different priorities were being set.[95]

4. THE HARSH SCHOOL OF THOUGHT

The mitigation of cellular confinement, the reduced imposition of the short sentence, the emergence of the educational view and the growing interest in the personalities of prisoners: all these are developments which were later interpreted as salutary results of the *New Direction* in penal law. The harsh forms of criminal politics which were also part and parcel of the *New Direction* have more or less been erased from penal memory, both in The Netherlands and other western countries. That is not any wonder considering penal practices in Nazi-Germany, but neither German *Kriminalbiologie* nor penal developments in The Netherlands can be understood without some knowledge of what was internationally acceptable in the area of crime prevention. The German *Kriminalbiologie* did not, as the criminologist, van Weringh, pertinently remarked 'appear out of thin air' but was 'an abominable excrescence' of ideas which were 'relatively generally' expressed in those years, even outside Germany.[96]

Two-track Policy in Penal Law: Moderate if Possible, Tough if Necessary

The harsh attitude to psychopathic and so-called professional or habitual criminals was surely just as characteristic of the penal climate between the two wars as was the mild attitude toward opportunistic criminals, a class to which the large majority of convicts were allocated. The harsh school of thought made the moderate school possible.[97] Mild reformers reassured themselves and the critics of 'sickly sentimentality' by pointing out what would today be called a 'two-track policy': moderation if possible and harshness if necessary.[98] This compensating of moderate feelings with intentional harshness lay to some extent at the root of the introduction of a new penalty in 1930: the combination of conditional prison sentencing and unconditional prison sentencing or fining. Conditional sentencing alone, it was thought, was seen by many as acquittal and as insufficiently deterrent.[99] This concerned a still relatively mild tightening up of the penal system. Other laws went much further.

As unanimous as penal Netherlands was for the educational view, mitigation of cellular confinement and forcing back of the prison sentence, just as unanimous were the same Dutchmen for putting psychopathic criminals in secure clinics for an indeterminate period and 'rendering harmless' habitual or professional criminals. In 1928, the 'Psychopatenwet' (Psychopath Law) came into being; convicts could, in principle, be placed in asylums for psychopaths for the period of two years. A judge's order could extend this term again and again by one or two years.[100] This was, thus, actually a punishment for an indeterminate period even though it was formally called a measure. Those put in a secure clinic or the 'mentally deficient' were completely surrendered to the judgement of psychiatrists who advised about any lengthening of the measure. The psychopath laws can, of course, not be seen purely as examples of harsh policy. Certainly, in the intentions of those who created them, moderate aspects existed as well. Not so, however, in the 'defusing' of so-called professional and habitual criminals after their sentence, for which there were also arguments. 'If nothing helps anymore, then the individual is stowed away for a good, long time,' proposed professor Pompe.[101]

In 1927, the Minister of Justice, J. Donner, presented a draft of a law in which judges could 'detain' recidivists with a lengthy criminal record *after* they had fulfilled their imposed sentence if demanded by 'the interests of public order'. Confinement in 'bewaringsgestichten' (preventive detention asylums) could be ordered for periods of at least five and a maximum of ten years.[102] The legal idea was formally a measure and not punishment. He estimated 200 to 250 to be the population of a future detention asylum.[103] The draft was accepted by the Lower House by a large majority of forty-nine to thirteen votes. Minister Donner emphasized the preventive purpose and made a comparison with the law dealing with contagious illnesses and the internment of 'the carriers of bacilli, whose freedom is offered up to the interests of public health'. The Upper House subsequently accepted the draft without poll.[104]

Strangely enough, discussion surrounding the detention law flared up noticeably only after the parliamentary proceedings.[105] This coincided

with the acceptance and bringing into operation of similar laws in many
Western European countries and American states. In England, as early as
1908, it had been possible to keep convicts in preventive detention who
had completed their sentence.[106] In spite of repeated pressure from the
Lower House, the detention law was never put into operation in The
Netherlands. This was due purely to high costs of building detention
asylums and not fundamental objections.[107] Bringing into effect of preventive detention came to be argued with more and more conviction,
outside parliament as well. Röling, professor in criminal law, spoke
consistently of the 'rendering harmless' of the mentally and physically
'deficient' and he compared the 'unmitigated scoundrels' with 'dangerous carriers of bacilli'. Very few protested against preventive detention
and those who did were concerned more with legislature than principle.[108]

The 'Public Effect' of Punishment

With their references to threatened society, early proponents of preventive
detention laid the foundation for acceptance of a harsh trend in penal
policy which entered The Netherlands from nazi-Germany around 1933.
The fact that the new, tough ways of thinking were so warmly welcomed in
The Netherlands by 'leaders of opinion in penal law' was surely connected to
the economic crisis which was also experienced by many as a social crisis.[109]
In The Netherlands and other Western European countries, harshening of
the penal climate was thus not *caused* by German developments but accelerated by them. Within a few months, progressive adherents of the educational view were forced into a defensive position, while they had occupied an
offensive position for a long time. Much emphasis on special prevention,
that is, on the effect of punishment on individual offenders, made way for
a single-minded stressing of the 'public effect of punishment'.[110]

In 1933, the police court judge, N. Muller, secretary of the Society for
the Moral Improvement of Prisoners and chief editor of the probation
monthly, put the cat amoung the pigeons in an article showing sympathy
for the harsh, partially eugenic treatment of crime by the National-
Socialists in Germany.[111] Muller was inundated with emotional criticism,[112] but this did not prevent him publishing an article in the authori-
tative *Tijdschrift voor Strafrecht* (Journal of Criminal Law) in 1934 which
caused a commotion. There he revealed the thought that the penalty also
had to have an effect on public morality which, in his opinion, left much
to be desired in many areas (tax evasion, traffic offenses, dole fraud, theft
of bicycle identity discs). He expected indeterminate sentences, imposing
ceremonial display in the courts and the publicizing of verdicts using the
press to strengthen the public morality in the area of 'epidemic crime'.
The educational view, passionately disseminated by Muller himself, had
to, with a view to the 'public effect' of punishing, take a step backwards.

The entire article was imbued with a tone of disappointment about failed tolerance. He took a giant step backwards in penal history by placing the emphasis upon external (societal) constraint instead of inner restraint: 'People must find, within the punishment, reason to refrain from offending because they do not know sufficient other reasons'.[113]

Muller seemed to have set free strong sentiments. People suddenly dared to say things 'which they shortly before had hardly dared to think'.[114] In parliament, at meetings, in journals and in reports fervent discussions took place about the new toughness in the interests of threatened society, about the reduction of rights for suspects and about the necessity of work camps for youth.[115] The harshening of the penal climate reached a high point in 1935 at the criminal law congress in Berlin. One cannot say that international resistence to the National-Socialist spirit of the times existed. Scholars the world over appeared to unanimously support the idea that, in penal law, 'the interests of society' had to have priority. Just as unanimously, they called for forced sterilization and castration of criminals.[116] Notably in the Scandinavian countries and in the United States, legal rules in this area already existed at that time. In The Netherlands, it went no further than 'volunteer' forms of castration whereby sexual delinquents could choose between long-lasting sentences or castration. Resistence against eugenic measures was based more on practice than on principle.[117]

Far-reaching eugenic intervention was openly spoken of, in The Netherlands as well. The professor of criminal law, van Bemmelen, spoke of 'racial hygiene' and called sterilization and castration a possibility to 'preserve the human race from mental ruin'. He thought it 'really' a huge danger 'that precisely the mentally weakest elements of the population reproduce more than the mentally stronger'.[118] Within a short time in Nazi-Germany, the authorities were faced with the practical consequences of such thoughts.

Tightening up the Prison Sentence

The new emphasis on societal interest and the 'public effect' of punishment led to new proposals, which revealed to what an extent prisoners could thank the stress upon special prevention for their improved position. Severity of punishment, the extent of imposition of suffering, was, all of a sudden, no longer judged with an individual prisoner in mind but for the resulting 'public effect'. The interests of convicts took the back seat to that of the whole society. The 'feeling of the common folk' became more important than the feeling of punishers and those punished. Special prevention and the educational view established maxima for retribution and infliction of punishment, but in striving for a 'public effect' it was hard to establish boundaries.

In 1933, the Roman Catholic Minister of Justice, J. R. H. van Schaik, had said that improvements in prison regime must keep pace with increases in the general welfare, but then with the clause that the prison regime stayed 'at a certain distance' from the 'regime in free society'.[119] He thought that the existing distance still allowed improvements to prison life, but many begged to differ. The judge from Rotterdam, A. J. Marx, for instance, argued for food 'with little taste', hard beds, continuous denial of all privileges, longer work hours, less reading material, no relaxation and 'no more sleep at night than strictly necessary'.[120] His proposals led to particularly fierce and emotional approbation and criticism.[121] He was attacked especially because he had come to overly drastic conclusions using the arguments for general prevention, but the importance of general prevention was also accentuated by his critics. It was only in the course of 1935 that earlier adherents of the educational view had enough gumption to deliver general criticism of the new spirit of the times. The aged member of the board of the Society for the Moral Improvement of Prisoners, René van Ouwenaller, thought the new toughness to be a product of a general feeling of depression, driven even further by fear. Going completely against the grain of the spirit of the times, he pointed out that a criminal was 'our neighbour'. New times surely brought new demands, but 'the demand for charity' remained in existence, in his opinion.[122] The socialist criminologist, W. A. Bonger, went much further in his criticism of the 'new' exercise of criminal law. He saw in this 'the law of dictatorships, the fascist and the communist'. Anyone who did not see that connection was 'blind'. The new way led only back to the past, back to criminal practice characterized by 'violence and then more violence in all areas of life, ignorance and impotence, fanaticism and lack of respect for the individual'. He saw nothing 'beautiful' at all in it. 'It is hideous and barbarian,' said Bonger, who, in 1940, a few days after the German invasion, could not 'bow to that scum that is now going to hold sway' and put an end to his life.[123]

People like Bonger and René van Ouwenaller still paddled against the current for a period of time, but as awareness that things were going in the wrong direction in Germany began to penetrate and as The Netherlands recovered economically to some extent, this current became less powerful and 'soft' publications began to reappear.[124] Even A. J. Marx wrote much more mildly about infliction of pain in 1940 than in 1934.[125] Special prevention again gradually became more important than general prevention.

5. MAKING UP THE BALANCE

Ex-member of the general committee of the Society for the Moral Improvement of Prisoners, René van Ouwenaller, feared, in 1939, when he was eighty-four-years-old, the cellular prisons would remain virtually unchanged for another twenty-five or fifty years. The cellular system would, he thought, have to wait until the twenty-first century to be judged as 'a deficient means of preventing crime'.[126]

The fact that René van Ouwenaller had an overly gloomy view of the future shows that he was too little aware of contemporary criticism of the prison sentence and the strengthened legal position of prisoners. He seems, in particular, not to have realized how extensively the network of experts within the prison system had broadened in the interbellum period and to what an extent these experts had expanded their influence on the treatment of prisoners. The pronounced professionalization of probation work, forensic psychiatry, psychology, penology and criminology had diminished the influence within the practice of penal law of retribution sentiments of common people and reasoning based on the common sense of crime and punishment. How criminals had to be punished was left more and more to experts and less to politicians who often thought and think just as superficially about punishment as the general public. Increasingly higher demands were placed on the training of warders and other prison personnel, so that criminological and psychological knowledge also made itself felt in the daily treatment of prisoners.

In the view of professor Pompe, an 'expert' attitude to criminals led indeed more easily to understanding and forgiveness than to feelings of retribution and revenge.[127] The psychiatrist, van der Hoeven, argued, that, within his profession, the attitude to criminals could 'not be other than an attitude of unfeigned, animated interest, and of unclouded humanitary commiseration'.[128] The role of experts in the penal process had increased greatly in the 1920s and 1930s. Judges had to take reports and advice about punishment from probation officers, psychiatrists and psychologists more and more often into account. Both the sphere of activity and the influence of civil servants working on probation were significantly increased by conditional sentencing and conditional release, especially because they kept tabs on the fulfilling of the set conditions. Apart from the harsh intermezzo in the 1930s, interests of prisoners were so prominently promoted by probation and after-care agencies that the decent unemployed asked themselves from time to time whether they could not ensure a better future for themselves by doing time.[129]

The influence of probation care could probably have been even greater if it had not been so split up by the 'verzuiling' ('pillarization', which means religious and socio-political segregation) of Dutch society. Instead of uniting forces, the 'pillarized' probation and after-care services made a governmental policy of divide and rule possible by competing with each other and disputing about subsidies. By taking over probation work, the 'pillarized' institutions moreover prevented the setting up of after-care facilities by the State and contributed to the vision the State continued to have of after-care as a 'sort of benevolence, a sort of philanthropy'.[130] Apart from that, it cannot be said whether more governmental control of after-care services would have led to better quality care of detainees than at present. The Dutch after-care institutions have managed, for instance, to maintain a greater independence with regard to the Public Prosecutor than is the case in many other Western countries.

The prison system was spared pillarization, but continuous attempts at and proposals for it had the effect of restraining the carrying through of the educational view.[131] This contributed in an important way to the fact that the Dutch prison system remained behind in international developments. Education was aimed at influencing prisoners mentally. But Protestants wanted Protestant influences and Catholics Catholic. Representatives of both faiths feared socialist or left-liberal influences. And because there was no funding for special Protestant, Catholic and public prisons, no educational reformatories at all were begun for adults. Prisoners remained confined to cells in which pillarization was expressed by the presence of a catholic, protestant or no bible at all and the religious faith of cell visitors. These often caused, with their hellfire and damnation speeches, serious psychic problems for some prisoners.[132] Others knew how to defend themselves. A preaching cell visitor was asked:

> Why come here to see me, why not give the guys who aren't yet doing time better food and a decent wage? I don't believe in God. I didn't ask to be born. Everything is unjust and miserable! ... Your 'moral improvement' is also self-serving.[133]

No tolerance would have existed for such contrariness even within pillarized prisons.

NOTES

1. Maurits Dekker, 1923, p. 9.
2. Iependaal, 1952, p. 177.
3. Law of 22 Feb. 1917, Sb, no. 225.
4. The draft was submitted by Royal Decree on 11 Oct. 1918 and entered as a law into the Sb., no. 607, on 22 Nov. 1918.
5. *wvhr*, 13 Nov. 1918, no. 10322.
6. Cf. Domela Nieuwenhuis, 1919, p. 75; Veen, 1949, pp. 105–6 and 114–15.
7. Bonger (1922), too, presented war crime 'somewhat triumphantly' as evidence of the environment theory. Cf. Weringh, 1986, p. 88.
8. Quotes in this paragraph come from: Meijer-Wichmann, 1979, pp. 134, 151–9, 167–76; 1985, pp. 29–30, 88; 1923, pp. 287–94;. See also Boeke and van Mierop, 1920, pp. 104–5.
9. Bonger, 1932, p. 218; see also Mesdag, 1924, p. 519.
10. Blok, 1925, p. 9; cf. Bonger, 1932, p. 213; Pompe, 1930, pp. 38–9.
11. Mierop, 1927, p. 490; cf Jongh, 1923, p. 124 (n.); René van Ouwenaller, 1925, p. 45; Holmes and Boeke, s.a., p. 101; Kohlbrugge, 1922, p. 141.

12. Circular no. 701, 7 Aug. 1919; Petersen, 1978, pp. 480–4; Circular 26 Mar. 1923; *MvBR*, 1923, p. 154.

13. *MvBR*, 1923, pp. 96–7; see also *MvBR*, 1922, p. 92; Vlugt, 1930, p. 145.

14. Based upon their word of honour, the honour system gave to prisoners certain freedoms such as work outside the walls or several days leave. cf. Haan, 1913, p. 1916. Experiments with self-government systems (cf. Veenstra, 1921/22) had begun in the United States at the end of the nineteenth century. Thomas Mott Osborne, a well-to-do man who had been chairman for several years of the supervisory board of the *George Junior Republic*, began self-government experiments with adults in Auburn in 1913. Daily management was to a large extent taken over by prisoners. A year later, he implemented the same system in the Sing Sing prison (see Osborne, 1920, in particular pp. 35–67, and the preface by Muller, v–xix.). The Auburn experiment was stopped in 1929 after a prison riot had brought self-government into discredit. Soon after, the Sing Sing prison followed. The American experiments were imitated in a diluted form particularly in English, Belgian and Scandinavian borstals (Eriksson, 1976, pp. 137–47.)

15. Cf. Domela Nieuwenhuis, 1921, p. 198; Vlugt, 1930, pp. 141–3; *MvBR*, 1924, pp. 314–16;

16. *Het Vaderland*, 10, 14 and 17 Oct. 1923; see also Elst, 1923/24.

17. *MvBR*, 1922, pp. 229–35, 1923, p. 247 and 1924, p. 164. See also Munnik, 1919, p. 382; Oostdam, 1922, pp. 310–11; Elst, 1922/23, p. 693.

18. Geldboetewet (fine law), Sb., 1925, no. 134, art. 1 (art. 23bis, wvs); See also articles against short sentencing in *MvBR*, 1922, pp. 93–6 and pp. 163–4.

19. Circular no. 788, 15 May 1923; cf *MvBR*, 1923, pp. 157–64.

20. *KB*, 18 July 1925.

21. Unabridged text of Circular no.800, 27 July 1925 and of the 'Wijzigingsbesluit' (Amendment Decision) in *MvBR*, 1925, pp. 290–9.

22. Cf. *AH*, 23 Oct. 1925; *De Maasbode*, 18 and 19 June 1927; *WvhR*, no. 11393, 16 Sept. 1925; *MvBR*, 1924, pp. 189–95, 256–9, 308, 319, and 1925, pp. 5, 60–4, 245–55, 292–3, 376–80; *NJB*, 1926, pp. 340–1; Bierens de Haan in *MvBR*, 1924, pp. 256–8; Mierop, 1927, pp. 490–2. About problems in keeping order see Arnoldus, 1921, and Noordhoff, 1922. See also prison statistics in which many paragraphs about behaviour and the system of deviations are reported.

23. *NCR*, 1 and 28 Nov. 1925, 10 Jan. 1926 and 23 Apr. 1926; cf chapter about time perspective and blowing up of details: Buitelaar and Sierksma, 1972, pp. 71–94.

24. Cf. Boeke and Van Mierop, 1920, pp. 23–34, 37, 40, 47–8.

25. Voo, 1929, quotes on pp. 16, 32, 33, 52, 56, 67, 85, 163. *HdSG*, 1928/29, Beraadslagingen Tweede Kamer, p. 2207. Eerste Kamer, Bijlage 68., no. 141, p. 2, and no. 141a, p. 2. See also Oostdam, 1929.

26. Bill of the law 'more detailed provisions for the carrying out of the prison sentence', *HdSG*, 1927/28, Bijlagen 257.4, pp. 6–7, art.1, 2 and 4; cf. *MvBR*, 1926, pp. 201–6.

27. Circular 27 July 1929, see prison statistics for 1929, pp. 14–16; Kleerekoper, 1928, p. 10.
28. *MvBR*, 1929, pp. 37–41. See also *MvBR*, 1926, pp. 5–16; 1928, pp. 33–68; Kleerekoper, 1928; *wvhR*, 27 Jan. 1928, no. 11763, and 7 Mar. 1929., no. 11926.
29. Gevangenismaatregel (Prison Ruling), Sb. 1932, no. 194.
30. Prison statistics for 1939, p. 109.
31. *MvBR*, 1927, pp. 36–9, 171–6; Eggink, 1958, pp. 231–2.
32. Law from 25 June 1929, art. 4a, Sb., 1929, no. 361; prison statistics for 1937, pp. 96–8; *MvBR*, 1939, pp. 151–64.
33. See for instance Muller, van Mesdag and Röling in *MvBR*, 1934, pp. 37–40; 1938, pp. 146–7; 1930, pp. 257–69; 1940, pp. 89–91; Molster, 1932, pp. 127–8; Pompe, 1930, p. 43; van Bemmelen, in *AH*, 14 Feb. 1935; Röling, 1933 (*De Opvoedingsgedachte...*), p. 28.
34. Vlugt, 1930, p. 164; cf. Kohlbrugge, 1922, p. 125.
35. See Elias, 1982, pp. 229–47, especially the quotation on page 230.
36. Gross, 1902.
37. A review of this is in Feber, 1934, pp. 76–84. See also Nagel, 1977, pp. 30–44.
38. Heymans, 1932, pp. 29–30, 67; see also Kohlbrugge, 1922, especially p. 61.
39. Cf. Verdoorn, 1941, p. 12; Feber, 1934, p. 75. Slightly different but related characteristics are summed up by Breuer, 1943, p. 57.
40. Feber, 1934, p. 92; see the special issue of the *Sociologische Gids* about 'Civilization and Violence', 1982, vol. 29, no. 3/4.
41. *MvBR*, 1924, pp. 8–10 (van Mesdag); See also *MvBR*, 1924, pp. 135–7, 190, 260–3 and *AH* (23 Oct. 1925).
42. See prison statistics for 1926, p. 34 and 1929, p. 31.
43. See Verdoorn, 1941 and Graaf, 1914.
44. Röling, 1933 (*De Opvoedingsgedachte...*), pp. 31–5. See also *MvBR*, 1933, pp. 73–5; *MvBR*, 1939, p. 152.
45. See Franke, 1991.
46. Dekker, 1923, pp. 6–8, 15–16 and 49.
47. Fuchs, 1931, pp. 113–18. Preface by Bierens de Haan, pp. 8–9; *AH*, 11 Dec. 1931.
48. Kohlbrugge, 1922, pp. 113–15.
49. Boeke and van Mierop, 1920, pp. 5–10, 33; *De Jonge Gids*, 1932, p. 125.
50. Kleerekoper, 1928, p. 1; cf. Gerlings, 1935.
51. Patijn, 1938, p. 16.
52. Handelingen NJV, 1928, beraadslagingen, p. 171.
53. Haas, 1932; *MvBR*, 1931, p. 71; *MvBR*, 1938, pp. 13–19, 51–3; 1939, 160–3; *wvhR*, 1930, no. 12126.
54. Pauwels, 1926, pp. 7–9, 191. See also Boeke, s.a., pp. 118, 122; *wvhR*, 1926, nos 11579, 11583, 11590, 11594.
55. Cf. Stipriaan Luíscius, 1927 and René van Ouwenaller, 1925.
56. Cf. *HdSG*, 1928/29, Tweede Kamer, p. 817.
57. *MvBR*, 1926, pp. 229–35.
58. Oostdam, 1927, p. 677. See also *MvBR*, 1924, p. 319.
59. Westerman, 1926.
60. *De Maasbode*, 18 and 19 June 1927.
61. Simons, 1929, p. 243; Blok, 1925, p. 17.

62. Cf. Vlugt, 1930, pp. 143–4;
63. Mesdag, 1924, p. 499; *De Nederlander*, 21 Nov. 1923.
64. *AH*, 10 Feb. 1935; *NRC*, 13 Oct. 1928.
65. Voo, 1929, pp. 27–8.
66. *MvBR*, 1925, p. 251.
67. Pompe, 1930, p. 41.
68. Noordhoff, 1922, p. 148; cf. Blok, 1927, p. 213.
69. Noordhoff, 1922, pp. 148–9, 156.
70. *MvBR*, 1935 (year-book), p. 27. For questions in the house, see: *WvhR*, 1925, 11292; 1925, no. 11518; 1926, and 1927, no. 11712.
71. *MvBR*, 1922, pp. 251–4; *MvBR*, 1924, pp. 64 and 91; cf. Oostdam, 1925, p. 363.
72. *MvBR*, 1922, pp. 308; 1923, pp. 279–80.
73. Mesdag, 1928, pp. 38–46.
74. *NJB*, 1930, pp. 53–4. See also Kleerekoper, 1928, p. 10 and Simons in *WvhR*, 1928, no. 11826.
75. Pompe, 1928, p. 47. See also Pompe, 1935, p. 206; Munnik, 1919, p. 380; Van Mesdag in *MvBR*, 1925, p. 3; Arnoldus, 1921, p. 285.
76. *AH*, 3 Oct. 1930; *AH*, 10 Feb. 1933.
77. *Bulletin de la Commission Pénitentiare Internationale*, October 1929, no. 5, pp. 5–7; Balans, 1974, no. 6/7, p. 9; *Prison Information Bulletin* (Council of Europe), 1987, no. 9, p. 4.
78. Circular from 21 May 1937; cf. *MvBR*, 1937, pp. 258–9, 309.
79. From 1918–1929, inclusive, an average of at least 4.25 prisoners per year, in an average population of just under 4,000, put an end to their lives. Slightly more, 5.25, prisoners attempted suicide (prison statistics for the years 1919 to 1929, inclusive). In the whole of The Netherlands, 1 in 8,000 people, aged eighteen or older attempted suicide (Tammenoms Bakker, 1941, p. 3). Prisoners who got into psychic problems were almost all initially placed in the Special Penitentiary at Scheveningen. The prison statistics of the CBS show that annually an average of just under a hundred 'unsuited to the cell' were admitted. The total number of those unsuited to the cell amounted to an average of almost 145 annually. The figures do not show a trend (cf. *MvBR*, pp. 232–5; speech of the prison doctor at Scheveningen, B. R. H. Portheine; see also Mesdag, 1924, pp. 503–7.) These were prisoners with serious psychic symptoms. Only if they became completely unmanageable were they generally sent on to the government mental asylum, opened in 1918, in Woensel near Eindhoven, or sometimes to a private asylum. From 1920–7, a total of eighty-six prisoners were admitted to an insane asylum (prison statistics for 1927, pp. 47–9). In the annual reports the government inspectorate for care for the insane, only total figures were provided for admissions from prisons and 'similar institutions' after the war. From 1919–36, inclusive, an average of almost eighty people per year were admitted. The figures do not reveal a trend.
80. Cf. Meijers, 1938; Tammenoms Bakker, 1941 and Amir, 1932.
81. *MvBR*, 1930, pp. 156–9.
82. *MvBR*, 1923, pp. 281–5; Wever, 1940, pp. 23–4, 75–92; cf. Hartog et al., 1988 (1960), p. 380.
83. The death rates for free men decreased, according to the Wever's data (1940, p. 99), between 1919 and 1936 from 1.37 to 0.88 per

100 men. Data about death among prisoners were, in this period of the annual CBS-prison statistics, provided very irregularly. In the years 1927, 1928 and 1929, the death rates in prisons (over an average population) were 0.22, 0.31 and 0.17 per cent, respectively. So in 1939 and 1940, this figure again was significantly higher.

84. According to CBS prison statistics (which, as a matter of fact, differ strongly from the figures of the Bureau for Health Inspection of the Ministry of Justice), an average of 8.7 prisoners per year died in the period 1977–1986, inclusive, in an average prison-population in that period of 3,665 prisoners. That amounts to a percentage of 0.24. Nationally, the percentage of deaths hovered around 0.82 per cent in that period.

85. Ruller, 1986, pp. 60 and 64–5; CBS publication *Vijfentachtig jaren statistiek in tijdreeksen, 1899–1984* (eighty-five years of statistics), 1984, p. 217; *Crimineele statistiek* (criminal statistics) for the year 1940 (CBS), pp. 23, 28–32; Pompe, 1959, pp. 344–5, 410–13; Pompe, 1938, pp. 266–7; CBS prison statistics, The Hague.

86. Bierens de Haan, preface by Fuchs, 1931, p. 5. See also Pompe, 1930, p. 19, and prison statistics for 1927 and 1929.

87. See prison statistics of the CBS. The calculations of Ruller, 1981, 1986 have also been based on these.

88. To what extent the system of 'deviations' really led to less disciplinary punishments is difficult to discover precisely because the data about this were extremely incompletely reported after the war.

89. Vrieze, 1927.

90. *MvBR*, 1949, p. 142; Iependaal, 1952, pp. 118–19.

91. Petersen, 1978, p. 484.

92. Prison statistics for 1928, p. 37; Patijn, 1938, p. 416.

93. *MvBR*, 1929, p. 9; see also *MvBR*, 1927, pp. 148–50.

94. Cf. *MvBR*, 1924, p. 259 and *NJB*, 1926, pp. 340–1.

95. *MvBR*, 1932, pp. 173–9; *MvBR* 1936, pp. 246–8; *Rapport over de Rijks-, Straf-, en Opvoedingsgestichten voor vrouwen en meisjes (…)*, 1935, p. 175; *MvBR*, 1935, pp. 25–7 (*year-book*).

96. Weringh, 1986, p. 119.

97. Garland points to a similar 'two-track policy' in England in the interbellum period, pp. 193, 221–2, 243–4.

98. Cf. Kleerekoper, 1928, p. 4; Bonger, 1932, p. 219; Röling in *MvBR*, 1938, p. 134; Pompe (1939), in *Gedenkboek, 1907–1957*, 1957, pp. 14–15.

99. See *HdSG*, Tweede Kamer, 1927/28, Bijlage 257.3, pp. 3–6. Wettekst (text of the law) in Sb, 1929, no. 360.

100. Cf. Simons, 1929, p. 123. See also Hamers, 1986, pp. 3–4 and Hofstee, 1987.

101. Pompe, 1928, p. 13.

102. *HdSG*, Tweede Kamer, 1927/28, Bijlage, 257.6, p. 10, 1 (43bis, 43ter).

103. Explanatory memorandum, *HdSG*, Tweede Kamer, 1927/28, Bijlage 257.7, pp. 11–12. See also 'Voorlopig Verslag' (interim report), *HdSG*, Tweede Kamer, 1928/29, Bijlage 68.1, pp. 37–8.

104. *HdSG*, Tweede Kamer, 1928/29, debates pp. 2209, 2220; and Eerste Kamer, 1928/29, p. 921. See Sb, 1929, no. 362.

105. *Gedenkboek, 1907–1957*, 1957, pp. 79–80; Röling, 1933 and 1934.
106. Cf. Röling, 1933, (*De wetgeving* (...)), Appendix I, 287–506. From this appendix, it appears that preventive detention laws were accepted and/or implemented in Australia, Austria, Belgium, Czechoslovakia, Denmark, Germany, England, Estonia, Finland, France, Greece, Hungary, Italy, North America (thirty-two states), Norway, Poland, Russia, Serbia, Spain, Sweden, Switzerland, and some South American, African and Asian countries.
107. Cf. Petersen, 1978, pp. 496–7.
108. Röling, 1934; Röling, in *Verslag van den criminologendag*, 1938, pp. 86–7; Hazewinkel–Suringa, 1939.
109. Cf. Ruller, 1980, pp. 19–20, 33 (note 6); see also Ruller, 1988 and Kempe in *Gedenkboek, 1907–1957*, 1957, pp. 80–1.
110. Cf. Veen, 1949, pp. 168–195.
111. *MvBR*, 1933, pp. 260–1.
112. Cf. Ruller, 1980. See particularly *WvhR*, 1933, no. 12653; Langemeijer, 1934 (*NJB*).
113. Muller, 1934, pp. 17, 23.
114. Polak in *MvBR*, 1935, p. 89.
115. Cf. *MvBR*, 1934 (year-book), pp. 12–25. About work camps see *MvBR*, 1935, pp. 173–9; 1937, pp. 174–7, 201–11, 246–57, and Jongh, 1943, Chapters xx and xi; cf. Ruller, 1980.
116. Report of this congress is in *MvBR*, 1935, pp. 260–8.
117. Cf. *MvBR*, 1936, pp. 46–8, 84–7; 1937, 1, pp. 25–36; Bonger, 1932, p. 212; Weringh, 1986, pp. 122–3.
118. Bemmelen, 1933, p. 36.
119. See Petersen, 1978, p. 485.
120. Marx, 1934. See also Marx, 1933 (*NJB*).
121. Cf. *MvBR*, 1934, pp. 318–29; *WvhR*, 1935, no. 12853.
122. *MvBR*, 1935, pp. 286–90; *MvBR*, 1935, p. 201; *MvBR*, 1936, pp. 290–5.
123. Bonger, 1935, p. 32; Heerikhuizen, 1987, pp. 160–1.
124. Cf. Patijn, 1938, p. 27.
125. *MvBR*, 1940, pp. 164–9.
126. René van Ouwenaller, 1939, pp. 14, 19, 21–2.
127. Pompe, 1941, p. 29.
128. Hoeven, 1941, p. 5.
129. *MvBR*, 1925, pp. 65–7.
130. *HdSG*, Tweede Kamer, 1928/29, pp. 2159, 2212, 2155, 2188, 2197, 2216.
131. Cf. Petersen, 1978, pp. 491–2, and Pompe, 1930, pp. 44–5. See also *HdSG*, Tweede Kamer, 1928/29, Bijlage 68.1, pp. 20–3, 27–8, 30, and *MvBR*, 1928, pp. 272–7; Simons, 1929, p. 148; *WvhR*, 9 Mar. 1929, no. 22937.
132. cf *MvBR*, 1935, pp. 82–3.
133. Holmes and Boeke, s.a., p. 111.

10

Radical Reforms after the Occupation: The Abolition of the Cell System

Prison fails because of the faulty assumption that changes in the personality of a delinquent can be brought about by merely shutting him up in the isolation of a prison. Here a revolutionary new idea is, however, beginning to develop. To wit: that the dynamics of change in the personality are determined by the healthy personal relationship with another person, and that it is the duty of the prison to provide the correct environment for this to take place.[1]

> *People all around him…*
> *with a door that suddenly opens*
> *Working with others,*
> *supervision!*
> *he hates it*
> *Because: 'I am searching for myself*
> *and that you can best do alone'*
> *He is saddened*
> *By lack of solitude*
> *In the prison.*[2]

In the course of the Second World War, solitary confinement disappeared more and more from prison practice. Halfway through the period of the German occupation (1940–5), prisons were already so crowded with perpetrators of typical war offences (such as clandestine butchering, black market and circumventions of rationing) and members of the underground that cellular confinement was not always possible anymore. In many places, two or three detainees occupied one cell. Thousands of convicts were communally confined in labour colonies and new prison camps.

After the war, prison experts were immediately struck with an almost revolutionary urge to reform.[3] This had much to do with 'their own suffering in prison' of many members of the underground. They were so shocked by penal reality that they decided to carry on 'a powerful and continued campaign' for reorganization of the prison system, even though this did not result in the 'mass-demonstrations' and 'surging protests' which ex-convict, van Iependaal, had so wanted. At the end of 1945, the national Society of ex-political prisoners proclaimed that the cellular system, for ordinary prisoners too, was 'antiquated, inhumane and inefficient'.[4]

The willingness of members of the underground to go into action was widely supported by penal experts. In 1949, 'de Vereniging tot Vernieuwing der Opvattingen omtrent Misdaad en Straf' (VOMS)(the Society for the Renewal of Concepts concerning Crime and Punishment) was founded, whose opinion was that the reaction of government to crimes should be directed on the one hand 'to protecting society' and, on the other, 'to resocializing the perpetrator'. Retribution was discarded as the foundation of penal measures.[5]

Now that the misery of prison had been felt by persons of one's own circle, even in those years of financially straitened circumstances, possibilities seemed to open up which for decades had been closed. In 1946, the Roman Catholic Minister of Justice, Kolfschoten had already set up a committee 'for the further expansion of the prison system'. In 1947 this *Fick committee* – named after the chairman – submitted a report which argued for a fundamental reorganization of the prison system. Not even a full two years later, parliament accepted a new Prison Act which abolished the cellular system.

This governmental dynamism went hand in hand with chaotic developments in prison practice. The already overcrowded prisons could no longer handle the stream of many thousands of political prisoners (members of the Dutch national socialist movement, members of the German SS, collaborators etc.). Shutting more than one person up in a single cell offered only partial relief. Camps in the southern mine region, concentration camps left by the Germans, cloisters, barracks, forts, factories and harbour sheds; anything remotely suited to the accomodation of detainees was used.[6] This situation, born of necessity, provided a large-scale opportunity to experiment with daring forms of communal confinement.[7] Political delinquents in the camps, for instance, were allowed to go home for the occasional weekend.

Thus, not only experiences of members of the underground during the war but also those with communal confinement of political delinquents after the war contributed to the reform of the prison system. These and the reforms that followed are often imagined as the intentional result of the aspiration towards a more decent treatment of prisoners. But these changes were much less intended, planned and aimed at than is often thought. Many changes took place, in fact, against the wishes and convictions of powerful persons involved. In connection with processes of bureaucratization and democratization which affected society as a whole, the position of power of prisoners became so much stronger that their punishers were only able to steer these reforms to a limited extent. Both in free society and within the prison, there was, as the sociologist de Swaan put it, a shift from 'management by command' to 'management by deliberation and negotiation'.[8]

In the long run one can see that the post-war reforms were mainly the result of acceleration of developments begun much earlier: 'socializing' of the problems surrounding crime and punishment and an increasing emphasis upon self-constraint. The 'socializing' of the prison sentence particularly was intimately connected with significant developments within the emancipation process of prisoners.[9]

I. SOCIALIZING AND SELF-RESTRAINT

The Fick committee for reform saw in arguments used by prison experts and politicians up to the twentieth century a 'truly frightening lack of psychological insight'. They deemed cellular confinement to have proved to be 'least of all suited' to moral improvement or moral edification because it went against 'human nature' and made those shut away 'egocentric and unsociable'.[10]

Without consultations, parliament accepted the articles of law in 1951 which led to the abolition of solitary confinement.[11] Thus, a system that for a century had caused fierce debates and much senseless prison misery was almost noiselessly written off.

Because the cellular system was going to be abolished, a review of the arsenal of disciplinary punishments became imperative. Solitary imprisonment in a normal cell was now put on the books as a new punishment. Corporal punishment, only allowed in the Special Penitentiary at Leeuwarden and confinement 'in a completely dark cell', was done away with. The Minister of Justice, Wijers called the latter punishment 'an unnecessary torment' of which the psychic effect was 'perhaps not undangerous' and the efficacy 'doubtful'. In spite of protests of some socialist Members of Parliament, the punishments of 'putting in chains' and restricting to bread and water were retained, because one should not lacking, in case of active resistance, 'a means of power'.[12]

Solitary confinement did not entirely disappear from prison practice. As a disciplinary punishment or to keep the order, convicts can still be shut up in an isolation or punishment cell for a period of time. Moreover, the examining magistrate can impose, with the preliminary investigation in mind, 'restrictions' on suspects during detention on remand. These restrictions can amount to a ban on every form of contact with the outside world and fellow-detainees.

The Rise and Fall of a New Ideal: Resocialization

Through the new Prison Act, which was put into operation in 1953 together with the new Prison Ruling, prison experts came under the influence of a completely new ideal: *resocialization*. The government should strive 'to give a convict back to society as a less socially disruptive element and, where possible, a better person'.[13] Following *moral improvement* and *education* the new theme was that the prison sentence should *prepare prisoners for re-entry into society*. This change in aim illustrates that the closed, cellular image of man from the nineteenth century had been replaced for good by the image of man as a social being. The concept that man 'solely through reflection and solitude, thrown upon his own reserves' could be brought 'to other thoughts, to a better way of living' had been, according to the Calvinist Minister of Justice, Scholten, in 1964 'completely abandoned'.[14] In article 26 of the draft of the Prison Act, this resocializing aim of imprisonment was, for the first time in history, also laid down legally. During Parliamentary discussions the calvinist Minister of Justice, Struycken, reassured Members of Parliament who feared that the punitive character of imprisonment was going to be sacrified, with a fundamental argument. He called the essential component of imprisonment the deprivation of what he deemed a right 'most loved by man': freedom. The punitive character, then was not lost when imprisonment was more directed 'to the social nature of man'. Still, the text of the resocialization article was adjusted and became:

> Upholding the character of the punishment or measure, the execution thereof must also serve to prepare convicts for their return to a life in society.[15]

A combination of cellular and communal confinement replaced uniform cellular confinement: nightly solitude and communal activities during the day. A huge differentiation of both institutes and regimes (from restrictedly to generally communal) was added to the new Prison Act in order to let the punishment, as far as possible, fit the criminal.

The Prison Act was accepted by the Lower House in June, 1951. The Upper House followed shortly thereafter. In the Prison Ruling of 1953, the accepted principles were worked out in detail. Many articles dealt with doing away with social isolation and were aimed at keeping up contacts with the outside world. Contacts with authorities, foundations and societies which could offer help in finding a solution to 'the social problems' of convicts were organized under the heading 'social care'.[16] Meanwhile, for the solution of such social problems, a completely new official had been appointed in diverse prisons: the 'sociaal ambtenaar' (social official). This official (later to be replaced by the *social-cultural* and *welfare worker*) was, as it were, the personification of the aspiration to resocialization, the 'ideal in the prison'.[17] Now equally salutary effects were expected from social contacts with officials, free citizens and fellow-prisoners (until just recently before this time a serious breach of prison discipline) as had been expected a century earlier from solitary confinement.

The new optimism lasted a relatively short time. In the first prison memorandum of 1964, the Minister of Justice, Y. Scholten, remarked that figures for recidivism showed that resocialization had not gone as well as had been hoped and expected. National and foreign literature had begun to locate sources of recidivism in a chief characteristic of the new prison system: living in group context. Donald Clemmer introduced the term *prisonization* to define the process by which prisoners begin to orient themselves more and more to the subcultural values, rules and demands of social life within the walls and become thereby less and less able to deal with the demands of a free life.[18] The Minister hoped, nevertheless, to be able to influence convicts sufficiently that they, after their sentence, would have 'better chances to make good' in free society. He had large expectations of 'group work' with welfare workers.[19]

Between 1964 and the appearance of the prison memorandum of the liberal State Secretary of Justice, H. J. Zeevalking, in 1976, diverse studies had pointed out the extremely negative effects of a prison sentence upon the personalities and social relationships of prisoners.[20] These so-called 'artefacts of detention' and high recidivism rates, according to Zeevalking, contributed to a growing awareness that societal reform, education and improved living conditions could be more instrumental in the battle against crime than judicial reactions. One had meanwhile 'retracted' one's 'great expectations' of confinement as a means to resocialization.[21]

The resocialization concept was almost stripped bare in the prison memorandum of the liberal State Secretary of Justice, M. Scheltema in 1982. He called the aspiration to make better persons of prisoners 'not very realistic'. He was more inclined to see an 'almost invincible contradiction' in such aspirations because 'important effects of alienation' were clearly brought to bear by the punishment. The State Secretary arrived at a new chief aim based upon this cynical-realistic assessment: 'The avoidance or at least limitation of damaging effects of detention.' In his explanation he pointed to the breakdown of relationships, loss of independence, initiative and responsibility for oneself, dangers of drug addiction and hospitalization and to 'criminal contagion' within subcultures of convicts, among other things. After almost one and a half centuries of optimism and idealism little more was expected of the prison sentence than that it prevented what it had itself caused.[22]

In 'Effective Detention', the latest prison memorandum of 1994, even the aim to limit damaging effects is called too optimistic. Its meaning is reduced to the prevention by the prison staff of 'detoriation of the (psycho)social and physical state of detainees'.[23] Only a small group of prisoners 'who want to improve their opportunities in society' will qualify for special treatment (education, occupational courses and work training programmes) specifically directed towards promoting their integration into society. At the same time resocialization is established prominently as a leading principle in the first draft of a new Prison Act which will be presented in parliament next year. In his explanation the Secretary of State, A. Kosto, stresses the 'unabated' importance of limiting the damaging effects of imprisonment. The future will show which words will become deeds.

In prison practice a significant broadening of the possibilities for social contact went hand in hand with this dissolution of the ideal of resocialization.[24] The convicts, who were allowed gradually to wear their own clothes,[25] saw and spoke to each other during airing, work, gymnastics and, when under a regime of 'general community', in their free hours too during recreational activities. Some prisons even made participation in group activities under the direction of socio-cultural trainers or group leaders a daily duty. The control of radio programmes, which enabled management to choose which programmes could be listened to in cells and communal rooms, gave way in the 1970s to the transistor radio. Then came the television. For a long time watching was restricted to the recreation halls, but, in the 1980s most prisons permitted television sets in the cell. The possibility to censure newspapers and magazines disappeared in 1977.

Limitations upon the number of letters that prisoners might receive or send were given up. Censure of contents was brought to bear less (random checks) and has since been done away with in some prisons. Many prisons have telephone boxes which can be used varying from once a day to once a week. During the 1960s and 1970s, more and more persons from outside were admitted to the prisons in the context of regime activities such as sport meetings, discussion groups and presentations. Moreover, especially in the penitentiaries, possibilities for visits have been expanded. Up until 1977, visits from other than direct family members were only allowed if this was considered good for the prisoner. This restriction no longer exists. The visit is often longer too than the minimum allowance of one hour per week and supervision is usually such that freedom of speech is possible.[26]

Open and Half-open Prisons

As the belief in resocialization *within* the classical prison diminished, confidence in the pedagogical effects of other forms of sentencing increased. Conditional sentencing had become rather debased from a pedagogical point of view. Hardly any special conditons were connected to conditional sentencing any more. But relatively quickly after the war, prison experts did speak and write with optimism about the pedagogical value of experiments with open and half-open prisons.

The first Dutch 'open institutions' came into use in the late 1940s for carefully selected political war-delinquents. They returned voluntarily from their work outside the institution, and almost never escaped. One convict compared himself with the latest acquisition of a pigeon flyer: 'Flying away and then returning, flying away again and then returning once more and finally you may take part in the great race.'[27] A serious appeal was made to the self-restraint of prisoners in the open prisons. The prison inspector, J. van der Grient, was of the opinion that only *trust* could form the basis for admission to an 'open institution':

> Trust in those confined who, as the only barrier to the road to freedom find ... the word which they have given, their own promise. Thus convicts become their own warders and that is exactly one of the reasons why this is done: to foster a feeling of responsibility to the direction and to fellow-prisoners.[28]

In the late 1950s the first open prisons for non-political adult prisoners were put into use in Eygelshoven and Hoorn with a capacity of twenty to twenty-five each.[29] The first experiences were hopeful. The convicts held their own under the mental 'burden-test', the content of their conversations became broader, they kept their distance from women, and after they 'had recovered from the first shock' it was thought that 'their true personality characteristics' would clearly surface. The experts were convinced that prisoner behaviour was hardly ever influenced just by fear of return to another institution or of forfeiting conditional release. They really wanted to show that they were worthy of the gift of trust.[30]

Prisoners in open institutions were very quickly allowed a number of weekend leaves. In the course of the 1960s and 1970s prisoners were more often allowed to spend a weekend at home and, since 1978, even every week. Thus an increasingly more demanding appeal was made upon self-restraint, will power and feelings of responsibility of convicts in the open institutions. After a weekend of complete freedom in the midst of family and friends they were expected to return themselves to prison. In 1982, State Secretary Scheltema found the 'pressure' of life in 'such a bound freedom' so severe that he deemed a stay of longer than five or six months unacceptable.[31]

In 1993, The Netherlands had eight open prisons with a total capacity of about 150 persons. Their intention is to prepare those who have suffered long sentences for their return to free society at the end of their sentence, but the pedagogical fervour felt at the beginning had disappeared in the 1970s, partially because the number of failures strongly increased.[32] Expansion is also hardly possible because the huge unemployment has made the finding of work outside the 'walls' consistently more difficult.

The problem of possibilities for work does not come up in the half-open or semi-open prisons which have gradually and rather quietly come into use since the beginning of the 1960s. These are prisons with a *minimal* or *less than normal* security. Until the 1980s, practically only those with short sentences with so-called 'lopende vonnissen' (outstanding verdicts) were placed here. Following a summons they voluntarily and independently report to undergo punishment. They are therefore called 'zelf-melders' (self-reporters) and the semi-open institution where they are housed has come to be called the 'self-reporters' prison'.[33] In connection with the wish to place convicts as much as possible in an 'open-detention situation', prisoners have also been admitted from the 'huizen van bewaring' and from closed institutions in the context of 'phasing out their detention'. In several half-open prisons, the daily program consisted in large part of formative and group therapeutic activities in which the increasing of insight into oneself, feeling of responsibility and self-restraint were, and still are, central. In 1993, approximately 1000 prisoners – that was about 25 per cent of the total number of sentenced prisoners – were housed in prisons with an open or semi-open character.[34] In 1988 an experiment was begun with day-detention at the end of the sentence. The prisoners, men and women together, had to take part in training 'in social skills' and practical manual skills, but were allowed to go home in the evenings. One of the expectations of this experiments with 'degrees of freedom' was that it would prove whether or not convicts are capable of returning to confinement every day to contribute to their own 'social rehabilitation'.[35] The experiment showed they were. In 1994 there were already five Day Detention Centres with a capacity of over fifty. In the first draft of a new Prison Act the possibilities to serve one's prison sentence outside the walls within a 'penitentiary program' has been extended to cover even the whole term of imprisonment.[36]

Together with the reduction in locks, bars, walls and surveillance, the possibilities for furlough or interruption of a sentence became significantly larger. In 1978 and 1979, it was stated that convicts in open prisons were permitted furlough each weekend and on official holidays. In half-open prisons, convicts may have a three-day weekend at home once in four weeks. Since 1982, the *Algemene Verlofregeling* (general rule of furlough) is in force. If they satisfy a certain number of conditions, convicts from closed prisons are also allowed a few instances of furlough in the last year of their sentence.[37] Pedagogical enthusiasm can be found nowadays especially in the sphere of 'alternative punishment' such as social services or 'taakstraffen' (to carry out a task as a punishment). In 1990, this punishment, after ten years of experimentation, was included in the Penal Code.[38] In 1993, 12,000 offenders were sentenced to carry out a task. Working in free society as a punishment: a greater contrast with cellular confinement is hardly imaginable. The same is true for the experiments with electronic house arrest and intensive supervision by social workers. 'The future of punishment lies outside the prison walls', the State Secretary of Justice, Kosto, wrote in 1994, pointing at favourable recidivism-rates.[39]

Self-restraint: from Aim to Means

The influence of post-war developments upon the lives of prisoners has not been felt equally strongly in all prisons, but, even in the old cellular domed and winged prisons, solitude has given way to busy social interaction. Much more than ever takes place as a result of trust and willingness and rough coercion has taken a back seat. However, for quite some time now, little has been seen of the pedagogical enthusiasm which accompanied the 'socializing' of prison life and the blurring of the boundaries between freedom and imprisonment. Evaluations and, particularly, research into recidivism were less positive than had been hoped.[40] Few persons within the prison system still believe that imprisonment leads to internal change, to 'resocialization from inside out'.[41] Still, the prison system developed further in a direction consciously argued for in the 1950s and 1960s and also in pre-war years with optimistic references to re-education, resocialization, feelings of responsibility, will power and self-discipline. Without the heavy pedagogical pretentions, more extensive appeals than ever were made to the social abilities and self-restraint of convicts in the open and half-open prisons. In half-open prisons, the majority of prisoners says good-bye to family, friends and freedom to then voluntarily register for months of imprisonment. 'Actually quite crazy to go and register at a prison', remarked a 'self-reporter' in 1981.[42]

In 1986, for instance, self-reporters in Veenhuizen worked outside the prison grounds in woods and public parks and on agricultural and horticultural sites with ample chances to slip away unnoticed. They spent their free time in pavilions and every prisoner had a room of his own for which he had a key. The 'walls' did not differ much from the usual fences built around storage places for building materials. Warders only now and then took a walk around the prison grounds. From time to time someone counted to see if everyone was still there. Security really only came into action if something went conspicuously wrong, such as fights and destruction of property. Serious offences against the rules or betrayals of trust were quickly punished with a solitary stay in the neighbouring cellular building ('De Rode Pannen') or return to a 'huis van bewaring' or a closed institution. Most prisoners managed, for fear of loss of privileges, to keep themselves under control. Added to this was the clever use by management of group coercion and self-restraint in punishing *every* participant in every fight, even when it was abundantly clear that one convict had provoked and challenged the other. Thus was the person in whose room drugs were found always punished even if the drugs had been hidden there by a fellow-prisoner.[43]

The unconcealed use of prisoners' self-restraint to ensure that things proceed in an orderly way illustrates just how far educational themes have become a background issue. A self-reporter in the first half-open women's prison, 'Ter Peel', in Sevenum (opened in 1987) even mentioned it a 'refined system' of 'self-oppression'.[44] Technical management considerations had always played a role in the granting of favours and freedom, but in the 1970s and 1980s they began to dominate. The pedagogical aim of self-restraint became a means of solving growing problems of management and capacity. The open and half-open prisons have shown that many convicts could also be held in confinement without expensive walls and warders and with less 'detentieschade' (damage caused by detention) than in closed prisons. Also with an eye to 'winning cells and saving money',[45] the experiment with *day-detention* and electronic house arrest was begun. The freedom of prisoners financed itself and surely that is one of the reasons prisoners got more of it.

2. PRISONER EMANCIPATION GATHERS PACE

The post-war penal climate was characterized by an atmosphere of fraternization. In professional journals and even warder-instructions prisoners were described as 'brothers' and 'fellow-men' who had the right to a 'decent' treatment.[46] There was much public interest in prison life. All of this formed a substrate for developments which were at one point the cause of and at another the consequence of fundamental improvements in the position of power and legal position of prisoners.

Meeting and treatment

The Criminological Institute of the University of Utrecht exerted a significant influence upon opinion forming. Within this 'Utrechtse School' (Utrecht school) differences between criminological, penal and psychiatric approaches to crime and punishment were reconciled by the common interest in the existential-anthropological body of thoughts of philosophers such as Heidegger, Jaspers, Sartre and Buber. The 'meeting' with 'the imprisoned person' (the 'I–Thóu relationship') was the central theme.[47] The Utrecht criminologist, Kempe, defined the fundamental problem of 'all' criminologists as how a criminal did 'experience and realize his potential as a person in this world, in the light of freedom and responsibility?' The professor of criminal law, Pompe, felt that 'respect for the fellow-man, the criminal included' would lead to respect of the criminal 'for his fellow-man'.

As late as 1967, warders were still being told during their training that they, with an 'understanding and willing attitude', were expected to steer towards 'a real meeting' with the prisoners.[48] The teachers' use of language was, at that point, somewhat dated because the Minister of Justice, Scholten, had meanwhile introduced the word 'bejegening' (treatment) by which he meant 'the human approach', 'a dignified meeting' or 'as normal a contact as possible'.[49] The word quickly came to be used to cover all contacts of personnel (warders, spiritual care workers, psychologists, social workers and other officials) with prisoners which were aimed at resocialization, education and well-being. State Secretary Scheltema defined 'treatment' in 1982 as 'interacting with convicts in a humane way'.[50] The 'task of treatment' became as important as the 'task of security' in most prisons. Much stress is laid upon the importance of a humane approach in recent Dutch books about the prison system too.[51]

Sounds of Abolition

In the 1960s and 1970s a critical disposition to society in general led not only to attacks upon prisons but also upon other *total institutions* such as psychiatric asylums. Crime and insanity were related to the power of the ruling classes. Many saw a societal ideal in *de-institutionalizing*. Penal scholars and criminologists such as Hulsman and Bianchi advocated not just the abolition of the prison sentence but criminal law in its entirety.[52] Their abolitionistic points of view and their arguments for non-penal forms of *conflict control* were packaged in extremely critical views of government power and the existing social organization.

The dissatisfaction about the administration of criminal justice was so general in circles of lawyers, criminologists, probation officers, politicians and journalists that the *Coornhert Liga*, established in 1971, attracted many members and much publicity. The formal goal of the liga was the 'active' striving for reforms of criminal law which would 'optimally' guarantee that 'the individual constitutional rights and freedoms' were taken into consideration.[53] Shortly thereafter, W. F. C. van Hattum, as chairman of the state committee about 'aims and function of remand prisons', called the deprivation of freedom 'a deeply to be regreted occurrence' and 'an intolerable encroachment' upon the personality. 'One asks oneself what sort of sensible reason there is for shutting someone away,' he added.[54]

In those years it really did seem that Dutch prisons were on the retreat. In spite of the fact that crime figures had increased sharply since the 1950s, the average prison population reached a historical low in 1975 of 18.6 persons per 100,000 citizens, one of the very lowest figures for detention in the Western world. Foreign countries looked on with wonder at the way in which *decarceration* took shape in The Netherlands.[55]

Even though the penal climate became more severe rather suddenly in the 1980s, in prison practice the forcing back of the prison sentence continued despite growth in the total of imposed sanctions. The average length of detention did increase from 95 days in 1981 to 165 days in 1990. The 'wet vermogenssancties' (Law of Property Sanctions) which came into being in 1983 enabled the judge to impose a fine instead of a sentence more often. Moreover, liability to conviction was discharged for increasing numbers of suspects by means of 'transacties' (deals with payment of a fixed penalty) and 'schikkingen' (settlements). From 26.3 per cent in 1976 onwards, an increasingly smaller percentage of all those declared guilty in criminal offences was sentenced to an unconditional prison sentence. In 1989, this was 22.5 per cent. In the harsh 1990s it increased to 30 per cent in 1994.[56] The Netherlands still had an unusually low detention figure in 1993 with its 49 prisoners per 100,000 citizens. In England, Germany and France this figure was almost twice and in the United States approximately ten times as large.[57]

Humanizing

Prison experts agreed with the well-known words of Alexander Paterson: 'Men come to prison as a punishment, not *for* punishment'.[58] In the first prison memorandum (1964), Minister Scholten remarked that the imposition of suffering could not be 'an aim in itself' and that 'the creation of conditions which increase the severity of suffering' had to be avoided wherever possible. In the light of the emancipation process of prisoners, his statement about the relationship between prison life and life in free society, also called 'the dilemma of penal reform', became very fundamental and important.[59] The Minister felt that material conditions of prisoners should not be any worse than 'living conditions considered reasonable in free society'. He thought that, to compensate unavoidable deprivations, the norms had to be even *higher* in certain areas. He further emphasized that the 'element of punishment' in a prison sentence had to lie 'in the deprivation of freedom itself'. He deemed the imposition of 'additional suffering' from the point of view of the resocialization goal to be altogether forbidden.[60]

State Secretary Scheltema concurred with this in his prison memorandum (1982), using almost identical words. Furthermore, he made of 'the striving to humanize detention' an aim in itself. He even called it a 'primary aim' of the prison system. Limitation of damaging effects and resocialization, in its eroded sense, placed second and third in his view. Prison personnel had to be aware 'in an even more pronounced way than before' that the convict 'is a fellow-man who, as such, occupies an equal position, is expected to take responsibility and even – within certain limits – must be permitted to and expected to make choices'.[61] Although in the

prison memorandum of 1994, 'Effective Detention', security is stressed
as a fundamental premise at the cost of humane treatment, 'the principle
of minimal restrictions' was, for the first time in history, laid down in the
first draft of a new Prison Act in 1993.[62]

Some criminologists saw the humane policy intentions of the prison
memoranda as so many empty words, as 'verbal frippery' and 'obfuscation'
of severe prison practice.[63] Still, these fine words give an indication of the
atmosphere within which prisoner emancipation could lead to actual
improvements in their position of power and their legal position. The
much-criticized empty words of scholars, members of government and
prison experts were, for the convicts, really significant sources of power from
which they could concretely draw, supported by committed free citizens.

Improvements in the Position of Power

Shortly after the war, prisoners were confronted with the new officials
(social workers, welfare workers, psychologists etc.) who had been given
the task of supporting them in their hour of need and preparing them for
life after prison. This created possibilities of playing officials off against
each other. And, the pressure to be humane while ensuring security and
keeping order grew both from outside and from above, both formally and
informally. There was pressure to *treat*, to show understanding, to restrict
detention damage, to resocialize and to use as little physical violence or
other severe measures as possible.

The criminologist, Zwezerijnen, described how significantly the balance
of power within prison walls had continued to shift in the 1960s in favour
of the prisoners. In prisons with a complete community regime (only
nightly separation in 'cell rooms') warders found themselves confronted
with groups of prisoners who could make keeping order a huge problem.
The use of severe means (physical violence, punishment cell) had, become
more and more condemnable. The task of treatment demanded consultation and the cultivation of trust. In this way, warders became dependent
to a large degree upon the cooperation of prisoners and, particulary, their
informal leaders. They attempted to placate these leaders with freedom
and favours, but, in doing so, they strengthened the positions of power of
the leaders within the group. This power was then used to get new favours
(more sport, more television time, more participation in daily decision-
making, etcetera). The ideal of the warders, in Zwezerijnen's view,
consisted of remaining 'as aloof as possible, while the convicts govern
themselves, but following official directions'. In reaching this ideal, they
leaned heavily 'upon the readiness of prisoners to comply with instructions'.

The relative increase in power of prisoners can be seen even more
clearly in Zwezerijnen's description of an old cellular domed prison in
which the transition from a strictly cellular to a limited community regime

gradually took shape. The prisoners here were continually involved in a boundary conflict with the warders. It was especially an 'elite' of verbal and 'insolent' prisoners who fought for more communal activities, while the warders tried to keep them as long as possible behind cell doors. These prisoners entered into relationships with officials who had something to offer (sport, recreation, work, discussions etc.) and ignored the ordinary warders. These warders had less and less sources of power. Favours, such as the little jobs outside the cell, were no longer there to give out and the use of force was also less permissible than it had been. 'For the rest, warders are left with "soft" means such as persuasion and encouragement, but these are often insufficient to keep convicts in line', Zwezerijnen reported. He saw this as a 'loss of power' for warders.[64]

Zwezerijnen came close, thus, to what the sociologist de Swaan, looking at similar developments in society, called a transition from 'management by command' to 'management by negotiation'.[65] Recent research shows that the balance of power between warders and convicts, during the course of the 1970s and 1980s, shifted further in favour of the latter and was based indeed more upon negotiation than upon orders. To keep order and peace without using force and exerting too much effort, judicial researcher, Grapendaal, maintained that one 'consciously took advantage of the self-interest of convicts'. He called attention to a 'dynamic balance' based upon the 'shared interest' that convicts and warders have in 'a peaceful, predictable and relatively pleasant course of events'. Grapendaal contends that when mutual dependence between groups is this large wielding the axe or using brute force no longer works and 'the necessity for consultation and mutual decision-making' increases. A study of Kommer permits us to see how warders feel themselves to be hedged in between their superiors and the prisoners.[66]

While prisoners inside the walls were beaten less often and became more vocal, the pressure to treat them humanely and with dignity also increased internationally. The minimum standards of the United Nations Organization (UNO) for the treatment of prisoners were renewed and accentuated in 1955. In 1988 the UNO accepted the 'Body of Principles for the Protection of all Persons under any Form of Detention'. Amended versions of the UN-prison rules were accepted by the committee of ministers for the Council of Europe in 1973 and 1987.[67] In The Netherlands, the international rules were seen as welcome support for its prison policy. Right up to the highest prison management circles, the rules were accepted or even criticized as not going far enough.[68] Even in 1986, when the penal climate had become significantly harsher, the conservative Minister of Justice, Korthals Altes, still recognized the minimum rules as an 'actual code' for the treatment of convicts and pushed for permission for 'an inspection at European level' as a means of 'strengthening' the rules.[69]

Sexual Emancipation

Prisoners could not derive any legal rights from the minimum standards. Their value was primarily moral and could be used by prison reformers to support their proposals and criticisms of existing practices. This was true long before passages defining standards were included in the Prison Act, the Prison Ruling and the prison memoranda. At the beginning, the usefulness of all the formulated criteria, rules and committees lay, from the prisoners' perspective, in the increasing problems their punishers had justifying prison suffering not inextricably connected to the prison sentence and not contributing to their resocialization. Sexual need is a suffering of this sort, described by a male prisoner in the 1950s as being in conflict with humane treatment. He felt that prisoners should 'morally have the right' to contact with a woman. 'This is completely natural and legal.'[70]

Before the war, the taboo on sex in prison had been lifted a little. But it was in the late 1950s and 1960s that the question received renewed attention. Ex-convicts called forced celibacy 'a torture'.[71] It was thought to develop homosexual tendencies and lead to 'excessive masturbation' and breakdown of the male or female self-image. Also mentioned was the sexual need in the free partners and the danger that they would solve this problem with relationships outside marriage. All of this was considered to be calamitous for the resocialization process. A ministerial committee 'conjugal distress in prisons' was formed in 1963. Shortly before that, the Dutch Society for Sexual Reform (NVSH) formed a committee to do research into the 'sexual need in judicial penal and health institutions'.[72] The problem was openly dealt with in publications and convicts themselves also told their story. Their descriptions of warders who forbade every form of homosexual contact and banged on cell doors if they, through the spy hole, caught a convict 'busy with himself' give a very oppressive image of the sexual problem.[73]

In the 1950s and 1960s, the sexual problem was primarily posed. After that the pressure grew to also do something about it. Sex was thought of more and more as something which prisoners too had a *right* to.[74] Upto the 1980s, this 'right' to sex was only translated into policy through a more flexible leave arrangement. Beside this, masturbation was not only seen as normal sexual behaviour but was also facilitated by pornofilms, photographs and sex literature. State Secretary Scheltema found a verbal solution for the moral protests against unsupervised visits in his prison memorandum of 1982. His opinion was that that form of visit had to be lifted out of the narrow atmosphere of 'means to resolve sexual need'. 'What it is all about is that the convict is given the opportunity of undisturbed togetherness with his relations,' said the State Secretary. In Winschoten (De Noorderschans), with his permission, experiments already had begun with unsupervised visits. Today, most prisoners in closed prisons can receive their permanent partner without supervision in a separate 'screwing room'. The frequency varies from once every two weeks to once per month.[75]

Legal Position

The sexual emancipation of prisoners was strongly connected to more relaxed sexual morals in free life. The equally significant improvement in their legal positions, of course, cannot be divorced from emancipatory changes in society as a whole either, but it is only really understandable from developments within the prison system itself. These led to changes in prison life which were quickly experienced by prisoners not as favours but as rights.

Up until the war there was actually no question of a legal position for prisoners. In the interbellum period, there was increased talk of rights for prisoners, but that took place primarily as verbal support for reform proposals. It concerned rights in their *moral* sense, just as the minimum standards possessed only moral force. In fact, prisoners could at most express their grievances either verbally or in writing to agencies or persons who did not have to answer and also did not possess any power of decision. Attempts of the Fick reform committee in 1947 to strengthen the legal position of prisoners in a legal sense largely failed. However, it is important that committees of supervision were founded in each prison as a consequence of the new Prison Act.

Notwithstanding the possibility to appeal against placement in a certain prison or against transfer, the no rights position remained unchanged until the 1960s. Significant changes in the legal position of convicts were only actualized in the 1970s.[76] A very stimulating influence upon this process emitted once again from the Criminological Institute in Utrecht. In 1962, a staff member from Utrecht received his Ph.D. based on a thesis about 'the legal position of the prisoner'. He argued for a better legal position with a view to prisoners' 'human dignity' and the fact that they were 'human beings'. The resocialization task itself called for 'the normal legal position' being violated as little as possible and 'as concrete as possible a description of permitted violations'.[77]

Two years later, in 1964, the Minister of Justice, Scholten, delved deeply into the legal position of prisoners in his prison memorandum.[78] He appointed a committee which produced a report in 1967. Based on this, the Roman Catholic Minister of Justice van Agt, produced a draft for amendments to the Prison Act in which a *right to complain* was proposed for prisoners. This meant that prisoners could complain in writing about the imposition of disciplinary punishments, the forbidding of correspondence or visits and the imposition of measures which deviated 'from the rights' which he could derive 'from regulations prevailing in the institution' to a *complaints committee* made up of members from the supervision committee. The complaints committee had the duty of facilitating a verbal explanation of his written complaint by the complainer, unless it was very clearly inadmissable or groundless. The complaints committee was given the authority to then alter a decision of the prison-management. It was thought that both the prison-manager and the complainer should be able to lodge an appeal to an independent appeals committee. Both in historical context and in comparison to other Western countries, this draft signified a fundamental improvement in the power and legal position of prisoners. It also indicated the large extent to which prisoners could count on support from the press, parliament, science and diverse interest groups.[79]

In 1974, a critical report appeared from the Coornhert Liga. The liga found that the draft, where it concerned conditions for 'an acceptable legal position for prisoners', still was inadequate on important points.[80] Critically, however, Members of Parliament almost became rivals of the Coornhert Liga. Debates held in 1976 in the Lower House and in the Senate formed the parliamentary high point in post-war developments directed at more understanding, more feeling and more interest for the position and the suffering of prisoners. The calvinist senator, Piket, saw confinement of persons as 'a human shortcoming' of society. In the admittedly radical draft, the government speakers of all the large parties wished to see little more than an 'initial impetus' to 'a reasonable detention management' or 'a first step' on the way to improving the prison practice. 'Elementary rights' were pointed to that were still denied the prisoners. One argued, partially supported by amendments, for more procedures tailor-made for prisoners, for more democracy and participation, for even more rights such as an active right to vote and sexual contact with the free partners and for better information about rights and procedures for prisoners. There was a push for further restrictions upon the power of the prison-management. The Coornhert Liga was repeatedly applauded in both houses for its criticism of the draft.[81] The entire draft, practically unchanged, was finally accepted without division in both houses. The law was instituted in May 1977.

'The balance of power would never again be what it had been', wrote a prison governor later. The 'almost unlimited power' of governor and personnel and the 'virtual absense of rights' of convicts had, in his opinion, been brought 'into better balance'. In the penal system, a silent revolution had taken place. For most warders the right to complaint came 'like a bolt from the blue'.[82] Prisoners fought the power of warders and governors with a flood of complaint letters.[83] In 1977, 126 complaints were lodged. After that, the number of complaints increased to 1,290 in 1985 and 2,323 in 1990. The number of complaints has risen explosively, particularly in recent years, something surely related to the harshening of the penal climate, but also explicable as a form of emancipatory resistance. Outsiders often tend to see these complaints as trifling affairs, but approximately a third of the complaints concern relatively important augmentations of suffering such as disciplinary punishments, bans on visits or restrictions on exchanges of letters. In 1990, a little over twenty per cent of the complaints was declared legitimate. Thus, warders and governors must regularly experience being told they are wrong in public. It is clear that this process, not only on the actual but also the psychological plane, strongly reduces power differences between prisoners and personnel.[84]

A contribution was certainly also made to this leveling out of power by the growing number of lawyers' and criminologists' publications about the right to complain, in which, without respect of persons, judgements were made about procedures and texts of laws were construed more often than not in favour of the weakest party, the prisoner. 'Penitentiary Law' grew into a judicial specialism, the jurisprudence of which was meticulously kept track of in special periodicals.[85] Based on this, warders and governors can form an impression of which complaints tend to be declared valid. On the job, they will have to keep in mind a possible judgement of the complaints committee about their performance, something necessitating more restraint and self-control. Janssen says that they reach less quickly for a punishment report, justify their performance better, make compromises with convicts and act less impulsively.[86]

In the first draft of a new Prison Act (1993) the right to complaint forms a central element. Many rules and favours are explicitly formulated as *rights*. The chairman of the appeals committee is given even the power to stay the execution of a decision by the governor awaiting the final judgment.[87] With the appointment of the National Ombudsman in 1982, prisoners moreover gained an extra possibility to complain of their treatment without censure. They can inform themselves in detail of their rights, once again, since 1982, in the *Bajesboek* (handbook for prisoners and those placed in secure clinics) of the Coornhert Liga and the Union for Lawbreakers (BWO). Just under 1,000 prisoners bought a copy of the last edition. The book is also very often lent out by prison libraries. The first chapter devotes 111 pages to 'Your rights as a convict'. A quarter of a century previously, this information would have filled perhaps a page, with great difficulty.

In the *Bajesboek* prisoners are also made aware that they can resist unlawful treatment by summary proceedings. This civil legal measure is used more and more often. In 1987, prisoners in Amsterdam were successful in forcing a leave of absense of their governor by giving information to the press and starting summary proceedings. They must have felt this result to be a huge victory. The psychological effect of these proceedings was perhaps even more significant than amendments to the Franchise Law in 1986 which gave prisoners henceforth the right to vote by proxy. For the critical outside world, though, this amendment was seen as fundamentally important. As a consequence of the granting of active voting rights, articles were written in the penal journal *Balans* which spoke of 'a milestone in the emancipation of the detained person'.[88]

As far as other democratic fundamental rights such as freedom of speech, right of association and assembly and the right to strike are concerned, prisoners are still discriminated against compared with free citizens. This does not keep them from expressing their opinion, striking and assembling, because, hand in hand with the improvement in their legal position, prisoners' assertivity and democratic awareness has been continually increasing since the war.

Opinions of Prisoners

In the 1950s, the penal system had to deal with written opinions of ex-prisoners which reached a large public.[89] The influence of their books could not compete, however, with the shock caused in 1958/59 by a study of the criminologist, Rijksen. In eight remand prisons and eleven penitentiaries Rijksen asked prisoners to put their opinions about and experiences with the penal system down on paper. Approximately 1,000 prisoners responded to his request. Fragments of their anonymous answers, ordered as to subject, were included literally and without comment in the over 300-page book *Meningen van gedetineerden over de strafrechtspleging* (Opinions of detainees about the penal system). The first edition in 1958 was distributed within a restricted circle of experts as a *secret* document.

Practically every fragment could be seen as lethal criticism of the resocialization objectives and numerous judicial officials were accused of cruelty, coldness, short-sightedness and injustice. All elements of prison life were raised by prisoners in a critical, emotional and revealing way.[90] The calvinist Minister of Justice, A. C. W. Beerman, thought the book of complaints should be kept from the public. If journalists had not got hold of the book, this most probably would have taken place. A great fuss was made about its secret character in page-long articles in the dailies. In 1961, a commercial edition appeared, but the Minister still managed to prevent free distribution by buying up the whole edition! The attempts at secrecy are sure to have contributed unintentionally to the enormous impact of its contents. The papers emphasized that the published opinions of prisoners had found their mark both inside and outside the penal system and had sparked off reconsiderations and self-criticism.[91] Doubtless the book also led to the immediate adjustment of their behaviour by a number of criticized officials, but, in retrospect, the significance of the book lay, above all, in its trail-blazing character. Critical opinions of prisoners were made public without censorship and these were listened to as well, even though this will often have been accompanied by gnashing of teeth as can be seen from the negative reactions to the book. One lawyer, for instance, saw it as pure 'propaganda' for the half-baked insights of the Utrechtse School and 'humanitarian rabble-rousing'.[92]

A critical attitude to *total institutions* became widespread following Rijksen's book. Prisoners both outside and inside prison walls became more assertive and they were more routinely listened to.[93] Journalists visited prisons and prisoners sought contact with journalists. After many failed attempts, a Union for Lawbreakers (BWO) was set up in 1970, which, in the course of the 1970s and 1980s, would develop into an active pressure group which arranged actions and published its own periodical: the BWO-*nieuws* (BWO news).[94] In 1971, the probation and after-care magazine KRI appeared; very soon it began to publish articles which were extremely critical of the prison system and other judicial institutions. This magazine appointed itself as a mouthpiece of detainees and was successful in the 1970s in gaining publicity for abuses in prisons and bringing them to the attention of politicians. Shortly thereafter, in 1974, the first *Bajeskrant* (Prison Journal) appeared with the support of the Coornhert Liga, 'an independent publication with an autonomous editorial board'. In the first number, the editors stressed the fact that they did not pursue 'the objectivity and detachment' which issued forth from most publications about the prison system. 'The *Bajeskrant* strives to be a paper for and by people who know what it is to do time. It will thus also be a paper wherein the emotional aspect occupies the foreground. The subjective opinion of those who sit on one side of the wall pitted against those who stand on the other side will be predominant,' according to the editors.[95] The KRI , the *Bajeskrant* and BWO-*nieuws* were effective in intensifying the pressure to reform which led to improvements in the power and legal position of prisoners. They functioned additionally as a publication platform for the increasing number of organizations that worked for prisoners and the many temporary solidarity and action committees. Under the coordinating authority of the BWO, a *prisoner movement* came into being which organized actions and manifestations. Around the middle of the 1980s, this movement focussed its efforts upon the underpaid prison work and prices in the canteen which were much too high; they called for a prison strike. The movement organized 'Bajesmanifestaties' (Prison Manifestations) which had a strongly emancipating character as far as points of conflict and criticism went.

It was not only ex-prisoners whose assertivity increased. The words of prisoners still within the walls also came to carry more weight. This increase went hand in hand with the call for more democracy and participation in society as a whole, but it also had it's own dynamics. To have a say in prison management was seen as important for resocializing.

After all, prisoners returned to a society in which participation and negotiation increasingly belonged to 'the normal human pattern of intercourse'. Management, moreover, also saw it as a means of controlling the internal tensions which were part and parcel of actions and strikes. The head of the directorate for the prison system, P. Allewijn, called the increase in democracy and participation in prisons a necessary development. Allewijn saw formalized negotiation with prisoners as an appropriate 'translation' of the changed balance of power within prison walls.[96]

'Democratization' was the subject of the annual meeting of prison governors in 1969. The governor of the remand prison in Utrecht thought that the task of resocialization and humanizing had led to huge tensions in the authority relationship between warders and detainees. He felt 'one solution' for this to be that prisoners had a say in affairs such as recreation, visits, radio, TV, food, sport, canteen, instruction, crafts and cultural forming. This participation could, additionally, help to put an end to a growing problem with the informal leaders who had become too powerful. Some colleagues raised serious Foucault-like objections to this calculating form of democracy. They feared that 'the persons in power' might intentionally or unintentionally be buying prisoners' resignation to their authority with this sort of favour.[97]

In 1971, warders bitterly vented their feelings of unhappiness at their weakened position of power and the soft treatment of prisoners in *De Telegraaf*, the largest newspaper in The Netherlands. 'Detainees have taken over', the heading said. The use of harsh measures and physical violence was absolutely forbidden, so that the warders actually had no trump cards at all in enforcing order. The drift of it was that, should prisoners complain, a whole team of welfare workers stood at the ready, but warders had to find their own way.[98]

Shortly thereafter, probably incited by the article, serious disturbances took place in the prisons of Breda and Veenhuizen. On the evening of 4 December 1971, a vicious uprising including severe vandalism, the setting of fires and taking warders as hostages broke out in the remand prison in Groningen. Just over forty predominantly young prisoners demanded more recreation, cheaper canteen articles and a better make-up of the 'contact committee', which, according to them, was being dominated by the oldest prisoners. The findings of a quickly established committee were that a large number of complaints about treatment and regulation of visits had led to the riot. Beside this, the diluted position of authority of warders, which had been portrayed in vivid colours in *De Telegraaf*, had played a role. It was thought that warders had become insecure in their way of acting because the participation committee of prisoners had been instituted without their knowledge and they no longer felt themselves 'covered' by their direction.[99]

The riot, which was followed by another in 1974, led to much publicity and many questions in parliament. It contributed substantially to the founding of a State Committee under the chairmanship of the ex-professor, Van Hattum. In its final report (1977), this committee made many recommendations for the improvement of the position of prisoners, which were also partially realized. In the prison system monthly, *Balans*, the riot led to arguments for a further liberalization of the regime, for more account to be taken of prisoners and for a far-reaching self-criticism. In 1979, prisoners achieved success with repeated work strikes and actions for increases in wages for work and pocket money. A sign of the strengthening of their position of power was that not only 'alternative penal lawyers' at the universities and social workers but also governors supported their actions to some extent. Insiders say that governors realized only too well that a better wage would improve the atmosphere inside the institution and would reduce tensions.[100] The voice of prisoners who were emancipating themselves was thus not only heard but led to actual results as well.

More prisoner participation was argued for in the 1976 and 1982 prison memoranda. Despite this verbal governmental support, full prisoner participation never completely got off the ground, even though the sounding out of prisoners' opinions has meanwhile become routine for judicial and scientific researchers and journalists. Prisoners are involved in working out a personal 'detention plan', that is, in decisions about how and where they will carry out the diverse phases of their imprisonment. Prisoner committees and prisoner associations are operational in many prisons, but they are seldom allowed to voice an opinion in affairs more important than sport, recreation or relaxation. Participation in such a committee or association is also not always thought a lot of by fellow-prisoners and is sometimes seen as being in league with the enemy or as promotion of purely personal interests. Governors are not formally obliged to pay any attention either.[101]

It is also of importance that the need for communal action and mutual solidarity in Dutch prisons is actually less urgent because of the relatively high quality of facilities and the individual right to complain than in foreign and, particularly in American prisons. The emancipation process of prisoners in The Netherlands has placed the new means to power, as it were, in the hands of individuals and, thus, the power of prisoners *as a group* has been broken to some extent; a development for which there is evidence in emancipation processes of other groups as well. As soon as the struggle provides that which was struggled for to the group, personal interest begins to exceed group interest. 'Solidarity as a dominant attitude even begins to be replaced by a certain mistrust focussed on fellow-prisoners and the placing of self-interest first,' concluded Grapendaal, who did research amoung prisoners in three Dutch prisons. In The Netherlands, differentiation of prisons (including differentiation of regime *within* prisons) and the development of individual detention plans has, to some extent, split the group interest of prisoners up into individual interests.[102]

Emancipation of Female Prisoners

Seen from the point of view of present-day concepts of *women's emancipation*, post-war changes in the situation and treatment of female prisoners can be only very partially characterized as emancipatory. The Fick committee (1947), in its argument for a central prison for women, found, for example, that account must be taken of 'the typical female need for more homeyness'. Moreover, work had to appeal to 'the inner life of women'. The deputy governor in Rotterdam, J. P. H. M. de Rooy, also charged with the women's department, stated around 1960 that women lived in 'the world of caring' and men in that 'of work'. The need to care was thought to focus itself on *others* in the form of cooking, washing, cleaning and on *themselves* in the form of paying a lot of attention to clothing, arrangement of hair, make-up and bodily care.[103]

Role-confirming arguments were also generally used by women in pleas for one central prison for women. At present, it is precisely traditional female work which is denounced in prisons for women.[104] In the 1970s women's groups involved themselves actively in the emancipation of female prisoners in the sense of *equal treatment*. This equal treatment is still not achieved, but differences with the situation of male prisoners are certainly less daunting than in the 1960s and 1970s. Then, the differentiation of institutions and selection of prisoners completely passed women detainees by, just as did the growing possibility to spend a portion of one's sentence in open or half-open prisons, in spite of the fact that, in practice, the danger of escape and aggressive behaviour appeared and still appears to be much less for women. In fact, their situation deteriorated because the number of prisons for women decreased severely and women's departments of prisons in many places were closed. From January of 1973, all female detainees, sentenced and pending trial, were housed in an old building in Rotterdam, often at great distances from those who wanted to visit them.

While there was no question at all of equal treatment of men and women, the striving toward resocialization and humanizing and the breaking up of solitary confinement had consequences for women as well. Relationships between female warders and prisoners came under the same pressures as their male counterparts. Or, as a convicted woman expressed it: 'The knowledge that we prisoners have access to higher authoritites has improved the attitude of the personnel'. Negotiations gradually replaced commands and mutual dependency increased. Various researchers maintain that solidarity among women prisoners was and is more pronounced than among men, something which probably strengthened their position of power versus personnel. Jealousy and gossip are said to play a role more often among women and this can, of course, threaten mutual solidarity.[105]

The balances of power changed too in women's prisons in favour of the prisoners, but, in contrast to their male fellows, they were much less successful in letting their opinions be heard outside the prison. This was the result of their small numbers and neglected position. A detailed and critical research report from the social official, K. H. Niekerk, completely focused upon 'the detained woman', was, characteristically, never published even though the Ministry of Justice had financed the research.[106] It was not until 1988 that, once again, an unpretentious report about 'women in detention' appeared; words of the women themselves were extensively used. After that, diverse reports appeared with the same title.[107] The important portion of the struggle for equal treatment had then already been fought.

In the 1970s, the battle had been the fiercest, with support from the women's movement. It pointed out the structural neglect of female prisoners in areas of psychiatric research, possibilities for care in crises, prisoner participation, selection and regime-differentiation. Women in Rotterdam with long sentences demanded the same wage as that given their male counterparts. The demand was refused, but, shortly thereafter, wages were equalized anyway.[108] Dissatisfaction about the bad housing and unequal treatment and indignation about two instances of death led to a few small riots. In the first month of 1978, these led to much publicity and visits from politicians.[109] Shortly thereafter, women prisoners moved to 'De Singel', a tower in the new *Bijlmerbajes* in Amsterdam. By defending their rights at different times with summary proceedings and by appearing on radio and television programs, they ensured that attention remained focussed on their situation.[110]

No such thing as an open or half-open prison existed either like those the men had in Amsterdam. Just as in Rotterdam, the women were sometimes allowed, in the last phase of their detention, to work outside the walls and the same rules applied for furlough as for the men, but they were subjected to the same regime as their fellow-prisoners in the same building until the end of their sentence. This situation was somewhat altered in 1978 by the coming into use of two pavilions in the new prison in Maastricht. At first, only those in preventive custody and with short sentences were housed there, but later it became an open prison (four places) and a self-reporters, prison (twelve places). This was followed by the opening of more female prisons in the 1980s and 1990s. In 1994 there were fourteen prisons for women, of which two had an open and two a half-open regime. This had, as a matter of fact, been stimulated by a significant increase in the number of female detainees from about fifty in 1977 to about 400 (almost five per cent of the average prison population) in 1994.

Even this rather revolutionary development has not made the level of emancipation of female as compared to male prisoners equal. Differentiation and selection possibilities are still more limited, care for mentally disturbed women is much worse and regionalization is less well implemented than for men.[111] Experiments with day detention include experiments with mixed activities, but outspoken protests against communal detention of men and women exist. Recent reports also no longer stress *equal* treatment but *specific* treatment of women.[112] Taking into account their not very aggressive behaviour and extremely low tendency to escape, women should more often be considered for extra-mural sentences and alternative punishment. Or, as a female researcher queried: 'So, abolitionism after all? Only for women?'[113]

Prisoner Emancipation and the Tough 1980s and 1990s

Due to economic decline, highly increasing crime rates, rising drugs problems and a shift to the right in politics, the tolerant Dutch penal climate quickly became harsher in the 1980s. Broadly speaking, this harshening arose from a renewed and increasing belief in punishment and police-action as accurate means of solving crime problems. Ideological questions, penological ethics and a critical view of society have taken a back seat to instrumental and technocratic visions of crime control. The judicial machinery was described more and more in terms of *management.*[114] The process of European unification caused increasing pressure on The Netherlands to adjust its relatively mild penal system to European standards. This also meant a revaluation of the deterrent or public effects of imprisonment at the cost of treatment and rehabilitative aims. In the prison memorandum of 1993, it is stated that security in society and retribution are among the main objectives of imprisonment.[115] Within prison walls, new problems have arisen such as a strongly increasing percentage of foreign prisoners (in 1994 about forty per cent of the prison population), drug-addicts (about thirty per cent),[116] the mentally disturbed, and people suffering from AIDS. The growing risks of escape by wealthy prisoners and restrictions on personnel have added to the problems.

The growing harsheness was, to a great extent, only verbal, but also expressed itself concretely in a nibbling away at the legal position of suspects, more police and less money for probation and welfare work. The influence of the hardening of the prison system was most felt in tackling drug-dealers, committers of serious violent crimes, sexual crimes and assault. Indeed, serious criminals received longer sentences, were more strictly guarded, were granted less furlough and recreation and were frequently housed in Reinforced Security Units (*EBI's*) for escape-prone prisoners.[117] Prison capacity was also drastically expanded under pressure of increasing crime rates and tougher public opinion. Still, this harshening was very one-sided, because, at the same time, the legal position of prisoners was strengthened instead of weakened, trust in self-control increased as did the number of open detention situations for both the long and short-sentenced, furlough possibilities improved further and, as we have seen, the percentage of unconditionally imposed sentences continued to decrease until late in the 1980s. Just as in the interbellum period, this situation reflected a two-track policy: tough where necessary, soft where possible.[118]

Proposals for tougher crime policies produced, in circles of criminologists and penal lawyers, an outspoken resistance which they gave voice to in scientific journals and on the opinion pages of dailies and weeklies.[119] This resistance made it obvious that, even within the harsher penal climate, historically grown feelings, insights and practices were obstinate. With regard to the prison system, it would become clear that the position of power of prisoners had meanwhile become so strong and their emancipation so well-developed that they ware rather successful in defending their achievements against attempts to save money and reorganizations.

Technocracy and Cutbacks within the Prison System

Resisting the spirit of the times, prison officials had to put up a fight against a worsening of their working conditions, or, stated more dramatically, 'the giving way of a penological ideal-nation'.[120] In this they sought and received support from prisoners.

The scope of the cutbacks revealed itself increasingly clearly in the early eighties. It was expected that, for several years in a row, tens of millions of guilders less would be spent on personnel costs and material provisions. To obviate the shortage of personnel, one of the proposals made was to limit the day program for detainees in the weekend and to allow them less freedom of movement. This implied that prisoners would spend more time in their cells and that less activities would be organized for them.[121]

In 1983, inmates in a large number of prisons inititated actions and 'work strikes' which were mainly aimed at gaining publicity. Shortly after, security personnel decided to work-to-rule. Newspapers carried extensive reports of the actions of personnel and prisoners. Finally, prison governors came into action. In the presence of State Secretary of Justice, Korte-van Hemel, they expressed their 'grave concern' about the 'very drastic effects' of the cut-backs. They feared 'an essential degrading of the quality' of detention and vandalism by inmates. All these actions made clear that prisoners, warders and governors took a united stand against the cut-backs and let each other take turns doing the dirty work of resisting. Fear of prison personnel for 'a worsening work climate' turned out to be a very significant source of power for prisoners.

At a governors' conference in 1983, the most important theme of discussion was described as 'special problems of the cut-back measures and compensation for prisoners'. It was thought that reduction of personnel would produce feelings of insecurity and intolerance and lessen the resilience. The governors formulated seven 'counter measures'. These measures appeared to be primarily focussed on 'a compensation effect' for prisoners: a television set in the cell, more extensive visiting allowances, earlier transfer to open and half-open prisons, intensifying of prisoner participation, more work projects and allowing prisoners to have more personal possessions in their cells.[122]

It became, thus, very clear to what an extent the balance of power within prison walls no longer permitted any serious attack on favours and freedoms. Prisoners were given back with one hand what the other had taken away. Television in the cell was, indeed, allowed within a short time. The furlough and visiting rules and the new ruling for personal possessions in the cell were extended. Even traditional protests against conjugal visits came to weigh less heavily because, here too, a 'compensation effect' was envisioned. This is not to say that a prisoner's existence was not negatively influenced by the cut-backs, the strongly increasing number of complaints lodged testifies to the contrary, but it does show that prisoners were certainly no longer powerless playthings for their warders and punishers. The central government, caught in the mesh of new *law-and-order* sentiments, was continually confronted with the hard-won rights, defended with conviction by inmates, personnel, governors and its own directorate for the prison system.

The prison memorandum of 1994, 'Effective Detention', announced the introduction of an 'austere, but decent standard regime' as the starting-point for inmates in closed instutions. But motivated prisoners (estimated at twenty per cent) who want to improve their opportunities in society will qualify for special treatment by means of education, occupational courses and work training programmes. The central feature of the standard regime will be work (twenty-six hours a week) as a productive effort. The current regime, based on the memorandum of 1982, is typified as 'excessive and non-committal' and 'too expensive' considering that the convicts' 'successful' return to society remains 'too invisible'. The standard regime will provide the prisoner with a number of statutorily guaranteed facilities and activities such as fresh air, visits, recreation and sport. There will also be some room for occupational education. The prison memorandum planned to introduce the standard regime from the outset in new penal institutions. The intention is that the standard regime be introduced into the existing prisons from 1995 onwards.[123]

The plans for 'Effective Detention' again caused protests by criminologists, lawyers and penal experts.[124] Perhaps more important is the resistance to the standard regime (which collides in some degree with the current decentralization of management) within the prison system. The governors fear aggressive reactions by inmates and growing insecurity within the prisons.[125] So it seems that prisoners still have governors on their side, albeit from motives of self-interest, in averting this serious threat to their standard of treatment.

Cell Shortages and Group Cells

In 1984 the professor of criminal law, Kelk, compared all the fuss about cell shortages to 'a true obsession'.[126] And indeed, the political discussion about the prison system would continue to be strongly dominated by cell shortages and pressure to change the policy of one person per cell right into the 1990s. Once again, it would become apparent how strong the position of power of assertive prisoners had become in the meantime.

The shortage of cells began as a result of increasing crime, longer sentences and, in particular, a tougher way of dealing with drug dealers.[127] Because the penitentiaries were full to capacity, many convicts sat out their time in remand prisons. This, in turn, caused a shortage of cells for suspects. In 1983, the Lower House rejected the solution of group cells out of fear for 'American conditions'.[128] Partially due to public pressure, caused by the setting free of suspects of serious offenses, some public prosecutors and journalistic opinion-makers argued that the House ought to reverse its decision.

The possible introduction of group cells caused great turmoil and would continue to do so up to the present day every time it became known that suspects were set free because of cell shortages. Governors, warders and prisoners initiated actions against these plans. In leading newspapers, a wealth of articles appeared in which people from 'the field' argued against plans for 'cell-sharing'. In professional journals as well, this question was avidly discussed. The House, just as the Minister of Justice and his State Secretary, switched sides several times. Only the small leftist parties were consistent in rejecting group cells. Every change of opinion was followed by excitement in the media.

By building new prisons, renovating existing institutions and arranging temporary facilities, the cabinet hoped to solve the cell deficit radically in years to come and stop the call for group cells. In 1985 these plans meant a virtual doubling of existing capacity.[129] Criminologists foresaw 'the end of decarceration' and feared that The Netherlands would become 'a classical case of recarceration' after having been a 'classical case of decarceration' for decades.[130] The 'Comité Bajes Stop' (Committee Prison Stop) was set up by the prisoners' movement as a 'platform against prison expansion'.

Very quickly it became apparent that the prognoses of prison capacity had to be adjusted. The cell deficit grew faster than expected and continued to gnaw away at the credibility of governmental policy. In 1987, Minister of Justice, Korthals Altes, said he was again considering group cells as 'a transitional measure'. The chairman, P. Koehorst, of the society of prison governors immediately responded that the Minister would be confronted with a 'uniquely constituted broad front' should he go further with his plans. He was referring to the warders' unions, the Coornhert Liga, the BWO, solicitors and 'even' to a few public prosecutors. He could easily have added criminologists and lawyers.[131] 'A unique army threatens to rise up in arms,' reported a leading weekly, *Vrij Nederland,* a few days later, referring to the unanimous resistance of inmates, warders and prison governors against 'cell-sharing'.[132] The prison section of the Central Advisory Council deemed the group cell 'undesired to a high degree' for fear of an 'insidious attack' on the regime and because the *privacy* of prisoners would be assailed by it. In the 'shrivelling of the mutual relationships', the section envisaged 'danger' for both warders and prisoners. Before the resistance had led to real action, minister Korthals Altes retreated from his standpoint.[133]

After this the group cell offered itself again and again as a solution of cell shortages, causing commotion in the media and in parliament. Warders and inmates announced actions. Prison governors predicted strife, sexual violence and rape. In editorial comments, *De Telegraaf* produced a different sound. Warders and their unions had to realize that 'here necessity breaks the law'. Arguments for group cells weighed so heavily that 'even rights (of prisoners) formulated in the past' had to be put aside.[134]

In 1988 Minister Korthals Altes and his State Secretary in a letter to the Lower House showed that they were still very seriously considering the 'placing together' of prisoners, although they predicted 'an increasing aggression' amoung prisoners which could lead to 'riots and disturbances', something The Netherlands, in contrast with other European countries, had been spared up to then.[135] In spite of this detached tone, warders unions were 'disconcerted'. Personnel strikes took place in some prisons. The inmates went into action as well. With complete cooperation of governor and personnel, prisoners in the domed prison at Breda held a strike. They remained in their cells. Photographers and cameramen got great chances to make telling pictures and shots of banners ('We won't swallow this' and 'On strike. No two men to a cell') and of warders, who wore union posters on their backs which predicted 'a riot's a dead cert' should the group cell be introduced.[136]

Readiness for action grew. The Coornhert Liga announced a demonstration in Amsterdam. 'Place more than one prisoner in a cell and step in an abyss', was the slogan on the poster for the demonstration. But, before the demonstration could take place, minister Korthals Altes accepted, against the wishes of the majority of the Members of Parliament, an alternative plan from the warders' unions.[137] This made prominent front-page news in the daily papers. The demonstration was cancelled. The prisoners' position of power had been under heavy fire and had held out in a period in which The Netherlands, as suggested by the Coornhert Liga, was 'obsessed with prison'.[138]

In recent years the whole discussion repeated itself several times, but group cells continued to meet a united front of prisoners, governors, warders and penal experts, including officials at the Ministry. The new Christian Democratic Minister of Justice, E. Hirsch Ballin, announced a further expansion of prison capacity to 12,000 cells (seventy-eight per 100.000 inhabitants) in 1998, which mean a tripling of the capacity compared with 1980. The average population of all prisons increased from 2,526 in 1975 to 7,432 in 1993 (forty-nine per 100,000 inhabitants).

Until the additional facilities are completed, emergency measures have been taken to increase the occupancy rate of the existing institutions. Whenever 'this is possible and justifiable', these measures also provide for the sharing of cells, mainly by aliens (awaiting expulsion) or prisoners who are (alternately) confined for refusal to pay fines. In case of emergency (for instance if someone suspected of a very serious crime would have to be released) even suspects can be forced to share a cell for a short period of time. The systematic placing together of either people in preventive detention or prisoners serving lenghty sentences is not being considered. 'This would pose too great a threat to the ability to control the prison situation and to the safety of the staff and fellow-prisoners', states the prison memorandum of 1994.[139]

Although The Netherlands still kept up, at least in principle, the policy of one prisoner per cell, the enormous expansion of the prison capacity points to more repressive penal policies, as was also illustrated by parliamentary calls (from both the left and the right) for tightening up the prison regimes and maximizing security conditions and reducing prisoners' rights. Some wishes are met in the latest prison memorandum, for instance the introduction of an austere standard regime and work institutions for young offenders ('marked by strict discipline'). The memorandum also announced that early release once again was to be made conditional. Conditional release after completion of two-thirds of a sentence was so generally granted that this began increasingly to be seen as a right by prisoners and was, in fact, laid down as such in 1987 in the law concerning 'early release'.[140]

So, in recent years, just as in the thirties, a stronger emphasis on public effects of punishment had negative repercussions for the process of prisoners' emancipation. This makes the Dutch efforts (albeit under pressure of prison governors, warders, penal experts, and prisoners) to preserve the principle of one prisoner to a cell, certainly in an international context, very exceptional indeed.

3. EMANCIPATION ON BALANCE

Has Dutch prison life become more endurable? Has emancipation decreased suffering? The actual developments suggest confirmative answers. Cellular solitude made place for social contacts with fellow-prisoners and the outside world. Material provisions improved, freedom of movement increased, the regimes became much less strict and the legal position improved fundamentally. Many of the improvements desired by reformers in the 1960s and 70s have been carried out. But prisoners at present have no idea of how things were in the past. They take the milder regime for granted. They compare life in prison primarily with life in free society.

The Gap between Freedom and Lack of Freedom

If one takes the gap between life in freedom and in captivity as a measure then it becomes very dubious indeed whether existence in prison has become more endurable. It might well be that prisoners experience this gap in certain ways as larger than in the past, in spite of, or perhaps because of, the emancipatory developments. As early as 1951, the Member of Parliament, Bachg, pointed out that a less strict regime would not do away with suffering but only change its nature. 'All the attention is focused then on the lack of freedom, which is nowadays more highly valued than ever. Suffering remains and is, in its refined form, even more difficult to bear,' said Bachg.[141] Following this reasoning, prisoners should have been suffering increasingly in recent decades. A prison chaplain pointed out in the 1960s, indeed, that prisoners experienced the new recreation and education activities 'as sheer torment', because they have been permitted to see the 'fruits of freedom' hanging, but 'they could not eat and enjoy them fully.' To 'almost have freedom' was thought to make life in open prisons extra difficult too. 'Golden bars' were often 'more painful' than bars 'of any other sort'.[142]

To this must be added the fact that material welfare improved more profoundly and relationships based on authority changed more drastically in society than in prisons. A leisure culture grew up around sport, recreation and pop music. Social intercourse became less formal and less hierarchical. The criminologist, Moerings, spoke for these reasons of an 'increasing discrepancy' between the disciplined life inside and the free-and-easy life outside the walls. State Secretary Scheltema added to this in his prison memorandum of 1982 that the 'sharper' the contrast the 'less inclined' a prisoner would be to 'resign himself to detention'.[143]

Looked at in these terms, it is difficult to judge the effect of post-war reforms upon the 'detention experience'. Data about disciplinary punishments, death, suicide, self-mutilation and psychic problems allow more to be said, but what do prisoners themselves think of all this?

One prisoner who, since 1910, had, with interruptions, experienced the 'appalling and stultifying system of that time' in different prisons saw only enormous improvements in 1949. He called fellow-prisoners who still complained 'spoiled brats'.[144] Ex-prisoner, Willem van Iependaal, found that prisoners after the war were treated 'much much more mildly, much much more humanely' than before. Around 1950 he visited a number of prisons. His opinion was that 'much of what was rejected as craziness a quarter of a century ago' had become reality. It was not completely ideal but the reforms could be seen as 'being on the turn, as a farewell to a barbarian system' that had existed before the war. Van Iependaal thought it ideal that light, air, relaxation, sport and everything possible within the limits of captivity, were no longer seen as favours but as rights.[145]

Thirty-five years later he would have been able to find this 'ideal' situation in many prisons, but he had other reference points and criteria than prisoners at present. This goes just as well for 'prisoner 1113' who, in his bitter revelations of prison practices (1960), also mentioned 'the blessings' and the 'material privileges' of the new prison regime.[146] Even in Rijksen's sensational opinions-book (1958) there was talk of 'a carefree life' compared with the past. 'Life which first much resembled that of an animal in a cage is now over, being human has returned,' a prisoner wrote.[147]

In the 1960s and 1970s a few books and articles were published by ex-prisoners. Less based on loose impressions of ex-prisoners is the image sketched in the 1980s by researchers from the scientific research bureau of the Ministry of Justice (WODC) based upon large-scale surveys and interviews. Again and again, prisoners and ex-prisoners seemed to mention, as the most important elements of detention, its meaninglessness and stupefying effect, the dependency, the distancing from family and friends, the solitude and the psychic derangements.[148] At the beginning of the 1990s, researchers at the Ministry of Justice developed so-called 'detention climate scales'. Prisoners were presented with fifty-two standardized questions covering areas such as safety, regime, contact with warders, privacy and leisure time. Since then the detention climate has been measured in seven prisons. These results confirm that, in Dutch prisons, there is hardly ever a question of the formation of a front between warders and prisoners. Contact with warders is generally called humane and relaxed. It is conspicuous in comparison to many foreign prisons that the large majority of respondents answered that they 'seldom' or 'never' had been sexually molested or felt threatened by fellow-prisoners. The complaints lie in the area of boredom, dependency, noise, telephone restriction, canteen regulations, confinement for too long to a cell and other aspects of daily regime.[149]

Disciplinary Punishments

Beatings with the pizzle and completely dark cells were abolished in 1951 as disciplinary punishments. In 1976, the abolition of chaining, bread-and-water punishment and the refusal of airings, visits and correspondence followed. The punishment cell was retained, but the maximum period was reduced from four to two weeks.[150] While in 1951 protests against chaining were disposed of as over-sensitivity and absolutely no one protested against bread-and-water punishment, Members of Parliament in 1976 seemed to want to surpass each other in their aversion to these punishments. 'That type of medieval thing', 'archaic disciplinary punishments' and 'prehistorical disciplinary punishments' were the qualifications heard from both left and right in the House. The right-wing senator, Polak, asked whether two weeks in the punishment cell was still compatible with the Treaty of Rome. The 'malnutrition of the senses' during the solitary stay in that cell was 'atrocious' in his view.[151]

After 1976, the punishment cell remained as the most severe punishment. 'Confinement squared' or 'the blackness in the dark', were the characterizations of criminologists of a stay in the punishment cell. The situation in these punishment cells has been alleviated somewhat in the last fifteen years. Light, air, visits and correspondence are at least guaranteed in the rules, 'even though it is all strictly limited'.[152]

From 1956 to 1992, the number of prisoners placed in a punishment cell or in an isolation cell (either as a means of keeping order or from fear of suicide and self-mutilation) were not separately entered into the prison statistics. That these are 'extreme measures' which are seldom used, as officials try to convince the outside world from time to time, is certainly not so. In the 1950s 500 to 600 prisoners were put in a punishment cell annually. From 1956 to 1973, about 1000 prisoners annually were isolated as disciplinary punishment, but this included prisoners who were not allowed to leave their own cell for a period of time. On the basis of incomplete data,[153] I estimated that in the 1980s 600 to 800 prisoners (roughly fifteen per cent of the average prison population) were placed in a punishment cell annually and 200 to 300 (roughly five per cent) in an isolation cell. The official data from 1992 and 1993 show that the situation has dramatically changed in recent years. In this period, about 3,000 prisoners (roughly forty per cent of the average prison population) were placed in a punishment cell and even more (about 3,500) in an isolation cell.[154] A growing number, moreover, are doing time in the new

Reinforced Security Units (EBI's). This form of confinement virtually amounts to isolation. Indeed, that was one of the reasons why a delegation of the European Committee for the Prevention of Torture (CPT) was very critical of the EBI's during a visit in 1992.[155]

Totals of figures kept until 1973 show that the number of disciplinary punishments declined from 5,546 in 1948 to 1,905 in 1955, rising again to 3,304 in 1972, in defiance of the significant decrease in the average prison population in that period. Further, one notices that the punishments of chaining and bread-and-water, abolished in 1976 as 'medieval' and 'barbarian', were certainly in use until at least 1973. Between 1957 and 1973, eighty-five prisoners were still put into chains as a disciplinary punishment. All in all, 256 prisoners were put on bread-and-water in that period, even though this punishment was hardly used at all after the 1960s.[156] Being bound with belts to a safety bed, also called 'the bicycle', still takes place. This is formally a method of coercion and not a punishment. In the 1970s, the safety bed was used about twenty to twenty-five times annually,[157] in 1993 thirty-seven times.[158]

The increase in the number of imposed disciplinary punishments in the 1960s and early 1970s is difficult to interpret. This appears to conflict with the liberalizing and mitigation of regimes in precisely that period. Some criminologists concluded from the rising figures that one could speak of 'an attitude of resistance' amoung prisoners.[159] The increase in numbers of punishments can, indeed, be seen as a symptom of the growing emancipation of prisoners. They became more assertive, stood up for their rights and became more intensely aware of the gap between life with and life without freedom. They fought a battle out with warders whose freedom to manoeuvre was increasingly restricted and who had to keep order using only non-violent means. One of these means was the making of a report, usually followed by a disciplinary punishment. The strong increase of disciplinary punishment in the 1990s clearly points to a growing resistance by inmates to the recent harshening of prison life.

Suicide, Self-mutilation and Natural Death

The psychiatrist Baan expected in 1953 that the number of suicides and self-mutilations amoung prisoners would decrease as they were treated with more care, interest, humanity and attentiveness.[160] The post-war developments very clearly show that his optimism was misguided. In spite of the 'humanizing' of the regime, the liberalization, and the improvements to their legal position, increasing numbers of prisoners appeared to find no other escape from suffering than to mutilate or even to kill themselves. Table 10.1 shows a noticeable increase.

Bernasco compared the number of suicides per 100,000 men between twenty and forty-nine years old in the whole society with the number of

TABLE 10.1 Average numbers of suicides per year in prisons, 1956–93
(five-yearly periods).[161]

Period	Absolute	Per 1,000 prisoners from the average population
1956–60	1.4	0.4
1961–5	2.2	0.7
1966–70	1.8	0.6
1971–5	2.4	0.9
1976–80	5.4	1.8
1981–5	7.2	1.9
1986–90	5.6	1.4
1991–3	6.3	0.9

suicides amoung the average population in prisons during the period from 1973–1984. It appeared that proportionately *ten times* as many suicides were committed in prisons as outside.[162] Table 10.1 shows that the largest increase took place in the tolerant 1970s and early 1980s. In the period 1956–75, an average of almost two suicides per year were committed, with peaks of three in 1970 and five in 1965. From 1976 to 1993, an average of approximately six suicides per year were committed with peaks of eight, twelve and nine in 1979, 1982 and 1985 respectively. Democracy and 'humanizing' had a flip side, even though other factors will also have played a role. Most prisoners hung themselves, some jumped from the ring and the rest inflicted mortal wounds upon themselves.[163] The English criminologist, Downes, established in his comparative study that the suicide figure for Dutch prisons was higher than that for English prisons 'despite a more humane regime and better medical facilities'. Recent data shows, however, that suicide figures per 1,000 prisoners are now almost the same in England and The Netherlands.[164]

Figures for self-mutilation and suicide attempts indicate how difficult prison life was to bear in the 1970s and 80s in a more pronounced way than do the figures for suicide. In the years from 1960 to 1964, the health inspection registered an annual average of twenty 'serious' suicide attempts. After this period, the number of suicide attempts and self-mutilations (also called parasuicide) increased strongly, as Table 10.2 reveals.

The number of hangings that did not lead to death varied from four to twenty per year, but these figures do not show a clear increase. That is also true of annual figures for jumping from the ring. The large increase was caused by the taking of an overdose of medicines and primarily by self-mutilations, the swallowing of 'strange objects' and refusal to eat. Psychiatric experts see the 'swallowing' as typical of 'the shut up, shut in and shut out person' because this form of self-wounding leads more readily to attention and treatment than the self-infliction of cuts 'which can be dealt

TABLE 10.2 Number of cases of parasuicide, 1965–93.[165]

Year	Parasuicide in prisons	Per 1,000 prisoners from the average population
1965	39	12.0
1970	49	18.5
1975	105	41.6
1980	198	61.2
1985	225	48.9
1990	263	39.8
1993	168	22.6

with with a dressing or stitches'.[166]

It is difficult to interpret the number of suicides and parasuicides. The Coornhert has suggested in 1989 that a harshening of the penal climate and cut-backs have led to 'a serious worsening of the detention situation' and consequently to more suicides and suicide attempts.[167] However, the rise in the number of suicides and suicide attempts could be seen clearly as early as the 1970s, long before cutbacks and harshening could possibly have been influential. Moreover, it was precisely in the second half of the 1980s and the early 1990s that the percentage of suicides and parasuicides decreased again. The development could, then, have much more to do with the emancipation of prisoners than with penal harshening. Through their emancipation, prisoners possibly became more aware of their situation which thereby became more difficult to bear. The swallowing or cutting also points to the need to do something, while the routes to this action are completely closed off. Prisoners who had become more assertive might have found it increasingly difficult to reconcile themselves to prison after living in a society which had become freer, even though they had more freedoms, rights and avenues of appeal than their fellows of the past. If one looks at it this way, the increased number of parasuicides and suicides would actually be an *expression* of their emancipation. The increased number of prisoners in the 1970s and early 1980s refusing food certainly points in this direction.[168]

The fact that suicide and parasuicide figures have significantly decreased the last years could be related quite specifically to penal harshening. Prisoners were perhaps forced by the harsh influences to concentrate their attention more inside than outside the prison and project their feelings of powerlessness and aggression more readily onto their punishers than themselves. The great number of severe disciplinary punishments in the 1990s and complaints by the prison personnel about aggressive and violent inmates point to this indeed.[169]

Natural death in prisons has gradually decreased since the 1950s from an average of 2.9 deaths (averaged per year per 1,000 prisoners) in the period from 1956–60 to 1.0 in the period from 1991–3, something which most likely is connected with improvement in material circumstances and care. On the other hand, in free society the number of deaths increased in the same period.[170] During almost the entire nineteenth century, death rates in prisons lay far above the national figure; now, comparatively speaking, the death rate is approximately eight times as small as in free society. Indeed, a set of figures which clearly illustrates the emancipation process of prisoners.

Psychic Disorders

It is not possible to say whether the abolition of solitary confinement and other changes in regime have led to a decrease in psychic problems. Meaningful statistical data are lacking.[171] But data dealing with the psychiatric service at the remand prison in Amsterdam do point to interesting changes in terms used to denote psychic problems. In 1950, this service concentrated its efforts upon prisoners who reacted to their detention 'in a singular way', 'either through suicidal tendencies, or food refusal or through showing other mental disturbances'. A few alcoholics and 'morphinists', a swallower of steel objects and prisoners with 'cell psychotic reactions' demanded special care.[172] Fourteen years later, in 1964, forty prisoners were admitted to the psychiatric department based on symptoms given totally different names: 'unmanagability, recalcitrance, depression or other reasons'. 'Danger of suicide' and 'maladjusted' were added shortly after. In 1968, prisoners were admitted 'in connection with troubles'.[173] These formulations point to an element of resistance in the psychic complaints, something which could be related to the increasing gap between life in freedom and in captivity.

The health inspectors spoke very explicitly about this gap later on. In 1979, they wrote in their yearly report that the contact with 'persons who were not free', such as prisoners, appeared to be becoming more difficult, 'in the medical area as well'. They felt that just as in free society, 'feeling well' and 'being healthy' tended to be interchanged, this was even 'more pronounced' in detention. 'The doctor cannot, alas, deliver the most coveted medicine, "freedom", on prescription.' The annual reports of the health services showed 'clearly' that an 'increasing number' of prisoners hovered 'on the edge of psychiatry'. A year later, the opinion of the inspectors was that society as a whole already exhibited 'great numbers of illness-inducing conditions' which led to 'socioses'. They thought it 'understandable' that, in such an 'extremely free welfare state' as The Netherlands, the detention situation 'will work even more strongly pathogenetically'. Finally, in 1985, the inspectors stated that in 'the luxurious-free-society of The Netherlands' it was becoming increasingly difficult to 'accept and undergo deprivation and curtailing of freedom, as well as authority, of no matter what sort'. They thought feelings of aversion were often expressed by prisoners as medical problems.[174]

It is, of course, not possible to establish how often feelings of aversion and not being able to reconcile oneself with imprisonment led to serious psychic complaints. Often psychic problems are the result of many factors which interact with each other. Just as in the case of suicide the so-called *import/deprivation model* is used: the causes lie in problems which already existed before imprisonment and have been 'brought along' or in the detention itself.

The Ministerial Committee Psychiatric/Therapeutic Facilities for the Prison System (Mulder Committee) came up in 1983 with hard conclusions about the nature and size of the psychic problems based upon a survey of the managements of all prisons. Mental disturbances were present in approximately ten per cent of all prisoners, according to the governors. In institutions for those with long sentences, as many as a quarter (24.3 per cent) of prisoners occasioned 'serious worries'. In contrast to the suicide problem, psychic problems are more often seen in the long-sentenced in the penitentiaries than in those prisoners kept in remand prisons. The already upsetting figures were made even more alarming by the committee which presented them as 'minimum estimates'. An investigation by the departmental research bureau (WODC) in 1988 confirmed the alarming figures. It appeared that the medical services were concerned about more than twenty-five per cent of those with long sentences. Welfare workers found more than forty per cent deserving of concern.[175]

The committee called it 'not unlikely' that the increase in mentally disturbed prisoners was connected with problems in mental health care. They thought that aggressive patients could less often be placed in psychiatric institutions which more often led to their appearance in the judicial circuit and the prisons. Taking into consideration the increase in the number of those with long sentences, the committee thought it 'probable' that prisons would be confronted more often with inmates who 'wasted away and threatened to capsize'. The committee did not address the problem of increasing resistance to imprisonment in connection with a growing gap between freedom in modern society and the lack of freedom behind 'golden' bars. Despite this omission, they still concluded:

> Earlier convictions that the undergoing of punishment could effect improvement and resocialization by means of reflection and adequate coping with feelings of guilt have not held up under the reality of hospitalization, augmentation of aggression, apathy, regression, deterioration of behavorial standards and estrangement from family and social environment.[176]

In short, much had changed within the prison system, but suffering remained and had, to some extent, even increased. The professor of forensic psychiatry, N. W. de Smit, maintains that there were only incidental cases of psychoses in the 1960s, while a survey from 1988 indicated, according to him, that there were 175 'extremely seriously disturbed' persons in prisons, 'a problem category of great intensity, both quantitatively and qualitatively'.[177] He sought the causes of the increase entirely outside the prison. He did not include the fact that prisoners could also become seriously disturbed just through their stay in prison. This is perhaps the most obstinate characteristic of many psychiatric dissertations about the prison system in this and the preceding century, both in The Netherlands and in other Western countries. The American criminologist, Gibbs, broke a taboo in 1987 when he looked for and found causes of psychopathology within the jail environment. His most important conclusion was that the criminogenic aspects of mental illness were seen as the main explanation of the large number of seriously disturbed prisoners. In his opinion this had obscured the prison environment itself as a cause of these illnesses. He added to this something which Dutch researchers also could take seriously:

> The uncritical acceptance of the person-centered perspective has shaped both research and programs concerning psychiatric disorders in jail. It is time to broaden our research framework and program perspective to include the environment.[178]

The Future

The professor of criminal law from Utrecht, Kelk, said in 1986 that it was 'not unthinkable, why, even probable that we would be called barbarians one hundred years hence because we deprived persons of their freedom for years on end'.[179] Shortly after 1986, one new prison after the other was opened in order to resolve the controversial cell shortage. A prisonless society seems highly unlikely in one hundred years' time.

The judicial researchers, Grapendaal and Kommer, saw not only a 'quantitative break with a trend' but they also feared 'a chilling of the penal climate'. They thought that, in the architecture of the new buildings, the emphasis had been so exclusively put upon surveillance that the development of a 'dichotomous, antagonistic structure of an inmates' society versus a warders' society' could be expected, something which the Dutch prison system has been spared until now.[180]

In this light, the future of prisoners does not look particularly rosy. It would seem their process of emancipation has been blocked for a while, although for the moment their sources of power, based on fundamental characteristics of society as a whole, seem too strong for a complete reversal of this process. But predictions are precarious. It is unclear, for example, what the effect of decentralization of management and an increasing differentiation of regimes *within* prisons, will have on the position of detainees. Will their chances for power increase or will they be more at the mercy of the capriciousness of governors?[181] There is also a chance that in the near future the prison system will unexpectedly have to deal with surplus capacity. The old, chilly, nineteenth-century prisons with little comfort, old facilities, insufficient space for activities and other faults would then be able to be disposed of, because brand new, more comfortable prisons have been built. The penal climate of the 1980s and 1990s would then unintentionally have led to an important improvement in housing for prisoners. Even this would not necessarily mean a significant decrease in subjective prison suffering. Grapendaal and Kommer have already pointed to a possible worsening of the climate in the new buildings, but they were using decidedly contemporary standards when they characterized the presence of 'living units' with separate 'sitting rooms' instead of separate 'pavilions' as a serious step backwards. Prisons with pavilions, such as the Bijlmerbajes in Amsterdam and the remand prison in Maastricht were, after all, shortly before their opening in 1978, still dreams of the future. In any case, complaints began to pour in quite quickly from these 'new panopticons.'[182] One prisoner, for instance, was of the opinion that the 'old-fashioned' little windows with bars were 'real and honest' and better recognizable as 'the concretizing of force' than the 'beautiful bullet-proof windows' with electric wires in Amsterdam and Maastricht. He saw the new building 'as the symbol of pseudo-soft, luxurious and refined force from the judicial side'.[183]

You can never win, that's how it seems.

And that's the way it is.

In prisons.

NOTES

1. From *The Prison Journal* of the Pennsylvania Prison Society. Cited in *MvBR*, 1949, p. 25.
2. Stilma, 1984, from the poem 'Berouw' (Remorse), pp. 36–7.
3. Kempe, 1946, pp. 6–7.
4. Iependaal, 1952, pp. 178–9; *MvBR*, 1946, pp. 14–15.
5. *TvS*, 1949, pt LVIII, p. 324.
6. Cf. Petersen, 1978, pp. 904–7.
7. Cf. Greven, 1989.
8. Swaan, 1981.
9. For a detailed overview of the differences in regimes after 1945 see Vegter, 1989, pp. 39–72.
10. Fick (...), 1947, 9; see also Kempe, 1946.
11. *HdSG*, 1948/49, Bijlagen 1189. 1–2.
12. Fick (...), 1947, pp. 33–4, 104–5, 115–6; explanatory memorandum, *HdSG*, 1948/49, Bijlagen, 1189.3, p. 12; *HdSG* 1950/51, Beraadslagingen Tweede Kamer, pp. 2141 and 2149; Memorandum in reply, *HdSG*, 1950/51, Bijlagen, 1189.5, p. 27.

13. Fick, 1947, p. 22.
14. *Gevangenisnota* 1964, 10.
15. HdSG, 1949/50, Voorlopig Verslag, Bijlagen, 1189.4, pp. 15–16; HdSG, 1950/51, Bijlagen. 1189.5, Reply memorandum, p. 22; Sb, 1951, no. 596, art. 26 and 41.
16. Sb 1953, no. 237.
17. Cf. *Gevangeniswezen* (...), 1954, pp. 66–8; K.H. Niekerk, 'De Sociale Dienst', in MvhG, 1963/64, pp. 12–18; Heijder, 1963, pp. 46–7; Heijder, 1966, p. 6.
18. Clemmer, 1940/1958; Heijder, 1963, pp. 95, 111; Rook, 1983, pp. 6–7.
19. Veen, 1961, p. 80; *Gevangenisnota*, 1964, in particular pp. 7–8, 10, 30.
20. See for instance Galtung, 1967; *Vrijheidsstraf*, 1969; Rijksen, Kelk and Moerings, 1972; Anjou, De Jonge and Van der Kaaden, 1975; Naafs, 1975.
21. *Gevangenisnota*, 1976, pp. 9–10, 32–6.
22. *Gevangenisnota*, 1982, pp. 21–5.
23. *Gevangenisnota*, 1994, pp. 11, 15.
24. Cf. Ruller, 1980 ('De Gevangenis (...)') and Abspoel, 1985.
25. Cf. Lissenberg, 1993.
26. Cf. Concerning contacts with the outside world, see Niekerk, 1965, pp. 92–3; Rijksen, Kelk and Moerings, 1980, pp. 88–9; *Gevangenisnota*, 1982, chap. VII about the contacts of prisoners with 'society', pp. 52–60; Kelk, 1983, pp. 179–93; *Bajesboek*, 1992, pp. 46–54.
27. MvhG, 1949, pp. 174–7.
28. MvhG, 1949, pp. 161–7 and 1956/57, pp. 134–50.
29. 'Open gesticht voor criminele gevangenen', MvhG 1957/58, pp. 134–5.
30. MvBR, 1959, pp. 125–44, particularly 138; MvhG, 1959/60, pp. 101–5, 117–24 and 137–43, particularly 122–4; 'Een penitentiair experiment' (A.G.) in TvCr, 1959, vol. 1, pp. 86–8; Geurts, 1963.
31. *Gevangenisnota*, 1982, p. 33.
32. Cf. *Balans*, 1976, no. 11–12, pp. 1–32.
33. Cf. Ratingen, 1983, pp. 73–6.
34. Cf. Key Figures of Penal Institutions, 1993; CBS-prison statistics for 1993.
35. *Vrijspraak*, 1987, vol. 1, no. 4, p. 6; Tulkens, 1987, pp. 107–8; Tulkens, 1988, 14.
36. Explanatory memorandum, 1993, art. 2, pp. 13–7.
37. Articles 46 and 47 of the Prison Ruling; MvhG, 1968/69, pp. 1–3; *Gevangenisnota*, 1976, pp. 48–50; *Balans*, 1982, no. 7, pp. 7–15; Rook and Sampiemon, 1985; *Bajesboek*, 1988, pp. 33–43;
38. Cf. *Dienstverlening*, 1984; Bol and Overwater, 1984; Haar, 1984; Anjewierden et al., 1986, pp. 432–6 and *Alternatieven voor de vrijheidsstraf*, 1988.
39. Kosto, 1994, p. 9; see also Laan, 1988
40. Denkers, 1969; Fiselier, Nijmegen, 1969; Caminada, 1973; Dijksterhuis, 1973; Linden, 1973, 1981; Werff, 1979; *Balans*, 1980, pp. 26–8; Kommer en Brouwers, 1986; Grapendaal, 1990.
41. Hutte et al., 1972, p. 104.
42. *Balans*, 1981, no. 6/7, p. 17.
43. The description is based on my visit in June 1986 to this prison ('Bankenbosch' in Veenhuizen). See also *Balans*, 1980, no. 6, pp. 10–19.

44. *BWO–nieuws*, 1988, vol. 11, no. 6, pp. 10–15.
45. See the second advice to the State Secretary of Justice about the day detention experiment by the *Centrale Raad voor Strafrechtstoepassing* (Central Council for the Application of Criminal Law), 27 June 1988, no. RA 91/88, June 27, 1988, p. 6.
46. *MvhG*, 1953/54, p. 178.
47. Pompe, *MvhG*, 1954/55, p. 257; Kempe, 1957, p. 96; see also Kempe, 1950; Moedikdo, 1976, pp. 90–154; Bianchi, 1980, pp. 163–87; Weringh, 1986, pp. 155–68; Downes, 1988, pp. 88–98.
48. *MvhG*, 1966/67, pp. 164–7.
49. *Gevangenisnota*, 1964, pp. 26–7.
50. *Gevangenisnota*, 1982, p. 45.
51. Cf. Buitelaar and Sierksma, 1972; Hutte, 1972; Griever, 1979, p. 140; Rijksen, Kelk and Moerings, 1980; Ratingen, 1983; Graaff, 1984; Jong et al., 1986; Sordam and Van de Vliet, 1987; Chorus and Van der Velden, 1989, Weringh, 1993. See also the criminal year-books of the Coornhert Liga.
52. Cf. Bianchi, 1964, 1980; Bianchi and Van Swaaningen, 1986; Buitelaar and Sierksma, 1972; Hulsman, 1986.
53. Cf. *MvBR*, 1971, pp. 229–32.
54. *Rapport commissie doelstelling en functie huis van bewaring*, 1977, p. 146. See also *Balans*, 1975, no. 8, pp. 29–33.
55. Cf. Doleschal, 1981; Smith, 1981; Downes, 1988.
56. Also see Anjewierden et al., 1986, pp. 428–32; Haan and Verpalen, 1989, pp. 99–102; Verhagen, 1989, pp. 7–16; Berghuis and Franke, 1992; recent statistics of the Ministry of Justice.
57. Cf. Council of Europe, *Prison Information Bulletin*, June 1987, p. 23, Tabel 1; Jaarverslag Openbaar Ministerie 1991, p. 14; prison statistics.
58. Paterson, 1951, p. 23; Veringa, 1964, p. 7; Heijder, 1966, pp. 12–13.
59. Cf. Mannheim, 1939.
60. *Gevangenisnota*, 1964, pp. 26–9.
61. *Gevangenisnota*, 1982, pp. 22–4; cf. Graaff, 1984, 123.
62. Voorontwerp Penitentaire Beginselenwet, 1993, art. 2.
63. Moerings, 1978, p. 14; Weringh, 1978, pp. 97–100; 1983, pp. 18–19; 1993; Kelk, 1983, p. 26; Ruller, 1983.
64. Zwezerijnen, 1972, pp. 19–21, 36–53.
65. Swaan, 1981.
66. Grapendaal, 1987, pp. 5, 78–9; Grapendaal, 1990; Kommer, 1991.
67. Cf. Kenneth Neale, 'The European Prison Rules', In *Prison Information Bulletin* (Council of Europe), June 1987, no. 9, pp. 4–6; *Bajesboek*, 1992, pp. 213–38; *Staatscourant*, 23 July 1990, vol. 140, pp. 2–3 (UN-report A/43/889, 9 December 1988)
68. *Balans*, 1974, no. 6–7, pp. 8–14.
69. *Symposium (...)*, 1987, pp. 11–12.
70. Rijksen, 1961 (1958), p. 250.
71. Rijksen, Niekerk, Baan and Pompe, 1957, 43–4; cf. *MvBR*, 1959, pp. 65–6; Iependaal, 1952, pp. 76–7, 83–4, 204; *Gevangene 1113 onthult*, 1960, pp. 243–55; Rijksen, 1961 (1958), pp. 250–1; *MvBR*, 1962, pp. 201–7; *MvBR*, 1963, pp. 23–5; *MvBR*, 1966, pp. 267–9; *MvBR*, 1967, pp. 38–42.
72. *MvBR*, 1963, p. 54; *MvBR*, 1965, pp. 150–2.
73. Ruschitska (1958); Niekerk, 1965, pp. 114–16 and 155; Zitman

(1965); Galtung, 1967, pp. 104–7, 132–3; Davidson, 1968, p. 103; Roman, 1972; Zuyderland and Bernlef 1974, pp. 75, 96; Nagel, 1977, pp. 100–1.

74. Cf. *Gevangenisnota*, 1976, p. 50; *Rapport commissie (...)*, 1977, p. 68; Griever, 1979, pp. 81–2, 125.

75. *Gevangenisnota*, 1982, p. 54; cf. *Balans*, 1984, no. 7, p. 4; *Balans*, 1988, no. 4, pp. 21–4; Zwering, 1988, p. 46; Chorus and Van der Velden, 1989, pp. 31, 72, 128; *Opzij*, May 1989, pp. 49–51.

76. Cf. Anjewierden et al., 1986, pp. 442–5.

77. Geurts, 1962, pp. 15, 140–1.

78. *Gevangenisnota*, 1964, pp. 18–19.

79. HdSG, 1972/73, Bijlagen, 12, 337, no. 1 and 2, pp. 1–2, also no. 4, p. 5; Alternatieve Justitiebegroting Coornhert Liga, 1973, pp. 34–5.

80. Kelk, 1976, pp. 64–5. See also Brucken Fock and Heijder, 1975.

81. Quotes in HdSG, 1975/76, Beraadslagingen Tweede Kamer, pp. 4033, 4035, 4037, 4039; HdSG, 1976/77, Beraadslagingen Eerste Kamer, p. 16.

82. Janssen, 1980, p. 255; *Proces*, 1987, no. 7/8, p. 202.

83. Ploeg and Nijboer, 1983.

84. Cf. Annual reports Ministry of Justice (directorate for the prison system); *Balans*, 1977, no. 9/10, pp. 1–6; Janssen, 1980, p. 255; Ploeg and Nijboer, 1983.

85. For example *Penitentiaire Informatie* (Penal Information, later included in *Sancties*) and *Balans*. In 1986, the *Vereniging voor Penitentiair Recht en Penologie* (The Society for Penitentiary Law and Penology) was set up. See also Jonkers, *Het penitentiair recht* (from 1975, Arnhem: Gouda Quint); Kelk, 1978, 1983; Balkema, 1979, 1986; Geurts, 1981; Ratingen, 1983.

86. Janssen, 1980, p. 256; see also Griever, 1979, p. 49.

87. Voorontwerp Penitentiaire Beginselenwet, July 1993, art. 65.

88. Griever, 1979, p. 67; Kelk, 1983, pp. 19, 91–6; *Balans*, 1986, no. 6, pp. 18–19; *Bajesboek*, 1988, pp. 97–9.

89. Iependaal, 1951, 1952; *Gevangene 1113 (...)*, 1960.

90. Rijksen, 1961 (1958), pp. xii–xiii.

91. *Het Parool*, 4, 6, 7, 12 and 19 Nov. 1959. See also MvBR, 1959, p. 209; MvBR, 1960, p. 131; TvCR, vol. 1, 1959, pp. 156–9; TvS, 1959, pt LXVIII, pp. 441–72; TvS, 1960, pt LXIX, p. 385; *Delikt en Delinkwent*, 1978, pp. 501–7.

92. NJB, 2 Jan. 1960, vol. 35, no. 1, pp. 10–11. See also MvhG, 1959/60, pp. 169–71, 183–4; MvBR, 1960, pp. 29–30, 80; TvS, 1960, pt LXIX, pp. 382–91; Downes, 1988, p. 96.

93. Davidson, 1968; Klijssen, 1968; Roman, 1971; See also Rijksen, 1967, particularly chapter IV.

94. Cf. MvhG, 1969/70, pp. 14–15; Hutte et al., 1972, pp. 61–2.

95. *Bajeskrant*, October 1974, no. 1, p. 3.

96. MvhG, 1968/69, p. 126; NRC, 15 Nov. 1968; *Het Parool*, 17 Feb. 1968.

97. MvhG, 1969/70, pp. 38–58; cf. MvhG, 1968/69, pp. 125–34; Denkers, 1971 (TvCr), p. 156; Buitelaar and Sierksma, 1972, pp. 58–9; Kelk, 1976, pp. 10–11; Kelk, 1983, p. 43.

98. *De Telegraaf*, 10 Apr. 1971; See also *De Telegraaf*, 2 Oct. 1969.

99. Cf. *Nieuwsblad van het Noorden*, 5 Nov. 1971; Griever, 1979, pp.

42–4; Leuw and van Weringh, 1980.

100. *Balans*, 1972, pp. 39, 59–62; Griever, 1979, pp. 58–60. See also Rijksen, Kelk and Moerings, 1980, pp. 80–1.

101. Kelk, 1983, pp. 62–3, 94, 107–9; Boer, 1988; *Proces*, 1989, no. 3, pp. 65–71. On opinions of prisoners, see Ploeg and Nijboer, 1983, pp. 53–79; Brand-Koolen and Overwater, 1987; Brand-Koolen, 1987; Grapendaal, 1987; Brouwers and Sampiemon, 1988; Zwering, 1988; Chorus and Van der Velden, 1989. On prisoner committees, see Rijksen, Kelk and Moerings, 1980, p. 99; Kelk, 1983, p. 212.

102 Grapendaal, 1987, pp. 61–2; see also Chorus and Van der Velden, 1989, pp. 70, 76 and Grapendaal, 1990.

103. Rooy, 1961 and MvhG, 1960/61, pp. 135–42; cf. MvBR, 1965, pp. 218–23; Niekerk, 1965, pp. 152–3, 172–5, 234 et seq.; Hutte et al., 1972, pp. 79–87;

104. Fick, 1947, pp. 50–1; Bemmelen, 1954, pp. 82–7; Niekerk, 1965, pp. 296–310; *Vrouwen in de bajes*, 1983, pp. 32–3; *Vrouwen in detentie*, 1991.

105. Cf. Niekerk, 1965, pp. 129, 136; Hutte et al., 1972, pp. 81–4.

106. Niekerk, 1965.

107. Brouwers and Sampiemon, 1988; Borst, 1991; Ketelaars, 1991; *Vrouwen in detentie*, 1991.

108. *Proces*, 1972, pp. 156–62; See also Kelk, 1983, pp. 62, 94.

109. *Proces*, 1977, p. 280, and 1978, pp. 25–6; *Vrouwen in de bajes*, 1983, p. 10.

110. Solidariteitsgroep Vrouwelijke Gevangenen, *Zwartboek over de vrouwengevangenis te Amsterdam*, Amsterdam 1979; Kelk, 1983, p. 15; *Vrouwen in de bajes*, 1983, pp. 12–13.

111. See *Geestelijk gestoorden in de strafrechtspleging*, 1988, p. 23; Zwering, 1988, pp. 28 and 58; *Vrouwen in detentie*, 1991.

112. Borst, 1991; Ketelaars, 1991; cf. *Vrouwen in detentie*, 1991.

113. Zwering, 1988, p. 59; cf. Lissenberg, 1992 ('vrouwen...'); Verrijn Stuart, 1992.

114. Cf. Peters, 1986; Anjewierden et al., 1986, pp. 422–3; *Tijdgeest en criminaliteit*, 1988.

115. Prison memorandum, 1994, p. 11.

116. Cf. Alem, 1989.

117. *Balans*, 1988, no. 1, pp. 12–14.

118. Cf. Anjewierden et al.,1986, pp. 427–8; Brand-Koolen *et al.*, 1988, pp. 61–3; Franke, 1990; Berghuis and Franke, 1992.

119. See for instance Kelk, 1984, 1993.

120. *Proces*, 1983, p. 125.

121. Cf. *Proces*, 1983, pp. 125–8.

122. *Balans*, 1983, no. 4, bijlage bezuinigingen (appendix cut–backs), pp. 1–3.

123. Prison Memorandum, 1994, pp. 4–6, 14.

124. See Tulkens, 1994; Wurzer-Leenhouts, 1994; Kelk, 1994; Verpalen, 1993; Wiewel, 1994.

125. Cf. NRC *Handelsblad*, 30 June 1994.

126. Kelk, 1984, pp. 904–5.

127. Cf. *Balans*, 1984, no. 4, pp. 24–5.

128. *Balans*, 1983, no. 1, separate appendix about cut-backs, p. 2; Kelk, 1984, p. 903.
129. *Samenleving en Criminaliteit* (policy plan), 1985, pp. 95–7, 145–7.
130. Ruller, 1985; Haan, 1986, p. 2.
131. NRC *Handelsblad*, 10, 11 and 18 Feb. 1987; *Proces*, 1987, no. 5, 138–143; VK, 18 Feb. 1987.
132. VN, 21 Feb. 1987.
133. *Balans*, 1987, no. 6, p. 29.
134. *De Telegraaf*, 24 Feb. 1987 and 16 Jan. 1988; cf. VK, 20 Jan. 1988.
135. Letter to the chairman of the Lower House, dated 20 Jan. 1988, pp. 6–9.
136. AD, 23 Jan. 1988; NOS-journaal (television news), 22 Jan. 1988; VK, 21 and 23 Jan., 10 Feb. 1988.
137. *Nederlandse Staatscourant* (Dutch Gazette), no. 38, 24 Feb. 1988.
138. Haan and Verpalen, 1989.
139. Prison memorandum, 1994, pp. 8, 33–4
140. Anjewierden et al., 1986, pp. 436–8, 445–8; *Bajesboek*, 1992, pp. 81–2; Prison Memorandum, 1994, pp. 37–8.
141. HdSG, 1950/51, Deliberations about the Prison Act in the *Tweede Kamer*, 2130.
142. MVBR, 1962, pp. 98–101.
143. Moerings, 1978, p. 14; *Gevangenisnota*, 1982, pp. 14, 20, 22; see also *Gevangenisnota*, 1976, p. 9.
144. MVBR, 1949, pp. 141–3.
145. Iependaal, 1951, p. 101; Iependaal, 1952, pp. 189–223.
146. *Gevangene 1113 onthult*, 1960, pp. 22, 151, 178–9.
147. Rijksen, 1961 (1959), pp. 258–9, fragment 827 and 831.
148. See, for instance, Tuynman, 1966; MVBR, 1966, pp. 11–17; Davidson, 1968; ex-gedetineerde, 1972; Klerk, 1978; Brand-Koolen et al., 1987; Zeeman, 1987; Brouwers and Sampiemon, 1988, pp. 43–5.
149. Department of Policy Information of the directorate for the prison system (M. D. Herbschleb and F. Zorge), Ministry of Justice, The Hague.
150. HdSG, 1972/73, Bijlagen, 12 337, no. 3, explanatory memorandum.
151. HdSG, 1975/76, Beraadslagingen Tweede Kamer, p. 4041; HdSG, 1976/77, Beraadslagingen Eerste Kamer, pp. 11, 14.
152. Kelk, 1983, pp. 150–1; Moerings, 1984, pp. 6, 23.
153. Thanks to Martin Moerings who figured out how many prisoners were actually confined to a punishment or isolation cell on two randomly chosen days in 1984. See also Moerings, 1984 and 1988, pp. 403, 410; Griever, 1979, pp. 111; Tuinen, 1986; Annual Report of the directorate for the prison system, 1987, pp. 52–3;
154. Key figures of penal institutions, 1992, 1993, Ministry of Justice, The Hague.
155. *Report to the Dutch government* (…), 1993, pp. 33–6.
156. From the CBS prison statistics, 1950 to 1972, inclusive.
157. Cf. HdSG, 1975/76, Beraadslagingen Eerste Kamer, pp. 14, 20–1; Dellen, 1987, p. 125.
158. Key Figures of penal institutions, 1993, Ministry of Justice, The Hague.
159. Buitelaar and Sierksma, 1972, p. 62.

160. *MvhG*, 1952/53, pp. 278–281; cf. Tammenoms Bakker, 1953.
161. Bron, Annual reports of the *Geneeskundige Inspectie* (Health Authorities), Ministry of Justice.
162. Bernasco et al., 1986, bijlage 1.3. See also Bernasco *et al.*, 1988 and *Suicidaal gedrag in detentie* (...), 1989.
163. From the Annual Reports of the Health Authorities, Ministry of Justice.
164. Downes, 1988, pp. 116–17; Downes, 1992, p. 204.
165. From Bernasco et al., 1986, bijlage 1.1, and the Annual Report of the Health Authorities.
166. *MvBR*, 1969, pp. 221–9. Quotes on pp. 227 and 229.
167. Brûle, 1989, p. 98.
168. Since 1965, the annual reports of the medical inspection have mentioned that a number of 'hunger strikers' have been admitted to hospital. At the beginning, these were about five per year. Only in 1971 was the hunger strike, now more passively called 'food refusal', included in the tables as a parasuicide method. The number of those refusing food increased steadily to more than 120 per year in 1985. In the period from 1986–90, the number of food refusals per year was an average of approximately 80. After that the number sharply decreased to only 16 in 1993 (Annual Reports of the Health Authorities).
169. In 1993 about 650 inmates received punishment for having used violence against prison personnel. Source: Key figures of penal institutions, 1993, Ministery of Justice.
170. Annual reports of the Health Authorities, Ministry of Justice, and *Negentig jaren statistiek in tijdreeksen, 1899–1989*, CBS, Den Haag, 1989.
171. Cf. Schnitzler, 1988.
172. *MvBR*, 1951, pp. 161–62.
173. Annual Reports of the Health Authorities, 1964, p. 2; 1967, p. 3; 1968, p. 3.
174. Ibid., 1979, p. 2; 1980, p. 2; 1985, p. 2.
175. *Rapport van de Commissie Psychiatrische/Therapeutische Voorzieningen Gevangeniswezen*, 1983. See also the report *Geestelijk gestoorden in de strafrechtspleging*, 1988.
176. Idem, pp. 31–42, p. 136.
177. Smit, 1989, quotes on pp. 64–5.
178. Gibbs, 1987, p. 308.
179. Kelk, 1987, p. 43.
180. Grapendaal and Kommer, 1988.
181. Cf. Franke, 1990.
182. Cf. Moerings, 1986 ('Fundamenten van (...)'), p. 355.
183. *Proces*, 1978, pp. 164–5.

11

Two Centuries of Imprisonment: Socio-Historical Explanations and Conclusions

No matter what, a criminal often has it very easy in comparison with the mental exertion to which he compels the scholars.[1]

At the end of the eighteenth century, penal reformers in England, France, Germany and the United States had expressed the opinion that fear of punishment did not constitute a satisfactory restraint on the realization of criminal intentions. They preferred that the lower classes be educated and habituated to an orderly and industrious way of life, in which bad intentions would not even arise. The prison, they felt, should not only deter people from doing wrong; it should improve them morally as well, by way of discipline and work, although the first penitentiaries in England were also meant to stop the abuses John Howard revealed. It seemed that prison guards could not accustom themselves to the disciplinary way of life they were to impose on their prisoners. The 'civilizing offensive' was failing because corrupt guards were neglecting the rules.[2] Very soon the penitentiaries resembled the old prisons, where people from outside were allowed to walk in at any time they liked on payment of some money, and where prisoners lived together in an atmosphere of sexual debauchery, hate and envy, excessive drinking, and violence.[32]

It was not until the 1820s and 1830s that in Pennsylvania (Philadelphia) and New York (Auburn) prison systems were developed where order and discipline could be enforced. Both systems were based on solitary confinement in cells, though in Auburn the isolation was not complete: during daytime the prisoners worked together, but they were not allowed to talk with or to contact each other. In Europe most governments and prison reformers were attracted by the Philadelphian system, whereas in the United States the Auburn system was practised more often. In 1842 the first 'Philadelphian' prison in Europe, Pentonville prison in London, was opened.[4] The members of its executive staff were trained disciplinarians from the army. Quite soon, but not before

heated political and juridical discussions had taken place, similar penitentiaries were put into use in France, Germany, Belgium, The Netherlands
and other countries on the continent.[5]

The rapid spread of the cellular prisons cannot be explained by
pointing to its superior results in the war on crime. In fact, the cellular
type of imprisonment appeared not to be successful at all. Again and
again, reports of insanity, suicide, and the complete alienation of prisoners from social life seriously discredited the new form of punishment.[6]
The observed effects on recidivism were more often negative than positive. In most European countries, the system of cellular imprisonment
had been extended in spite of continuously rising crime rates.

The apparent failure of the system had repeatedly been attributed to
the inadequate realization of an idea which was adequate in theory. The
way in which the documented criticism of the cellular system was defused
seems to indicate that there were other factors which favoured the
introduction and extension of the penitentiaries. According to Michel
Foucault, the disciplined life in prisons harmonized better with a new
'strategy of power' by comparison with the former 'spectacle of suffering'[7]
on the scaffold,. The prisons shaped a criminal class of listed ex-convicts
that could be more easily controlled than the heterogeneous group of
artisans, farmhands, tramps, beggars and criminals who constituted the
former 'dangerous class'.[8] Consequently the prisons led to a growing
animosity between poor yet decent workmen and their rebellious peers of
the criminal class. Their unity was broken. The control of criminal groups
had been extended even further by the knowledge and investigations of
psychiatrists, criminologists, probation officers, social workers, and
other professionals, increasing numbers of whom earned their living in
the expanding *système carcerale*. Those professionals related the entire
personality of prisoners to the crimes they had committed. Lawbreakers
became 'delinquents'. In Foucault's vision, the apparent failure of the
system of imprisonment had in fact been an extraordinary *success* in
producing delinquency that was politically and economically harmless. At
the same time the delinquency thus produced distracted attention from
the crimes of the rulers. 'The penality of detention seems to fabricate
hence no doubt its longevity an enclosed, separated and useful illegality,'
Foucault argued.[9]

It seems that Foucault confused the unintended consequences of
judicial reactions with the intended results of power politics and strategies.[10] This point brings me to an important shortcoming of many
historical explanations: their failure sufficiently to stress the relatively
autonomous character of social developments and the unintended consequences of human strivings.

Blind Forces or Well-thought-out Strategies?

Historical phenomena are very often explained either as the effect of purposeful actions or as the effects of blind forces and processes to which people had to adapt themselves. In some explanations it is not clear at all whether the wishes and aspirations of individuals or groups had any impact on social developments.

This shortcoming is obvious in the explanations of the rise and spread of cellular prisons in the Western world. The most voluntaristic – often to a degree implicit or hidden – are the explanations in the work of scholars and laymen who try to understand the abolition of the scaffold and the rise of cellular prisons in the light of the humane or inhumane feelings of powerful penal reformers and politicians. In their view, for instance, the scaffold had been abolished out of pity for the criminals, or the cellular system had been erected to put an end to 'pleasant' residence in the old, communal prisons. At the opposite extreme we find interpretations in which the personal influence of powerful individuals is almost totally neglected, and in which the march of scholarly and humanitarian 'progress'[11] or the 'requirements' of the socio-economic 'system' are offered as explanations. Most explanations, however, combine character-istics of both perspectives.[12] Rothman and Ignatieff stress the guiding influence of upperclass individuals who demanded the building of cellular prisons because they intensely feared social crisis and social disorganiza-tion in their society. But the reason for their fear – the supposed disrup-tion of society – is not seen as an effect of individual intentions but as the unintended effect of changing socio-economic conditions. Yet the voluntaristic vision dominates in their work, as Rothman, perhaps quite unintentionally, reveals in the title of his book by calling the rise of prisons and asylums a 'discovery'.

In their well known study *Punishment and Social Structure* (1939), Rusche and Kirchheimer also adopt aspects of both perspectives, al-though an economic and deterministic vision remains dominant. They try to understand long-term changes in the judicial punishment of criminals in interconnection with socio-economic conditions. At the same time they frequently oppose the view that humane intentions caused those changes. In their opinion the real incentives, that is to say the economic springs, have only been obscured by philanthropic storytelling. The rise of cellular prisons in the nineteenth century, was, according to Rusche and Kirchheimer, closely linked with the free labour market and the labour surplus within an emerging capitalistic, industrial system of production. While the control of 'free' labour for economic exploitation may have been one of the early advantages of the houses of correction (*Rasphuizen* in The Netherlands, 'Bridewells' in England and *Hôpitaux Généraux* in France), increased industrialization quickly undermined their economic foundation. Prison labour came to be seen by unemployed workmen and factory foremen alike as unfair competition. Also, it became increasingly difficult to exploit prison labour in a profitable manner.[13] Hence the new cellular prisons were intended only to deter criminals and to reform them morally. Purposeless labour was used to prevent prisoners in solitary confinement from going mad; sometimes its sole object was to augment the penalty. On the treadmills in England, for instance, the bodies of prisoners were ruined for no other reason than to chastise them.[14]

Although Rusche and Kirchheimer pay considerable attention to general socio-economic conditions, it ultimately becomes clear that they see the ruling classes as having wittingly carried through the main penal reforms in pursuit of their direct economic interests. Consequently, their perspective becomes a version of conspiracy theory. Such theories are in fact very dominant in Marxist or radical analyses, for instance, in the work of Melossi and Pavarini. This makes their work very hard to accept, although one may be attracted by those analyses for precisely that reason. Melossi and Pavarini call the penitentiaries an 'essentially bourgeois creation' and a cruel 'invention', meant to intimidate the grumbling proletariat and to transform prisoners into the disciplined and docile factory workers needed within the capitalist mode of production.[15] At the same time the factories, with their strict rhythm of work and long working hours, came to resemble prisons.

Melossi and Pavarini recapitulate the bourgeois umbrella ideology of both developments succinctly: 'prisoners must be workers, workers must be prisoners'.[16] About the same time as they finished their study, however, Foucault's *Surveiller et Punir* was published, and in an epilogue Melossi and Pavarini outlined their dissatisfaction with Foucault.[17] This is understandable, for it seemed that their analysis had been immediately overruled by another. Foucault's analysis incorporated many of the attractions of Marxist explanations, but apparently by-passed their conspiratorial overtones. In Foucault's work, power is treated not as a relational concept but as *something* which pervades social life totally and develops its own strategies and desires although it must be said that its desires often bear an uncomfortable resemblance to those attributed to the bourgeois capitalists in Marxist analyses. Foucault defines the shift of the object of punishment from body to soul, and the growing enforcement of discipline inside prisons and other institutions, as elements of a new and better 'strategy' of power.[18] He also interprets the 'normalizing' of criminals inside Panopticon-like prisons, and the modelling of unruly prisoners into 'docile bodies', as a new 'technology of power', better suited to the changing socio-economic conditions. Thus Foucault successfully avoids the conspiratorial elements of Marxist theory in part by decentring the subject and by depersonalizing his concept of power; this decentring has the limitation, however, of reducing individuals and groups to instruments of a willful, omnipresent, and all-pervading force: power.[19] People have to comply with the wishes and desires of that power. They even do so unconsciously. From this point of view Foucault's analysis very much resembles that of the structural functionalists, who try to explain social life in terms of the functions that have to be performed for the maintenance of a social system. People – structural functionalists prefer to talk about 'actors' – have to comply with this strategy of survival whether they like (and are aware of) it or not.[20] Notwithstanding this, many advocates of Foucault interpret him in such a way as to restore the subject so that power becomes once again a 'thing' owned, worked upon or manipulated by actual individuals, so that their analyses regain all the characteristics of a clearly structured conspiracy theory.[21] One cannot always blame them for this, because Foucault himself sometimes seems to forget that power is not the same as influential gentlemen in three-piece suits. In an interview with *Le Monde* in 1975, he even showed himself to be very surprised about the cynicism with which the nineteenth-century bourgeoisie 'said very precisely what it did, what it wanted to do, and why it wanted to do so'. For the bourgeoisie this cynicism would have been a matter of pride. 'Only in the eyes of naive persons is the bourgeoisie stupid and cowardly. It is intelligent and cool. It said very precisely what it wanted.'[22]

In the most important explanations of penal changes, either the guiding influence of powerful individuals is emphasized or the changes are presented as the results of anonymous forces such as 'power' or 'the system'. Human plans and intentions seem to explain everything or nothing at all. By asking the question why some processes did and why other processes did not develop in accordance with the wishes or plans of powerful people, it seems possible to avoid both extremes. It then becomes clear that influential people seldom agreed with each other about the desirability of penal changes. The cellular prisons, for instance, were strongly opposed by those people who feared a mitigation of the system of punishment, and who wanted to retain public punishment on the scaffold. The fact that public punishment was abolished and penitentiaries were built all over Europe is not comprehensible without seeing those events in interconnection with long-term social developments that possess a structure which cannot be reduced to specific human plans and intentions, and at the same time is not completely detached from them. As Norbert Elias puts it, these developments or processes are 'relatively autonomous' with respect to the intentions of even the powerful.[23]

I will shortly show how the important changes in imprisonment in The Netherlands were closely linked with blind, yet structured, long-term social processes, such as a growing aversion to physical violence and a gradual internalization of external social constraint. For the moment, I want to stress that most penal changes also have their own dynamics; that often there is no way back once reforms are set in motion. By the end of the nineteenth century, for instance, the state had invested so much money in the building of new cellular prisons, and so many prison experts and politicians had aligned themselves with the cellular system through the spoken and the written word, that it was not possible to take account of the growing criticism. Even influential people had to put up with these circumstances and to confine themselves to realizable reform proposals.[24] This makes it easier to understand why the cellular system was introduced in The Netherlands on a large scale by the adoption of a new penal code in 1886 at the very moment that in other Western countries solitary confinement was losing its appeal and was maintained fairly rigidly until the 1950s. This being so, the revolutionary changes in Dutch prison policy after the Second World War would be better explained by reference to embedded bureaucratic resistance and material interests during the first half of the twentieth century than by such a concept as the mythical 'Dutch tolerence'.[25] Instead of a 'restraining lead', The Netherlands had a 'stimulating arrear'. The old prison buildings badly needed renovation; and besides, it was a long time since vast investments in the cellular system had been made.

Ad-hoc Explanations of the Phenomenon

Another usual shortcoming of historical explanations is that they are sought in the social conditions and political circumstances that character-ized a nation at the time when plans for the building of penitentiaries were made and executed. Those conditions and circumstances are not seen as interconnected with long-term processes which concern the entire West-ern world. David Rothman, for instance, argues that prison reformers in the United States worried seriously about the perceived disorganization of their society after the war of independence. They saw growing problems of crime, poverty and insanity, and hoped that the disciplinary way of life in the new penitentiaries and asylums would serve as a model of society. 'The well-ordered asylum would exemplify the proper principles of social organisation and thus insure the safety of the republic and promote its glory,' Rothman writes.[26] Michael Ignatieff finds his explanations for the rise of the penitentiary in social phenomena which are specific to England in that period. The American civil war temporarily frustrated the deportation of criminals to the New World; the numerous death sentences meted out to minor offenders weakened the authority of the government; there was growing fear of a revolution like the French and of Jacobin radicalism; a great number of soldiers without livelihood or residence returned to England after the American war of independence and the Napoleonic wars; the modernization of agriculture caused high unemployment outside the peak seasons; and in the cities large groups of orphaned or dissolute youngsters threatened public security. These and other factors should have strongly convinced the upper classes that the nation found itself in a serious social crisis. The penitentiaries, Ignatieff continues, had such a strong appeal because they promised to be a perfect remedy for the perceived social problems. They formed 'a part of a larger strategy of political, social, and legal reform designed to re-establish order on a new foundation'.[27]

Similarly, some part of the explanations of 'the birth of the prison' offered by Michael Foucault is related strongly to the specific French situation during the *ancien régime* and the revolutionary period which followed. He related the heyday and decline of public executions and corporal punishment on the scaffold to the weakening power of the absolutist ruler (sovereign) and the transition to the sovereignty of the people.[28] Although Jacques-Guy Petit, in his voluminous study on the rise of penal prisons in France, strongly criticized Foucault's analysis and its empirical basis, he also stressed the influence of the French Revolution in relation to the rise of the penal prison.[29] Finally, Patricia O'Brien connects the rise of the penitentiaries with the formation of a French national state in the nineteenth century. By requiring certain virtues of orderliness, punctuality, and self-restraint, O'Brien argues, the new prison was aligned with the emerging national community, and with the new moral consensus of an industrial society.[30]

The problem with these ad-hoc explanations is that they shed little light on similar penal developments in other Western societies. The Netherlands, for instance, was never ruled by an absolute monarch. The Batavian revolution in 1795 even constituted a transition from a republic to a monarchy. In the first half of the nineteenth century the ruling classes in The Netherlands did not fear social disorganization and social crisis as strongly as did their counterparts in the United States and England. Moreover, the cellular system of imprisonment was put into use in a period of social calm, bourgeois contentment, and stabilizing crime problems rather than one characterized by strong fears for a collapsing social order.[31]

Abrupt Changes

In identifying the shortcomings of many historical explanations, I first showed the ways in which a blindness to the relatively autonomous character of social changes had led historians to favour onesided explanations in terms of human specific intentions or blind forces;[32] next, I stressed their ad hoc nature. A third shortcoming is closely bound up with the two just mentioned: the history of imprisonment is commonly described in terms of 'discoveries', 'births', 'inventions', and 'transformations'. The impression is given that radical changes took place abruptly, whereas, I shall contend, those changes actually came about gradually. There have always been long periods during which old and new elements of the penal system coexisted. Foucault, for example, suggests that prisons took the place of corporal and capital punishment on the scaffold, but in fact those forms of punishment coexisted for a long period of time. In The Netherlands, for instance, the public execution of a three-fold murderer in 1854 even took place in front of the first brandnew cellular prison in Amsterdam.[33] In European countries, most prisoners were still locked up in large, communal, disorderly and unclassified prisons during the nineteenth century, notwithstanding the 'invention' of the disciplinary system of cellular imprisonment.[34] The view that 'transformations' completely changed the penal system within short periods of time is also dominant in David Garland's study of penal and criminological changes in England around 1900. He describes the rise of the criminological discipline, the spread of views in which the *protection* of society and the *treatment* of criminals were paramount and the experiments with *reformatories*. All this, he says, led to 'a new structure of penality' within a period of about twenty years, which formed the foundation of the modern 'penal-welfare complex'.[35] Garland is certainly right in suggesting that people were thinking very differently about problems of crime and punishment at the beginning of the twentieth century than they had at the end of the nineteenth century; but the practice of imprisonment hardly changed at all. In The Netherlands, the new way of thinking about crime problems initially resulted only in the introduction of conditional sentences in 1915. That form of punishment, and later changes such as the mitigation of solitary confinement and the new confidence in the re-education of criminals, were very much in line with developments that started long before. In general it appears that long-term changes in the penal system took place much more gradually than concepts like 'transformation' or 'birth' suggest. Such images of abrupt change in the history of punishment distract attention from the apparent trend and structure of penal development, especially in the field of imprisonment, since the end of the eighteenth century.

I. TREND AND STRUCTURE OVER TWO HUNDRED YEARS

From the late middle ages the manners and emotions of people in West European societies manifested changes which show a certain relationship and a certain trend. Feelings of hatred, love, joy and sadness were gradually expressed less passionately and overtly. Many functions of the human body became loaded with feelings of shame and were removed behind the scenes of social life. Human conduct became more calculating and bound by standards. People developed a more psychological and rational view of one another. Norbert Elias connects these long-term developments with state-formation processes, which went hand in hand with the monopolization by the state authority of the use of physical violence. In the course of the 'civilizing process' people grew ever more interdependent. In more and more social spheres they were forced to consider more and more other individuals, and greater demands were made upon their self-control and empathy. People in the higher social classes also tried to distinguish themselves by self-control, the regulation of behaviour and good manners from people lower on the social scale, and especially from those who attempted to climb up the social ladder, and who themselves started to behave like people of the higher classes. The growing interdependency and the social urge to distinction functioned, as it were, as the engines of what Elias called the civilizing process. At the same time, Elias convincingly shows how in the course of this process external social constraint became a pressure that people exerted on themselves. What one initially had refrained from doing or had done simply out of calculation, the urge for distinction, or fear of social reactions, now increasingly became embedded in human personality and emotional life. Many 'civilized' forms of acting, thinking, and feeling were gradually taken for granted in such a way that the awareness of external pressure was lost.[36] In some earlier studies, Spierenburg and I showed how the growing opposition to public executions and corporal punishment on the scaffold and finally the abolition of those penalties in The Netherlands must be seen in the context of changing sensibilities.[37] Jim Sharpe argues that, 'though stimulating and benefitting from being founded on extensive empirical research', the interpretation of Spierenburg has its drawbacks, for 'there is still the problem of why it is that sensibilities change'.[38] I think Sharpe does not conceive the internal dynamic of the civilizing process as sketched above.

If one takes into account that 'civilized conduct' was self-evident for the upper classes, one can understand their endeavours since the end of the eighteenth century to get the lower classes, whom they thought to be riotous, to behave the same way by means of social constraint. In these 'civilizing offensives' the importance of regularity, orderliness, and a division of tasks in family life was pointed out to members of the lower class, as well as the necessity of controlling impulses of aggression, emotional urges and sexual desires.[39]

From this viewpoint, unlike Foucault's, the training of people in general and the life in institutions such as psychiatric homes, schools, orphanages and prisons in particular, is not regarded as a power strategy which was developed rather suddenly, but as a development characteristic of a certain stage in the civilizing process. What was pleaded by prison reformers, philanthropists and politicians in the middle of the nineteenth century, and which began to be implemented, I would rather interpret as a 'penal civilizing offensive' than as the 'birth' of a new punishment technology. Also, other changes in the way criminals were imprisoned appear to be linked with the characteristics of the West European civilizing process.

Increasing Social Pressure towards Self-constraint

'For obedience based on fear does not persist', a prisoner wrote to the Dutch criminologist Rijksen in the 1950s. He put into words what had begun to dawn on some criminal lawyers and prison experts more than a century earlier: that the prison sentence ought to have an educational as well as a punitive purpose; solitary confinement was considered to be a suitable means for this. Before this time, the punishment of imprisonment had focused on intimidation and exclusion. Convicts were deported and killed or – in order to set an example to others and as a means of deterrence – they were grievously maltreated in public and left to their own devices in jail. All these punishments resulted in their expulsion from society, even after they had served their time. The penitentiaries, on the other hand, aimed at readopting criminals into society, all reformed, in due course of time. Yet, halfway through the century, there was more going on in the penitentiary field. By means of punishment, prison reformers and politicians wanted to achieve the development of feelings and attitudes among convicts that would prevent them from performing criminal acts in the future; not the fear of punishment, but the awakening conscience should keep people on the rails; they would not even want to commit them any longer. Reformers hoped to achieve this moral improvement by subjecting prisoners to strict discipline, order and regular labour. They had to learn to resist sudden emotional impulses and ignore desires for immediate satisfaction of material and non-material needs.

The feelings and the rules of behaviour that were to be transferred to prisoners were virtually identical to what was considered to be civilized conduct in the upper classes. The 'penal civilizing offensive' which was quite overtly launched by the Dutch Society for the Moral Improvement of Prisoners in 1823, acquired a very specific character halfway through the century due to the great importance attached to solitary confinement. It was thought that when prisoners were entirely left to their own devices, tendencies towards proper behaviour would win out over their evil proclivities. The emphasis on solitary confinement reflected the replacement of social constraint exerted by the external forms of corporal punishment and deportation by a confidence in an internalized constraint. This increasing shift from *Fremdzwang* to *Selbstzwang* (social constraint to self-constraint), which is so characteristic of the West European civilizing process in general, remains characteristic of the prison system up to the present. Not only did successive generations of prison reformers and politicians emphasize again and again that inner constraint was far preferable to external constraint, but an appeal also was made for self-discipline and self-control in practice. The very awareness of the fact that good intentions and a virtuous conscience are of little value if willpower and the capacity for self-control are missing led to criticism of the cellular system and experiments with self-government and half-open prisons. One may doubt whether the growing confidence in self-restraint should be regarded merely as a development within the penitentiary history of ideas and not above all as a symptom of state-formation and democratization. At the beginning of the nineteenth century, social constraint from above and outside might have been more necessary because emotional ties with the home country and the social order among the lower classes were less strong than later in the century.

In the first half of the last century, for instance, the Dutch prison system was still dominated, both theoretically and in practice, by deterrence through public executions and prisons comprised of enormous, unhealthy dormitories and workshops. After 1850 the emphasis shifted to moral improvement. Experiments with solitary confinement, which had begun in 1851, were extended in 1854 and 1871. In 1886, cellular confinement became the core of the new penal code. In this period, public corporal punishment such as flogging, branding and exposition on the scaffold was abolished in 1854; the abolition of the death penalty followed in 1870. Forms of communal confinement became subject to a growing number of regulations for order and discipline, and after 1886 were used only for children, old people, suspects and long-sentenced prisoners who already had five years of solitary confinement behind them.

Theoretically, moral improvement remained a subsidiary purpose of imprisonment, but, in practice, advocates of the 'the educational view' in the interbellum period and of the striving for resocialization after the Second World War considered the extension of self-constraint to socially acceptable behaviour as its main purpose. Whereas the champions of solitary confinement hoped that in a cell conscience would be roused all by itself, the subsequent educators and probation officers stressed the importance of training of the will, self-discipline and self-control in contacts with fellow-prisoners and free citizens. With the introduction of conditional release (in 1886; extended in 1915) and the conditional sentence (in 1915), a strong appeal was made to the capacity of people to force *themselves* to lead regular and decent lives. The constraint from outside meant nothing more than the threat of an extra severe punishment if conditions were not fulfilled. Already before the Second World War in the open-air prison of Veenhuizen and after the war in the half-open and open prisons and so-called 'self-reporters prisons', even higher demands were made on the self-control of prisoners. The same applies to the intermediate furloughs and the latest experiments with 'day detention' (where prisoners go home at night) and other form of 'imprisonment' outside the walls. Looking forward to future favours, the detained keep themselves imprisoned without walls and guards and report voluntarily at the gate after being summoned or after a period of leave. Such demands, and the capacity of prisoners to live up to them, confirm the course of the civilizing process, but can also be better understood as part of that process.[40] In the light of this long-term development it becomes clear that the ad-hoc solutions which were repeatedly sought for problems in the prison system including the new problems arising from such solutions did show a trend and a structure.

Homo Clausus *and the Socializing of Imprisonment*

Comparing the cellular system and the unsocial 'cellular' image of human beings which prison reformers had over the last century to the socializing of the prison sentence and the ideas of reformers in our own century, it is more difficult to identify a trend and a structure. After all, around the turn of the century, views on crime and punishment that used to dominate the penal and criminological fields were challenged. Concepts such as free will and sin were undermined by the new deterministic views of human behaviour. The protection of society or *défense sociale* became a more important purpose of punishment than deterrence and retribution.[41] Less and less did experts believe in the improving effect of solitary confinement. Yet this 'break' with nineteenth-century ideas of crime and punishment is closely connected with other developments which had actually become manifest much earlier. One of these developments relates to the image of man as *homo clausus*, which was so strikingly expressed in the experiments with babies by Friedrich II von Hohenstaufen (1194–1250) and the Scottish King James IV (1472–1513). They wanted to find out what language children speak by themselves if they are excluded from any contact with speaking educators. The subjects of the experiments died before they could say a word.

Only those who consider their own and others' inner nature as something set apart from the outside world will design such experiments. In *Imagining the Penitentiary* (1987), the English linguist, John Bender, shows how this isolated image of man was also expressed, albeit less rigidly, in eighteenth-century novels by Henry Fielding and especially in Daniel Defoe's solitary islander, Robinson Crusoe. A contemporary Dutch version of Defoe's book was published: in *De Walcherse Robinson* an anonymous writer tells about a little boy growing up all by himself on an uninhabited island and educating himself into a decent, rational and yet religious man.[42] Bender argues that this literature laid the foundation

for the later penitentiaries, because people became familiar with the idea
of character development from psychological insight gained all by oneself.
He compares the omnipresent novelist who models his heroes' characters
with the central management and supervision in Jeremy Bentham's
Panopticon and the later cellular prisons. 'The interior personification of
juridical presence as character' is, according to Bender, the central
element of 'the penitentiary idea'.[43] Using a quotation from the Scottish
moral philosopher, Adam Smith, Bender shows how Smith, in his *Theory
of Moral Sentiments* (1759), in spite of a relatively strongly developed
concept of the social basis of moral judgements, did consider it possible
for people who grow up completely isolated to have a character, sentiments and thoughts:

> Were it possible that a human creature could grow up to manhood
> in some solitary place, without any communication with his own
> species, he could no more think of his own character, of the
> propriety or demerit of his own sentiments or conduct, of the beauty
> or deformity of his own face... Bring him in society, and he is
> immediately provided with the mirror which he wanted before.[44]

All the same, Smith was much closer to an image of the self as a social
construction than the later advocates of solitary confinement were, even
though his psychological analysis of the conscience contributed to the
cellular reform philosophy. According to the strongly religious percep-
tions of prison reformers in the nineteenth century, it was possible for
prisoners to resocialize themselves in solitude with the help of God and
the Bible.[45] Those prisoners were, so to speak, also prisoners of the
cellular image of man held by their punishers.

Obviously, the enthusiasm for solitary confinement cannot be seen in
isolation from the highly individualistic concept of sin and evil avowed by
the confessional politicians and members of the society for the moral
improvement of prisoners. Yet, their image of man as a *homo clausus* also
strongly reflects the greater differences of power between the upper and
lower classes. Much more easily than in our time, judges, scholars,
members of parliament, ministers and successful merchants could regard
themselves as independent, autonomous individuals who owed their
places at the top of the social pile to their own moral standing and abilities.
They did not have to take account of other people as much as their
counterparts nowadays do; particularly not of lower class people. Seen in
the long term, it is true that the elite too had become dependent on more
and more people, but in the middle of the nineteenth century this clearly
did not yet prevent its members from viewing themselves as *homo clausus*.
It also enabled them to think about the causes of crime in terms of
individual shortcomings and ill-nature and to barely consider crime as a
social phenomenon.

Solitary Confinement in The Netherlands

Not everyone thought and felt alike. Although in The Netherlands – and even more so in England, France and the United States – criminality was linked to social crises, disorganization and social conditions, in none of these countries did these thoughts dominate.[46] Solutions were sought not in social measures but in the moral improvement of individuals. In France, however, the cellular system never got off the ground completely, even though in the 1840s, after a passionate debate, a parliamentary majority expressed itself in favour of solitary confinement of unlimited maximum duration. The revolution of 1848 destroyed the enthusiasm for prison reforms.[47] Around 1880, France had only nine strictly cellular prisons.[48] In the United States the Auburn system with communal labour was dominant. In England the 'progressive system', with increased social contacts and a gradual transition to freedom, was being developed, although it was vigourously opposed in The Netherlands. Moreover, in England the maximum duration of solitary confinement was soon reduced from eighteen to nine months.[49] This development led the Dutch penal law expert, Pompe, in 1930 to raise the question why, especially in The Netherlands, the cellular system had gained the upper hand towards the end of the nineteenth century. He assumed that this 'curious phenomenon' should be attributed to 'the professors'. 'In a study,' he wrote, 'problems were posed and solved, including the problems which were pre-eminently important in the practical sense. The cell was pre-eminently satisfactory to those who never left their study.'[50] The influence of armchair scholars of course only partly accounts for the great and longlived enthusiasm in The Netherlands for year-on-year confinement, unless it is assumed that scholars in other European countries left their studies more often than did their Dutch counterparts.

The historian, Spierenburg, has tried to assemble material for a completely different, more comprehensive explanation. In an article about the rise of imprisonment in seventeenth-century Holland and nineteenth-century America (1987) he asks the question why the Auburn system was dominant across the Atlantic and the Philadelphian or Pennsylvanian system in Europe. Spierenburg thinks that the Europeans liked to experiment with new forms of confinement because of their former experiences with workhouses and houses of correction, whereas the Americans, as it were, started with a clean slate. 'Most Americans did not want to experiment,' Spierenburg states, without any justification:

> they were just starting with the prison and the Auburn system suited them well. The Pennsylvania-style remained a minority-system because it served the needs of its society less adequately.

To this somewhat obscure, undeveloped structural-functionalistic notion he adds that in Europe state-formation processes had led to 'a new transformation in repression', referring to the shifting from public sentences involving physical violence to sentences in which discipline and 'confrontation of the offender with his inner self' were central. 'Mind control became a major objective, and solitary confinement fit into this model. This is why Europeans admired Pennsylvanian practice'.[51]

Spierenburg does not make very clear, however, the steps by which these developments occurred and how precisely state-formation led to this 'transformation'. His explanation is therefore rather circular: solitary confinement met with such response in Europe because it met with such response. In addition, the Auburn system was also based on solitary confinement, although prisoners were allowed to see each other but definitely not talk to each other during working hours. Besides, in America various systems were actually busily experimented with before the Auburn system gained the upper hand, whereas in Europe there was much dispute about style differences, mainly on the basis of those American experiments.[52]

Neither Spierenburg's interpretations nor those of Pompe shed much light on the exceptionally great and prolonged enthusiasm for strictly cellular confinement in The Netherlands. As well as with its relation to the Calvinistic tradition of *innerweltlichen Askese* (innerworldly asceticism),[53] this enthusiasm was definitely connected with the absence of social and political disturbances of the magnitude of French, English or American experience. Similar experiences did not affect Dutch merchants, gentry and patricians. Their very atomistic, unsocial (in the sense of not viewing human beings and their moral character as products of social conditions and relations), or cellular image of human beings was less strikingly contradicted by the social reality. In 1848, while practically the whole of Europe was on fire, the bourgeois revolution in The Netherlands was carried out by a Royal Decree. The increasing power of other social classes revealed itself in a less shocking way than elsewhere in Europe. This makes it more clear why the cellular images of man could only be defeated by more sociological views when Dutch society too was confronted with grave social disturbances in the form of socialist opposition, riots and strikes at the end of the nineteenth century. At first, large scale prison reforms were prevented by material circumstances in the form of newly built cellular prisons; however, after the Second World War, the socializing of the prison regime took shape in a sequence of reforms. Social contacts with fellow-prisoners and free citizens were assigned a pre-eminent rehabilitating role.[54] Instead of special prisons for those unfit for a cell, prisons for those 'unfit for the community' were created for people who could not cope with social and therapeutic group work.

From all this, it appears that both the enthusiasm for and the later dislike of isolated images of man on which the cellular system was based are related to decreasing power differences and increasing interdependencies. Their strong position of power and their relatively weak ties with others enabled upperclass people to seek the causes of social problems mainly in the individual's inner life and the solutions in the social isolation of the wrongdoers. However, as the lower classes gained more power and the upper classes were forced to show them more consideration, the old opinions on crime and punishment were put under strain, and the causes of crime came to be sought in social circumstances. The aim of punishment now was to teach social skills to prisoners instead of entirely throwing them back upon their own resources.

Explanations by Foucault and Others

Unfortunately, hardly any attention is paid to such long-term developments in the explanations offered by historians and criminologists for the rise of cellular prisons. This leads them not only into dubious interpretations, but also to a disregard of the pedagogical core of cellular prisons: solitary confinement. Foucault does not make any distinction between cellular prisons and prisons with communal confinement. His explanations in terms of power and knowledge relate specifically to strict order and discipline; they do not, however, relate to the complete isolation in the new penitentiaries. The same goes for the strongly Marxist-tinged explanations by Scull and by Melossi and Pavarini. Rusche and Kirchheimer, who link penitentiary reforms with socio-economic developments, have great difficulty in explaining solitary confinement as a dominant type of punishment in the nineteenth century. Once economic advantages are ruled out, they emphasize the cruel character of the cell-sentence as an explanatory factor. They also see intimidation of the working class as having played a major part. 'What European society with its industrial reserve army needed was a punishment which would strike fear even into the hearts of the starving,' they write;[55] for this purpose the torture of solitude was considered very suitable. The authors themselves are of the opinion that 'the barbarous treatment of the past' was 'almost merciful' compared to the mental misery of the cell-sentence. Strangely enough, they immediately go on to say that the prison reformers did not want to inflict torture; no, on the contrary, they wanted to reform and had high expectations from the cellular system. These reformers blamed 'intemperance and thoughtlessness' as the causes of crime. 'Alone in his cell' the criminal would enter into a struggle with his conscience which would lead to 'insight, remorse and a change of attitude'.[56] Rusche and Kirchheimer throw doubt upon these ideas. Besides, according to them, the cell system failed completely. For most convicts, solitary confinement led only to 'illness, lunacy and agony'; yet those in favour of solitary confinement continued to maintain that this punishment had a beneficial effect. As a compromise between their sympathy for the benign intentions of philanthropists and their own economic-deterministic explanatory model, Rusche and Kirchheimer describe solitary confinement as symptomatic of a mentality 'which, as a result of surplus population, abandons the attempt to find a rational policy of rehabilitation and conceals the fact with a moral ideology'.[57]

This forced solution of their problems of explanation manifests a strong resistance to the view that prison reformers and politicians really and sincerely believed in solitary confinement as a solution to the problems of crime. This is a pity, because I am convinced that it is only from the unsocial *homo clausus* image of man and the individualistic images of society shared by reformers and politicians in the last century, that one can properly understand the enthusiasm for the cellular system. This enthusiasm had nothing to do with direct economic advantages, even though these images of man and society fitted the existing economic structure well. It is difficult to see which form of power, which group or which interest was being served by the destructive effect of prolonged solitude on the psyche and the social functioning of prisoners. They definitely did not learn how to cooperate, as required for factory work. The sight of all these broken-spirited cell prisoners at the very best flattered the individual feelings of power of prison governors, guards and visitors.

Nor do Ignatieff and Rothman make it clear why, of all forms of punishment, *solitary* confinement could be regarded as a solution to the social crisis and social disorganization which they had described. The worldwide enthusiasm for solitary confinement at the beginning of the nineteenth century should rather be understood as a refutation of the assumption that causes of crime were to be sought in social circumstances: for social causes of crime and social causes of character-building were exactly the causes that were denied in the cellular system. The only social dimension was to be found in the fear of moral contagion which was to be prevented by means of cellular hoods, cellular chapels and cellular airings; however, this fear too was based on a strongly individualistic conception of sin, and definitely not on social criticism. Therefore I think that Rothman and Ignatieff strongly overestimated the meaning and effect of statements made by reformers and politicians about the social dimensions of crime. This is indicated not only by my own findings on the Dutch situation, but also by the impresssions gained by Garland about England and by Wright about France. In connection with the liberal *laissez-faire* individualism of the nineteenth century, Garland points out how eagerly attempts were made to find the causes of poverty and crime within the terms of doctrines of 'individualism, self-help and freedom'. He does not think that unemployment, poverty and crime were considered to be social problems but rather 'moral problems' in terms of traits of character, righteousness and individual responsibility.[58] Wright convincingly shows how in France social explanations of crime were 'too unorthodox' to gain wide support. 'Occasionally there had been passing suggestions that crime might have social roots in misery or ignorance, but few reformers had seen fit to develop these ideas in any depth,' according to Wright. Some socialists who did try to do so were regarded as cranks and not taken seriously.[59]

The image of man as *homo clausus* which, to the present-day observer, was so strongly revealed in the pedagogical justification of cellular confinement, was already being attacked by those people who took a more social image of human beings in the middle of the nineteenth century; but they were a minority. Not until the twentieth century did sociological interpretations of crime and criminals come to the fore. Yet the image of criminals propagated by the first prison reformers was already richer in the psychological sense and less static than the strongly religious view of man as a sinful person in the sixteenth and seventeenth centuries.[60] The fact that moral improvement was linked to imprisonment as a secondary purpose itself refers to a changing view of the human soul and inner life. The new penal views of Beccaria and their enthusiastic reception illustrate how much more rational that view of man became in connection with the *Entzauberung der Welt* (disenchantment of the world).[61] Looking back to the middle ages onwards, both the cellular philosophy and the later socializing of imprisonment show that the view people had of themselves and others became much less static, gained psychological depth and revealed increasing awareness of the way human beings are built socially and of their interdependency. In the light of that development, connected with changes in human relations, it becomes even clearer that changes in views on crime and punishment in the eighteenth and nineteenth centuries should not be characterized as 'breaches'. They fitted within the trend and structure of long-term social developments.

Miserable Suffering behind the Social Scenes

The abolition of public corporal and capital punishment in the last century is often seen as an intentional 'humanizing' of penal practice. But well-to-do citizens were not motivated as much by compassion for criminals as by their own 'civilized' aversion to public physical violence.[62] Appeals that the death sentence and scaffold punishments be carried out in out-of-the-way places or inside prison walls so that one did not have to witness the common and barbarian scaffold tableaus are telling evidence of this attitude. In other Western countries the death sentence was, indeed, carried out in this way and pressure for abolition disappeared to a large extent. The horrible scenes were out of sight and out of mind. This did not take place in The Netherlands and the death sentence was abolished in 1870. Why the secret execution of the death sentence was so much more objectionable in The Netherlands than in France, England and the German states is difficult to interpret. The 'dispatching' of criminals in out-of-the-way places was associated by opponents of the punishment with illegal practices which could not bear the light of day. The fact that this association was made was most likely connected to the long democratic (and the lack of an absolutist) tradition in The Netherlands and a relatively broad openness of management. One thing that is certain is that the punishment of criminals was pushed away behind the social scenes, just as many other facets of life.[63] Only during transfers were prisoners still exposed to mocking or compassionate glances of the public. Suffering imposed upon them in the name of justice had henceforth to be undergone behind thick walls – at first still in the presence of fellows, later in complete solitude.

Even though the abolition of public punishment cannot be seen as an expression of increased compassion with criminals, it did arise from an increased ability to imagine the pain and suffering of fellow-men as one's own. This ability was finely described by Adam Smith as the basis of his *Theory of Moral Sentiments* (1759). Because in his time the rack was still used to the full, he unintentionally illustrates how relatively weak this ability still was:

> Though our brother is upon the rack, as long as we ourselves are at our ease, our senses will never inform us what he suffers ... It is the impressions of our own senses only, not those of his, which our imaginations copy. By the imagination we place ourselves in his situation, we conceive ourselves enduring all the same torments, we enter as it were into his body, and become in some measure the same person with him.[64]

Opponents of scaffold punishments did, indeed, give evidence that they felt the welts of the flogging on their own backs, as it were. During capital punishment their breath was also taken away for a moment as the hangman's rope tightened around the neck of the convict.[65]

The fact that the sight of physical torture on the scaffold seems to have been more difficult to stand in the nineteenth century than in centuries past was connected to changes in social relations. In many areas people became more dependent on each other and were forced to put themselves in another's shoes, to form a more accurate image of someone else's goals and feelings and to adjust their behaviour accordingly. Thus it became more and more difficult to escape noticing the suffering of fellow-men, and also that of criminals. State-authorized infliction of suffering became increasingly problematic. The first expression of this with reference to criminals was directed to the clearly visible physical forms of suffering on the scaffold. The first complaints about the treatment of prisoners were also directed at the physical deprivations they suffered in extremely filthy and unheated hovels and holes. Later on the formulation of the problem of prison suffering came to include psychic forms as well, bound to the deprivation of freedom, the breaking of (sexual) contacts with loved ones and longlasting solitude.[66]

How difficult it was for people of the upper class in the nineteenth century to identify themselves with the psychic life of the less fortunate is apparent from the tenacious blindness to the suffering in cellular prisons. Lawyers' and politicians' own civilized, studious personalities made it seem that the suffering imposed by communal imprisonment was much more severe than cellular misery. They said that they could imagine themselves peacefully reading a good book in the cell and making exciting excursions into a rich mental world. Even in our century psychiatrists have been known to ask themselves, full of wonder, how it could be that prisoners in cells developed fullblown psychoses which quickly disappeared as soon as they had people around them again. Present-day views of 'isolation torture' and sensory deprivation actually make it very surprising that apparently so many were able to stand the cellular solitude without becoming severely deranged or profoundly depressed.

Even though the awareness that cellular confinement implied severe suffering grew, it was still only after the Second World War that this suffering was generally recognized and deemed unacceptable. The extent to which the recognition of cellular misery was connected with the ability to identify oneself with one's fellow man became quite clear through the role played by the members of the resistance. Their own experience of cellular misery during the German occupation opened their eyes to the misery that normal prisoners already had been suffering for many decades. It was not the first time that political prisoners had served as pioneers in penal and prison reforms.[67] Dirk Volkertsz Coornhert, who was seen as the 'spiritual father' of the 'rasp' and 'spinhuizen', wrote his famous *Boeventucht* (Discipline for scoundrels) in the prisongate in The Hague where he was imprisoned in 1567 because of difficulties with the Spanish occupiers.[68] During the Batavian Republic and the French occupation many Orangeists also made acquaintance with prison life. The French had hardly taken to their heels when King William I set up a commission to deal with the bad treatment of prisoners. Around the turn of the century vocal socialists went into fierce battle against solitary confinement based on their own experiences. After the First World War, conscientious objectors gave expression to their horrid experiences in the cell by actively helping in founding the Committee for Action against existing Opinions concerning Crime and Punishment. In the 1960s a number of Provos converted their prison experiences into solidarity with other detained victims of consumer society. It is easiest to identify with suffering if one has felt the same pain. Nevertheless, the Orangeists, the socialists and the members of the resistance from the Second World War would never have received as much attention as they did if their descriptions of the horrors suffered had not had a larger appeal. Their influence especially consisted of their divulging of conditions unknown to the upper classes and to the majority of the public. The fact that their revelations aroused feelings and led to changes illustrates a long-term development that had forced people to more intense forms of identification, empathy and commiseration. Sufferings of others came more and more to be felt and experienced as one's own.

All of this is in a certain sense affirmed by the marked contribution of writers and poets, whether or not they themselves had personal prison experiences, to protests against the poor treatment of prisoners. Their tendency, enforced by their profession, is to identify more with fictive or non-fictive fellow men than their fellow citizens do. On the other hand, the development of more life-like forms in novels of the eighteenth and nineteenth centuries shows that people in general, and not only writers, were socially forced to identify more with each other. Seen in this way it is understandable that the philologist, Bender, sees the literature of the eighteenth century as the substrate for later penitentiary notions, but he does not arrive at the more sociological insight that both literature and the abolition of public punishment and the emergence of *penitentiaries* went hand in hand with certain long-tern developments in human feelings, manners and social relations.[69]

Social Control and Dialectic

Halfway through the 1980s judicial policy was strongly oriented to 'restoration' of formal social control through the appointment of new supervisory officials and the encouragement of expansion of private security services. Seen in the light of two centuries of judicial reactions to crime, this policy gains a meaning which is definitely missing from the a-historical perspective of its designers. It does not appear to be concerned with restoration but with a further *expansion* of formal social control.

Spying cameras in warehouses and on underground stations give society today, in Foucault's terms, a panopticon-like character. The criminologist, Stan Cohen, points out that the growing army of welfare and social workers can also be seen as *agents of social control* who have expanded formal control to deep in the private lives of citizens. The so-called alternative punishments such as community service and obligatory education do not usually replace, as intended, other punishments, but greatly widen the net of social control. The call to bring criminals and other deviants back to society from *total institutions* in the 1960s appears unintentionally to have resulted in a profound increase in control of the offenders outside prison walls without leading to a decrease in numbers of prisoners. In England, the United States and recently also in The Nether-lands detention rates have even increased strongly.[70]

The network of supervisory departments and officials has become larger and more intricate. In the last two centuries this expansion of formal control has been expressed clearly in the development of a professional police organization and the growing number of police per 100,000 citizens.[71] Psychiatrists, psychologists, doctors, probation and aftercare workers and social workers have found work within the *carceral system*, as Foucault calls the growing network of formal social-control officials. Within the Dutch prison system the expansion of control and surveillance outside the walls started in the beginning of the nineteenth century with care for ex-prisoners by the Society for the Moral Improvement of Prisoners. This supervision was formalized and expanded in 1886 and once again in 1915 by the introduction of conditional leave and conditional sentencing. After the Second World war this control was primarily expanded by means of alternative punishments, *diversion*,[72] and technical means. At present computers keep a detailed record of persons who have once come into contact with the law. Meanwhile, possibilities are being explored for imprisoning suspects and convicts in their own homes by means of electronic monitoring.[73]

This development of increasing surveillance and control in the private lives of people is interpreted by Foucault and his disciples, of course, in terms of a strategic exercise of power and of power technology. My conviction is that it is much better to see these structured developments as largely unintentional results of the new 'solutions' which are continuously being sought for changing problems of crime and punishment.[74] The problems are often also the unintended result of earlier 'solutions'.[75] Thus the prison sentence gained strongly in importance because public corporal punishment and banning became problematic. And this led to the problem of moral decay in the 'universities of crime', as prisons were soon called, becoming an issue. I have shown that, in the long run, the chain of ad hoc solutions possessed a certain trend and structure. One can imagine this graphically as a series of wave-like movements which point to a dialectic dynamic and not as straightforward developments.

The dialectic nature of penal developments was most succinctly expressed in the transition from communal (thesis) to cellular confinement (antithesis), followed by a combination of both forms of confinement (synthesis). From the descriptions of 'far-reaching depravity' in nineteenth-century communal prisons it is obvious that reformers and politicians were more driven by civilized feelings than by penal convictions. Their aversion to overcrowded dormitories and workshops, as to public execution of punishment, was connected strongly with a broad civilized rejection of rough forms of social intercourse and uncontrolled expressions of feelings and desires. The cellular 'antithesis' was in that sense a civilized punishment. The mental suffering which accompanied cellular confinement was, to a certain extent, recognized but was less identified with and did not go as much against the grain. In the cellular improvement philosophy images of man and society were expressed which revealed a far-reaching blindness to the social forming of man. The 'synthesis' which took shape with mixed forms of confinement after the Second World War cannot be seen disconnected from long-term civilizing processes. The misery of long-lasting solitude was identified with more strongly. The large majority of politicians and reformers now characterized cellular practice as 'cruel' and 'barbarian'. They spoke of a 'unconscionable lack' of psychological insight. The dissolute togetherness in former communal prisons made way for a purposive *socializing* of the punishment, whereby, contrarily, a resocializing effect was expected of social contact. Now the new reformers saw not solitude but group pressure as the pre-eminent therapeutic and pedagogical tool.

The dialectic nature of this development was thus strongly linked to other long-term developments which I have described. This is even more true of the emancipation process of prisoners as it progressed – relatively autonomously – over a period of two centuries. At the beginning prisoners came into possession of more means of power, against the explicit intentions of their punishers and without realizing it themselves, let alone having fought for it. Only in the second half of the twentieth century did their emancipation process develop the character of an active prisoner movement.

2. THE EMANCIPATION PROCESS OF PRISONERS

In 1828 the *Zedekundig Handboek voor Gevangenen* (Moral Handbook for Prisoners) was published by the Society for Public Welfare. More than one-and-a-half centuries later (1982) quite a different handbook, the first *Bajesboek* (Handbook for prisoners and those placed in secure clinics), appeared. The expectations of the moral handbook were that it would bring to life 'the not yet completely dead seeds of Virtue and Religion' and that therefore many 'would both be given back to the Society of citizens, and prepared for Heaven'. The authors of the *Bajesboek* wanted to offer prisoners 'the chance to learn something more about their own rights'. In a later edition (1988) they stated that the book provided information to 'prisoners and their legal-aid workers in their unequal struggle with the judicial machinery'.[76] The *Zedekundig Handboek* did not point out the rights of prisoners but the importance of 'love for our duty'.[77]

Sources of Power

The *Zedekundig Handboek*, in spite of its moralistic tone, formed nevertheless the expression of a growing interest in the fate of prisoners. This growing interest went hand in hand with an increasing sensitivity to the physical suffering that was inflicted upon prisoners by the state. Doctors and other prison visitors published their descriptions of misery, filthiness and depravity. These reports were joined, shortly after the French occupation, by complaints of well-to-do political prisoners. This led in 1821 to a Royal Decree in which the treatment of prisoners was bound to rules for the first time, even though these rules were certainly not enforced everywhere in practice. Still, the rules gave critics of this practice some grip.

While interest in the treatment of prisoners grew further, insights concerning the goal of their confinement changed too. Prison had not only to deter but must also contribute to the moral improvement of criminals. The increasing sensitivity to the suffering of prisoners contributed significantly to this 'subsidiary goal'. As justification of this suffering, deterrence, retribution and revenge *alone* were no longer acceptable. Revenge and retribution as bases for punishment came gradually to be associated with primitive passions. The prison sentence, wrote the later Minister of Justice, Modderman, in 1864, had to be an 'ostensible evil' as far as deterrence was concerned and an 'essential good' as far as moral improvement went.[78] Clearly he did not make it easy for future defenders of the punishment. After all, the more the essential good of the prison sentence could be doubted, the more the ostensible evil grew into an essential evil. He thus formulated a criterion from which, based on later experiences and insights, no sort of prison sentence at all could be justified.

With moral improvement bound to the punishment as a goal prisoners came to be, as it were, subjected to this sentence for their own good. For prisoners these developments meant that they came into possession of an important source of power which would slowly but surely gain in significance in the course of the nineteenth and twentieth centuries. They could repeatedly undermine and cast doubts upon the justification of their punishment by *not* improving morally and by continuing to repeat offences, even more so as the improving effect of punishment came to be seen as increasingly important. Moreover, and this constituted the *second* important source of power, their punishers were increasingly forced to justify any extra suffering (other than the deprivation of freedom) imposed on prisoners as they became more sensitive to this suffering and as their belief in moral improvement or other positive effects diminished. Unintentionally and unaware, both prisoners and their punishers worked together to shift the balance of power in favour of the prisoners: prisoners by remaining bad and continuing to suffer; their punishers by continually expecting new positive effects of the punishment and making retribution, revenge and deterrence as bases of punishment increasingly problematic. At the beginning it was only a potential strengthening of prisoners' position of power, wherein they fulfilled a passive role. Later, particularly in the twentieth century, the growing power materialized in rights, rules and facilities and prisoners made active use of the decreasing power differences. Their *emancipation process* became an *emancipation movement* as well. The differences in power have naturally remained large right up to the present day, but bit by bit the chances of prisoners to influence and control their punishers have become remarkably larger.

Public Interest and Opinions of Prisoners

The choice between solitary and communal confinement dominated scientific, political and public discussions about crime and punishment for a large part of the nineteenth century. Both in connection with a series of drafts for a new Penal Code and the bills about solitary confinement and the abolition of corporal and capital punishment all the arguments for and against both forms of confinement were brought to the fore emotionally in parliament again and again. The parliamentary discussions found their reflection in scientific journals and newspapers. They must have been much discussed in clubs and salons. The question forced people to imagine themselves in the position of prisoners and to reflect about causes of crime.

In view of the emancipatory process of prisoners it is important that this discussion meant that public interest for their situation grew significantly and knowledge about the inside workings of prisons increased. Where other emancipation movements actively must seek public attention, prisoners got it given to them through no fault of their own. During the nineteenth-century system struggle it even occurred on a large scale that their opinions about cellular versus communal confinement were sollicited, although it contributed to the final introduction of the cellular system. Using Foucault's frame of reference, this knowledge was primarily a new means of power in the hands of the punishers, but in the long run and retrospectively it points particularly to a certain levelling out of power. At the beginning of the century ministers and the king still could, without citing chapter and verse, issue decisions about the treatment of prisoners. Now decisions about changes in the penal system had to be justified with evidence of the salutary effect that they had upon prisoners. Politicians, journalists and members of the Society for the Moral Improvement of Prisoners wanted to know the details of recidivism, suicide and mental illness. To convince them the minister even needed the opinions of prisoners.

Around the turn of the century ex-prisoners offered their opinions *unsollicited*, for the first time. Socialists, who included leaders such as Ferdinand Domela Nieuwenhuis and Pieter Jelles Troelstra, expressed extremely sharp criticism of the agonizing solitude in cellular prisons. Thanks to this to some extent, just before the breaking out of the First

World War little cellular optimism remained among politicians and prison experts. Not only the socialists but also conscientious objectors contributed to the first careful breakthroughs of the cellular system after the First World War. The belief in the improving effect of cellular confinement had not yet completely disappeared but its supporters had to defend themselves much more avidly than in the nineteenth century against politicians, scholars, journalists, criminologists and prisoners who thought otherwise.

In 1929 a report of the answers more than a thousand prisoners had given to questions about the pros and cons of 'cell or community' unintentionally gave a detailed account of the lonely life in cellular penitentiaries and the social jungle in communal remand prisons. Not even twenty years later the Fick-committee for reform, partially based on pre-war literature about cellular punishment, would express its surprise about the 'terrifying lack of psychological knowledge' possessed by proponents of cellular confinement. Ex-prisoner members of the resistance mobilized public opinion with their actions for reform of the prison system. The cellular system was abolished in 1951. In a new Prison Act and a new Prison Ruling a system of mixed cellular and communal confinement was organized.

Once again it was the prisoners themselves who convinced a large public that the reforms had failed to address a great deal of prison suffering. The books of ex-prisoners caused only slight breezes compared with the storm caused by Rijksen's *Meningen van Gedetineerden* (Opinions of Prisoners) in 1959. Both the appearance of this book and the unusually incensed reactions in newspapers and magazines to its revealing content illustrate to what an extent prisoners had won in power.[79] Prisoner opinions were henceforth not only important outside the prison for the evaluation or preparation of new reforms, but also within the walls themselves. Physical violence and rough intimidation were seen as incompatible with the new aspiration of resocialization. Warders and governors came to be increasingly dependent on the cooperation of prisoners for the keeping of order and discipline. Within the prisons too a 'management by command' gave way slowly to a 'management by negotiation'. Participation committees and prisoners associations ensured that opinions of prisoners played an institutionalized role in decisions about their treatment. Outside the walls ex-prisoners organized themselves in unions, societies, action committees and pressure groups. In their own periodicals they were allowed to vent their uncensored critical opinions about the exercise of criminal justice. At present prisoners have almost unhindered access to the mass media.

These developments within the emancipation process of prisoners can only be understood when one realizes the increasing size of the problem experienced by their punishers in justifying the punishment and the suffering accompanying it. In a society where the sensitivity to physical and mental suffering of fellowmen had clearly increased, prisoners could draw more and more upon the sources of power which had been developed at the beginning of the nineteenth century.

Penological Disarmament: Growing Problems with the Legitimation of the Prison Sentence

Within a psycho-analytic historical perspective the present-day cynical-realistic attitude to resocializing effects of the prison sentence would certainly have to be linked to the *trauma* of the cellular failure. To have welcomed cellular confinement with such boundless optimism halfway through the past century as *the* means against crime was asking for a profound disappointment. Cellular dreamers unsuspectingly steered straight for this disappointment which began to manifest itself towards the end of the century. Then they continued to try to defend the core of the system, solitary confinement, by ascribing the failure to faulty execution like too little individual attention or insufficient education. Furthermore – and this argument was already used by the governor of the first cellular prison in Amsterdam – 'society' did not properly care for the prisoners after their release whereby the salutary effect of the punishment was lost.[80] This is one of the ways in which later failures of the prison sentence as pedagogical institute also repeatedly were reasoned away. Not the punishment itself but the execution thereof and the after-care were said to be faulty and open to improvement.[81]

The cellular deception was an important factor in undermining the legitimation of the prison sentence. It was precisely the passionate proponents of cellular confinement who argued that retribution, retaliation and deterrence were insufficient justification. The punishment had also to improve prisoners. When recidivism figures did not decrease and moral improvement was doubted on other grounds as well, they stood there, as it were, empty-handed. These were first filled a few times with new ideals and goals but these finally made the legitimation of the punishment only more problematic. Within the so-called New Direction in criminal justice *défense sociale* was made the central goal and legitimation of the punishment. By emphasizing protection of society the penal innovators completely relinquished retribution and retaliation. They leaned heavily on the criminal-anthropological opinions of the Italian positivists and the Frence environment theorists and rejected concepts like sin, guilt and responsibility. Criminals were determined by biological, psychological and social factors so that, ethically, nothing more could be held against them. Society had to be protected from them by removing them from it for a long period and subjecting them to drastic treatments. Now the legitimation of the punishment was based, at least in theory, completely on future effects. The treated would no longer want to and the long-sentenced no longer be able to repeat offences. In the interbellum period proponents of the 'educational view' too committed themselves to the expected improvement in behaviour as legitimation of the prison sentence. Because positive results again failed to appear or at least did not express themselves in falling figures for recidivism or crime, the legitimation problems increased again.

Even though the cellular trauma was mitigated by the new optimism surrounding education and treatment of criminals up until the Second World War, imposition of suffering other than the deprivation of freedom could hardly be defended any more. It was precisely this 'additional suffering' to which committed critics of the prison sentence, and among them several ex-prisoners, directed their protests in the interbellum period. They portrayed in emotional tones the psychic and physical misery in prisons which were still modelled on the cellular system. This resulted in nothing much more than marginal mitigations of punishment in the form of so-called 'deviations' but the groundwork for the post-war 'humanizing' of the prison sentence had been done. Emotionally and rationally the deprivation of freedom could only still be defended by assigning to the punishment a new goal within which a milder and less intimidating treatment was not only deemed desirable but also functional: the resocialization or rehabilitative ideal.

Very quickly much more came to be understood under the term resocialization than 'the preparation for the return of prisoners to life in society', as the new goal had been described in the Prison Act. In reports and memoranda resocialization also came to have the meaning of enlargement, or at least preservation of self-respect, self-reliance, a feeling of responsibility, one's own initiative and social skills. Degrading behaviour of warders and the use of physical force were increasingly difficult to rhyme with this. The liberalization of prison regimes in the 1960s and 1970s was carried out with a view to the 'resocialization task'. At the same time scientific research was showing that the resocializing treatment of prisoners certainly did not have positive effects on recidivism. Furthermore, quickly rising crime figures compelled one to a suitable humility with regard to the possibility of judicial crime prevention. To use psycho-analytic imagery once more, the trauma of the cellular failure was again felt in the collective emotional life of prison experts and politicians after it had been repressed for a time by the new resocialization ideal. This time there was no escape left. The hard reality had to be confronted: the prison sentence, no matter how it is executed, does not make better people of those sentenced. They also do not let themselves be deterred by it. The punishment actually hinders resocialization.

In policy memoranda the consequences were faced. Resocialization took the back seat to a much humbler goal: prevention of damage wrought by detention. Of course the definitive forfeit of the striving for improvement did lead to attempts to reinstitute deterrence, 'affirmation of moral standards',[82] or retribution as goals of punishment. Just as in the 1930s, a strong harshening of the penal climate in the 1980s and early 1990s did show how important a stress on special prevention was within this development. As soon as the goals of imprisonment are primarily located in the deterrence of the public in general (general prevention) the prisoners' position of power is weakened. Recent pleas for tightening up the prison sentence illustrate this.[83] Within such goals, however, the imposition of any suffering additional to the deprivation of freedom itself is more difficult than ever to justify; actually it is forbidden in the Bill for a new Prison Act of 1993. Research into the deterrent (general-preventive) effect on potential criminals indeed repeatedly shows that the nature and the length of punishment is only very relatively influencial. The same goes for the effect of affirmation of moral standards. It is apparently of prime importance that some sort of punishment or judicial reaction, no matter what sort, follows. To impose suffering from sentiments of retribution means numerous justification problems. Retribution is in the first place not a goal but a foundation of punishment. No future effect is desired from imposed suffering. A conscious and aimless hurting of people collides with historically developed sentiments and penal concepts. Retribution finds its justification in concepts such as sin, guilt and responsibility, but it is precisely these concepts which are difficult to reconcile with widespread insights into social causes of crime. In the final analysis, it will still be expected of retributive punishments that detention damage be limited as much as possible, if they are not to, in Minister Modderman's terms, be transformed from an 'ostensible evil' into an 'essential evil'.

To prisoners the thorough undermining of possible goals of punishment provided a source of power of great significance. Especially after the Second World War numerous mitigations of the regime were implemented because failure to do this could no longer be justified. Only in the 1960s and 1970s did prisoners actively push for such improvements. Their emancipation process also became an emancipation movement, but the fact that they were heard and were successful at that time was connected with the *penological disarmament* of their punishers. This disarmament formed a structural characteristic of a relatively autonomous development, which had already showed itself at the beginning of the previous century. This makes it look improbable that the tough 1980s and 1990s will really cause a lasting deterioration of the treatment of prisoners and their position of power.

Rights of Prisoners

Growing public interest was indispensable to the emancipation process of prisoners, but it also constituted an expression of that process. Thus prisoners did not only win in power as a consequence of problems of legitimation and the growing sensitivity to the suffering imposed on them but the problems and sensitivities were also caused by shifting balances of power. Together with these and other developments within the prison system, such as the socializing of the punishment and the increasing reliance on internal constraint and self-control, politicians, judges and prison personnel were forced to take the feelings and interests of prisoners more and more into account. An emancipation, meaning the granting of civil rights, equality before the law, increasing assertivity and freedom gained from an oppressive authority, existed in only an extremely limited way in the nineteenth century. Prisoners did not possess formal rights. Even if the punishment of being declared infamous was not formally imposed, prisoners found themselves *de facto* in a state of suspended animation as far as society went. In parliament prisoners with rights were seen as something preposterous. Prisoners were, first and foremost, people who had lost all their rights by committing a crime. At the time of deliberations about the draft for the Penal Code in 1881 there were even strenuous protests against the idea that the long-sentenced had the 'right' to reject favours and mitigations of punishment, such as conditional leave and communal confinement after five years in solitary. They could, at most, file a request.

At the beginning of the nineteenth century, prisoners were completely handed over to the power of a gaoler who hardly had to answer for his actions at all. Until into the twentieth century, prison governors too could do practically anything they pleased with prisoners, even though inspections and supervision of their work increased. Increasing assertivity was at the most expressed by the possibilities to complain about their treatment, first to philanthropic cell visitors and later to prison inspectors, but such complaints were quickly termed deviant behaviour and punished.

Still, their situation at about the turn of the century differed greatly from that at the end of the eighteenth century. They no longer lay suffering in cold, filthy and dilapidated rooms which no one took any notice of, but were busily visited and stared at in their cells within newly built prisons. On the other hand, they were confronted with new forms of severe suffering such as cell psychoses, nervous disorders and self-mutilation. With regard to their clothing, food, bedding, health care, order, discipline and management, governors had to conform to a Prison Act, a Prison Ruling and innumerable ministerial missives and circulars. The number of prisoners per 100,000 inhabitants decreased from 150 in the 1840s to approximately fifty-five in the first decade of the twentieth century.[84] The high death rates were significantly decreased. Halfway through the nineteenth century the mortality fluctuated between four and five per cent with peaks of ten up to thirty per cent in some prisons. In the twentieth century this figure came to lie further and further under one per cent and under the death rate for society as a whole.

While they did not have any formal rights, the moral pressure upon their punishers grew to take into account standards connected to the rights of *every* person, such as the right to fresh air, daylight, sufficient food and the permission to read a newspaper. Just before the First World War and in the inter-war period this pressure was made increasingly stronger by socialist and left-liberal politicians, journalists, lawyers, probation officers and scholars. Magistrates argued for the right of prisoners to lodge an appeal against certain decisions. For the first time psychiatrists demanded public attention for the right to sexual contact that was denied prisoners. They also pointed out the very adverse effects of forced celibacy. Until that moment the sexual problem had not been voiced or sexual profligacy had been causally linked with crime. Masturbating prisoners proved, as it were, that they had not been unjustly imprisoned.

Between the two world wars international interest in the treatment of prisoners also increased significantly, and this resulted in the formulation of minimum rules, accepted in 1934 by the League of Nations. In The Netherlands these minimum rules were quite quickly violated by people pushing for a substantial harshening of prison practice, following in the footsteps of the National Socialist revolution in Germany. These tough sounds were muted rather quickly, making way after the war for an unprecedented passion for reform among politicians and prison experts. Formal rights, however, were not yet granted to prisoners in the new Prison Act of 1951. Their opportunities for complaint were somewhat broadened and they could lodge an appeal against placement or transfer in the context of the regime-differentiation of the prison system. In 1955 an amended version of the minimum rules was accepted by the United Nations, strongly increasing their status. Later these rules were sharpened and expanded several times.

Towards the end of the 1960s pleas for strengthening of the legal position of prisoners were given support by what could be called a prisoner movement indeed. The Coornhert Liga and the Union of Lawbreakers (BWO), supported by active splinter groups in the country and committed individuals, increased the pressure to arrive at a better legal position for prisoners. A serious rebellion in the remand prison in Groningen in 1971, followed by actions and minor rebellions in other prisons and a second rebellion in Groningen (1974), placed the situation of prisoners in the center of political and public interest.

This turbulent and momentous period within the emancipation process of prisoners was followed by a fundamental improvement in their legal position, at least when seen from the point of view that they had been without rights for centuries. The improvements were not only expressed in the prisoners' right to complain but also in the amendments to the Prison Act and Prison Ruling which followed. Quite quickly extensions to furlough and visiting possibilities were instituted which, it is true, did not include any formal recognition of the right to sexual contacts but did imply a practical recognition. Applications for a temporary injunction by prisoners show how they are increasingly leaving behind the image of themselves as persons without rights. They can refer to national and international rules, laws and treaties. They are, moreover, supported by lawyers who have specialized in detention law, and institutions such as the National Ombudsman. Illustrative of their emancipation in the sense of rights and equality before the law is the fact that prisoners also were granted an active vote in 1986. In the bill for a new Prison Act in 1993 minimum rules have been formulated explicitly as prisoners' rights.

Prisoners' Emancipation in an International Perspective

The emancipation of prisoners is not a typically Dutch development, even though the Dutch prison system has several unique characteristics. Seen in the long run, the emancipation process of prisoners appears to be universal. The process is not developed to the same extent in every country but it does have the same characteristics everywhere: growing interest in prisoners and sensitivity to their suffering, increasing problems with the penological legitimation of this suffering and, connected to this, a continuing improvement in their legal position. The growing awareness that physical deprivation of freedom forms the core of imprisonment and that extra aggravations of punishment are unacceptable makes it increasingly difficult to justify lasting infringements of the civil rights of prisoners and to withhold from them detention rights. The increasing importance of prisoner movements in the whole Western world since the 1970s points to this. At a scientific level this movement was expressed in the critical work of Foucault, Christie, Cohen, Mathiesen, Rutherford, and, specially directed at women prisoners, Carlen and Dobash et al.[85] In countries such as England, Germany, France, Belgium, Scandinavia and the United States many groups threw themselves behind prisoners' rights.[86] There is an international movement which fights for the abolition or reduction of the prison sentence.[87] This extramural pressure for an improvement in their legal position was supported by actions and rebellions of the prisoners themselves intramurally in both the 1970s and 1980s.[88] Their protests had, for instance in England and Belgium, emancipatory consequences in the form of bettered treatment and legal position.[89]

Both the League of Nations and the International Penitentiary Congress in London (1925) attempted, before the Second World War, to arrive at minimum rules. In 1929, such rules were, indeed, published. In 1934 they were accepted by the General Assembly of the League of Nations. No coercive power was exercised upon governments of the member states through these rules, but they did offer prison reformers, critics and prisoners the possibility to compare existing practices with international standards. The minimum rules confirmed the increasing sensitivity for the suffering inflicted on prisoners. Practically at the same time it became clear from writings of ex-prisoners and from real riots that prisoners were aware that their chances to gain power were growing.[90] For example, the violent resistance of prisoners in Dartmoor, England in 1932 to the frequent use of punishment cells, the maltreatment and bad food was, admittedly, put down heavy-handedly but a research committee was appointed which declared a number of complaints well-founded and the large public learned of this through the media.[91]

General pressure for human rights and fundamental freedoms emanated from the European Treaty of 1950, better known as the *Treaty of Rome*. This treaty followed upon the *Universal Declaration of Human Rights* by the General Assembly of the United Nations in 1948. An international pressure, especially focussed upon the treatment of prisoners, emanated from the new minimum standards. At the request of the United Nations (UNO) the *Commission Internationale Pénale et Pénitentiaire* designed a new system of 'minimum standards for the treatment of prisoners' that was first accepted in 1955 by the UNO-congress 'on the Prevention of Crime and the Treatment of Offenders' in Geneva, and then by the *Economic and Social Council* followed by the *General Assembly*.[92] The new system primarily contained highlights and refinements of the minimum standards formulated in 1929. Thus corporal punishments and shutting up in a completely dark cell as punishment were totally rejected, while such punishments still had been deemed acceptable in 1929, albeit under strict conditions.

The new standards differed more fundamentally in their formulation of general principles. The rules of 1929 lacked such principles. At that time the goals of treatment were briefly described as getting used to order and work and moral improvement. Now it was stated that the punishing nature of a stay in prison consisted primarily of deprivation of freedom. The goal of detention was thought to lie in re-education and resocialization. The regime of the prison had to be directed to restricting any differences between life inside its walls and life in normal society 'to a minimum', wherever these differences could damage 'the personal awareness of responsibility' of the convicts or 'the respect for their human dignity'. In the 'treatment' of the convicts the stress was not to be laid upon their exclusion from society but upon the fact that they still were part and parcel of it. With regard to those sentenced, it was separately stated that the treatment was expected to increase their self-respect and their feeling of responsibility.[93]

Just as in 1929, no government was formally bound to these minimum standards but their acceptance by the United Nations did increase their status. In 1973 the minimum standards gained in consequence through their acceptance (in a lightly amended and adjusted form) by the committee of ministers of the Council of Europe. As a guiding principle, rules were added about inspection of prisons and independent checks on the enforcement of the legal prescriptions. Article 58 stated that the deprivation of freedom as such constitutes the punishment and that the way in which prisoners are treated may not have the character of punishment. The governments of the member states were urged strongly to let themselves be led by the rules in their law-making and policies. The committee moreover exerted pressure to report to the Secretary-General once in five years which activities had been undertaken based on these minimum standards.[94] Dutch proposals to set up an independent inspection office and to make the minimum rules known to the prisoners were, however, rejected.[95]

In 1987, the Ministers' Committee of the European Council again accepted an amended version of the *European Prison Rules*. The *first* ('the Rule of first priority and principle') of the six guiding principles, which, according to the compilers, reflected 'the fundamental philosophy on which our prison systems are based' now said that deprivation of freedom had to take place under physical and mental conditions which ensured 'respect for human dignity'.[96] Following internationally acceptable standards prisoners now had to be treated in the first place in a dignified way. In 1988 the United Nations accepted the 'Body of Principles' for the protection of all persons under any form of detention or imprisonment. In 1987 the Council of Europe accepted the *European Convention for the prevention of torture and inhuman or degrading treatment or punishment*, very actively supported by a committee of the same name.[97]

Just as had happened during the Dutch prisoners' emancipation process, international writers, poets and journalists played an important role. Heine, Dickens, Victor Hugo, Dostoevsky, Chekhov and Oscar Wilde put prison suffering that others did not know or could not feel into words. More recently Breyten Breytenbach, Arthur Koestler, Václav Havel, Jean Genet and Nawal El Saadwi have fulfilled a similar role. Journalistic reports about prison misery in the former Soviet Union, China, South America and other countries, no matter how minimal, had and still have emancipatory effect. Ex-political prisoners have a large influence worldwide, as in The Netherlands. Again and again they appear to be better than ordinary prisoners at bringing to the attention of the large public their suffering and their criticism of prison systems. And, again and again, their indictments and protests have a radiating effect upon the treatment of ordinary prisoners. Especially the reports of Amnesty International about prison situations in numerous other countries arrest the attention for prison suffering and force, sometimes more and sometimes less successfully, the possessors of power to take measures under the pressure of world opinion. In Czechoslovakia, Poland and South Africa ex-political prisoners (Havel, Walesa, Mandela) recently became president of their country. One of the first things they ordered was to release a lot of prisoners.

The changing treatment of prisoners can, thus, also be analyzed and characterized as an emancipation process on a world scale. The question now is whether Dutch prisoners are in a better situation than their foreign fellow-prisoners? Have Dutch prisons indeed become 'little paradises' compared with their foreign counterparts?[98] Prisoners themselves are rather clear about this. 'It's not just bull shitting for Holland. The prisons there are really better stay in there for two days or so and you'll see,' was what the English criminologist David Downes was told by a countryman detained in The Netherlands. Others expressed themselves in similar ways.[99] Ex-convict, Peter de K., remarked after a stay of years in Belgian prisons that the Dutch prison, compared with that in Belgium, is 'a five-star hotel'.[100] A Dutch prison pastor visited numerous foreign prisons in the last decade. 'In foreign prisons you are a nobody', was his general opinion. Both the electronically over-regulated prisons of Scandinavia and the non-regulated social jungles of southern European countries cannot, in his opinion, be compared to the relatively good Dutch prisons. Prisoners live in more isolation, there is less checking up from outside, they have fewer rights and there is more violence.[101]

Literature, too, shows that conditions in Spanish, Italian, French, British, Belgian, Scottish and American prisons are poorer in many areas than the Dutch.[102] The confinement of more than one person to a single cell is more the rule than the exception in those countries. Prisoners generally have less contacts with the outside world, less detention modalities (open, half-open, day detention) and less chances to influence their own treatment. Usually they also are given longer sentences for equally serious crimes. Based on most indicators (not only the imprisonment rate) The Netherlands appears to be less punitive than other European countries.[103] In 1992 a delegation of the European Committee for the Prevention of Torture and Inhuman or Degrading Treatment or Punishment (CPT) visited The Netherlands. In general the delegation concluded that the conditions in prisons were 'satisfactory and on occasion were of a very his standard'.[104]

Why is the situation of Dutch prisoners better than that of prisoners in other Western countries? Stated differently: why is their emancipation process further advanced? Without detailed, comparative analyses one can, of course, only speak in very general and speculative terms. The old tradition in The Netherlands of relatively strong social contact among political, penal and scientific circles is an important factor. Many judges, public prosecutors, criminologists, prison experts, professors of criminal law, members of parliament and ministers who contributed partially unintentionally and partially intentionally to the emancipation process of prisoners in the course of the last two centuries were not only each other's contemporaries but they knew each other as well. They belonged to the same social circles, were members of the same committees and visited the same conferences and meetings. This most likely has led to a deeper and faster permeation of knowledge and insight about crime and punishment than in other countries. Added to this is the smaller gap between the classes. There is no real Dutch aristocracy. The division between middle and upper classes seems less sharp than in France and England, for example. The feeling of being mutually interdependent could be more intense in a strongly democratic society like that in The Netherlands and, connected to this, the ability to identify with people of other classes. The influence exerted by educated people in lower social positions on decisions about methods of dealing with problems of crime was and is relatively large. Compartmentalized Dutch society (Catholics, Calvinists, socialists) created, furthermore, a system of political decision-making which leans heavily upon conciliation and compromise. Law-and-order sentiments were smothered in The Netherlands by the necessity of making political compromises. In this context it is important to mention that the influence exerted by laymen and feelings of common people within the Dutch execution of criminal justice is extremely small. In contrast to Belgium, England and France, for instance, there is no jury system and public prosecutors have a relatively large discretionary jurisdiction.[105]

These characteristics taken together make it understandable why the practice of criminal law lay much closer to the decision-makers and why extreme opinions gained and still gain little ground. It is probably so that the *process of penological disarmament* as I have called the undermining of justifications for punishment is, for some of these reasons, further advanced in The Netherlands. One must also remember that The Netherlands has had a critical, independent and influential press for a very long time. It was precisely this press which played an important role in the breaking open of the prison system and criticism of prisoner treatment. That this press was able to radiate a less punitive attitude than in other countries is probably due to the relatively limited scale of crime and, particularly, serious violent crime in The Netherlands. Until far into the 1970s The Netherlands had the lowest figures for crime in the western world, though comparisons can only be made with great difficulty. Political terrorism and violence hardly form a part of Dutch history. Even at present fewer people per 100,000 inhabitants in The Netherlands lose their lives because of crime than in practically every other western country.[106]

Finally, the influence of religious conviction on decision-making in criminal law is very important. That began with the rather late separation between church and state in The Netherlands. But, even when this separation had been formally carried out, Dutch politicians, criminal law experts and even the journalists remained deeply religious until far into the twentieth century. Religious beliefs, far more than political conviction, served as the foundation for the formation of political parties. The adoption of a humanitarian attitude to sinners and underdogs was an important element of that religious, primarily Calvinist conviction. Neither the rise of the cellular system nor the relatively large sympathy for the needs of prisoners is understandable without this strong religious consciousness. The fact that a hard judicial wind has picked up in The Netherlands too in the 1980s could easily have a lot to do with both the secularization and the 'depillarization' of Dutch society. Tough common sense has won out over neighbourly love.

With this speculative analysis I have tried to make it to some extent understandable why the emancipation process of prisoners in The Netherlands has progressed further than in other western countries. It is not my intention to provide more than an impetus to a more inclusive interpretation. From possible explanations it is obvious that there is a very different and far more complicated relationship between crime and punishment than many people think. In spite of its relatively mild punishment system, The Netherlands has never had larger problems with crime than other western countries. On the other hand, the harsh punishment system of the United States has gone hand in hand for a very long time with huge crime problems. Developments in crime patterns and penal reactions are evidently more or less autonomous processes. They influence each other much less directly than is often assumed and they are both connected to broad, societal long-term developments. That is, no matter how imprecise, an important criminological insight that should admonish tough judicial policymakers to be humble and reserved.

For the time being, it seems that in The Netherlands and in other western countries belief in a harsh, judicial tackling of crime problems is, however, actually on the rise.[107] The unique Dutch prison system, that for years has been an example to foreign reformers, is being threatened by both national and foreign forces. The humane principle of one prisoner per cell is continuously attacked by politicians, journalistic opinion-makers and police spokesmen. They also repeatedly push for severe preventive measures against escape and tightening up the prison sentence. Added to this, the European unification process leads to constant pressure to adjust the Dutch penal system to European standards.[108] Perhaps this book will contribute to the realization that The Netherlands has much to lose and very little to gain should this happen.

NOTES

1. Robert Musil, pt. II, 1988, p. 700.
2. Cf. Ignatieff, 1978, pp. 104–8.
3. See Ignatieff, 1978, pp. 15–43; Bender, 1987, particularly chs 1 and 2, pp. 11–61; O'Brien, 1982.
4. See Ignatief, 1978, pp. 3–14, for a description of the strict cellular regime in Pentonville with its cellular hoods, cellular chapels and cellular airings.
5. In The Netherlands, the first cellular prison was put into use in 1850 in Amsterdam. In France existing prisons were partly rebuilt at first. The main cellular prison was built in Paris (Mazas) during the 1840s. See Wright, 1983, pp. 48–81, 100. The first German penitentiaries (Prussia and Baden) were built in Bruchsal (1848) and Moabit in Berlin (1849). The construction of the Berlin prison was ordered by the Prussian King Friedrich Wilhelm IV after he visited the Pentonville prison in London. The first cellular prison in Bruchsal was especially recommended by the well-known prison experts Julius and Wichern. See Krebs, 1978, pp. 64, 490–1. In Belgium the first cellular prison was built in Tongeren (1844). Prison-inspector E. Ducpétiaux particularly recommended the new form of imprisonment. See Dupont-Bouchat, 1988, pp. 13–16.
6. Cf. Ignatieff, 1978, pp. 9–11, 199–200; Rusche and Kirchheimer, 1968, pp. 36–7; O'Brien, 1982, pp. 23–4, 27–8; Wright, 1983, pp. 100, 105–6;
7. Spierenburg, 1984.
8. Weisser (1982, p. 155) also points at the attempts to differentiate between the honest poor and the lower-class criminals. Later on a differentiation was stressed between docile and socialist working men.
9. Foucault, 1979, pp. 276–9, quotation on p. 278.
10. This criticism of Foucault is also stressed by Garland, 1990, pp. 160, 165.
11. Jim Sharpe, 1990, also repeatedly criticizes the 'transition from barbarism' model which is so dominant in a lot of historical studies of penal developments.
12. Dutch examples of both perspectives are dominant in the work of Hallema, 1958; Petersen, 1978; and Bianchi, 1980.
13. For a similar, though less detailed, analysis, see Weisser, 1982, pp. 127–71.
14. See Ignatieff, 1978, p. 177.
15. Melossi and Pavarini, 1981, p. 95. They adopt the word 'invention' in the title of the second part of their book, 'The Penitentiary Invention'. In his 'radical view' of the rise of penitentiaries Andrew Scull (1977, pp. 25–6) also points at the connection with the

growing capitalist market system: the new penal institution produced the discipline and order which the factory-like way of production needed.

16. Idem, p. 188.
17. Idem, pp. 191–6.
18. This way of thinking in terms of strategies and tactics is also dominant in Garland, 1987.
19. For a similar criticism of Foucault's use of the term 'power', see Garland, 1990, pp. 168–75.
20. An overall picture of structural functionalism (grounded in Talcott Parsons and Robert Merton) is given by Johnson, 1968.
21. This is very dominant in a study by Robert Ros (1986) of the Dutch Society for the Moral Improvement of Prisoners.
22. Foucault, 1976, pp. 44–5. The tension in Foucault's analysis between blind forces and well planned actions of the bourgeoisie is also stressed by de Wit in his criticism of *Discipline and Punish* (Wit, 1981, p. 331).
23. Cf. Elias, 1978 (1970).
24. That penal institutions and crime-control policies have their own internal dynamics is stressed and analyzed in detail by David Garland, 1987. See also Young, 1983 and Garland, 1990, pp. 126–30.
25. Cf. Downes, 1988, and my criticism of his study (Franke, 1990).
26. Rothman, 1971, p. xix.
27. Ignatieff, 1978, p. 210.
28. Foucault, 1979, pts 1 and 2.
29. The first part of his book (pp. 17–180) deals with the emergence of the penal prison in the period 1780–1815.
30. O'Brien, 1982, pp. 300–2. A more general and detailed analysis of punishment as 'an active generator of cultural relations and sensibilities' has been presented by David Garland in his magnificent *Punishment and Modern Society*, 1990, ch. 11, pp. 249–76.
31. Cf. Franke, 1981, pp. 44–6.
32. In a critical reflection on the main studies of penal developments, including his own study, Ignatieff points at similar shortcomings (1983, pp. 77, 32). A clarifying analysis of the different historical explanations of penal changes (especially the failure of prison reforms) is presented by Cohen (1985, ch. 1), although he also seems to be attracted by the idea of abrupt changes or transformations.
33. See Faber, 1989.
34. Cf. de Wit, 1981, p. 318; Petit, 1990, pp. 72, 545.
35. Garland, 1987. In his most recent study Garland shows himself to be aware of this and other criticisms of Foucault. See Garland, 1990, ch. 7, esp. p. 158.
36. Cf. Elias, 1978, 1982 (1939).
37. Spierenburg, 1984; Franke, 1985. The importance of Elias' work for the historical study of punishment is quite elaborately stressed by Garland, 1990, ch. 10, pp. 213–47.
38. Sharpe, 1990, pp. 129–30.
39. Kruithof, 1980; De Regt, 1984.
40. By stressing *rationality* in their plea for alternatives for incarceration, Morris and Tonry (1993) illustrate this.

41. Garland, 1987; 1990, pp. 267–71; Vries, 1986.
42. Incorporated in Leonard de Vries (ed.), *Imaginaire reizen* (Imaginary travels). Houten: Agatahon, 1988.
43. Bender, 1987, esp. ch.2, pp. 43–63 and 218 (quotation).
44. Bender, 1987, p. 222.
45. Garland, 1990, p. 269.
46. Wright, 1983; Ignatieff, 1978; Garland, 1987; Weisser, 1982; Rothman, 1971.
47. Wright, 1983, pp. 48–9; Petit, 1990, pp. 219–60.
48. O'Brien, 1982, pp. 25–8.
49. Cf. Ignatieff, 1978, p. 4. According to Rusche and Kirchheimer (1968, pp. 128–9), the American preference for the Auburn system has to be explained by the scarcity of labour. In sharp contrast to the European situation with its surplus of labour, in the United States solitary confinement was seen as an unacceptable waste of manpower.
50. Pompe, 1930, p. 31.
51. Spierenburg, 1987, pp. 448, 455.
52. Apart from this, one can seriously doubt whether one can put the emergence of workhouses in seventeenth-century Holland on the same level as the rise of the penitentiaries in nineteenth-century America. I think, in this case, Spierenburg's model of explanation shares too many characteristics with models used in the natural sciences.
53. See Weber, 1984 (1920), pp. 115–65.
54. Vegter, 1989, pp. 11–72.
55. This intimidating effect of the cellular system is also stressed by Weisser, 1982, pp. 168–9.
56. Rusche and Kirchheimer, 1968, pp. 132–7.
57. Rusche and Kirchheimer, 1968, p. 137.
58. Garland, 1987, pp. 40–5, 50–1.
59. Wright, 1983, pp. 4–5, 61, 77.
60. Bender, 1987.
61. To this phrase attributed to Friedrich Schiller, Max Weber gave a comprehensive religious-sociological meaning: 'Der Ablehnung der sakramentalen Magie als Heilsweg (to give up sacramental magic as a road to salvation). Weber, 1984 (1920), p. 123, n. 20.
62. Franke, 1985.
63. Cf. Pratt (1992, pp. 99–104), who argues (wrongly, I think) that not only the punishment of criminals but prisons too were removed from public view.
64. Bender, 1987, p. 220.
65. Spierenburg makes this sort of interpretation, 1984.
66. Cf. Garland, 1990, ch. 10.
67. In France as well penitentiary reforms were instituted shortly after revolutions and wars. After the Second World War, French experts and politicians were overwhelmed by a similar spirit of reform to that in The Netherlands, but resistance to this was stronger and came earlier to the fore than in The Netherlands. Cf. Wright, 1983, pp. 190–8.
68. Cf. Bemmelen, 1954, pp. 35–8, 48.

69. Cf. Bender, 1987; Davis, 1990.
70. Cohen, 1985.
71. Groeneweg and Hallema, 1976; Fijnaut, 1979; see also Hoogenboom and Morre, 1988.
72. Attempts to supervise young law-breakers and teach them better behaviour outside the judicial machinery.
73. Cf. Cohen, 1985, p. 146; Fox, 1987; Schalken, 1989.
74. Cf. Ruller, 1989.
75. Cf. Goudsblom (1977, p. 127), who defines sociology as the studying of the ways 'in which people cope with the problems of social interdependence'. Much of what I have described in this book bears out the fruitfulness of this definition. See also Franke, 1990.
76. Suringar, 1828, p. iv; *Het Bajesboek*, 1st edn, 1982, p. 6, 2nd edn, 1988, p. 4.
77. See Suringar, 1828, pp. 189–94.
78. Modderman, 1864, pp. 4–5, 27.
79. Cf. Downes, 1988, pp. 95–6.
80. See Faber, 1989, p. 81.
81. Cf. Cohen, 1985, pp. 14–18.
82. See Knigge, 1988.
83. Cf. Burt, 1993.
84. Data about the average daily population are taken from prison statistics. Differing from Ruller, 1981, appendix I–A, I have worked out the detention figure per 100,000 inhabitants of all ages.
85. See Foucault, 1979; Cohen, 1972, 1985; Christie, 1981, 1993; Mathiesen, 1974, 1990; Rutherford, 1986; Carlen, 1983; Dobash *et al.*, 1986.
86. Cf. Rudovsky, 1973; Jacobs, 1980; Zyl Smit and Dünkel, 1991.
87. Cf. Bianchi and Van Swaaningen, 1986.
88. Cf. Fitzgerald, 1977; Mary, 1988; Scraton et al., 1991.
89. After the riot in Strangeways in Manchester, the *Woolf Report* appeared in which various proposals were made to improve the legal position of prisoners. Cf. Vagg, 1991, pp. 163–4; Smaers, 1994.
90. Cf. Neale, 1991.
91. Fitzgerald, 1977, pp. 121–9. See also Priestley, 1989, pp. 104–13.
92. Cf. Kenneth Neale, 'The European Prison Rules', in *Prison Information Bulletin* (Council of Europe), June 1987, no. 9, pp. 4–6.
93. 'Ontwerp Minimum-Normen voor behandeling van gedetineerden' (Bill Minimum Standards for the treatment of prisoners). Included in *MvhG* as an appendix, November 1951, pp. 6–7.
94. Resolution (73) 5, *Standard minimum rules for the treatment of prisoners*, adopted by the Committee of Ministers on January 19, 1973 at the 217th meeting of the Ministers' Deputies.
95. *Balans*, 1974, no. 6/7, p. 10.
96. *Prison Information Bulletin*, Council of Europe, 1987, no. 9; see the translation of this in *Bajesboek*, 1988, pp. 207–30; J. P. Balkema wrote an editorial comment on the European Prison Rules in *Penitentaire Informatie*, 1988, no. 3, pp. 81–2.
97. Cf. Parmentier, 1992.
98. Griever, 1979, p. 22.
99. Downes, 1988, pp. 163–88, quotation on p. 180.

100. Chorus and Van der Velden, 1989, pp. 145–8.
101. *VK*, 11 January 1992. In December 1992 I also had several talks with the prison pastors, J. Spoor and M. G. Boeschoten, who keep in touch with the more than 800 Dutch prisoners in foreign countries (of whom almost 700 in European countries).
102. Cf. Zyl Smit and Dünkel, 1991; Berghuis and Franke, 1992; Muncie and Sparks, 1991. To what an extent the situation in American prisons is worse is apparent from the gripping descriptions of Rideau and Wikberg, 1992.
103. Cf. Kommer, 1994.
104. *Report to the Dutch government* (...), 1993, p. 53. For a critical review of this report, Fiselier, 1993.
105. Downes points out some of these points as well, 1988, pp. 74–7.
106. Cf. Franke, 1994.
107. Cf. Rothman, 1994.
108. Cf. Berghuis and Franke, 1992.

Bibliography

JOURNALS

I consulted systematically (index, table of contents) all volumes of the following journals; other journals were only consulted partly or for specific articles.

Balans (a prison journal).
Delikt & Delinkwent (Delinquency and Offender).
Liefde en Hoop, tijdschrift voor gevangenen en gevangenissen (Charity and Hope, a journal for prisoners and prisons).
Maandblad voor Berechting en Reclassering (Monthly for Adjudication (Trial) and Rehabilation (After-care and probation).
Maandblad voor het Gevangeniswezen (Monthly about Imprisonment).
Proces (a criminological journal).
Rechtsgeleerd Magazijn Themis (Themis, a legal journal).
Tijdschrift voor Criminologie (Journal of Criminology).
Tijdschrift voor Strafrecht (Journal of Penal Law).
Weekblad van het Regt (Recht) (Weekly of the Law).

STATISTICS, ANNUAL REPORTS, LAWS ETC.

Gevangenisstatistieken (Prison statistics), from 1837.
Handelingen der Nederlands(ch)e Juristen Vere(e)niging (Proceedings of the Dutch Society of Lawyers).
Handelingen der Staten-Generaal (Official Parliamentary Reports).
Jaarverslagen van de geneeskundige inspectie bij het Ministerie van Justitie (Annual reports of the health authorities at the Ministry of Justice).
Jaarverslagen van het gevangeniswezen (Annual reports of the prison department of the Ministry of Justice).
Jaarverslagen van het staatstoezicht op krankzinnigen en krankzinnigengestichten (Annual reports of the Government Inspectorate on the Insane and Insane Asylums), period 1885–1936.

Verzameling van wetten, besluiten en voorschriften betreffende het gevangenis-
wezen. Verzameling van J. J. de Jongh, period 1791–1959 (Collection of
laws, decrees, instruction, official letters concerning prisons and imprisonment. Collection of J. J. de Jongh, period 1791–1859): series
1960–1905, 1905–1939, de zogenaamde 'Blauwe Boekjes' (the so-
called 'Blue Books').

ARCHIVES AND LIBRARIES

The municipal and provincial archives in Groningen, Alkmaar, Arnhem,
Den Bosch, Amsterdam and Haarlem.
Amsterdamse Universiteitsbibliotheek (Amsterdam University Library).
Koninklijke Bibliotheek in Den Haag (the Royal Library at The Hague:
catalogues, newspaper archives.
I also visited other archives and libraries for specific ends.

WORKS CONSULTED

Most newspaper articles and short articles in periodicals like *WvhR*, *MVBR*,
MVhG, *Proces* and *Balans* are not entered in this bibliography. Complete
references of them can be found in the relevant notes.

Abbott, Jack Henry, *In the Belly of the Beast: Letters from Prison*, New York,
1982.
Abspoel, J. J., *Tralies zijn geen medicijn, bespiegelingen van een strafrechter*,
Utrecht/Antwerpen, 1985.
Alem, V. C. M., and L. H. Erkelens et al., 'Verslavingsproblematiek in de
penitentiaire inrichtingen', in *Justitiële Verkenningen*, vol. 15, no. 2,
1989: 39–61.
Aletrino, A., *Twee opstellen over crimineele anthropologie*, Amsterdam, 1898.
—, 'Over de Elmira Reformatory', in *Psychiatrische en Neurologische*
Bladen, vol. 2, 1898: 488–513; vol. 3, 1899: 75–104.
—, *Handleiding bij de studie der crimineele anthropologie*, Amsterdam, 1902.
—, *Is celstraf nog langer geoorloofd en gewenscht?*, Amsterdam, 1906.
Alstorphius Grevelink, P. W., *Rapport van de Inspecteur der Gevangenissen,*
betreffende zijne inspectiereis gedaan in 1857 uit het oogpunt van cellulaire
opsluiting, The Hague, 1857.
—, *Ons cellulair stelsel. Een woord tot mr. M. H. Godefroi naar aanleiding*
zijner rede in de Tweede Kamer der Staten-Generaal van den 11 Junij 1868,
The Hague, 1868.
—, *Bijdrage tot de kennis van het Iersch gevangenisstelsel, in verband met het*
beheer onzer gevangenissen en bedelaarsgestichten, The Hague, 1870.
Alstorphius Grevelink, P. W. et al., *Rapport aan zijne Excellentie den*
Minister van Justitie van Mr. P. W. Alstorphius Grevelink, J. A. H.
Netscher en A. C. Pierson der door hen gedane opneming van eenige

buitenlandsche gevangenissen, met daaruit voortvloeiende beschouwingen en voorstellen nopens het gevangeniswezen in Nederland, The Hague, 1858.

Alternatieven voor de vrijheidsstraf, special issue of *Justitiële Verkenningen*, vol. 14, no. 3, 1988.

Amir, M., 'Over gevangenispsychosen', in *Geneeskundig Tijdschrift voor Nederlandsch Indië*, vol. 72, no. 14, 1932: 926–32.

Anjewierden, O., A. M. van Kalmthout and J. Simmelink, 'Ontwikkelingen in het Nederlandse strafrecht in de afgelopen decennia' (part I), in *Panopticon*, 1986: 420–53.

Anjou, L. J. M. d', G. de Jonge and J. J. van der Kaaden, *Effektiviteit van sancties, een overzicht van het onderzoek naar generale en speciale preventie*, WODC-report, The Hague, 1975.

Appert, B., *Bagnes, Prisons et Criminels*, vol. 2, Paris, 1836.

Arnoldus, Chr. A, 'Tucht en straffen in de gevangenissen', in *Tijdschrift voor Strafrecht*, vol. 31, 1921: 267–86.

Asser, C., *Vlugtige beschouwing van eenige voorname beginselen des Strafregts in verband met het ontwerp des lijfstraffelijken wetboeks*, The Hague/ Amsterdam, 1827.

Het Bajesboek (...), Handboek voor gedetineerden en ter beschikking gestelden, Breda, 1982 (1st edn), 1985 (2nd edn), 1988 (3rd edn), 1992 (4th edn).

Balkema, J. P., *Klachtrecht voor gevangenen*, Alphen aan den Rijn, 1979.

—, et al. (eds), *Gedenkboek. Honderd jaar Wetboek van Strafrecht*, Arnhem, 1986.

Balkema, J. P. and G. J. M. Corstens, 'Het straffenarsenaal', in Balkema et al. (eds), Arnhem, 1986: 303–32.

Beaumont, Gustave de, and Alexis de Tocqueville, *Du système pénitentiaire aux Etats-Unis et de son application en France*, Paris, 1833.

Beccaria, Cesare, *Over misdaden en straffen* (Dutch translation by J. M. Michiels of *Dei delitti e delle pene*, 1764), Antwerpen/Zwolle, 1971.

Beknopt overzigt van het gevangenisstelsel in Nederland, in verband met dat van afzonderlijke opsluiting; door Een Gerehabiliteerd Gevangene, Amsterdam, 1843.

Bemmelen, J. M. van, *Van Zedelijke Verbetering tot Reclassering, geschiedenis van het Nederlandsch Genootschap tot Zedelijke Verbetering der Gevangenen, 1823–1923*, The Hague, 1923.

—, 'Voor- en nadeelen van een wettelijke regeling der sterilisatie en castratie', in *Verslag van de bijeenkomst van het Psychiatrisch-Juridisch Gezelschap*, 25 maart 1933, Rotterdam, no. 7: 33–52.

—, *Criminologie, leerboek der misdaadkunde*, Zwolle, 1948 (2nd edn).

—, *Gedenkt den Gevangenen, opstellen over hervorming van het strafrecht en gevangeniswezen*, The Hague, 1954.

Bender, John, *Imagining the Penitentiary. Fiction and the Architecture of Mind in Eighteenth-Century England*, Chicago/London, 1987.

Bentham, Jeremy, *Panopticon, or The Inspection House*, London, 1791.

Berg, J. H., van den, *Metabletica of leer der veranderingen*, Nijkerk, 1968 (1956).

Berghuis, B. and H. Franke (eds), 'Foreign views on Dutch penal policy', special issue of *Tijdschrift voor Criminologie*, vol. 34, no. 3, 1992.

—, 'Dutch tolerance under pressure?', in *Tijdschrift voor Criminologie*, vol. 34, no. 3, 1992: 189–97.

Bernasco, Wim, *Zelfdestructief gedrag van gedetineerden*, Publication Vakgroep Klinische Psychologie Rijksuniversiteit Leiden, Leiden, 1986.

—, et al., 'Suicidaal gedrag van gedetineerden in Nederland', in *Tijdschrift voor Criminologie*, vol. 30, no. 1, 1988: 61–76.

Bertillonage, handleiding voor den Beambte belast met de toepassing der lichaamsmeting enz. volgens het stelsel van Alphonse Bertillon, about 1895.

Bianchi, Herman, *Ethiek van het straffen*, Nijkerk, 1964.

—, *Basismodellen in de Kriminologie*, Deventer, 1980.

Bianchi, Herman and René van Swaaningen (eds), *Abolitionism. Towards a non-repressive approach to crime*, Amsterdam, 1986.

Bije, P. J. de, 'Kort overzigt van den tegenwoordigen toestand der Gevangenissen in het koningrijk der Nederlanden, volgens het nieuwe stelsel ingericht', in *Annual Report 1826* of the *Nederlandsch Genootschap tot Zedelijke Verbetering der Gevangenen*, appendix: 61–80.

Binsbergen, W. C. van, *Algemeen Karakter van het Crimineel Wetboek van het Koningrijk Holland*, Utrecht, 1949.

—, *Poenaal Panorama*, Zwolle, 1986.

Blok, A. J., *De ontwikkeling van het strafstelsel in Nederland*, Leiden, 1925.

Blok, Anton, *Wittgenstein en Elias*, Amsterdam, 1976.

Blok, P. R., 'De celstraf', in *Nederlandsch Juristenblad*, 1927: 210–13.

Bloom, F. E., et al., *Brain, Mind, and Behavior*, New York, 1986.

Boeke, C. and L. van Mierop, *De Vergetenen*, Blaricum, 1920.

Boeke, I. H.: see Holmes and Boeke.

Boer, Marieke de, *De gedetineerdenvereniging in het Huis van Bewaring*, Publication Wetenschapswinkel Utrecht, Utrecht, 1988.

Bol, M. W. and J. J. Overwater, *Dienstverlening. Eindrapport van het onderzoek naar de vervanging van de vrijheidsstraf in het strafrecht voor volwassenen*, WODC report, no. 47, The Hague, 1984.

Bonger, W. A., *Criminality and Economic Conditions* (translation of *Criminalité et conditions économiques*), Boston, 1916 (1905).

—, *Over de evolutie der moraliteit*, Amsterdam, 1922.

—, *Inleiding tot de criminologie*, Zwolle, 1932.

—, *Het 'nieuwe' strafrecht*, Amsterdam, 1978 (1935).

Borst, E. J. de, *Vrouwen in detentie. Een inventarisatie van grondkenmerken*, Afdeling beleidsinformatie D & J, Ministerie van Justitie, The Hague, 1991.

Bouricius, L. G., *Over de gevangenissen in Nederland*, Leeuwarden, 1838/ 1840.

Brand van Langerack en Cabauw, J., *Iets over de gevangenissen in het Koningrijk der Nederlanden*, Amsterdam, 1819/1841.

Brand-Koolen, M. J. M. (ed.), *Studies on the Dutch Prison System*, Berkeley/Amsterdam, 1987.

Brand-Koolen, M. J. M. and Jan Overwater, 'Gedetineerden, wat vinden zij ervan?', in *Symposium, 100 jaar vrijheidsstraf*, 1987: 110–35.

Brand-Koolen, M. J. M., et al., *Strafrecht en Rechtshandhaving*, publication 67 of the B. M. Telderstichting, The Hague, 1988.

Brauw, J. de, 'Vervolg der beschouwingen omtrent de groote strafgevangenis te Woerden gevestigd, met opzigt tot de hygiëne in dat gesticht', in *Nederlandsch Tijdschrift voor Geneeskunde*, 1860: 561–69.

Breuer, J. H., *Mensch en Misdadiger*, Heerlen, 1943.

Brouwers, M. and M. Sampiemon, *Vrouwen in detentie*, WODC report, no. 83, The Hague, 1988.

Brucken Fock, E. P. and A. Heijder, *De rechtspositie van de gedetineerde in Nederland en België*, preadviezen voor de Vereniging voor de vergelijkende studie van het recht van België en Nederland, Zwolle, 1975.

Brueys, J. R. de, 'Iets over de beginselen, waarop het Strafwetboek in het jaar 1827 aan de tweede kamer der Staten-Generaal van het Koningrijk der Nederlanden overgegeven, rust', in *Bijdragen tot Regtsgeleerdheid en Wetgeving*, vol. 4, 1829: 385–409.

Brugghen, J. J. L. van der, *Mededeelingen en gedachten over het Iersche Gevangenisstelsel*, Nijmegen, 1863.

Brûle, Ineke van den, 'Sterfgevallen in handen van justitie en politie', in *Crimineel Jaarboek '87–'88*, publication Coornhert Liga, Breda, 1989: 79–103.

Buitelaar, Wout and Rypke Sierksma, *Gevangen in de gevangenis, beschouwingen over gevangenis, misdaad en maatschappij*, Meppel, 1972.

Burt, Robert A., 'Cruelty, hypocrisy, and the rehabilitative ideal in corrections', in *International Journal of Law and Psychiatry*, vol. 16, 1993: 359–70.

Calkoen, Henricus, *Verhandeling over het voorkomen en straffen der misdaaden*, Amsterdam, 1780.

Caminada, H. P. G. M., 'Het PTK-evaluatieproject, tweede fase van de wetenschappelijke begeleiding', in *Tijdschrift voor Criminologie*, vol. 15, December 1973: 270–9, 280–6.

—, *Het P.T.K.-evaluatieonderzoek; een vergelijkend onderzoek naar het directe effect van twee kortdurende vrijheidsstraffen*, Nijmegen, 1973.

Carlen, Pat, *Women's Imprisonment: A Study in Social Control*, London, 1986.

Casparie, J., 'Ervaringen uit de Bijzondere Strafgevangenis te 's-Hertogenbosch', in *Uit Zenuw- en Zieleleven, uitkomsten van psychologisch onderzoek*, vol. 1, 1912: 191–233.

Celstraf, *De toepassing der (...) en hare werking. Verslag van de door het Nederlandsch Genootschap tot Zedelijke Verbetering der Gevangenen op donderdag 16 mei 1907 in 'American Hôtel' te Amsterdam gehouden vergadering*, Haarlem, 1907.

—, *De toepassing der (...). Verslag, door eene commissie van onderzoek uitgebracht aan het Hoofdbestuur van het Nederlandsch Genootschap tot Zedelijke Verbetering der Gevangenen*, 1917.

Chesnais, Jean-Claude, *Histoire de la violence, en occident de 1800 à nos jours*, Paris, 1981.

Chorus, Boudewijn and René van der Velden, *Gevangenen. De werkelijkheid achter de tralies*, Utrecht, 1989.

Christie, Nils, *Limits to Pain*, Oxford, 1981.

—, 'Beschouwingen over geweld', in René van Swaaningen et al., *A Tors et à Travers. Liber Amicorum Herman Bianchi*, Amsterdam, 1988: 205–13.

—, *Crime Control as Industry. Towards Gulags, Western Style?*, London, 1993.

Clemmer, Donald, *The Prison Community*, New York, 1958 (1940).

Cohen, Stan, *Psychological Survival*, Harmondsworth, 1972.

—, *Visions of Social Control. Crime, Punishment and Classification*, Cambridge, 1985.

Cohen, Stanley and Andrew Scull, *Social Control and the State*, Oxford, 1983.

Cool, S., *Het cellulaire stelsel verdedigd tegen de zienswijze van de Minister van Justitie*, Amsterdam, 1856.

Cooper, David D., *The Lesson of the Scaffold*, London, 1974.

Corbin, Alain, *Pestdamp en bloesemgeur. Een geschiedenis van de reuk*, Nijmegen, 1986 (1982).

Davidson, Steve, *Lessen in overleving, 26 brieven uit het huis van bewaring te Amsterdam en de gevangenis Nieuw-Vosseveld te Vught*, Amsterdam, 1968.

Davis, Ioan, *Writers in Prison*, Oxford, 1990.

Deinse, A. J. van, *Strafregt, ontwikkeld en in verband beschouwd met de Algemeene Bepalingen der Nederlandsche Strafwetgeving*, Middelburg, 1860.

Dekker, C. M., *Schetsen uit de strafgevangenis*, The Hague, 1910.

Dekker, J. J. H., *Straffen, redden en opvoeden. Het ontstaan en de ontwikkeling van de residentiële heropvoeding in West-Europa, 1814–1914*, Assen, 1985.

Dekker, Maurits, *Doodenstad, schetsen uit het gevangenisleven*, Amsterdam, 1923.

Deknatel, J. W., 'De bijzondere strafgevangenis te Scheveningen', in *Nederlandsch Tijdschrift voor Geneeskunde*, vol. 2, 1913: 158–73, 422–5.

Dellen, Paul van, *Misdaad en Straf in Nederland*, Assen, 1987.

Denkers, F. A. C. M., *Ervaringen van gedetineerden in open gestichten*, Publication Criminologisch Instituut Katholieke Universiteit Nijmegen, Nijmegen, 1969.

—, 'Democratisering in het gevangeniswezen', in *Tijdschrift voor Criminologie*, vol. 13, 1971: 154–68.

Derks, Willem, 'De tbr: een historische vergissing', in *De Gids*, no. 6/7, 1987: 455–69.

Dickens, Charles, 'Philadelphia, and its solitary prison', in *American Notes for General Circulation*, Paris, 1842: 121–37.

Diederiks, Herman and Pieter Spierenburg, 'L'enfermement non criminel en Hollande, XVIIIème–XIXème siècles', in Petit (ed.), 1984: 43–55.

Dienstverlening, special issue of *Justitiële Verkenningen*, vol. 10, no. 6, 1984.

Dijk, Jan van et al. (eds), *Criminal Law in Action. An Overview of Current Issues in Western Societies*, Arnhem, 1986.

Dijksterhuis, F. P. H., *De gevangenis Bankenbos II. Beleving en invloed van een verblijf in de gevangenis voor verkeersdelinkwenten*, Assen, 1973.

Dobash, R. P., R. E. Dobash and S. Gutteridge, *The Imprisonment of Women*, Oxford, 1986.

Doleschal, E., 'Proportie en duur van gevangenisstraffen', in *Justitiële Verkenningen*, vol. 7, no. 2, 1981: 32–6.

Domela Nieuwenhuis, J., *De straf der afzonderlijke opsluiting, historisch en kritisch beschouwd* (Ph.D.), Amsterdam, 1859.

—, 'Welk gevangenisstelsel is voor ons land het meest aanbevelenswaardig', proposals, *Handelingen der Nederlandsche Juristen-Vereeniging*, 1872: 160–91.

—, *De gevangenisstraf, overeenkomstig de eischen van het recht en het maatschappelijk belang ingericht, de beste der straffen*, Groningen, 1884.

—, 'Een dreigend gevaar voor het welslagen der cellulaire gevangenisstraf in Nederland', in *Tijdschrift voor Strafrecht*, vol. 1, 1886–7: 523–41.

—, 'Eene bijdrage tot de kennis der geschiedenis en der uitvoering van de vrijheidsstraffen', in *Tijdschrift voor Strafrecht*, vol. 5, 1891: 381–402.

—, 'Een terugblik op den strijd voor de invoering der afzonderlijke opsluiting in Nederland', in *Tijdschrift voor Strafrecht*, vol. 7, 1893: 256–89.

—, *Het wezen der straf*, Groningen, 1899.

—, 'Bijdrage tot de kennis der Straffen in Nederland', in *Tijdschrift voor Strafrecht*, vol. 14, 1902: 1–29.

—, 'Strafrecht, geen misdaadrecht', in *Stemmen des Tijds*, vol. 1, 1912: 286–310.

—, 'Bedenkelijke reactie op strafrechtelijk gebied', in *Tijdschrift voor Strafrecht*, vol. 30, 1919: 75–88.

—, 'De cellulaire gevangenisstraf in het gedrang', in *Tijdschrift voor Strafrecht*, vol. 31, 1921: 194–207.

Donker Curtius van Tienhoven, W. B., *Iets over de theorie der Straffen en het bewijs der misdaden naar aanleiding van het ontwerp van het Strafwetboek voor de Nederlanden*, Utrecht, 1827.

Dostoyevski, Fyodor, *The House of the Dead*, Harmondsworth, 1985 (1864).

Douglas, Jack D., *The Social Meanings of Suicide*, Princeton, 1967.

Downes, David, *Contrasts in Tolerance: Post-war Penal Policy in The Netherlands and England and Wales*, Oxford, 1988.

—, 'The case for going Dutch. The relevance of post-war penal policy in The Netherlands for Britain', in *Tijdschrift voor Criminologie*, vol. 34, no. 3, 1992: 198–209.

Drooge, J. van, 'Voorwaardelijke Veroordeeling', in *Sociaal Weekblad*, no. 42, 20 October 1900; no. 44, 3 November 1900.

Drost, T. R., 'TBR – Wetgeving: op wat voor gronden?', in Fiselier et al. (eds), 1980: 279–91.

—, *Wikken en wegen. Een onderzoek naar het wel of niet verlengen van een terbeschikkingstelling*, Groningen, 1991.

Dupont-Bouchat, M. S., 'Ducpétiaux ou le rêve cellulaire', in *Déviance et Société*, vol. 12, no. 1, 1988: 1–27.

Durkheim, Emile, *Les règles de la méthode sociologique*, Paris, 1973 (1895).

Duyl, D. Z. van, *De voorwaardelijke invrijheidstelling, historisch en kritisch beschouwd* (Ph.D.), Leiden, 1881.

Eggink, J. W., *De geschiedenis van het Nederlandse gevangeniswezen* (Ph.D.), Assen, 1958.

Elias, Norbert, *The Civilizing Process. I. The History of Manners*, Oxford, 1978 (1939).

—, *The Civilizing Process. II. State Formation and Civilization*, Oxford, 1982 (1939).

—, *What is Sociology?*, London, 1978 (1970).

—, *Involvement and Detachment*, Oxford, 1987.

Elst, A. van der, 'Celstraf, theorie en praktijk', in *Vragen des Tijds*, vol. 1, 1899: 119–58, 226–62.

—, 'De gevangeniscourant', in *De Opbouw, democratisch tijdschrift*, vol. 5, 1922–3: 687–95.

—, 'Tuin- en veldarbeid voor gevangenen', in *De Opbouw, democratisch tijdschrift*, vol. 6, 1923–4: 812–19.

Engelen, D. O., 'Iets over het Elmira-stelsel', in *Rechtsgeleerd Magazijn*, vol. 19, 1900: 250–87.

Enquête over de behandeling van Politieke misdadigers in Nederlandsche gevangenissen, in *De Jonge Gids*, vol. 1, 1897–8: 681–726; vol. 2, 1898–9: 1–35, 108, 224–37.

Ensemble de règles pour le traitement des prisonniers, in *Bulletin de la Commission Pénitentiaire Internationale*, no. 5, October 1929.

Eriksson, Torsten, *The Reformers: An Historical Survey of Pioneer Experi-*

ments in the Treatment of Criminals, New York/Oxford/Amsterdam, 1976.

Ex-gedetineerde, 'Een huis van bewaring van binnenuit', in *Tijdschrift voor Criminologie*, vol. 24, 1972: 20–7.

Faber, Sjoerd, *Strafrechtspleging en criminaliteit te Amsterdam, 1680–1811, de nieuwe menslievendheid* (Ph.D.), Arnhem, 1983.

—, 'Een zachte botsing. Celstraf en schavot te Amsterdam in 1854', in Faber et al., 1989: 69–83.

Faber, Sjoerd and Bert Krikke, 'De psychiatrische expertise in de zaak Harmen Alfkens: een Bataafse primeur?', in *Tijdschrift voor Gezondheidsrecht*, 1977: 262–4.

Faber, Sjoerd, et al., *Criminaliteit in de negentiende eeuw*, Hollandse Studiën 22, Publication Historische Vereniging Holland, Hilversum, 1989.

Fabius, D. P. D., *Schuld en Straf*, Amsterdam, 1900.

—, *Voorwaardelijke veroordeeling*, Utrecht, 1914.

Feber, G. H. A., *Beschouwingen over crimineele psychologie*, Zwolle, 1934.

Feith, Jan, *Het verhaal van den dief*, Amsterdam, 1909.

Fick, *Rapport van de commissie voor de verdere uitbouw van het gevangeniswezen* (committee Fick), The Hague, 1947.

Fijnaut, C., *Opdat de macht een toevlucht zij? Een historische studie van het politieapparaat als een politieke instelling*, 2 vols, Antwerpen/Arnhem, 1979.

—, 'In de klem der verdeeldheid', in Balkema et al. (eds), 1986: 125–56.

Fiselier, J., *Open gestichten en recidive*, Publication Criminologisch Instituut Katholieke Universiteit Nijmegen, Nijmegen, 1969.

—, 'The state of the prisons: geen reden tot juichen', in *Sancties*, no. 5, 1993: 267–71.

Fiselier, J. et al. (eds), *Tegen de Regels, een inleiding in de criminologie*, Nijmegen, 1980.

Fitzgerald, Mike, *Prisoners in Revolt*, Harmondsworth, 1977.

Fleers, G. J. F., *Voorwaardelijk in vrijheid, de voorwaardelijke invrijheidstelling in Nederland* (Ph.D.), Amsterdam, 1976.

Fliedner, Theodor, *Collektenreise nach Holland und England, nebst einen ausführlichen Darstellung des Kirchen, Schul-, Armen- und Gefängniswesens beider Länder, mit vergleichender Hinweisung auf Deutschland, vorzüglich Preussen*, Essen, 1831.

Fokkens, J. W., *Reclassering en Strafrechtspleging*, Arnhem, 1981.

Foucault, Michel, *Mikrosphysik der Macht. Ueber Strafjustiz, Psychiatrie und Medizin*, Publication Internationale Marxistische Diskussion 61, Berlin, 1976.

—, *Discipline and Punish: The Birth of the Prison* (translation of *Surveiller et Punir, Naissance de la Prison*, Paris, 1975), Middlesex, 1979.

Fox, Richard G., 'Dr. Schwitzgebel's machine revisited: electronic monitoring of offenders', in *Australian & New Zealand Journal of Criminology*, vol. 20, 1987: 131–47.

Franke, Herman, *Van schavot naar krantekolom. Over de ontwikkeling van de misdaadverslaggeving in het Algemeen Handelsblad vanaf 1828 tot 1900*, Amsterdam, 1981.

—, *De dood in het leven van alledag. Twee eeuwen rouwadvertenties én openbare strafvoltrekkingen in Nederland*, The Hague, 1985.

—, 'Dutch tolerance: facts and fables', in *The British Journal of Criminology*, vol. 30, no. 1, 1990: 81–93.

—, 'De mythe van het achterstallig onderhoud', in *Tijdschrift voor Criminologie*, vol. 32, no. 4, 1990: 323–33.

—, 'De verloren eer van Maurits Dekker', in *Het Oog in 't Zeil*, vol. 8, no. 4, 1991: 1–15.

—, 'Violent crime in the Netherlands. A historical-sociological analysis', in *Crime, Law and Social Change*, vol. 21, 1994: 73–100.

Frieswijk, Johan and Hans Sleurink, *De zaak Hogerhuis*, Leeuwarden, 1984.

Fuchs, G., *Wij achter tralies, herinneringen van no. 2911 in de gevangenis geschreven*, 1931.

Gall, F. J., *Voorleezingen, gehouden te Berlijn, over de werksaamheden der herssenen en de mogelijkheid om den aanleg der eigenschappen van den geest zoowel, als die van het gemoed, uit de vorming der schedels van menschen en dieren te erkennen*, Amsterdam, 1805.

Galtung, Johan, *Gevangenis en maatschappij. Een sociologisch-kriminologisch onderzoek naar strafbeleving*, The Hague, 1967.

Garland, David, 'The Criminal and his science: a critical account of the formation of criminology at the end of the nineteenth century', in *The British Journal of Criminology*, vol. 25, no. 2, April 1985: 109–37.

—, *Punishment and Welfare. A History of Penal Strategies*, Aldershot, 1985.

—, *Punishment and Modern Society: A Study in Social Theory*, Oxford, 1990.

Gedenkboek 1907–1957, Publication Psychiatrisch-Juridisch Gezelschap, Amsterdam, 1957.

Geestelijk gestoorden in de strafrechtspleging, report of the Werkgroep Inventarisatie geestelijk gestoorden in de strafrechtspleging, Ministry of Justice, The Hague, 1988.

Gerlings, H. Th., 'Wie worden door ons strafrecht gegrepen?', in *Verslag bijeenkomst Psychiatrisch-Juridisch Gezelschap*, no. 11, 5 May 1934, Amsterdam, 1935.

Geuns, S. J. M. van, 'Misdadige krankzinnigen en krankzinnige gevangenen', in *Rechtsgeleerd Magazijn Themis*, vol. 60, part 3, 1899: 389–423.

Geurts, A. C., *De rechtspositie van de gevangene* (Ph.D.), Assen, 1962.

—, 'Enkele beschouwingen met betrekking tot het systeem van de open gevangenis', in *Tijdschrift voor Criminologie*, vol. 5, 1963: 162–76.

—, *De rechtspositie van de gevangene, of hoe het was, is en zou kunnen zijn*, Deventer, 1981.

Gevangene 1113 onthult. Verbeteren onze rechtspraak en gevangenissen de mens?, Amsterdam, 1960.

Gevangenisnota, see Prison Memorandum

Gevangeniswezen, Het Nederlandse (...) in de jaren 1945 tot en met 1953, The Hague, 1954.

Gevers van Endegeest, D. T., *Gevangenissen in Holland*, about 1838.

Gevolgen, De (...) van huisselijke achteloosheid, wanorde en verkwisting in voorbeelden, Verhandelingen van de Maatschappij tot Nut van 't Algemeen, vol. 20, Amsterdam, 1927.

Gezangen in den Kerker. Ten voordeele van den dichter uitgegeven door W. Goede, Christen-Leeraar te Rotterdam, Rotterdam, 1819.

Gibbs, John J., 'Symptoms of psychopathology among jail prisoners', in *Criminal Justice and Behavior*, vol. 10, no. 3, September 1987: 288–310.

Goffman, Erving, *Asylums: Essays on the Social Situation of Mental Patients and Other Inmates*, Harmondsworth/New York, 1984 (1961).

Goossens, G. (ed.), *Verzameling van stukken over de oogmerken der straf, de lijfstraffen en de eenzame opsluiting van gevangenen*, Amsterdam, 1843.

Goudsblom, Johan, *Sociology in the Balance. A Critical Essay*, Oxford, 1977.

—, *De sociologie van Norbert Elias, Weerklank en kritiek, De civilisatietheorie*, Amsterdam, 1987.

Graaf, A. de, *Opvoeding van gevangenen* (translation of A. Winter, *The New York State Reformatory at Elmira*, 1891), Amsterdam, 1899.

Graaf, H. T., *Karakter en behandeling van veroordeelden wegens landlooperij en bedelarij*, Groningen, 1914.

Graaff, Klaas de, *De som der hoeken blijft eenzaamheid, omgaan met gedetineerden*, Amsterdam, 1984.

Grapendaal, M., *In dynamisch evenwicht. Een verkennend onderzoek naar de gedetineerdensubcultuur in drie Nederlandse gestichten*, WODC report, no. 78, The Hague, 1987.

—, 'The inmate subculture in Dutch prisons', in *British Journal of Criminology*, vol. 30, no. 3, 1990: 341–57.

Grapendaal, M. and M. M. Kommer, 'Een koekoeksei voor de komende honderd jaar, kritische kanttekeningen bij de nieuwbouw van het gevangeniswezen', in *Delikt & Delinkwent*, vol. 18, no. 4, 1988: 306–15.

Grevelink, see Alstorphius Grevelink

Greven, M. E., 'De opsluiting van jeugdige politieke delinquenten in de

Rijkswerkinrichting Marum, 1947–1951', in *Tijdschrift voor Criminologie*, vol. 31, no. 4, 1989: 317–32.

Griever, Lukas, *Achter tralies. Het gevangeniswezen in Nederland*, Deventer, 1979.

Groeneweg N. and A. Hallema, *Van Nachtwacht tot Computermacht, vijftig eeuwen politie en justitie*, Zaltbommel, 1976.

Gross, Otto, *Die cerebrale Sekundärfunktion*, Leipzig, 1902.

Haan, Jacob Israël de, 'Amerikaansche en Hollandsche Crimineele Politiek', in *De Beweging*, vol. 9, no. 2, 1913: 27–47.

—, 'Amerikaansche Crimineele Politiek (Het Honor-system)', in *De Beweging*, vol 12, no. 3, 1916: 171–91.

Haan, Willem de, 'Explaining expansion: the Dutch case', in Bill Rolston and Mike Tomlinson (eds), *The Expansion of European Prison Systems*, Working Papers in European Criminology, no. 7, 1986, 1–14.

Haan, Willem de and Rino Verpalen (eds), *Bezeten van de bajes? Strafrechtelijk klimaat en gevangeniswezen in een zorgzame samenleving*, uitgave Coornhert Liga, Breda, 1989.

Haar, Wouter ter, 'Niet in de bak maar nuttig werk doen. Alternatieve sancties voor jongeren', in *Jeugd en Samenleving*, vol. 14, no. 12, December 1984: 771–82.

Haas, A. de, 'Water en Brood', in *Nederlandsch Juristenblad*, vol. 7, 1932: 238–42.

Haastert, J. van, *Justitie in Breda (1811 [hk] 1838)*, uitgave Vrije Universiteit Amsterdam, Amsterdam, 1984.

Haffmans, Ch., 'De plaats van de TBR in het geheel der strafrechtspleging', in D. H. de Jong, et al. (eds), 1986: 149–62.

—, *De berechting van de psychisch gestoorde delinquent* (diss.), Arnhem, 1989.

Hallema, A., 'De oudste Nederlandsche gevangeniscourant', in *Nederlandsch Juristenblad*, vol. 8, 1933: 665–70.

—, *De geschiedenis van het gevangeniswezen, hoofdzakelijk in Nederland*, 's-Gravenhage, 1958.

Hamel, G. A. van, *Verspreide Opstellen* (2 vols), Leiden, 1912.

—, *Inleiding tot de studie van het Nederlandsche strafrecht*, 3rd impression, Haarlem, 1913.

—, 'Het "Borstal"-stelsel', in *Tijdschrift voor Strafrecht*, vol. 20, 1909: 279–89.

—, 'Strafrechtspolitiek van voor honderd jaar', in *De Gids*, part 2, 1909: 11–40.

Hamers, H. J. A., *Het kristallen paleis* (Ph.D.), Lisse, 1986.

Hare, E. H., 'Masturbatory insanity: the history of an idea', in *The Journal of Mental Science*, vol. 108, no. 452, 1962: 1–25.

Hartog, C. den, et al, *Nieuwe voedingsleer*, Utrecht, 1988 (9th edn).

Hazewinkel-Suringa, D., 'De invoering der bewaring. Zijn de velden wit om te oogsten?', in *Tijdschrift voor Strafrecht*, vol. 49, 1939: 365–93.

Heerikhuizen, Bart van, *W. A. Bonger, socioloog en socialist*, Groningen, 1987.

Heijder, A., *Bewakers en bewaakten. Een bijdrage tot de studie van het gevangeniswezen* (Ph.D.), Meppel, 1963.

—, *Resocialisatie. Een ideaal in de gevangenis*, Deventer, 1966.

Heijermans, Herman, 'Rijksopvoedingsgestichten' and 'Feiten', in *De Jonge Gids*, vol. 2, 1898–9: 276–320, 378–84.

Heine, Heinrich, 'Gefängnisreform und Strafgesetzgebung', in *Sämtliche Werke*, vol. 12, herausgegeben von Hans Kaufmann, *Lutetia*, vol. 2, München, 1964 (1843): 127–33.

Heldring, O. G., *Leven en Arbeid*, vol. 1, Leiden, 1881.

Heymans, G., 'Uitwassen der crimineele anthropologie', in *De Gids*, vol. 1, 1901: 50–91.

—, *Inleiding tot de Speciale Psychologie*, 2 vols, Haarlem, 1932.

Hoeven, H. van der, *Celstraf*, series 'PRO EN CONTRA', Betreffende vraagstukken van Algemeen Belang, Baarn, 1908.

Hoeven, H. van der, and W. P. J. Pompe, *Psychiater en criminoloog tegenover den misdadiger*, series Criminologische Studiën, vol. 6, Nijmegen, 1941.

Hofstee, E. J., *TBR en TBS. De TBR in rechtshistorisch perspectief* (Ph.D.), Arnhem, 1987.

Hofstee, E. W., *De demografische ontwikkeling van Nederland in de eerste helft van de negentiende eeuw, een historisch-demografische en sociologische studie*, NIDI publication, Deventer, 1978.

Holmes, Thomas and I. H. Boeke, *In en buiten de gevangenis*, Amsterdam, (no year)

Hoogenboom, A. B. and L. Morre, 'Honderden Kleine Theaters van Bestraffing: de verspreiding van de politiefunctie', in *Delikt & Delinkwent*, vol. 18, no. 5, 1988: 429–45.

Howard, John, *The State of the Prisons in England and Wales*, Abingdon, 1977 (1777, 1st impression), London, 1780 (Appendix), 1784 (3rd impression).

Hughes, Robert, *The Fatal Shore. A History of the Transportation of Convicts to Australia, 1787–1868*, London, 1987.

Hulsman, Louk, *Afscheid van het strafrecht. Een pleidooi voor zelfregulering*, Houten, 1986.

Hutte, P. E. et al., *Mensen in onvrijheid, gevangeniswezen, dwangverpleging en hulpverlening in menselijk perspectief*, Alphen aan den Rijn, 1972.

Iependaal, Willem van, *De commissaris kan me nog meer vertellen*, The Hague, 1951.

—, *Bef, Boef en Bajes*, The Hague, 1952.

Iets over lijfstraffen, eenzame opsluiting en het poenitentiair stelsel, Amsterdam, 1840.

Ignatieff, Michael, *A Just Measure of Pain. The Penitentiary in the Industrial Revolution, 1750–1850*, New York, 1978.

—, 'State, civil society and total institutions: a critique of recent social histories of punishment', in Cohen and Scull, 1983: 75–105.

Jacobs, J., 'The prisoners' rights movement and its impacts, 1960–1980', in N. Morris and M. H. Tonry (eds), *Crime and Justice: An Annual Review of Research*, vol. 2, Chicago, Chicago University Press, 1980.

Janssen, J. J., *De bibliotheek in onze gevangenissen*, s.a.

Janssen, Niek, 'Het beklagrecht van gedetineerden in de praktijk', in *Tijdschrift voor Criminologie*, vol. 22, no. 5, 1980: 249–63.

Janssen, P. C. and J. M. M. de Meere, 'Het sterftepatroon in Amsterdam 1774–1930. Een analyse van doodsoorzaken', in *Tijdschrift voor Sociale Geschiedenis*, vol. 8, no. 26, 1982: 180–223.

Jelgersma, G., 'De geboren misdadiger', in *Tijdschrift voor Strafrecht*, vol. 6, 1892: 97–117.

—, *Leerboek der Psychiatrie*, 3 vols, Amsterdam, about 1908.

Jelgersma, H. C., *Galgebergen en galgevelden in West- en Midden-Nederland*, Zutphen, 1978.

Johnson, Harry M., *Sociology: A Systematic Introduction*, London, 1968 (1960).

Jong, D. H. de et al. (eds), *De vrijheidsstraf*, Arnhem, 1986.

Jonge, G. de, 'Totale inrichtingen en hun effecten', in Fiselier et al. (eds), 1980: 332–42.

Jongh, G. T. J. de, *Bestraffen en Bestrijden*, Haarlem, 1923.

—, *Bedreigde levens, over reclasseering, strafrecht en kinderrecht*, Arnhem, 1943.

Jongh, J. J. de, *Verzameling van wetten, decreten, besluiten, reglementen, instructiën en bepalingen, betrekkelijk het gevangeniswezen in de Nederlanden*, vol. 1 (1791–1844), Leeuwarden, 1846; vol. 2, (1845–1859), Leeuwarden, 1860.

Jonker, E., M. Ros and C. de Vries, *Kriminologen en reklasseerders in Nederland*, Publication Utrechtse Historische Cahiers, no. 1, Utrecht, 1986.

Kat, J., 'De verpleging van gevaarlijke en schadelijke krankzinnigen', in *Tijdschrift voor Strafrecht*, vol. 18, 1907: 215–63.

Kelk, C., *Rechtspositie gedetineerden*, report Coornhert Liga, Utrecht, 1976.

—, *Recht voor gedetineerden* (Ph.D.), Alphen aan den Rijn, 1978.

—, *Kort begrip van het detentierecht*, Nijmegen, 1983.

—, 'Het gevangeniswezen: een afbraak van verworvenheden?', in *Nederlands Juristenblad*, vol. 59, no. 29, 1984: 897–907.

—, 'Het wel en wee van de vrijheidsstraf', in *Symposium, 100 jaar vrijheidsstraf*, 1987: 43–58.

—, 'Het gevangeniswezen in de gevarenzone?', in *Delikt & Delinkwent*, vol. 23, no. 3, 1993: 195–201.

—, 'Sobere vooruitzichten voor het gevangeniswezen', in *Delikt & Delinkwent*, vol. 24, no. 2, 1994: 107–12.

Kelk, C. et al. (eds), *Recht, macht en manipulatie*, Utrecht/Antwerpen, 1976.

Kempe, G. Th., 'Penitentiaire toekomstproblemen in Nederland. Detentie, differentiatie, selectie', in *Geschriften van Reclasseeringsinstellingen*, vol. 1, 1946: 5–26.

—, *Schuldig Zijn*, Utrecht, 1950.

—, '50 jaar criminologie in Nederland', in *Gedenkboek 1907–1957*, 1957: 65–101.

—, *Inleiding tot de criminologie*, Haarlem, 1967.

Kenny, Anthony, *Wittgenstein*, Utrecht/Antwerpen, 1974.

Het Kerkerleven, (…) in Nederland, schetsen en tooneelen uit de nagelaten papieren van gevangenen, bijeenverzameld door een geestelijke, Amsterdam, 1870.

Ketelaars, Gerdie, *Vrouwen in detentie. Verslag van het onderzoek naar de behoeften van vrouwen in detentie*, Clara Wichmann Instituut, Amsterdam, 1991.

Kikkert, J. G., *Koning van Holland, Louis Bonaparte 1778–1846*, Rotterdam, 1981.

Kleerekoper, A. B., *Misdaad en Boete*, Publication Centrale Nederlandsche Ambtenarenbond, 1928.

Klerk, Peter de, *Zitten, hoe zit dat?*, Amsterdam, 1978.

Klijssen, Wil, *Op de punt van een naald*, Amsterdam, 1968.

Knigge, G., *Het irrationele element van de straf*, Arnhem, 1988.

—, 'Van abolitionisme en vergelding', in *Rechtsgeleerd Magazijn Themis*, no. 6, 1988: 260–71.

Koenraadt, Frans and Michael Zeegers (eds), *Trends in Law and Mental Health. Proceedings of the 13th International Congress on Law and Mental Health, Amsterdam, June 1987*, Arnhem, 1988.

Kohlbrugge, J. H. F., *Het zieleleven van den misdadiger, een maatschappelijk vraagstuk*, The Hague, 1922.

Kommer, Max, *De gevangenis als werkplek*, Arnhem, 1991.

—, 'Punitiveness in Europe – a comparison', in *European Journal on Criminal Policy and Research*, vol. 2, no. 1, 1994: 29–43.

Kommer, M. M. and M. Brouwers, *Vrijheid in gevangenschap. Een inventarisatie in de inrichtingen met een half-open regiem*, WODC report, no. 71, The Hague, 1986.

Kosto, A. 'Straffen buiten de muren', in *Justitiële Verkenningen*, vol. 20, no. 2, 1994: 8–21.

Kramps, J. M. A., 'Misdaad en Misdadiger', in *Vragen des Tijds*, vol. 7, 1891: 179–210.

Krebs, Albert, *Freiheitsentzug. Entwicklung von Praxis und Theorie seit der Aufklärung*, Berlin, 1978.

Kruithof, Bernard, 'De deugdzame natie. Het burgerlijk beschavings-offensief van de Maatschappij tot Nut van 't Algemeen tussen 1764 en 1860', in *Symposion*, vol. 2, no. 1, 1980: 22–38.

Laan, P. H. van der, 'Nieuwe pogingen om de vrijheidsstraf terug te dringen: dienstverlening, intensief reclasseringstoezicht en electronisch huisarrest', in *Justitiële Verkenningen*, vol. 14, no. 3, 1988: 9–47.

Lammers, J. A. N., *Voorwaardelijke Veroordeeling* (Ph.D.), Amsterdam, 1889.

Langemeijer, G. E., 'Volksopvoeding door den strafrechter', in *Nederlandsch Juristenblad*, vol. 9, no. 18: 293–300.

Laurillard, E., *Uit de cel, schetsen en beelden uit de gevangenis*, Amsterdam, 1876.

—, 'Een en ander over gevangenisstraf', in *Nieuws van den Dag*, 15 August 1899.

—, 'Bedenkingen tegen het stelsel van opvoeding van gevangenen in 't Elmira-Instituut te New York', in *Het Paleis van Justitie*, vol. 28, no. 42, 1899: 3–4.

Leuw, Ed. and Jac. van Weringh, 'Bewaarders en gedetineerden: laveren tussen voldongen feiten', in *Balans*, vol. 11, no. 2, 1980: 3–8.

Linden, B. van der, *Regiem en recidive. Een onderzoek naar het effect van twee verschillende gevangenisregiems op de recidive van middellang-gestraften*, WODC report, no. 3, The Hague, 1973.

Lissenberg, E., *Kinderen spreken recht, een onderzoek naar denkbeelden van kinderen over misdaad en straf* (Ph.D.), Alphen aan den Rijn, 1979.

—, 'Vrouwen uit detentie', in *Sancties*, no. 5, 1992, 267–71.

—, 'Prisoners' Clothing in the Netherlands', in *Textile History*, vol. 24, no. 1, 1993: 49–51.

Liszt, Franz von, *Der Zweckgedanke im Strafrecht*, Frankfurt am Main, 1968 (1883).

Lombroso, Cesare, *L'Homme Criminel* (French translation of *L'uomo delinquente*), Paris, 1887 (1876).

—, *Boeven-litteratuur*, Amsterdam (no year).

Lurasco, C. F., *Over de bezoeken in de cellulaire gevangenis te Amsterdam in overeenstemming met het penitentiair stelsel*, 1850.

Mannheim, H., *The Dilemma of Penal Reform*, London, 1939.

Marx, A. J., 'Het practische nut van strafoplegging volgens het beginsel der algemeene preventie', in *Nederlandsch Juristenblad*, vol. 8, no. 42, 1933: 653–9.

—, 'Onze celstraf, gezien in het licht der algemeene preventie', in *Maandblad voor Berechting en Reclasseering*, 1934: 288–95.

Mary, Philippe, *Révolte carcérale: Changements et logique pérenne de la prison*, Université Libre de Bruxelles, Brussels, 1988.

Mathiesen, Thomas, *The Politics of Abolition. Essays in Political Action Theory*, Oxford, 1974.

—, *Prison on Trial*, London, 1990.

Maür, G. in der, 'Nederlandsche Rijksopvoedingsgestichten', in *De Jonge Gids*, vol. 2, 1898–9: 170–84.

Mead, George Herbert, *Mind, Self and Society*, Chicago/London, 1974 (1934).

Meij, R. van der, 'Over straf en schuld', in *Tijdschrift voor Wijsbegeerte*, 1908: 279–315.

—, 'Het zoogenaamde vraagstuk der "minderwaardige" misdadigers', in *Tijdschrift voor Strafrecht*, vol. 20, 1909: 211–40.

Meijer, L. S., 'Psychiatrische beschouwingen omtrent de gevangenis en hare bewoners', in *De Gids*, vol. 63, 1899: 391–411.

—, 'Staatszorg voor krankzinnige gevangenen', in *De Gids*, vol. 63, 1899: 435–66.

Meijer-Wichmann, Clara, *Mensch en Maatschappij*, Arnhem, 1923.

—, *Bevrijding* (eds F. Holterman and H. Ramaer), Amsterdam, 1979.

—, Bundel voor Studium Generale Rijksuniversiteit Utrecht, Utrecht, 1985.

Meijers, F. S., 'Een psychische enquête onder gevangenen en hunne psychisch-hygiënische behandeling', in *Verslag van den Criminologendag*, 1938: 112–22.

Melossi, Dario and Massimo Pavarini, *The Prison and the Factory: Origins of the Penitentiary System*, London, 1981.

Mesdag, S. van, 'Cel of gemeenschap?', in *Leven en Werken, maandblad voor meisjes en vrouwen*, vol. 9, 1924: 497–520.

—, 'Prae-advies (II) over de tenuitvoerlegging van de gevangenisstraf', in *Handelingen der Nederlandsche Juristen-Vereeniging*, 1928: 1–84.

Metz, G. H., *De strafgevangenis en hare bewoners. Eene zielkundige leidraad*, The Hague, 1904/1905.

Mierop, L. van, 'Meeningen over de celstraf', in *Haagsch Maandblad*, vol. 7, 1927: 485–92.

Mijn verblijf in de gemeenschappelijke en afgezonderde gevangenis en eenige beschouwingen over die beide inrigtingen, beschreven door een ontslagen gevangene (…), Utrecht, 1858.

Modderman, A. E. J., *De hervorming onzer strafwetgeving, kritische beschouwing der wet van 29 junij 1854 (staatsblad no. 102)* (Ph.D.), The Hague, 1861.

—, *Straf – geen kwaad*, Amsterdam, 1864.

Moedikdo, P., 'De Utrechtse school van Pompe, Baan en Kempe', in Kelk et al. (eds), 1976: 90–154.

Moerings, Martin, *De gevangenis uit, de maatschappij in. De gevangenis en haar betekenis voor de sociale kontakten van ex-gedetineerden* (Ph.D.), Alphen aan den Rijn, 1978.

—, 'Isolatie: gevangenschap in het kwadraat', in C. Kelk, P. Moedikdo et al. (eds), *Grenzen en mogelijkheden. Opstellen over en rondom de strafrechtspleging*, Nijmegen, 1984: 6–23.

—, 'Fundamenten van de gevangenis. Huisvesting en detentie-opvattingen', in D. H. Jong et al. (eds), 1986: 347–62.

—, 'Isolation in prison', in Koenraadt and Zeegers (eds), 1988: 401–11.

Moll A., *Leerboek der geregtelijke geneeskunde voor genees- en regtskundigen*, Vol 1, Arnhem, 1825.

Mollet, J. S., 'Het Boetstelsel', in *Liefde en Hoop, tijdschrift voor gevangenen en gevangenissen*, vol. 2, 1828: 247–53, 309–31.

Mollet, J. A., *Rapport fait au Comité de Direction de la Société Neêrlandaise, pour l'amélioration morale des prisoniers (…)*, Amsterdam, 1840.

Molster, A., 'De ontwikkeling van ons strafstelsel', in *Jonge Gids, halfmaandelijks tijdschrift voor de jeugdbeweging*, vol. 6, 1932: 125–8.

Moorman van Kappen, O., W. Frouws and B. H. A. van der Woude, *Ontwerp-Lijfstraffelijk Wetboek, 1801, 1804*, Werken der Stichting tot uitgaaf der Bronnen van het Oud-Vaderlandsch Recht, nos 9 and 10, Zutphen, 1982.

Moreau-Christophe, M. L., *Rapport à M. le Comte de Montavilet, pair de France, ministre secrétaire au département de l'intérieur, sur les prisons de l'Angleterre, de l'Ecosse, de la Hollande, de la Belgique et de la Suisse*, Paris, 1839.

Morris, Norval and Michael Tonry, *Between Prison and Probation: Intermediate Punishments in a Rational Sentencing System*, Oxford, 1993.

Muller, N., 'De straf in het strafrecht (taak en schoonheid van de onvoorwaardelijke straf)', in *Tijdschrift voor Strafrecht*, vol. 44, 1934: 15–72.

Muncie John and Richard Sparks (eds), *Imprisonment: European Perspectives*, Hemel Hempstead, 1991.

Munnik, H. J. van der, 'De celstraf na den oorlog', in *Vragen des Tijds*, 1919: 370–83.

Musil, Robert, *De man zonder eigenschappen* (translation of *Der Mann ohne Eigenschaften*), vol. 2, Amsterdam, 1988.

Naafs, Joost, *Onvrijheid tussen gevangenismuren*, Publication stichting ivio, series ao, Lelystad, 1975.

Nagel, W. H., *Het werkschuwe tuig*, Alphen aan den Rijn, 1977.

—, *De funkties van de vrijheidsstraf*, Alphen aan den Rijn, 1977.

Neale, Kenneth, 'Aspects of the European Prison Rules', in Muncie and Sparks (eds), 1991: 203–18.

Neckeben, J., *Ein Vorblick auf das Jahr 2000 oder ein Tag in einer Strafanstalt des XXI Jahrhunderts; ein gefängnisswissenschaftlicher Zukunftstraum*, Breslau, 1891.

Nederburgh, J. A., 'Verantwoordelijkheid, straf; vergelding en veiligheidsmaatregel', in *Tijdschrift voor Strafrecht*, vol. 20, 1909: 47–99.

Nederlandsche Juristen-Vereeniging, Debat over voorwaardelijke veroordeeling, in *Handelingen der (...)*, 1890: 80–199.
—, Over wijzigingen in gevangenisstraf, in *Handelingen der (...)*, 1901.
Niekerk, K. H., *De gedetineerde vrouw*, unpublished report with appendices, Willem Pompe Instituut, Utrecht, 1965.
Nieuwe Berigten omtrent het Pennsylvanische Gevangenisstelsel en gedachten over lijfstraffen, deportatie en gevangenisstraffen, anonymous, Groningen, 1844.
Nieuwenhuis, C. J. N., 'Opmerkingen over de bedreigde straffen en de wijze van hare uitvoering volgens het thans bij de Tweede Kamer der Staten-Generaal ingediend ontwerp-strafwetboek', in *Nieuwe Bijdragen voor Rechtsgeleerdheid en Wetgeving*, vol. 6, 1880: 501–50.
Nieuwenhuys, Cs. Js., *Proeve eener geneeskundige Plaatsbeschrijving (Topographie) der Stad Amsterdam*, vols. 1–4, Amsterdam, 1816–20.
Noordhoff, M., 'Tucht en straffen in gewone strafgevangenissen', in *Tijdschrift voor Strafrecht*, vol. 32, 1922: 137–60.
O'Brien, Patricia, *The Promise of Punishment: Prisons in Nineteenth-Century France*, Princeton, 1982.
Olnon, L. M., *Van Bewaking naar Bescherming. De zorg voor misdadige en verwaarloosde kinderen gedurende de 19e eeuw in Nederland*, Amsterdam, 1986.
Oostdam, A. J., 'Een gevangeniscourant', in *Katholiek Sociaal Weekblad*, vol. 21, 1922: 309–11.
—, 'Ons gevangeniswezen', in *Katholiek Sociaal Weekblad*, vol. 24, 1925: 363–4.
—, 'Cel of gemeenschap?', in *Katholiek Sociaal Weekblad*, vol. 26, 1927: 677–8.
—, 'Cel of Gemeenschap', in *Katholiek Sociaal Weekblad*, vol. 28, 1929: 458.
Opzoomer, C. W., *De weg tot hervorming onzer gevangenissen*, Amsterdam, 1857.
Osborne, Thomas Mott, *Gevangenis en samenleving* (translation of *Prison and Society*), Amsterdam, 1920.
Oud, P. J., *Honderd jaren. Een eeuw van staatkundige vormgeving in Nederland 1840–1940*, Assen, 1987.
Parmentier, Stephan, 'Kijken achter tralies. België en het Europees verdrag voor de preventie van foltering en onmenselijke en vernederende behandeling', in *Panopticon*, 1992: 468–99.
Paterson, Alexander, *Paterson on Prisons* (ed. S. K. Ruck), London, 1951.
Patijn, J. G., 'Misdaad en atavisme', in *Tijdschrift voor Strafrecht*, vol. 5, 1891: 209–50.
Patijn, J. H., *De voorwaardelijke invrijheidstelling*, The Hague, 1938.
Pauwels, François, *Boeven en burgers*, Amsterdam, 1926.

Penitentiair gevangenissstelsel, Het (...) en dat der gemeenschappelijke opsluiting, anonymous, Arnhem, 1856.

Pennsylvanisch of eenig ander gevangenisstelsel, Is het (...) zonder lijfstraffen ter bevordering van afschrik doeltreffend?, anonymous, Amsterdam, 1844.

Peters, A. A. G., 'Main currents in criminal law theory', in van Dijk et al. (eds), 1986: 19–36.

Petersen, M. A., *Gedetineerden onder dak, geschiedenis van het gevangenis-wezen in Nederland vanaf 1795, bezien van zijn behuizing* (Ph.D.), Alkmaar, 1978.

Petit, Jacques G. (ed.), *La prison, le bagne en l'histoire*, Geneva, 1984.

—, *Ces peines obscures: la prison penale en France (1780–1875)*, Paris, 1990.

Piccardt, S., *De cellulaire gevangenissen in Nederland, eenige opmerkingen, wenken en wenschen, betrekkelijk hare inrichting en de bevordering van het doel met eenzame opsluiting beoogd*, Goes, 1866.

Pisciotta, Alexander. W., 'Scientific reform. The "new penology" at Elmira, 1876–1900', in *Crime and Delinquency*, 1983: 613–30.

Ploeg, Gerhard and Jan Nijboer, *Klagers achter slot en grendel, een evaluatie van het funktioneren van de gewijzigde beklagregeling voor gedetineerden*, Kriminologisch Instituut Rijksuniversiteit Groningen, Groningen, 1983.

Pols, M. S., *Het bestaan, de ontwikkeling en de tegenwoordige toestand van het Nederlandsche Strafrecht*, Utrecht, 1879.

Pompe, W. P. J., Prae-advies (I) over de tenuitvoerlegging van de gevangenisstraf, *Handelingen der Nederlandsche Juristen-Vereeniging*, 1928: 1–84.

—, *Verleden en toekomst van het strafstelsel*, 's-Hertogenbosch, 1930.

—, *Handboek van het Nederlands(ch)e strafrecht*, Zwolle, 1935 (1st edn, 1938 (2nd edn), 1959 (5th edn).

—, see Hoeven, 1941.

—, *Geschiedenis der Nederlandse Strafrechtswetenschap sinds de codificatiebeweging*, vol 2, section 3, Amsterdam, 1956.

Pouw, Anke, 'Het rijkskrankzinnigengesticht Medemblik (1884–1922); De verpleging van krankzinnige misdadigers en misdadige krankzinnigen', in Leonie de Goei and Joost Vijselaar, *Het ongelukkig lot der krankzinnigen*, NCGV series, Utrecht, 1988.

Pratt, John, 'Punishment and the lesson from history', in *Australian & New Zealand Journal of Criminology*, vol. 25, July 1992: 97–114.

Priestley, Philip, *Victorian Prison Lives: English Prison Biography, 1830–1914*, London, 1985.

—, *Jail Journeys. The English Prison Experience since 1918*, London and New York, 1989.

Prison memorandum, Het Nederlandse gevangeniswezen (Scholten), Ministry of Justice, The Hague, 1964.

Prison memorandum, Nota beleidsvraagstukken gevangeniswezen (Zee-valking), Ministry of Justice, The Hague, 1976.

Prison memorandum, Taak en Toekomst van het Nederlandse gevangenis-wezen (Scheltema), Ministry of Justice, The Hague, 1982.

Prison memorandum, Werkzame Detentie (Kosto), Ministry of Justice, The Hague, 1994.

Querido, A., 'De eerste psychiatrische expertise in foro', in *Tijdschrift voor Gezondheidsrecht*, no. 3, 1977: 134–41.

Quintus, J. J. A., *De cellulaire straf in Nederland, sinds hare invoering van de wet van 28 juni, 1851* (Ph.D.), Groningen, 1887.

Ranitz, S. M. S. de, 'De celstraf', in *Nieuwe Rotterdamsche Courant*, 30 August 1898.

Rapport commissie doelstelling en functie Huis van Bewaring (committee Van Hattum), The Hague, 1977.

Rapport over de Rijks-, Straf- en Opvoedingsgestichten voor vrouwen en meisjes, van een commissie samengesteld door het Nederlandsch Genootschap tot Zedelijke Verbetering der Gevangenen, Amsterdam, 1935.

Rapport van de Commissie, belast met de beantwoording der vraag: 'of zoogenaamde prisons-asiles voor Nederland wenschelijk worden geacht', in *Nederlandsch Tijdschrift voor Geneeskunde*, 1895: 998–1,015.

Rapport van de Commissie Psychiatrische/Therapeutische Voorzieningen Gevangeniswezen, The Hague, 1983.

Rapport van, de Staatscommissie, ingesteld bij Koninklijk besluit van 31 juli 1902, no. 30 (over krankzinnige misdadigers en misdadige krank-zinnigen), The Hague, 1904.

Ratingen, P. van, *Recht en gevangenschap*, Deventer/Zwolle, 1983.

Reek, J. van, and W. M. van Zutphen, 'Sterfte naar sociale klasse bij volwassenen in Nederland sinds de negentiende eeuw', in *Bevolking en Gezin*, no. 2, 1985: 179–90.

Reenen, P. van, *Overheidsgeweld, een sociologische studie van de dynamiek van het geweldsmonopolie*, Alphen aan den Rijn, 1979.

Regt, Ali de, *Arbeidersgezinnen en beschavingsarbeid. Ontwikkelingen in Nederland, 1870–1940*, Meppel/Amsterdam, 1984.

René van Ouwenaller, E., 'Celbezoek', in *Woord en Daad, tijdschrift voor inwendige zending*, vol. 4, 1925: 40–54.

— *Onbevredigd, een beschouwing over ons gevangeniswezen*, 1939.

Report to the Dutch Government on the visit to the Netherlands carried out by the European Committee for the Prevention of Torture and inhuman or degrading Treatment or Punishment (CPT), Council of Europe, Strasbourg, 11 June 1993.

Rideau, Wilbert and Ron Wikberg, *Life Sentences. Rage and Survival Behind Bars*, New York, 1992.

Rijksen, R., *Meningen van gedetineerden over de strafrechtspleging*, Assen, 1961 (1958).

—, *Vijf jaar tot levenslang, langgestraften in de gevangenis te Breda*, Alphen aan den Rijn, 1967.

Rijksen, R., C. Kelk and M. Moerings, *Achter slot en grendel*, Alphen aan den Rijn, 1972, 1980 (3rd edn)

Rijksen, R., K. H. Niekerk, P. A. H. Baan and W. P. J. Pompe, *De lange gevangenisstraf*, Assen, 1957.

Rochefoucauld-Liancourt, F. A. F. de la, *Over de gevangenhuizen van Philadelphia, door een Europeër in Philadelphia*, Amsterdam, 1796.

Röling, B. V. A., *De opvoedingsgedachte in het Strafrecht*, The Hague, 1933.

—, *De wetgeving tegen de zoogenaamde beroeps- en gewoontemisdadigers*, vol. 3, series 'Strafrechtelijke en Criminologische Onderzoekingen', The Hague, 1933.

—, 'Leidende beginselen in een wetgeving tegen de gevaarlijke recidivisten', in *Verslag van de bijeenkomst van het Psychiatrisch-Juridisch Gezelschap*, 24 maart 1934 te Amsterdam, no. 10, Amsterdam, 1934.

Roman, Tjakko, *Van harentwege verpleegd*, Amsterdam, 1971.

—, 'Seksuele problemen in de gevangenis', in *Delikt & Delinkwent*, 1972: 356–63.

Romein, Jan and Annie Romein, *Erflaters van onze beschaving, Nederlandse gestalten uit zes eeuwen*, Amsterdam, 1976 (1938).

Rook, A., 'Subculturen in penitentiaire inrichtingen', in *Justitiële Verkenningen*, vol. 9, no. 10, 1983: 5–38.

Rook, André and Marianne Sampiemon, *De algemene verlofregeling gedetineerden. Een evaluatie-onderzoek*, WODC report, no. 64, The Hague, 1985.

Roos, J. R. B. de, *De strafmiddelen in de nieuwere strafrechtswetenschap* (Ph.D.), Amsterdam, 1900.

—, 'Het Ve congres over Crimineele Anthropologie', in *Tijdschrift voor Strafrecht*, vol. 14, 1902: 293–338.

Rooy, J. de, 'Vrouwen in detentie', in *Tijdschrift voor Ziekenverpleging*, vol. 14, no. 1, 1961: 580–6.

Rooy, P. de, *Een revolutie die voorbij ging. Domela Nieuwenhuis en het palingoproer*, Bussum, 1971.

Ros, Robert, 'Het Nederlandsch Genootschap tot Zedelijke Verbetering der Gevangenen, een Foucaultiaanse visie op de macht van een reklasseringsvereniging', in Jonker et al., 1986: 5–70.

Rothman, David J., *The Discovery of the Asylum. Social Order and Disorder in the New Republic*, Boston/Toronto, 1971.

—, 'The crime of punishment', in *New York Review of Books*, 17 February 1994: 34–8.

Rudé, George, *Criminal and Victim. Crime and Society in Early Nineteenth-Century England*, Oxford, 1985.

Rudovsky, David, *The Rights of Prisoners. The Basic ACLU Guide to a Prisoner's Rights*, New York, 1973.

Ruller, Sibo van, 'Strafrechtsopvattingen in de jaren dertig, 1930–1935: van opvoedingsideaal naar generale preventie', in *Tijdschrift voor Criminologie*, vol. 22, 1980: 19–35.

—, 'De gevangenis in de nadagen van het resocialisatie-ideaal', in Fiselier, et al. (eds), 1980: 254–78.

—, *Het getal der gevangenen, 1837–1977, De omvang van de bevolking van de Nederlandse strafinrichtingen in de afgelopen 140 jaar*, Criminologisch Instituut Vrije Universiteit Amsterdam, Amsterdam, 1981.

—, 'Humanisering van de gevangenis: een fictie', in *Intermediair*, vol. 19, no. 27, July 1983: 19–25.

—, 'The end of decarceration', in *Working Papers* van *International Congres on Prison Abolition*, 24–27 June, 1985, Amsterdam: III.5: 1–20.

—, 'Honderd jaar vrijheidsbeneming in cijfers', in D. H. de Jong, et al., (eds) 1986: 57–75.

—, *Genade voor recht, gratieverlening aan ter dood veroordeelden in Nederland, 1806–1870* (Ph.D.), Amsterdam, 1987.

—, 'Ideeën over misdaadbestrijding in de jaren dertig', in *Tijdschrift voor Criminologie*, vol. 30, no. 2, 1988: 98–109.

—, 'De jaren tachtig en het strafrecht', in Haan en Verpalen (eds), 1989: 66–73.

—, 'De rechtspraak van het Zuidhollandse Hof van Assisen (1811–1838)', in Faber et al., 1989: 13–23.

Rusche, George and Otto Kirchheimer, *Punishment and Social Structure*, New York, 1968 (1939).

Ruschitska, W., 'Het sexuele probleem tijdens de gevangenisstraf', in *Documentatieblad*, Ministry of Justice, The Hague, 1958: 117–26.

Rutherford, Andrew, *Prisons and the Process of Justice*, Oxford, 1986.

—, 'Stemmingen in strafrechtelijk beleid, merkwaardige gebeurtenenissen in Engeland in de jaren tachtig', in Haan en Verpalen (eds), 1989: 17–36.

Sagra, Ramon de la, *Reis door Nederland en België, met toepassing op het lager onderwijs, de instellingen van liefdadigheid en de gevangenissen in die beide landen*, 2 vols, Groningen, 1839.

Samenleving en criminaliteit. Een beleidsplan voor de komende jaren, The Hague, 1985.

Schaaff, J. A., *De lijfstraf als disciplinaire straf* (Ph.D.), Groningen, 1886.

Schalken, T. M., 'Vormen alternatieven voor de voorlopige hechtenis een echt alternatief?', in Schalken et al. (eds), 1989: 47–59.

Schalken, T. M., et al. (eds.), *Voorlopige hechtenis*, Arnhem, 1989.

Schama, Simon, *The Embarrassment of Riches. An Interpretation of Dutch Culture in the Golden Age*, New York, 1987.

—, *Patriotten en bevrijders. Revolutie in de Noordelijke Nederlanden 1780–1813*, Amsterdam, 1989 (1977).

Schneevoogt, G. E. Voorhelm, 'Het Pennsylvanische gevangenisstelsel', in *De Gids*, vol. 2, 1848: 182–233.

Schnitzler, Johan G., 'The treatment of mentally ill prisoners in the Dutch prison-system and the ways to achieve this treatment according to Dutch law', in Koenraadt and Zeegers, 1988: 341–46.

Schopenhauer, Arthur, *The World as Will and Representation*, vol. 1, New York, 1969.

Scraton, Phil, Joe Sim and Paula Skidmore, *Prisons under Protest*, Milton Keynes/Philadelphia, 1991.

Scull, Andrew, *Decarceration. Community Treatment and the Deviant: A Radical View*, Englewood Cliffs, 1977.

Sharpe, Jim, *Judicial Punishment in England*, London, 1990.

Simons, D., 'De beginselen van ons gevangeniswezen', in *Themis*, vol. 62, 1901: 533–58.

—, 'Het congres van Crimineele Anthropologie te Amsterdam', in *De Gids*, vol. 4, 1901: 483–519.

—, 'Nieuwe strafrechtspolitiek', in *De Gids*, vol. 2, 1901: 253–96.

—, 'De celstraf in Nederland', in *De Gids*, vol. 2, 1907: 239–74.

—, *Problemen van het Strafrecht*, Amsterdam, 1929.

Sitter, L. U. de, 'Prae-advies over voorwaardelijke veroordeeling', in *Handelingen der Nederlandsche Juristen-Vereeniging*, 1899: 37–109.

Slingenberg, J., *De wet op de voorwaardelijke veroordeeling*, Haarlem, 1916.

Smaers, G., *Gedetineerden en Mensenrechten*, Antwerpen, 1994.

Smit, N. W. de, 'Psychose en gevangenis', in *Justitiële Verkenningen*, vol. 15, no. 2, 1989: 62–76.

Smith, P. D., 'Zo kan het bij ons ook: enkele gedachten over het Nederlandse strafstelsel', in *Justitiële Verkenningen*, vol. 7, no. 2, 1981: 43–9.

Sociologische Gids, special issue 'Beschaving en Geweld', vol. 29, nos 3/4, 1982.

Sordam, M. and P. van de Vliet, *Van bewaker tot bewaarder, 20 jaar gevangeniswezen in Nederland*, Schoten, 1987.

Spierenburg, Pieter (ed.), *The Emergence of Carceral Institutions: Prisons, Galleys and Lunatic Asylums 1550–1900*, uitgave Centrum voor Maatschappijgeschiedenis, Erasmus Universiteit Rotterdam, Rotterdam, 1984.

—, *The Spectacle of Suffering*, Cambridge, 1984.

—, 'From Amsterdam to Auburn. An explanation for the rise of the prison in seventeenth-century Holland and nineteenth-century America', in *Journal of Social History*, vol. 20, 1987: 439–61.

—, *The Prison Experience. Disciplinary Institutions and Their Inmates in Early Modern Europe*, New Brunswick/London, 1991.

stelsel, Het (...) *van afzonderlijke opsluiting, beschreven door een gevangenisdirecteur*, Rotterdam, about 1905.

Stilma, Liza, *Zitten, zat, gezeten, schetsen over (ex)gedetineerden en hun familie*, Nijkerk, 1984.

Stipriaan Luïscus, J. M. van, 'De celstraf', in *Nederlandsch Juristenblad*, 1927: 39–40.

Stuart, A. A., *De strafgevangenis te Woerden*, Amsterdam, 1865.

—, *Handboek voor direkteurs en bewaarders in gevangenissen, inzonderheid bij cellulaire opsluiting*, Leeuwarden, 1869.

—, *Onze gevangenissen*, Leiden, about 1870.

Suringar, W. H., *Godsdienstig en zedekundig handboek voor gevangenen, geschikt voor Zon- en Feestdagen*, Amsterdam, 1828.

—, *Bezoeken in de gevangenissen*, 1840.

—, *Een woord om over na te denken*, about 1840.

—, *Gedachten over eenzame opsluiting der gevangenen*, Leeuwarden, 1842.

—, *Eene stem uit Nederland over de cellulaire gevangenis te Bruchsal en de strafwetgeving in Baden en elders. In verband tot het gevangeniswezen en de strafwetgeving in Nederland*, Leeuwarden, 1859.

Swaan, A. de, 'The politics of agoraphobia. On changes in emotional and relational management', in *Theory and Society*, vol. 10, no. 3, 1981: 359–85.

Symposium. 100 jaar vrijheidsstraf. Verslag Groningen 15–18 April 1986, Rijksuniversiteit Groningen, Ministry of Justice, The Hague, 1987.

Tammenoms Bakker, S. P., 'Psycho-pathologische reacties in het Huis van Bewaring te Amsterdam', in *Verslag bijeenkomst Psychiatrisch-Juridisch Gezelschap*, 26 October 1940, no. 23, Amsterdam, 1941.

—, 'Zelfmoord en zelfverminking in de Huizen van Bewaring te Amsterdam', in *Nederlands Tijdschrift voor Geneeskunde*, 31 January 1953: 263–8.

Teeters, Negley K. and John D. Shearer, *The Prison at Philadelphia Cherry Hill. The Separate System of Penal Discipline*, New York, 1957.

Tex, C. A. den, 'Monomanie. – Voorbijgaande waanzin. – Toerekening van misdaden', in *Bijdragen tot Regtsgeleerdheid en Wetgeving*, vol. 5, 1830: 495–514.

—, 'Geschriften over onderscheidene stelsels van Gevangenissen. – Beschouwing van dit onderwerp in betrekking tot ons Vaderland', in *Nederlandsche Jaarboeken voor Regtsgeleerdheid en Wetgeving*, vol. 4, 1842: 529–608.

—, 'Gevangenisstelsels, zoo elders, als in betrekking tot Nederland', in *Nederlandsche Jaarboeken voor Regtsgeleerdheid en Wetgeving*, vol. 5, 1843: 393–407.

Theunissen, W. F., 'Bijdrage tot de kennis der gevangenispsychosen', in *Geneeskundig Tijdschrift voor Nederlandsch-Indië*, vol. 16, 1916: 406–39.

Thijssen, H. F., 'Brandstichting-zucht in verband met geslachts-ontwikkeling', in *Bijdragen tot Regtsgeleerdheid en Wetgeving*, vol. 1, 1826: 358–67.

—, 'Ligchamelijke oorzaken, welke de toerekening van daden wegnemen of verminderen. – Brandstichtingzucht. – Wat behoort over dit geheele onderwerp in een Wetboek van Strafregt bepaald te worden?', in *Bijdragen tot Regtsgeleerdheid en Wetgeving*, vol. 5, 1830: 461–95.

Tijdgeest en criminaliteit, special issue of *Tijdschrift voor Criminologie*, vol. 30, no. 2, 1988.

Tijn, Th. van, 'De sociale bewegingen van 1876 tot 1887', in *Algemene Geschiedenis der Nederlanden*, vol. 13, Bussum, 1978: 90–100.

Tulkens, Hans J. J., 'Strafrechtelijke alternatieven', in *Symposium, 100 jaar vrijheidsstraf*, 1987: 98–109.

—, *Graden van vrijheid*, Arnhem, 1988.

—, 'Over de rechtspositie van gedetineerden', in *Sancties*, no.1, 1993: 3–7.

Tuynman, Hans, *Full-time provo*, Amsterdam, 1966.

Vagg, Jon, 'Prison grievance and inspection procedures', in Muncie and Sparks (eds), 1991: 146–65.

Veen, C. J. F., *Correctioneel groepswerk*, brochure van het Centraal Opleidingsinstituut van het Gevangeniswezen, 1961.

Veen, Th. W. van, *Generale preventie*, The Hague, 1949.

Veenstra, S. L., 'Zelf-opvoeding van gevangenen', in *Volksontwikkeling*, vol. 3, 1921–2: 225–7.

Vegter, P.C., *Vormen van detentie. Een onderzoek naar verschillen bij de tenuitvoerlegging van de gevangenisstraf en de bemoeienis van de strafrechter* (Ph.D.), Arnhem, 1989.

—, 'Straffen en andere sancties', in Jan Fiselier, et al. (eds), *De Staat van Justitie*, Nijmegen, 1992: 137–58.

Veldhoen, Lex and Frank van Ree, *Eenzame opsluiting. Een aanklacht tegen de machtigen in politiek, wetenschap en maatschappij*, Utrecht/ Antwerpen, 1980.

Verdoorn, Johan, *Experimenteel onderzoek naar den invloed der gevangenis op de secundaire functie van gevangenen* (Ph.D.), Assen, 1941.

Verhagen, J. J. L. M., 'Veranderingen in de gedetineerdenpopulatie in de afgelopen tien jaar', in *Justitiële Verkenningen* vol. 15, no. 2, 1989: 7–16.

Veringa, G. H., *Het gevangeniswezen in de branding*, Nijmegen/Utrecht, 1964.

Vernée, L. G., *Het cellulaire gevangenhuis te Amsterdam*, Medemblik, 1849.

Verpalen, M. J. M., 'Voorontwerp Penitentiaire Beginselenwet. Verschil tussen theorie en praktijk blijft', in *Sancties*, no. 6, 1993: 334–44.

Verrijn Stuart, H., 'Gevangen vrouwen. Naar een detentiebeleid voor vrouwen als vrouwen', in *Proces*, no. 7, 1992: 170–81.

—, 'Gevangen in onzichtbaarheid', in *Nemesis*, no. 2, 1992: 1–4.

Verslag van de vergadering, gehouden den 7den Juni 1917 des namiddags 1.30 in het gebouw van het genootschap 'Liefdadigheid naar Vermogen' te Amsterdam ter behandeling van het verslag door eene commissie van onderzoek uitgebracht aan het hoofdbestuur van het Nederlandsch Genootschap tot Zedelijke Verbetering der Gevangenen over: 'De toepassing der celstraf'.

Verslag van den Criminologendag, gehouden op Zaterdag 26 november 1938 in het Wilhelminagasthuis te Amsterdam, georganiseerd door de Nederlandsche Vereeniging voor Geestelijke Volksgezondheid en het Psychiatrisch-Juridisch Gezelschap.

Verzameling van wetten, besluiten en voorschriften betreffende het gevangeniswezen, series 1860–1905.

Vijselaar, Joost (ed.), *Honderd jaar krankzinnigheid. Geschiedenis van de krankzinnigenwetgeving in Nederland,* Utrecht, 1985.

Vinson, Tony, 'Impressions of an Australian visitor', in Brand-Koolen (ed.), 1987: 11–17.

Visser, H. L. A., *Psychiatrisch toezicht in gevangenissen* (Ph.D.), Amsterdam, 1896.

Vlaming, Willem de, 'Strafrechtspleging, strafwet en socialisten (1884–1894)', in Faber et al., 1989: 125–40.

Vlugt, E. de, *De toepassing der progressiegedachte in het Nederlandsche gevangeniswezen* (Ph.D.), Amsterdam, 1930.

Vollemans, Kees, 'Inkerkering en celgevangenis in Nederland 1780–1900', in *Te Elfder Ure,* 24/26, 1978: 692–726.

Voo, H. van der, *Cel of gemeenschap?,* The Hague, 1929.

Vries, Colette de, 'De "Nieuwe Richting" in de strafrechtswetenschap in Nederland, 1880–1910', in Jonker, et al., 1986: 71–122.

Vries, J. de, *Het vraagstuk der celstraf in zijn tegenwoordige stand* (Ph.D.), Amsterdam, 1901.

Vriesaard, W., *Schetsen uit de Regtszaal en den Kerker, naar het leven geteekend,* Schoonhoven, 1840.

Vrieze, J. de, 'De celstraf', in *De Telegraaf,* 29 November 1927 (Ab.).

Vrijheidsstraf, De, Publication Wiardi Beckmanstichting, Amsterdam, 1969.

Vrouwen in de bajes. Een boekje open over hoe men veroordeelde vrouwen opbergt, Solidariteitsgroep vrouwelijke gevangenen, Amsterdam, 1983.

Vrouwen in detentie, rapport van de werkgroep (...), Delinquentenzorg en Jeugdinrichtingen, Ministerie van Justitie, The Hague, 1991.

Weber, Max, *Die Protestantische Ethik I, Eine Aufsatzsammlung,* herausgegeben von Johannes Winckelmann, Gütersloh, 1984 (1905).

Weisser, Michael, *Crime and Punishment in Early Modern Europe,* Brighton, 1982 (1979).

Werff, C. van der, *Speciale preventie,* The Hague, 1979.

Weringh, Jac. van, *Onrust is van alle tijden. Opstellen over criminaliteit in Nederland,* Meppel, 1978.

—, 'Het Nederlandse gevangeniswezen: van nota tot nota tot nota', in *Socialisme en Democratie,* no. 1, 1983: 16–19.

—, *De afstand tot de horizon. Verwachting en werkelijkheid in de Nederlandse criminologie*, Amsterdam, 1986.

—, *De ideale gevangenis*, Amsterdam, 1993.

Westerman, W. M., 'De celstraf', in *Haagsch Maandblad*, vol. 7, 1926: 240–54.

Wever, H., *De bijzondere strafgevangenis te Leeuwarden, een medisch-hygiënisch onderzoek* (Ph.D.), Assen, 1940.

Wiersma, D., *Moord en sensatie in de negentiende eeuw*, Leiden, 1969.

Wiewel, P. G., 'Onwerkbare detentie. Bespreking van de beleidsnota voor het gevangeniswezen 1994: Werkzame detentie', in *Sancties*, no. 1, 1994: 8–20.

Wijsman, J. W. H., *Diagnostiek der Zielsziekten in voorlezingen voor studenten, artsen en juristen*, Amsterdam, about 1890.

Wilde, Oscar, *De Profundis and Other Writings*, Harmondsworth/New York, 1987 (1949).

Willeumier, C. M., 'Is eene centrale cellulaire gevangenis voor vrouwen wenschelijk?', in *Themis*, vol. 12, no. 42, 1881: 252–64.

Winkels, M. J., *De binnenkooi. Een onderzoek naar de toepassing en toetsing van dwangmaatregelen binnen de terbeschikkingstelling*, Groningen, 1991.

Winkler, C., 'De verpleging van misdadige en gevaarlijke krankzinnigen, naar aanleiding van het rapport van de Staatscommissie, ingesteld bij Koninklijk Besluit van 31 juli 1902, no. 30', in *Rechtsgeleerd Magazijn*, vol. 24, 1905: 328–50.

Wit, H. de, 'De beginselenwet 1886, onthullende beraadslagingen', in D. H. de Jong et al. (eds), 1986: 77–101.

Wit, John de, 'Empirie en methode bij Foucault. Kritiese beschouwingen over "Surveiller et Punir"', in *Recht en Kritiek*, vol. 7, no. 3, 1981: 313–33.

Wittgenstein, Ludwig, *Philosophische Untersuchungen*, Frankfurt am Main, 1977.

Wöretshofer, J. and J. P. Balkema, *Penitentiary disciplinary Law* (congress paper), Maastricht, 1984.

Wright, Gordon, *Between the Guillotine and Liberty. Two Centuries of the Crime Problem in France*, New York/Oxford, 1983.

Wurzer-Leenhouts, S. M., 'Het voorontwerp Penitentiaire Beginselenwet', in *Sancties*, no. 1, 1994: 41–6.

Young, Peter, 'Sociology, the state and penal relations', in David Garland and Peter Young (eds), *The Power to Punish. Contemporary Penality and Social Analysis*, London, 1983: 84–100.

—, *Punishment, Money and Legal Order*, forthcoming, Edinburgh.

Zeeman, J., 'De sterfte in de gevangenissen van 1841–1864', in *Nederlandsch Tijdschrift voor Geneeskunde*, vol. 2, 1867: 97–103.

Zeeman, Michaël, 'Bericht van een onverhoedse aanval. Brief aan een verre vriend', in *Hollands Maandblad*, no. 3, 1987: 24–34.

Zitman, J., 'Gevangene en seksualiteit', in *Tijdschrift voor Criminologie*, vol. 7, 1965: 77–82.

Zuyderland, Siet and J. Bernlef, *Bajesmaf, een bijzonderhedenboek over Nederlandse gevangenissen*, Amsterdam, 1974.

Zwering, Atie, *Om een hoekje gekeken: een blik op resocialisatiebeleid in een vrouwengevangenis* (doctoral thesis), Amsterdam, 1988.

Zwezerijnen, J. J. A., *Dwang en vertrouwen, een empirisch onderzoek naar de machtsrelatie tussen bewaarders en gedetineerden*, Alphen aan den Rijn, 1972.

Zyl Smit, Dirk van and Frieder Dünkel (eds), *Imprisonment Today and Tomorrow. International Perspectives on Prisoners' Rights and Prison Conditions*, Deventer, 1991.

Index